T0300574

This book deals with the industrialisation of Russia during the crucial period of its transformation into a major industrial power. This was a transformation which enabled the defeat of the German onslaught of 1941, but it was achieved with great human suffering and at considerable material cost. The upheavals of World War I, civil war, Stalinism and German invasion also provide the historical context of the collapse of the Soviet system in 1991.

The book carefully examines Soviet successes and failures using the Soviet statistical record and the alternative estimates of Western and Russian economists. The contributors, all leading authorities, consider major sectors of the economy, foreign economic relations, and the war economies of 1914–1921 and 1941–1945. The major controversies are presented and reconsidered. How strong was the Tsarist economy? Did the mixed economy of the 1920s succeed? Did the Soviet economy overtake the major industrialised powers between the wars? How important were the defence industries? How extensive were the population losses due to war and repression?

This book will be used as a text and reference by students of Russian and Soviet history, politics, economic history, and comparative economics.

The economic transformation of the Soviet Union,
1913–1945

The economic transformation of the Soviet Union, 1913–1945

Edited by

R. W. Davies
Mark Harrison
S. G. Wheatcroft

CAMBRIDGE
UNIVERSITY PRESS

CAMBRIDGE UNIVERSITY PRESS
Cambridge, New York, Melbourne, Madrid, Cape Town, Singapore, São Paulo

Cambridge University Press
The Edinburgh Building, Cambridge CB2 8RU, UK

Published in the United States of America by Cambridge University Press, New York

www.cambridge.org
Information on this title: www.cambridge.org/9780521451529

© Cambridge University Press 1994

First published 1994

A catalogue record for this publication is available from the British Library

Library of Congress Cataloguing in Publication data
The economic transformation of the Soviet Union, 1913–1945 /
edited by R. W. Davies, Mark Harrison, S. G. Wheatcroft.
    p.   cm.
Includes bibliographical references and index.
ISBN 0 521 45152 3. – ISBN 0 521 45770 X (pbk.)
1. Soviet Union – Economic conditions – 1918–1945 – Statistics.
2. Soviet Union – Economic policy.   3. Soviet Union – Industries – Statistics.
4. Russia – Economic conditions – 1861–1917 – Statistics.
5. Russia – Economic policy.
I. Davies, R. W. (Robert William), 1925–   .   II. Harrison, Mark, 1949–   .
III. Wheatcroft, S. G.
HC335.T7362   1993
330.947′0842–dc20   93-25112   CIP

ISBN 978-0-521-45152-9 hardback
ISBN 978-0-521-45770-5 paperback

Transferred to digital printing 2008

Contents

Contents

Figures

Maps

Tables

xiv *List of tables*

52.	Sources of Soviet imports, 1913–1940	319
53.	Labour productivity in large-scale industry, 1913–1921	319
54.	Capital stock in large-scale industry, 1914–1923	320
55.	Grain production and procurement, 1909–13 to 1921	320
56.	Gross industrial production, 1913–1921/22	321
57.	Real GDP by sector of origin, 1937–1944	321
58.	Real burden of defence outlays, 1940–1944	322
59.	Employment, 1940–1945	322
60.	Recruitment into public sector employment, by sector of economy, 1942	323
61.	Estimated net output per worker in material production, 1940–1944	323

Notes on contributors

J. D. BARBER is a Lecturer in Soviet Politics and Fellow of King's College at Cambridge. He is the author of *Soviet Historians in Crisis*, and of many articles on Soviet working-class history, and (with Mark Harrison) of *The Soviet Home Front, 1941–1945*. He is preparing a collection of previously unpublished Russian archival material on the defence of Moscow in 1941.

R. W. DAVIES is Emeritus Professor of Soviet Economic Studies at the Centre for Russian and East European Studies of the University of Birmingham and was Director of the Centre from 1963–78. He is the author of *The Development of the Soviet Budgetary System, Foundations of a Planned Economy 1926–1929*, vol.1 (with E. H. Carr), and a multi-volume history of Soviet industrialisation. The third volume of this history, *The Soviet Economy in Turmoil, 1929–1930*, was published in 1989.

PETER GATRELL is Senior Lecturer in Economic History, Department of History, University of Manchester. His PhD thesis at the University of Cambridge concerned Russian industry in the First World War, and he is now completing a book on the same subject. He is the author of *The Tsarist Economy, 1850–1917*, and of many articles on Russian pre-revolutionary economic history. His book on government, rearmament and industry in Russia on the eve of World War I is now in press.

MARK HARRISON is Reader in Economic History, University of Warwick. He is the author of a number of articles on World War II, *Soviet Planning in Peace and War, 1938–1945*, and (with John Barber) *The Soviet Home Front, 1941–1945*. His current research interests include long-run Russian and Soviet economic development, the Soviet defence sector, and the Second World War.

ROBERT LEWIS is Senior Lecturer in Economic History, University of Exeter. He obtained his PhD at CREES, University of Birmingham in 1975. He is the author of *Science and Industrialisation in the USSR: Industrial Research and Development, 1917–1940*, and of articles on Soviet economic history and the organisation of Soviet science and technology.

J. N. WESTWOOD is an Honorary Research Fellow at CREES, University of Birmingham, and previously held posts at Florida State University and the University of Sydney, and as an economist in a large North American Railway company. He is the author of many books on the Russian railways, including *Soviet Locomotive Technology during Industrialization, 1928–1952*, and of several general histories of Russia.

S. G. WHEATCROFT is Director of the Centre for Soviet and East European Studies and Associate Professor in the Department of History, University of Melbourne. He is also Honorary Research Fellow of CREES, University of Birmingham, where he was variously Research Associate and Research Fellow from 1973 to 1985. He is the author of many articles on Soviet agricultural and demographic history, and on the history of Soviet statistics. He is collaborating with Professor Davies on a study of Soviet agriculture, *The Years of Hunger, 1931–1933*.

Preface

This volume examines the main quantitative features of the economic development of the Russian Empire and the Soviet Union from the eve of the First World War in 1913 to the end of the Second World War in 1945.

It is primarily intended as a textbook for students taking courses in comparative economic history, economic and social history of the Great Powers, and Russian or Soviet history. We hope that it will also prove to be a useful handbook for graduate students and for teachers of economic history, Russian and Soviet history and Communist affairs; the book is accordingly equipped with full references to text and tables, and with an extensive bibliography.

The years from 1913 to 1945 were a crucial period in Russian industrialisation. Between 1913 and 1939 the urban population increased from 26 to 56 million people, rising from 17.5 per cent to nearly 34 per cent of the total population. By 1914, the foundations had already been laid of modern iron and steel, fuel and cotton textile industries; some important branches of engineering had also been established. But these were islands in a sea of peasant agriculture and urban and rural handicrafts; Russia was industrially by far the most backward of the Great Powers. By the time of the German invasion in 1941, these industrial foundations had been greatly enlarged. Major new industries had also been established; these produced tractors, combine harvesters and motor vehicles, most kinds of capital equipment (including machine tools) and a wide range of sophisticated armaments. On the eve of the Second World War, the Soviet Union was already a major industrial power.

Economic developments in the thirty-four years dealt with in this volume were overshadowed by war and revolution. Between 1914 and 1920, world war, revolution and civil war resulted in a catastrophic fall in production from which the economy took some years to recover. By 1927 industrial production was only slightly higher than in 1913; the Soviet period of industrialisation began only in that year. In 1941, the Soviet Union was subjected to the devastating German invasion, during which most of the major industrial areas were occupied by the enemy; and industrial production did not exceed the pre-war level until about 1949. The first phase of Soviet industrialisation was thus concentrated in the fourteen years from mid-1927 to mid-1941. These peace-time years will receive particularly close attention in this volume; but it should be borne in mind that even in these 'peace-time' years fear of war strongly influenced the pattern of economic development.

The role played by the state in Soviet industrialisation in the 1930s and after was without precedent. In Imperial Germany industrial development was facilitated by import tariffs imposed by the state and by the national banks under the influence of the state, but industrial development was carried out by private capitalists working for the market. In the Tsarist Empire, the state strongly influenced and encouraged industrial development. As a consumer, the state purchased a substantial part of industrial production, mainly for the state railways and the Ministry of War. And import tariffs imposed by the state protected Russian industry. But the Tsarist economy was primarily a market economy, in which individual peasant households and private capitalist firms were responsible for the bulk of agricultural and industrial production. In contrast, in the 1930s the Soviet state owned nearly the whole of industry and trade, and assumed ownership of agriculture, or control over it, by compelling peasants to join collective and state farms, and subjecting these farms to its will. The state endeavoured to plan all production and investment through administrative orders. While markets continued to play a certain role, all economic activity was subordinated to the relentless industrialisation drive organised by the state.

There were some resemblances between the processes of industrialisation in pre-revolutionary and post-revolutionary Russia. In both eras, the state encouraged industrialisation with the political objective of strengthening Russia as a great power. In both eras, industrial production increased more rapidly than agricultural production, and within industry the production of capital goods increased more rapidly than the production of consumer goods. But the pattern of industrialisation differed considerably under the two regimes. Before 1914, agricultural production in the Russian Empire as a whole increased somewhat more rapidly than the size of the population, and food available per head of population increased. In contrast, in the 1930s and 1940s, while the production of capital goods rose much more rapidly than in the Tsarist era, agriculture suffered the twin disasters of forced collectivisation and German invasion. Even by the time of Stalin's death in 1953, agricultural production per head of population, particularly of foodstuffs, was lower than on the eve of the First World War.

With the dissolution of the Soviet Union at the end of 1991, the Soviet process of industrialisation has proved to be a unique event in world economic history. The developments analysed in this book were only the first crucial phase of Soviet industrialisation. In the years after the Second World War, Soviet industry greatly expanded. For a period of over forty years after 1945 the Soviet Union was one of the two military super-powers. When Gorbachev assumed office in 1985, 65 per cent of the population, 180 million people, lived in the towns – three times as many as on the eve of the Second World War. But neither Gorbachev nor his predecessors were able to reform the Soviet system. The Soviet economic system discussed in this volume was able, at great human cost, to cope with the first stages of industrialisation in a developing country. But it was unable to cope with the problems of economic growth and technical change in a more advanced industrial society. This was a major factor – perhaps the most important one – in the collapse in 1991 of the Soviet experiment in state socialism launched in 1917, which had been seen by the Soviet leaders as a blueprint or starting point for the establishment of a planned socialist economic order throughout the world.

The economic changes described in this book cannot in themselves explain the collapse of the system which was established in the inter-war period. Political and social factors, and their implications for the morality and the morale of Soviet society, appear only as essential background to the economic factors. And the story of the economy ceases in 1945; during the forty years of economic growth before the launching of *perestroika* in 1985 the weaknesses of the system became much more profound. But the reader will notice that economic problems characteristic of the mature – and dying – system of the 1970s and 1980s had already appeared in the 1930s. These included a tendency to over-investment, over-taut planning, the inability to innovate, and – perhaps most important of all – the failure of the grandiose efforts to modernise agriculture. The 'faulty foundations', diagnosed in the recent study by Hunter and Szyrmer (see Bibliography), were never repaired.

Although Soviet communism has come to an abrupt end, Soviet industrialisation has exerted a profound and lasting influence on world economic development. The inhumanities and social inequalities of the Stalinist version of socialism antagonised both the elites and the ordinary people in the Western democracies. But the great Soviet industrial advances took place in the 1930s – the years of the Great World Depression. The ability of the Soviet state to produce a dynamic economic system exercised a profound influence on Western economic thinking, and was undoubtedly a factor in the emergence of the mixture of state and private control and ownership that was characteristic of most Western industrial countries in the first thirty years or so after the Second World War.

Soviet industrialisation also exercised a major influence on the four-fifths of the world which was not yet industrialised. Soviet success convinced many Third World countries that it was possible for a relatively backward country to leap into the twentieth century in a comparatively short time. Some Third World countries endeavoured to develop their economies by adopting a modified form of the Soviet model of state socialism. In spite of the failure of these endeavours, and the shift of the Third World towards capitalism, the pace and scope of Soviet industrialisation remained a yardstick against which the economic success or failure of ex-colonial countries tended to be measured. Soviet industrialisation was a crucial stage in spreading the economic and social transformation which began in England in the middle of the eighteenth century to the thousands of millions of peasants who lived on the borders of starvation.

A careful assessment of the Soviet experience is therefore of great importance. Excellent general studies already exist of Soviet economic policy and the Soviet economic system, such as Alec Nove's Pelican *An Economic History of the USSR.* The present volume, while devoting some attention to policy and system, sets as its main task an assessment of Soviet economic successes and failures in quantitative terms, by evaluating the available economic and social statistics.

The difficulties in establishing the main quantitative features of economic growth are now familiar to all students of economic history through the painstaking work of Dean, Cole, Feinstein and others on British economic statistics, and of Mitchell on European historical statistics. Paul Gregory has initiated similar work on the national statistics of the tsarist period. (For these titles, see References.)

The statistics of the Soviet period present special difficulties. This is not because of any weakness in the Russian statistical tradition. As we show in chapter 2, pre-revolutionary national and regional statistics were relatively well-developed (they were certainly far fuller and more reliable than the statistics for Britain in the early nineteenth century!). The Russians were pioneers in the collection and analysis of national income statistics, peasant budgets, and even certain branches of industrial statistics. In the 1920s, several important statistical series were the subject of political contention; but detailed and reliable statistics continued to be published until the end of the decade.

The economic statistics of the 1930s, however, confront us with major problems. First, the speed of economic change, particularly in the capital goods industries, led to extremely severe index-number problems, which makes an 'objective' statement about the rate of industrial growth in the 1930s extremely problematic (see chapter 7). Secondly, from the end of the 1920s onwards, the quantity and range of published statistics greatly diminished, until by the end of the 1930s no more than a few isolated figures were available for many branches of the economy. These restrictions on publication were often designed to prevent knowledge of failures in the Soviet economy. Thirdly, the Soviet authorities in the 1930s deliberately distorted their published statistics in order to present a more favourable view of economic progress: the most famous examples here are the falsification of the grain harvest (see chapter 2), and the concealment and falsification of population data (see chapter 4).

In an endeavour to assess the true magnitude of the Soviet economic achievement, Western economists have struggled valiantly to remove the veil of mystery and falsification from Soviet statistics. In the first decade or so after the Second World War, major efforts were undertaken in the United States by Abram Bergson and his colleagues on national income and its components, by Warren Nutter on industrial production, and by individual scholars such as Naum Jasny. More recently a number of Western scholars, including the authors of the present volume, have undertaken more detailed work on several sectors of the economy, using previously unpublished Soviet data. The results of all this work have been published in numerous monographs, articles and mimeographed papers. In the present volume, we review the two generations of Western work and endeavour to draw conclusions from it.

With the advent of *glasnost'*, the story of the search for objective statistics has taken an unexpected turn. A number of Russian economists and journalists have attacked Soviet official statistics with far more radical criticisms than those of their American and British colleagues, and have made drastic further downward revisions of major statistical series. Much of this fresh criticism of Soviet statistics is made in rather general terms; and most of it is directed against the statistics of the Brezhnev years rather than of the period with which we are dealing on this volume. These recent Russian commentaries are also considered in this volume.

The debate is certainly not at an end. Since 1989, an increasing amount of statistical material has became available in the Soviet archives. The present volume uses this recently available material in several chapters, particularly those on population, employment, agriculture, the defence industries and the Second World War. These data do not substantially change our assessment but they considerably enrich it. More detailed data which are now available in the Soviet archives – for instance on industrial production, capital investment and internal and foreign trade – will require a great deal of work before new findings are available. To this extent the present volume should be regarded as an interim report.

Some of the conventions followed in this volume should be explained at the outset.
Boundary changes. The territory of the former Russian Empire underwent

several major changes during the period covered by this volume. By 1920, at the end of the civil war, the Baltic republics, Poland, parts of Ukraine and Belorussia, and Bessarabia, had been lost; in 1939–40, the first year of the Second World War, most of this territory was regained. The inter-war boundary before 17 September 1939, and the boundary on the eve of the German invasion in 1941, are both shown in map 1.

Except where otherwise stated, all statistics in this volume refer to the boundaries during the inter-war period 1922–1939, including statistics for the pre-revolutionary period.

Calendar. Pre-revolutionary Russia used the Julian calendar, which in 1917 was thirteen days behind the Western calendar. Hence the two revolutions of 1917 are known variously as the February or March revolution and the October or November revolution.

Between 1 October 1922 and 30 September 1930, most statistics referred to the *economic year*; at the end of 1930, a 'special quarter', 1 October–31 December intervened; and from 1931 the calendar year and economic year coincided. Crop statistics, however, both before and after the revolution, and before and after 1930, were often presented in terms of the *agricultural year* 1 July–30 June.

The economic and agricultural year are both denoted by a diagonal line (e.g. 1926/27), a two-year period by a hyphen (e.g. 1926–7).

Weights and measures. Traditional Russian measures (puds, versts, etc.) have been converted into metric tonnes (written as 'tons') and kilometres (km) throughout.

Regions. The main agricultural and industrial regions are shown on maps 2 and 3. We have used S. G. Wheatcroft's agricultural regions (CPR, EPR, NCR, SCR, SPR). These are explained in the Glossary. The statistics have been regrouped accordingly.

To assist non-specialist readers, a list of major events precedes the text, and a Glossary of Russian and specialist terms and abbreviations follows the text, together with tables and notes. Chapter 2 provides a guide to the main English-language sources on Soviet statistics, and each chapter ends with a short list of books and articles in English for further reading. Except for the first background chapter, these are primarily concerned with quantitative aspects of economic and social development.

Individual issues of the 'SIPS' (Soviet Industrialisation Project Series) Discussion Papers, when still in print, may be obtained from:

The Secretary,
Soviet Industrialisation Project Series,
Centre for Russian and East European Studies,
University of Birmingham, Birmingham B15 2TT.

RWD, MH, SGW

Acknowledgements

This book is a product of the Soviet Industrialisation Project at the Centre for Russian and East European Studies of the University of Birmingham. The project, which brings together British historians and economists working on this topic, has been supported since its inception by the British Economic and Social Research Council, which enabled the employment of Dr Wheatcroft before his departure for Australia, and of Melanie Ilič as part-time Research Associate. The ESRC also financed the Project Secretary, Mrs Betty Bennett, to whom we are grateful for her indispensable role in organising our regular seminars at Birmingham, and in preparing this book for publication. The University of Birmingham provided essential facilities.

Preliminary versions of the main chapters were presented at a meeting in Birmingham in September 1989 and at a session of the International Work-Group in Inter-war Economic History held during the International Congress of Soviet, Slavic and East European Studies at Harrogate in July 1990. We should like to thank the members of the Work-Group for their comments, and are particularly grateful to the following for their valuable advice and information: Professors H. Hunter and M. Dohan, Drs A. Heywood, E. A. Rees and J. Shapiro; Melanie Ilič, who prepared the Bibliography and Glossary; and Isobel McLean, who prepared the index.

R. W. Davies wishes to thank Drs J. M. Cooper and V. P. Danilov, O. Khlevnyuk and N. Simonov, and Mr E. Bacon, for advice and assistance. P. Gatrell acknowledges with thanks financial help from the Leverhulme Trust and the Kennan Institute for Advanced Russian Studies, which enabled him to make two research visits to the US. M. Harrison expresses thanks to Dr N. Simonov and Mr E. Bacon for their assistance and to the Leverhulme Trust for their support.

Major events in Russian and Soviet economic development

1694–1725		Reign of Peter I ('the Great')
1861		Emancipation of the serf peasantry
1890s		First industrialisation drive
1899		Economic depression begins
1905		First Russian revolution
1906–11		Stolypin's agrarian reforms
1909–13		Industrial boom
1914	August	Outbreak of First World War
1917	February/March	Revolution overthrows Tsar
	October/November	Revolution establishes Bolshevik or Soviet government
1918–20		Civil war; 'War Communism'
1921–9		New Economic Policy (NEP)
1924	January	Death of Lenin
1926–8		Pre-1914 industrial and agricultural output restored
1927–8	Winter	Grain crisis
1928(Oct.)–1932(Dec.)		First five-year plan
1929		Rationing of food and consumer goods in towns
1929	End of year	Mass collectivisation of agriculture and 'dekulakisation' begin
1930	March	Collectivisation drive halted, resumed at end of year
1930	25 April	Completion of Turkestan–Siberian railway (Turksib)
1932	May	Collective-farm market (free market) legalised
1932	7 August	Death penalty for theft of *kolkhoz* grain
1932–3		Widespread famine
1933	January	Hitler appointed Chancellor of German Reich

1933–7		Second five-year plan
1935	30–1 August	Stakhanov establishes coal-cutting record
1936–8		The 'Ezhovshchina' ('Great Purge')
1938		Third five-year plan begins
1941	22 June	Nazi Germany invades USSR
1941	October	Moscow under seige
1942	November	Soviet offensive in Stalingrad
1943	July	Soviet victory in Kursk tank battle
1945	8/9 May	Victory over Germany
1949		Pre-Second World War output of industry and agriculture restored
1953	March	Death of Stalin

Map 1   Republics, major cities and towns of the USSR at the end
of the 1930s

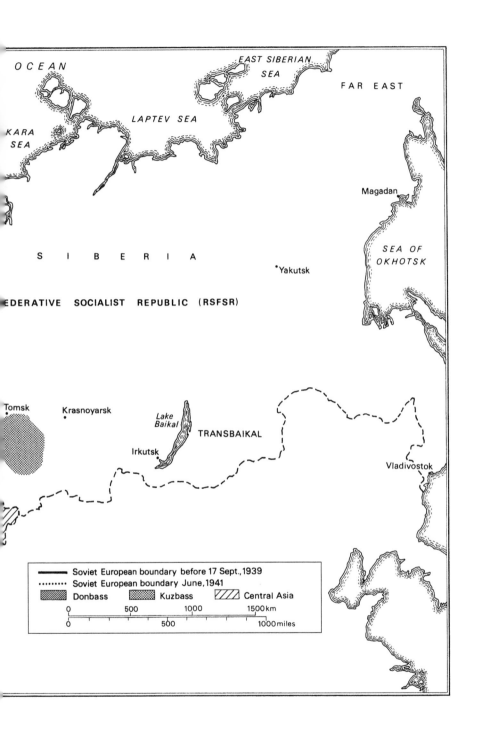

OCEAN

EAST SIBERIAN
SEA

KARA
SEA

LAPTEV SEA

FAR EAST

Magadan

S   I   B   E   R   I   A

•Yakutsk

SEA OF
OKHOTSK

EDERATIVE   SOCIALIST   REPUBLIC   (RSFSR)

Tomsk   Krasnoyarsk

Lake
Baikal   TRANSBAIKAL

Irkutsk

Vladivostok

	Soviet European boundary before 17 Sept., 1939
....	Soviet European boundary June, 1941
▨ Donbass	▦ Kuzbass ▨ Central Asia

0   500   1000   1500 km

0   500   1000 miles

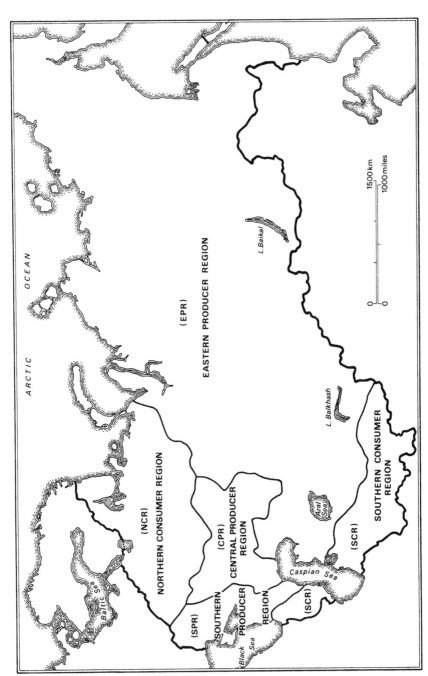

Map 2 USSR agricultural regions

Map 3   USSR industrial regions

OCEAN

S I B E R I A

FAR EAST

Lake Baikal

| 0 | 500 | 1000 | 1500 km |
| 0 | 500 | 1000 miles |

1 Changing economic systems: an overview

R. W. Davies

In examining economic development between 1913 and 1945 we shall be concerned with four substantially different economic systems.

(1) The economy of late Tsarism was in large part a *capitalist market economy*, but one in which the state played a considerable role and in which peasant households themselves produced a large part of the food they consumed.

(2) Following the two revolutions of February/March and October/November 1917, during the civil war (1918–20) a highly centralised system was established, later known as '*War Communism*': the state owned nearly all industry and sought to manage all economic activity (in practice, however, an illegal free market was responsible for a substantial proportion of goods circulation).

(3) Between 1921 and 1929, the *New Economic Policy* (NEP) led to the establishment of a mixed economy: the state continued to own nearly all large-scale industry, but state industry traded with the 25 million individual peasant households through a market which was partly in private hands, partly in state hands. NEP was a period of coexistence, collaboration and conflict between state planning and the market.

(4) Following the breakdown of the market economy at the end of the 1920s, from 1930 onwards economic development was planned or managed by a *centralised state administrative system*. Capital investment and industrial production were administered largely through physical controls; individual peasant households were forcibly combined into collective farms, and the market relation with the peasants was largely replaced by administrative or coercive control of agricultural output. Markets, legal and illegal, continued to exist, but were secondary in importance to the administrative controls.

(A) The Tsarist economy

The Tsarist economy on the eve of the First World War was still primarily an agrarian peasant economy. Agriculture was responsible for over half the national income, and three-quarters of all employment; over 90 per cent of the sown area was cultivated by some twenty million peasant households, the remainder consisting of landowners' estates. Following the emancipation of the peasantry from serfdom in 1861, agricultural production expanded greatly, and the peasant economy was increasingly involved in the market. But a large part of peasant production of food, and to some extent of consumer goods, was consumed by the families which produced it, or by other families within the same village. The villages were still to a considerable extent self-sufficient. In most regions peasant households were members of their village commune, in which the main fields were divided into strips; these were periodically redistributed among the households, and cultivated by the traditional three-field system.

Since the 1860s the development of the railway network and of factory industry had launched the modern industrialisation of Russia. The production of large-scale industry in 1913 has been estimated at over eleven times the 1860 level. Large-scale manufacturing and mining employed some 2½ million workers in 1913. Much of this development was in response to market demand: pride of place here was occupied by the cotton textile industry, which by 1913 employed about 20 per cent of all workers in large-scale industry. But the capital goods industries, especially fuel, iron and steel and machine building, expanded more rapidly than the consumer goods industries. In contrast to the consumer industries, the capital goods industries were encouraged and strongly influenced by the state. Railway construction fostered the development of these industries. From its inception, railway development was managed by the state, and by 1913 most of the railway network was nationalised. The state purchased a substantial proportion of all the capital goods manufactured by Russian industry, as well as some industrial consumer goods; the main state consumers were the railways and the armed services.

The capital goods industries also differed from the consumer goods industries in other respects. Unlike the consumer goods industries, they were largely foreign-owned, particularly by British, French and German capital; to a somewhat lesser extent they were also foreign-managed. And, following the depression of 1900–3, in most capital goods industries, including iron and steel, coal, oil and railway engineering, syndicates (the Russian equivalent of cartels) were formed. The syndicates decided on sales quotas for their member firms, and determined the wholesale prices. Thus capital goods industries, with some exceptions, were financed from abroad, managed by the state and had marked oligopolistic tendencies.

In the Tsarist economy, then, a number of economic structures coexisted: foreign-owned oligopolies in the capital goods industries, freely-competing Russian firms producing consumer goods, landowners' estates, small-scale artisan units, and an immense number of individual peasant micro-economies. This was a market economy strongly influenced by the state, but in which most of the participants still themselves produced many of the goods which they consumed.

There is no agreed view among historians on either the systemic features or the dynamics of the Tsarist economy. The American-Russian economic historian, Alexander Gerschenkron, writing in the late 1950s, argued that in the 1890s Russian economic backwardness was overcome by the state, which provided the motive force for industrial development in the absence of a sufficiently developed market. According to Gerschenkron, however, the economy had entered a new phase by the eve of the First World War. He argued that the boom of 1908–13 was primarily due to an increase in consumer spending; the role of the state was declining. Russian capital and entrepreneurship were replacing foreign capital. The state-induced industrialisation of the 1890s had been transformed into the market-led progress of the capitalist economy of 1908–13.[1]

In our view the balance of evidence does not confirm Gerschenkron's view that the role of the state declined in these years. It is true that the consumer goods industries expanded rapidly during the boom of 1908–13. But state orders also increased rapidly during the boom, largely as a result of the huge expansion in defence expenditure.[2] Nor is the relative role of Russian and foreign capital and entrepreneurship at all clear-cut. While the role of Russian capital and management was increasing in a number of well-established industries, foreign capital was dominant in the new industries such as electrical engineering, and its overall role had not diminished.

The debate among Soviet historians has focussed on rather different issues. Until the past few years the dominant view, expressed by V. I. Bovykin and others, was that 'monopoly capitalism' (in Western terms, 'oligopolistic capitalism') had triumphed by the 1900s; the role of the state was secondary, and pre-capitalist structures should be seen as no more than survivals from the past. The alternative view, advocated by Tarnovsky, Volobuev and others, emphasised the coexistence of competing economic structures, including pre-capitalist structures, and stressed the mixed transitional character of the late Tsarist economy. This approach was first clearly formulated at the end of the 1960s; but it was treated as a 'departure from Marxism-Leninism'. Its protagonists were demoted and their writings were banned.[3]

These debates are directly relevant to the problem of interpreting the collapse both of Tsarism and the two revolutions of 1917: the liberal-democratic revolution of February/March and the Communist revolution in October/November led by Lenin and the Bolshevik wing of the Social-Democratic Labour Party. Bovykin supported the orthodox view that the maturity of Russian capitalism meant that the Bolshevik revolution was a classical socialist revolution led by the revolutionary industrial working class. In contrast, Volobuev and his associates stressed that the plurality of economic structures had given rise to social and economic problems which had revolutionised a variety of social classes; the relatively immature Russian working class could not have succeeded on its own.

Both these Soviet schools of thought assume that contradictions within the economy and the society were the fundamental causes of the breakdown of the old order and its overthrow in 1917. On this general issue Western historians are divided. Some strongly emphasise the fundamental conflicts within Tsarist economy and society. Leopold Haimson argues that the structure of Russian industry, with its large units, poor working conditions and oppressive discipline, made for social unrest and political radicalisation.[4] Shanin notes that the Russian economy produced 'crowded city slums' and 'the growing hopelessness of villagers in the most populous part of rural Russia'; the poor became 'reservoirs of poverty and class hatred ever arrayed against the manor houses and the "nice quarters"'.[5]

Other Western historians reject these economic and social explanations. They regard the collapse of Tsarism as due to the failure of its political system to adapt to the needs of a modernising society. On the reasons for this failure opinions are divided. Some consider it was a profound structural problem;[6] others, including Hugh Seton-Watson, blame the narrow-mindedness and obstinacy of the tsar.[7]

So far we have only briefly mentioned the international context of Russian pre-revolutionary economic development: the mounting crisis which culminated in the First World War. Some Western historians, including Gerschenkron, see the war as an unlucky accident, which interrupted the progressive course of Russian evolution towards capitalism and parliamentary democracy.[8] In contrast Soviet historians, following Lenin and other pre-revolutionary marxists, saw the Russian economy as part of the international capitalist system. According to Lenin, 'imperialist war' between capitalist states was inevitable, and the half-developed Russian economy was bound to be shattered by the impact of war. Some influential Western historians, such as von Laue and Geyer, while rejecting Lenin's general view of the economic causes of war, argue that the drive to war was deeply rooted in the pre-war international system. Russia as a great power was inevitably involved in the drive to war. The Russian attempt to catch up the West placed enormous strains on the system, and these were greatly exacerbated when Russia confronted economically more advanced Imperial Germany.[9] On this view, the collapse of the Tsarist economy must be seen in the context of the profound contradictions within the European political order.

(B) War Communism

In Russia, as in the other combatant states, the First World War led to a major enhancement of the role of the state. The state regulatory agencies were headed by a Special Council for Defence, which assigned military orders to industry. This was supported by more specific agencies such as the Metals Committee, which controlled the distribution of metals and fixed their prices. A Special Council for Food Supply attempted to set maximum prices; and the Provisional Government which came to power after the February/March revolution established a state grain monopoly. After the Bolshevik revolution, the new Soviet government took over much of this war planning apparatus and adapted it to its needs.

The Bolsheviks came to power with far-reaching objectives. Following Marx, they believed that the October revolution was the first victory of a world proletarian (working class) revolution which would transfer factories, the land and other means of production into social ownership. A planned economy directly controlled by the community would replace the market, and money, the medium for market exchange, would cease to exist. In the first, socialist, phase of post-revolutionary development the social product would be distributed according to the work done by each individual. The abundance of production achieved by the planned economy would enable the transition to the higher phase of Communism, in which the social product would be distributed according to needs. Classes and the state, and all national barriers, would disappear.

The immediate aims of the Bolsheviks were far more modest. Marx anticipated that proletarian revolutions would take place in industrially advanced countries with a strong working class. But Russia, though the most advanced of the major peasant countries, was the most backward of the great European powers; it was perhaps just because of this duality of the Russian economy that the first successful working-class revolution took place there. In the summer of 1917, Lenin and his colleagues did not call for the establishment of a fully socialist economy in Russia, but for measures of state control and partial state ownership which would bring economic chaos to an end. Five months after the October revolution, in April 1918, Lenin renewed his call for relative moderation: the offensive against private capital must be temporarily halted; the modern achievements of capitalist organisation must be brought into industry; the currency must be stabilised.[10]

These proposals were soon superseded. By the summer of 1918 civil war and foreign intervention were well under way, and for two years the Soviet government was engaged in a desperate struggle for survival. In the autumn of 1919 its territory was no more extensive than that of sixteenth-century

Muscovy; the rest of the former Russian Empire was controlled by various anti-Communist 'White' governments.

Within a few months of the outbreak of civil war, the system later described as 'War Communism' was firmly established. The core of 'War Communism' was the compulsory acquisition of grain and other foodstuffs from the peasants, by the state and its agencies, using armed force where necessary. The peasants received little or nothing in return. In theory, the central authorities allocated a quota to each region, and the quotas were in turn divided among the villages. In practice, requisitioning was extremely arbitrary. The requisitioned foodstuffs were distributed to the army and in the towns; in the towns an elaborate rationing system was introduced, graded according to the occupation of the consumer.

Industrial consumer goods were also brought under close central control, at least in principle. In industry, all firms of a substantial size, and many smaller firms, were nationalised. The central planning apparatus inherited from the Tsarist regime was greatly extended. Compulsory labour service, and centralised direction of labour, were also introduced, though more cautiously.

Inflation was rampant. With the near-collapse of the taxation system, the government sought to fund its activities through currency issue. By 1 January 1921, currency in circulation amounted to 1,168,597 million rubles as compared with 1530 million rubles on 1 July 1914, but its purchasing power had declined to a mere 70 million pre-war rubles. Prices were estimated to have reached 16800 times the 1914 level.[11]

One further important feature of War Communism should be noted. The peasant economy remained more or less intact. During the agrarian revolution of 1917–8, which began spontaneously before the Bolsheviks took power, the land and property of the private estates were distributed among the peasants; and some equalisation took place between peasant households. Attempts by the government to encourage the collective or state ownership of former estates, and of the peasant economies, had almost no practical effect. State agencies had to deal with millions of peasant households.

The official economy was intended to embrace all economic activity, but in practice it was supplemented by illegal and semi-legal free markets. It was estimated that at the end of 1919 even workers' families in provincial capitals received less than half their grain, flour and potatoes from their official ration.[12] With the collapse of the currency, barter increasingly replaced money as a medium of exchange. War Communism could not have survived without this unofficial market economy.

Historians continue to debate the origins and function of War Communism. Some claim that it was primarily a result of the application of marxist ideology, with its hostility to private property and the market; others stress, in Dobb's famous phrase, that it was 'an improvisation in face of economic scarcity and military urgency'.[13] This question can be tackled in two ways. First, by an examination of the emergence of each of the characteristic institutions of War Communism. The truth seems to be that each major step was undoubtedly a response to emergency. Thus during 1918 and 1919 Lenin and his associates made valiant efforts to stabilise the ruble, but were driven inexorably along the road of inflationary currency issue. Similarly, the coercive measures to collect grain were a response to the grave food shortages in the towns and the needs of the Red Army: 'we do it', one leading official declared, 'because there is not enough food'.[14] But measures introduced in response to emergency were often strongly influenced by Bolshevik ideology. For example, in requisitioning grain, the Bolsheviks exaggerated both the importance of the rich peasants (the *kulaks*) and the extent to which the poor peasants would be prepared to cooperate with the Bolsheviks against the *kulaks*. As Alec Nove put it, 'there was a process of *interaction* between circumstances and ideas'.[15]

The second way to examine the question of improvisation versus ideology is to compare experience on Soviet territory with experience on the territories occupied by the White governments, which were all strongly biassed in favour of private ownership and the market. No detailed studies of the economic policies of the White governments have yet been made. But available evidence indicates that on a number of crucial issues the White leaders were confronted by the same problems as the Bolsheviks and adopted similar solutions. Even in the grain-rich areas of South Russia and Ukraine, following initial successes in feeding the population at relatively low prices, the governments of Hetman Skoropadskii, Denikin and Wrangel soon resorted to administrative measures and coercion to obtain grain. By the end of 1919 peasants were merely given paper receipts in exchange for requisitioned food. Wrangel invaded the Crimea in search of grain; and he even had to introduce a foreign trade monopoly in order to prevent grain being exported by private dealers. From mid-1919, the White governments in the South were also impelled to issue paper money in huge quantities, to the point of financial collapse. In the White as well as the Bolshevik areas, industrial production fell drastically.[16]

For the White governments, however, these measures of administrative control were purely a temporary expediency, to be cast aside in conditions of peace. Expediency had also driven the Bolsheviks towards a planned socialist moneyless economy far more rapidly than they had intended. But, in contrast to the Whites, the victorious Bolsheviks assumed throughout 1920 that the methods successful in war should be continued in time of peace. In February 1920, Lenin declared that the system of food requisitioning at fixed prices was a victory for socialism and should be used in economic reconstruction.[17] The requisitioning system was continued after the harvest of 1920 and during the winter of 1920–1, when the civil war had already come to an end. Moreover, in the winter of 1920–1, the Soviet government and its advisers sought to consolidate the moneyless economy, assuming that it would be a permanent feature of the peace-time economy.[18]

(C) The New Economic Policy

The Soviet government abandoned its efforts to transform 'War Communism' into 'Peace Communism' only in response to a profound crisis. From the summer of 1920 peasant disturbances were widespread. From the beginning of 1921, the country plunged into a disastrous fuel, transport and food crisis, and unrest spread to the industrial workers. Against this tense background, in March 1921 the X Communist party congress decided to replace requisitioning by a food tax, which was fixed in advance at a lower level than the previous grain quotas. The peasants would retain any surplus, and their incentive to grow more food would thus be restored.[19]

These decisions of March 1921 amounted to a quite limited reform. They assumed that peasants would dispose of their surpluses through local barter or by exchanging them for consumer goods provided by state agencies. Otherwise, 'War Communism', including the moneyless economy, would remain intact. This partial retreat did not prove viable; Lenin later frankly admitted that 'the private market proved stronger than us'.[20] Within a few months, what became known as the New Economic Policy (NEP) had emerged from the ruins of civil war.

The central feature of NEP was the right of individual peasants to sell their products freely, locally or nationally, to private traders, direct to other individuals, or to state agencies. Trade was resumed on a national scale, with most retail trade in private ownership. This was a retreat towards capitalism.

Nearly the whole of large-scale industry remained in state ownership. But artisan workshops and some small factories were rented or sold by the state to individual owners, and state industry was instructed to operate on principles of profit-and-loss accounting (*khozraschet*), and to adapt itself to the needs of the market. The wage system was restored, and enterprises were permitted to hire and fire workers in accordance with their needs. For the workers, all restrictions on changing jobs were removed; but they had to suffer the emergence of substantial urban unemployment.

The restoration of the market implied the restoration of the money economy. From the summer of 1921 the currency was gradually stabilised. Drastic reductions were made in every kind of state expenditure, and the taxation system was restored. The process culminated in the currency reform of March 1924. Simultaneously the tax in kind on peasant households gave way to a tax in money.

The NEP economy was thus a mixed money economy, in which state industry traded with individual peasant agriculture through a market which was partly in state hands, partly in private hands. The market operated within definite constraints. On the one hand, the state refrained from the use of coercion against the peasant: the state as well as the market was required to offer prices to the peasant which they were prepared to accept voluntarily. On the other hand, firm limits were imposed on the development of capitalism. All major banking institutions as well as large-scale industry remained in state hands. Stringent conditions were imposed on foreign firms seeking to invest in Soviet industry. The state maintained its monopoly of foreign trade, so that all imports required a licence, and the earnings from all exports were managed by the state. And the market economy operated within a strict political framework. While much freedom of discussion was permitted, during 1921–2 the one-party Communist dictatorship was consolidated, discipline within the party was tightened up, and an elaborate system of preliminary censorship was established. This political dictatorship continued for nearly 70 years.

After the initial set-back of a serious famine in 1921–2, the pace of recovery was extremely rapid. By 1928 both agricultural and industrial production exceeded their pre-war level. The extent of the recovery is disputed. According to the lowest Western estimate, in 1928 Soviet net national income had reached only 93 per cent of the 1913 level; according to the official Soviet estimate, it reached 119 per cent of the 1913 level.[21] Our own revised estimate of 111 per cent lies between these two limits: it implies that national income per head of population had just recovered to the pre-war level (see chapter 3 below).

In spite of the remarkable speed of the recovery, the economy failed to attain the pre-war level in several important respects. In an international perspective, the restored Soviet economy in 1928 was in a less favourable position than the Russian Empire in 1913. The other Great Powers had suffered less from the war and its aftermath than Soviet Russia. By 1928, the industrialised capitalist economies were at the peak of the inter-war trade cycle. The gap in production per head of population between Soviet and West European industry was as wide as ever, and the gap with the United States had widened. Even more significantly, as a result of technological advances in the West, particularly in Germany and the United States, the technological gap between Russia and the other Great Powers was considerably greater than in 1913.[22]

A more immediate preoccupation of Soviet policy-makers was the changed relation between agriculture and industry and, more broadly, between the countryside and the town. Although agricultural production had recovered to the pre-war level, agricultural marketings throughout the 1920s were substantially lower than before the war. We estimate that the share of agricultural output leaving the village had fallen from 22–25 per cent of the total in 1913 to 16–17 per cent in the mid-1920s. Grain marketings had fallen to little more than half the pre-war level.[23]

One important consequence of this decline was that foreign trade utterly failed to recover to the pre-war level. In the economic year 1926/27 exports amounted to only 33 per cent and imports to only 38 per cent of the 1913 level. This decline, entirely attributable to the decline in agricultural exports, was itself primarily a consequence of the decline in agricultural marketings, particularly of grain, the main pre-revolutionary export. Even in the best year of NEP, grain exports amounted to only one-quarter of the 1913 level.[24]

Why did agricultural marketings decline? One significant factor, strongly emphasised by Soviet historians, was the change in the socio-economic structure of the countryside. The abolition of the market-oriented landowners' estates, and the marked decline in socio-economic differentiation among the peasantry following the agrarian revolution of 1917–8, may both have had a negative effect on marketings.[25]

A second important factor in the decline of marketings was the reduced level of peasant taxation and the elimination of land rents. According to our rough estimate, direct taxation and land rents taken together had fallen from 9.5 to 4.9 per cent of farm incomes between 1913 and 1926/27.[26]

Thirdly, terms of trade for agricultural produce had generally deteriorated in comparison with 1913, and this probably discouraged peasants from marketing their output. From the 'scissors' crisis' of 1923 onwards, the ratio of the retail prices of manufactured goods to the prices received by the peasants for their produce was less favourable to the peasants than before the war (in Trotsky's striking image, the graph showing these two price-levels was compared to the open blades of a pair of scissors). In the 1920s, Soviet economists of all schools of thought believed that the 'scissors' would discourage the peasants from selling their produce, and encourage them to retain it for their own consumption. More recently, the American economist James Millar has argued that peasant demand for manufactured goods was price-inelastic. In consequence, when the terms of trade deteriorated, peasants were forced to sell *more* products in order to obtain essential manufactured goods. Strenuous attempts to check this hypothesis have been unsuccessful.[27] It is chastening to reflect that we are perhaps being unreasonable to expect Soviet politicians to have adopted sensible agricultural price policies in the 1920s, when we are unable nearly 70 years later to agree even the general direction in which prices should have moved ...

Whatever may be the truth about terms of trade as a whole, it is certain that the particularly low level of grain marketings was due to the low price of grain relative to other agricultural products. The authorities were confronted with a delicate balance. If they relatively increased grain prices, as they did in the summer of 1925, peasants tended to switch resources away from industrial crops essential for industrial development. If they reduced grain prices too far, as they did a year or so later, the peasants withheld grain and reduced their grain sowings. A further problem for the authorities was that meat and dairy produce were mainly sold on the private market; these prices could not be controlled without a considerable increase in direct state management.

Agricultural marketings were unstable as well as insufficient. Only two harvests in the 1920s – those of 1922 and 1926 – escaped serious economic difficulties resulting from inadequate marketings. These fluctuations were partly due to Russian climatic conditions which resulted in great variations in the harvest. But they were also a result of failures in policy. Maintenance of equilibrium on the market between a relatively small number of state enterprises and 25 million individual peasant households proved a delicate task. But a more fundamental dilemma lurked behind the successive crises. On the one hand, the Soviet authorities were constantly preoccupied with the danger that supplies of food to the towns and the army and of agricultural raw materials to industry would be inadequate. On the other hand, the urgent desire of the same authorities to increase the share of resources available to industry constantly threatened the economic basis of the relationship between the regime and the peasantry.

Matters came to a head with the grain crisis of 1927–8. In October-December 1927 peasants sold only half as much grain to the official grain collection agencies as in the same months of 1926. With this amount of grain the towns and the army could not be fed.

The grain crisis had complex causes, which have been much debated by historians. Until 1987, Soviet historians, reflecting Stalin's contemporary analysis, attributed the failure to supply grain to the changed post-revolutionary socio-economic structure of agriculture, combined with sabotage by the *kulaks*. In contrast, some Western political historians treat the grain shortages as merely an artificial crisis, used by Stalin as a pretext to crack down on the peasants.[28] Some Western economic historians, however, have placed more stress on the substantial increase in industrial investment during the economic year 1926/27. The increase was particularly rapid in the capital goods industries, which did not provide an immediate return in the form of consumer goods, and was accompanied in the summer of 1927 by a substantial unplanned increase in short-term credits to industry.[29] Other Western economic historians regard the crisis as primarily a con-

sequence of erroneous price policies, which themselves were rooted in
Bolshevik attitudes to the market.[30] A striking example in favour of this
view is provided by the reduction of industrial retail prices in the spring of
1927. This greatly exacerbated the goods shortage in the countryside, and
thus contributed to the peasants' reluctance to sell their grain.[31] In our
opinion, both the expansion of the resources devoted to industry and the
erroneous price policies played a major role in bringing about the crisis.

The dramatic grain crisis illustrated the general dilemma of NEP. NEP
had proved successful in bringing about the revival of the economy to the
pre-war level. But could it provide an effective framework for the industrialisation of the Soviet Union, for achieving the goal accepted by all wings of
the Communist Party – to catch up and overtake the advanced capitalist
countries?

Historians are equally strongly divided on this issue. At least four rival
approaches may be distinguished. First, many economists hold that NEP
restricted market forces too greatly, even in the years of the mid-1920s when
the greatest freedom was allowed to the private sector. Central price controls, in operation since 1923, and detailed state management of investment,
meant that the efficient allocation of resources was impossible. Alexander
Gerschenkron argued that the Bolshevik revolution was a fundamentally
reactionary event, which reversed the rise of democratic capitalism. According to Gerschenkron, by the mid-1920s 'the conditions for economic growth
would seem to have been rather unfavourable'.[32] This view is broadly
shared by the many present-day Russian economists who believe that
post-Gorbachev Russia must be transformed into a capitalist country, and
that no 'Third Way' between capitalism and centralised state socialism is
possible. According to Grigorii Khanin, for example, the last chance for a
successful development of the Russian economy 'was lost at the beginning
of the 1920s, and even then it was small'.[33]

A second group of historians, among whom the late E. H. Carr is the most
prominent, concurs that the economy of NEP was inherently unstable, if
not a blind alley. But Carr's standpoint was radically different. He believed
that the world economy is evolving from private capitalism to forms of state
planning, and that in this context there was 'a latent incompatibility
between the principles of the New Economic Policy and the principles of
planning'.[34] This general viewpoint, applied to the specific Soviet conditions of the 1920s, is also advocated by some modern Russian historians.
Thus M. M. Gorinov assesses the potential of NEP very pessimistically,
concluding that 'the threat of technical backwardness, the permanent
danger of war, and the instability of the market cast very grave doubt on the
effectiveness of this variant.'[35]

A third group, very influential in recent Western discussions, argued that

NEP was compatible with successful long-term economic development. Stephen Cohen, the biographer of Bukharin, and Robert Tucker, the biographer of Stalin, strongly sympathise with the viewpoint of Bukharin, chief figure in the 'Right Wing' opposition to Stalin in 1928–9, who insisted that the only acceptable solution to the grain crisis was to restore equilibrium on the market and fit industrialisation into the NEP framework.[36] And James Millar, logically applying his hypothesis that peasants would sell more of their production if its relative price was reduced, argued that NEP was compatible with at least as rapid a rate of industrialisation as that actually achieved.[37]

The American economist Holland Hunter and his associates broadly belong to the same school of thought. Using a series of computer models to project alternative policy variants, they assume an NEP-type framework, without such taut planning and without the collectivisation of agriculture; and seek to demonstrate that with these alternative policies much better results could have been achieved. However, unlike Millar, Hunter assumes that it was 'low prices for farm products in 1928 [which] made peasants less willing to produce and deliver output to the state'.[38]

The view that NEP provided a viable system for successful industrialisation dominated Soviet popular publications about the Soviet past in 1988, and was the subject of several serious historical studies.[39]

The fourth group of historians, including the editors of the present volume, takes an intermediate position between the second and third group. In our opinion, the economy of the mid-1920s had not yet reached an impasse. In the economic year 1926/27, net investment in the economy as a whole had probably reached 90 per cent of the 1913 level, and net industrial investment was higher than in 1913.[40] This success for planned industrialisation was accomplished before the grain crisis, and within the framework of NEP. In our opinion, given sensible price policies, a moderate rate of expansion of both industry and agriculture could have continued. On the other hand, we do not believe that NEP was capable of sustaining much higher rates of industrialisation than those achieved on the eve of the First World War.

(D) The Stalinist administrative economy

By the end of 1927 Stalin was already the dominating figure in Soviet politics; and the reaction of Stalin and his associates to the grain crisis was firm and unhesitating. The 'emergency measures' of the winter of 1927–8 are strikingly different from the methods by which a similar crisis was handled in 1925, only two years earlier. In the summer and autumn of 1925, the first substantial capital construction since the revolution had resulted in a considerable increase in demand; and serious shortages of goods resulted. The peasants, confronted by empty shelves, reduced their sales of grain. The state reacted by increasing the price of grain and reducing the resources supplied to industry, so as to restore equilibrium on the market.[41] At the end of 1927, however, the authorities kept the price of grain stable and pressed ahead with industrialisation. The 'emergency measures' at the beginning of 1928 involved the extensive use of compulsion to obtain grain. As in the civil war, the authorities also unsuccessfully endeavoured to win the support of the mass of peasants against the *kulaks*. This was the beginning of the end of NEP.

(i) Policy and practice

All wings of the Communist Party were committed to industrialisation and to the establishment of a socialist society in the Soviet Union. On the Right, Bukharin and his associates stressed the importance of moving towards socialism through market relations; the peasants would be won over to cooperative agriculture by strictly voluntary means. On the Left, Trotsky and his associates argued that the complete construction of socialism in the USSR could not be assured until the proletarian revolution was successful in more advanced countries. In the intervening period, according to Trotsky, the socialist sector of the economy would survive only if the party supported industrial development, and waged a determined struggle against private trade and capital, and against the petty capitalism of the *kulaks* in the countryside. Trotsky and the Left opposition did not deny, however, that the market economy should be maintained. Resources for industrialisation should be obtained from the *kulaks* and other peasants not by the forcible methods of 'War Communism' but by taxation and price policy.

Until 1927, Stalin and his associates were allied with Bukharin and broadly identified with his policies. But from the autumn of 1927 onwards, while vigorously denying that any departure from NEP was intended, they forced through an increasingly ambitious industrialisation programme, incompatible with market equilibrium.

During the 13½ years between the beginning of 1928 and the German invasion on 22 June 1941, economic policy and practice were dominated by the all-out drive to catch up and overtake the capitalist countries in level of production and technology, and above all in military might. This was seen as the prerequisite for the survival and triumph of socialism in a single country. Contrary to the programme of Trotsky and the Left Opposition, Stalin's industrialisation involved the use of coercion against the peasants, and the strengthening of the political dictatorship. These years also saw the consolidation of a hierarchy of status and privilege dominated by an élite of party and state officials ('the bureaucracy').

In 1928–41, the economy went through many vicissitudes. Five main phases may be distinguished.

(1) *1928–1930.* Industrialisation, with strong emphasis on the capital goods industries, proceeded at an accelerating pace. The succeeding drafts of the first five-year plan and the annual plans became increasingly ambitious. The climax was reached when the XVI party congress in July 1930 approved very high five-year plan targets for key industries. These targets were reached not in the economic year 1932/33 as planned, but some years after the Second World War.

In 1928 and 1929 the use of coercion by the state replaced the market relation with the peasants; the 'emergency measures' of the beginning of 1928 became a permanent feature of the system. From the autumn of 1929, the forcible collectivisation of agriculture strengthened state control over agricultural output. Collectivisation was accompanied by the mass deportation of hundreds of thousands of *kulak* households; heads of households believed to be particularly dangerous were summarily executed.

Simultaneously, the increase of industrial production and construction involved the rapid expansion of the urban labour force. To meet the higher national wage-bill, the flow of paper money was increased. Prices began to rise, but inflation was partly repressed through price controls; private shops and trading agencies were taken over by the state to facilitate this. With the breakdown of the market in 1929 a rationing system was introduced in the towns; following the practices of the civil war, rations were differentiated by occupation. Rationing continued until 1935. As in the civil war, foodstuffs were also sold extensively by the peasants on the free market – partly legal, partly illegal – at much higher prices. In this way, the available supply of consumer goods and food was distributed over the old and the new urban population, and consumption per head in the towns was forced down.

Within industry, a rudimentary system of physical controls already existed in the 1920s. This was gradually extended in 1928–30, so that virtually all capital goods and raw materials were physically allocated. In industry – and in the towns generally – many 'bourgeois' engineers, economists and other specialists who were suspected of resisting party policies, or even of insufficient enthusiasm, were arrested and accused of sabotage.

In this period Utopian concepts of the emerging socialist order prevailed in official circles. During the collectivisation drive of January–March 1930 attempts were made to socialise all livestock and close down peasant markets. Leading economists and officials announced that the transition to socialism would soon be completed; this would involve a moneyless economy, in which trade was replaced by physical product-exchange (exchange in kind or barter).

(2) *Spring/summer 1930–summer 1932*. Economic policy and practice were confused and ambiguous. On the one hand, feverish attempts continued throughout 1931 and 1932 to achieve the over-ambitious plans approved in July 1930. By 1932 the number of people employed in large-scale industry had more than doubled, and the number employed in construction quadrupled, as compared with 1928. Currency continued to be issued in large quantities to provide finance for this expansion. But industrial projects took much longer to complete than planned, and the strain placed on industry by the over-ambitious plans led to much disorder. In consequence, industrial production grew less rapidly in 1931 and 1932 than in previous years.

In agriculture, widespread peasant disturbances in February 1930 compelled a temporary retreat from collectivisation; but both the relentless collectivisation drive and dekulakisation were resumed at the end of 1930. By the end of 1932, over 60 per cent of all peasant households had joined collective farms. The state continued to compel both collective farms and individual households to surrender very large quantities of grain and other products, for a purely nominal payment, and offered virtually no economic inducement to the peasants to work on collective land.

So far the policies we have described involve no important departure from the previous period. But in the course of 1930–2 greater realism gradually came to prevail. As early as the spring of 1930, at the time of the retreat from collectivisation, Stalin called a halt to the compulsory socialisation of all livestock, and to the attempts to eliminate the peasant free market. In the autumn of the same year the flirtation with the moneyless economy was abandoned in favour of a policy of strengthening the ruble and strict financial discipline, though this could not be put into effect while the ambitious plans continued. From the spring of 1931 the authorities relinquished their enthusiasm for product-exchange in kind, and began to insist on the necessity for 'Soviet trade' and on the eventual need to abolish consumer rationing. Simultaneously the pressure on 'bourgeois specialists' was relaxed, though never completely removed. In May 1932 the free peasant market (the so-called 'collective-farm (*kolkhoz*) market') was legalised, the compulsory delivery quotas imposed on agriculture were reduced, and strenuous efforts were made to provide economic incentives to the collective farms; taken together these measures were unofficially known as 'neo-NEP'.

(3) *1933*. The measures of relaxation in the spring of 1932 were too little and too late. Following a poor harvest in 1932, the peasants failed to meet even their reduced delivery quotas. In the winter of 1932–3 the state pursued the grain quotas with particular brutality and exiled recalcitrant households. A

terrible famine followed in the spring of 1933; millions of peasants died from starvation. The poor condition of agriculture in 1932 was undoubtedly in large part the result of the excesses of collectivisation and the size of the food quotas imposed on the peasants. Was poverty turned into disaster by the deliberate actions of Stalin, determined to force the peasants to submit to the requirements of the state? Or was Stalin impelled to enforce the food quotas because the desperate food situation in the towns threatened the whole process of industrialisation? No agreement has been reached by historians on this grim topic.[42]

In the economy at large, the authorities committed themselves to more realistic policies. The production plan for 1933 was much more modest than in previous years, and the level of investment was actually reduced for the first time since the early 1920s. The 1933 plan, and the draft second five-year plan (covering 1933–7) stressed that top priority should be given to completing investment projects started during the first five-year plan, and assimilating them into production. Budgetary expenditure was curbed, and in consequence the amount of currency in circulation declined in 1933.

(4) *1934–6*. This was a period of spectacular economic development. The factories started during the first five-year plan were brought into operation, and agriculture began to recover from crisis. According to Harrison's estimate, national income per head increased by about 55 per cent between 1932 and 1937 (see chapter 3). Labour productivity rose substantially in agriculture as well as industry. The standard of living improved greatly, from the low level of 1933. In 1935 all consumer rationing was abolished.

Greater prosperity did not carry with it relaxation of repression, except for a brief period in 1934. Following the assassination in December 1934 of Kirov, a prominent member of the Politburo, many party members, as well as those outside the party, were arrested and executed. The first major public trial of Old Bolsheviks was held in August 1936. The international scene was grim and foreboding. Following the Japanese invasion of Manchuria in September 1931 and the seizure of power by the Nazis in Germany in January 1933 tension grew throughout Europe and Asia; in response Soviet military expenditure increased.

(5) *1937 – 22 June 1941*.[43] These years were haunted by the political purges, involving in 1937–8 mass arrests of leading economic officials and industrial managers. In Europe, tension mounted: the start of the Spanish Civil War in July 1936 was followed by the invasion of Austria in March 1938 and the dismemberment of Czechslovakia later in the year. Soviet war preparations greatly intensified. The armed forces expanded from 1.5 million men in 1937 to over five million on the eve of the German invasion, while armaments' production increased at a similar rate: in 1940 it was nearly 2½ times as great as in 1937.[44] And by 1937, consequent upon the high levels of

investment during the previous three years, the economy entered a new crisis of over-accumulation, similar to though less acute than the crisis of 1931–2. In 1938–40, as in the first years of the second five-year plan, considerable efforts were devoted to completing unfinished projects. Purges, rearmament and overaccumulation together resulted in a considerable slowing down of the growth of industry.

Economic policy was dominated by the rearmament drive, particularly intensive from 1939. The large increases in defence expenditure had repercussions throughout the economy. Purchasing power rose more rapidly than state retail sales. In consequence prices on the collective-farm free market rose considerably, and in 1940 and 1941 official retail prices were also increased. Numerous austerity measures were introduced to restrict budget expenditure on civilian purposes. The working day was lengthened, and labour discipline was tightened up.

(ii) The economic system

After the end of consumer rationing in 1935, few substantial modifications were made in the economic system, which remained more or less unchanged throughout the upheavals of the next half-century. Let us summarise its main features.

First, agriculture as well as industry was under close state control. A fairly small sector of state farms (*sovkhozy*) operated on the same principles as state factories. The vast majority of the 25 million peasant households which existed in 1929 were combined into some 250,000 collective farms (*kolkhozy*), one or several to each village. The old boundaries between the strips of land were removed, and most land was pooled, and worked in common. Agricultural machinery was made available to the *kolkhozy* through some 8,000 state-owned Machine-Tractor Stations (MTS). Through the system of compulsory deliveries the *kolkhozy* were required to supply a large part of their output to the state collection agencies at low fixed prices.

Secondly, within industry production and investment were administered through physical controls. Prices were fixed, and materials and capital equipment were distributed to existing factories and new building sites through an allocation system; through central allocations the state sought to give priority to key construction projects and to widen the bottlenecks in existing industries. The plan set targets for the output of materials, intermediate products and final products. These planning methods resembled both War Communism and the wartime planning controls used in capitalist economies to shift resources to the war effort.

Thirdly, the imposition of the priorities of the state through an economic hierarchy was supplemented by horizontal relations between state enter-prises. These horizontal inter-connections, involving unplanned and even illegal exchanges and agreements, complemented the rather crude controls of the central plan, and made them workable. Moreover, while the central authorities could always have the final say, a process of bargaining between all levels in the hierarchy, from Politburo to factory department, was crucial to the effectiveness of the plans.

Fourthly, several important market or 'quasi-market' features were incorporated into the planning system between 1930 and 1935.

(i) Each peasant household was permitted to work a personal plot, and to possess its own cow and poultry; this private or household sector was responsible for a substantial part of food production.

(ii) After the compulsory deliveries to the state had been completed, each household, and each collective farm as a unit, was permitted to sell its produce on the free market ('collective-farm market') at prices reached by supply and demand. Their large income from these sales on the free market partly compensated the peasants for the low prices they received from the state.

(iii) After the abolition of rationing, consumers were free to spend their income, in the state shops or on the free market, on whatever goods were available. In state-owned retail trade, prices were fixed, but the authorities endeavoured – with indifferent success – to balance supply and demand through the use of fiscal measures, particularly the 'turnover tax' (a purchase tax sharply differentiated according to the product).

(iv) Most employees were free to change their jobs. Wages were differen-tiated according to skill and intensity of work, but the existence of the very imperfect labour market meant that wage-levels were modified in response to supply and demand. There were major exceptions. The labour of some employees was subject to direct allocation from the centre, especially of course the growing forced-labour sector, which involved at least three million people by 1939.

(v) All state enterprises were subject to financial controls through so-called 'economic accounting' (khozraschet). Cost reduction targets, set for every Ministry and enterprise, were an auxiliary but significant part of the annual plans.

(vi) This was then a money economy as well as a physically-planned economy. Money flows corresponded to all the physical flows, and some money-transactions (for example, wage payments and sales on the free market) were not accompanied by physical controls. The government sought to achieve financial equilibrium by means of a plethora of taxes, credit and cash controls, and currency plans. In practice, however, financial stability was achieved only for a few years (1933–6) in the middle 1930's before preparations for war and the war itself led to a recrudescence of inflation. (The post-war years from the currency reform of 1947 to Stalin's death in 1953 were the great years for financial stability in which retail prices were actually reduced.)

The retention of market and quasi-market elements in the economic system led to a shift in the Soviet definition of socialism. 'Socialism' continued to mean a system in which the means of production were owned by the state or by society at large. But from the mid-1930s a moneyless economy based on product exchange was no longer a requirement of socialism; this would only come with the higher stage of communism. Instead socialism as officially redefined involved a money economy, and a socialist form of trade. And the personal plot of the collective-farm household, and the free market associated with it, were regarded as part of this socialist economy; it was for this reason that the 'free market' became known as 'the collective-farm market'. This shift in definition enabled the Soviet authorities to proclaim in 1936 that the USSR had 'already in principle achieved socialism'.

(iii) Effectiveness of the system

The difficulties involved in attempting a quantitative measure of the efficiency of the Soviet economic system in this period are discussed in chapter 9. No reliable measure has proved possible.

General measures of the efficiency of an economy or of one of its sectors are based on a 'production function', which compares the rate of growth of output and the rate of growth of inputs, particularly capital and labour. (For 'production function', see Box in chapter 9). That part of the growth of output which cannot be attributed to the growth of inputs is taken as a measure of efficiency; it is referred to as total factor productivity (or alternatively as 'the residual', the amount which remains after the rate of growth of the combined inputs is deducted from the rate of growth of output.[45]) Many technical difficulties complicate the task of estimating production functions for any economy. In a Soviet-type economy the absence of a capital and labour market makes it particularly difficult to determine the relative weights to be attributed to the inputs.

But, as we shall see in the course of this book, the greatest problem is that estimates of the basic Soviet economic quantities for the years 1928–40 vary widely. Only the rate of growth of labour inputs is known with some certainty. Measurements of the annual rate of growth of output (gross national product or national income) vary from 3.2 to over 9 percent (see chapter 3), and estimates of the rate of growth of capital also vary. Western estimates of the share of total factor productivity in the growth of GNP/NNP cited in chapter 9 vary from 2 to 24 per cent.(In the industrial sector even quite high estimates of the rate of growth of production lead to the conclusion that total factor productivity accounted for only 10–12 per cent of the growth of large-scale industry between 1928 and 1937, and that almost all this increase took place after 1933 (see chapter 9 and Tables 41 and 42).[46] It is tempting to see these results as confirming the commonsense view that substantial increases in efficiency would be unlikely to have occurred in this period of economic upheaval and social disorder.

In the absence of reliable quantitative assessments, we have to turn to more general considerations of effectiveness. The Stalinist administrative system was effective in the sense that it succeeded in achieving several of its major aims. It enforced the allocation of a very high proportion of GNP to investment in general and to investment in the capital goods and defence industries in particular. Central control of investment enabled advanced technology to be diffused rapidly throughout the USSR in certain priority sectors. Important economies of scale were achieved through the standardisation of products. The production drive successfully induced managers and workers to exert great efforts to fulfil the plans. Moreover, the whole economy was transformed into a 'socialist' economy, in the sense that agriculture and trade as well as industry were now socialised. However, whether Soviet society, with its privileged ruling élite and its centralised state system, can properly be described as having achieved 'socialism' remains a matter of controversy.

The system also had great failures and weaknesses. In agriculture, output declined drastically; by 1940, food output per head of population had not recovered to the 1928 level. Consumers suffered generally: the increase in the urban housing stock, for example, was far smaller than the increase in the urban population. Millions of people died prematurely as a result of the famine, and of the harsh repressions that were endemic in these years.

The centralised system also proved inherently clumsy in its effects at the point of production. Control of quality through centrally determined indicators proved very difficult. And the central planning indicators greatly restricted initiative throughout the system. By the end of the 1930s it was already becoming apparent that the system which had managed to bring about technological revolution and economic growth from above was incapable, without drastic reform, of encouraging technological innovation from below. The deficiency, which ultimately proved fatal for the Soviet economic system, is examined more closely in chapter 9.

The repressed inflation and sellers' market which was an integral part of the system reinforced these difficulties. At the same time it led each industrial Ministry or sub-Ministry to become a self-contained 'Empire', carrying out wasteful backward integration in order to control its supplies. If advertising and inflated sales organisations are a costly feature of modern capitalism, inflated supply organisations were a high cost of administrative planning.

In Western discussions about the effectiveness of the Soviet system, most attention has naturally been devoted to the relation between industry and agriculture. The collectivisation of agriculture, accompanied as it was by state requisitions of a large part of its output, failed to increase yield or total production. But were collectivisation and requisitioning effective means of transferring resources to industrialisation?

Until the early 1970s almost all Western historians assumed that agriculture was the main source of labour and capital for industry, and that collectivisation was the crucial though brutal mechanism by which this was achieved. Three achievements were particularly emphasised. First, the increase in compulsory delivery of grain to the state. In 1938–40, deliveries averaged 30 million tons from an average harvest of some 77 million tons (39 per cent), as compared with 10.7 million out of 73 million tons in 1928 (14.7 per cent). Secondly, the increased production of cotton and other products which were previously imported saved foreign currency and provided essential materials for industry. Thirdly, the agricultural sector provided most of the increase in urban labour. The scale of the migration was a consequence of state pressure on the peasants and the deterioration of conditions in the countryside, together with the lure of ample employment in the towns. This was not due to deliberate state policy; it was rather an unintended consequence of the priorities of the central authorities. But it greatly facilitated the increase in industrial production and in construction generally.

This positive view of the effects of collectivisation has been strongly challenged by Barsov, a Soviet economic historian, and by James Millar. Barsov claimed that the terms of trade for agriculture did not deteriorate in 1928–32, and improved in 1933–7. While some agricultural commodities, especially grain, were transferred to the state at low prices, others were sold on the free market at high prices; in physical terms, while the supply of grain by the peasants increased, their supply of meat and dairy products declined. Thus peasants' money incomes were higher and their supplies to the town lower than was previously believed. On the side of supply to the peasants from the towns, their high money earnings enabled them to buy industrial consumer goods, while agriculture also received greatly increased supplies of machinery from industry through the state Machine-Tractor Stations. The flow of industrial products to the countryside was therefore higher than previously believed.[47]

Other economists, including Alec Nove, while concurring with much of this general account, do not accept its implications. Nove argues that in the circumstances of forced industrialisation the state could not have obtained increased supplies of agricultural products without a drastic shift in the terms of trade in favour of agriculture (thus he rejects Millar's view of peasant behaviour in response to prices). Nove also points out that food and other consumption declined more rapidly in the countryside than in the towns, so that in this sense peasants made a major sacrifice for industrialisation.[48] Collectivisation also enabled agriculture to be treated as a residual sector, which absorbed shocks such as bad harvests.[49]

Whatever the outcome of this controversy, it seems clear that collectivisation of agriculture, together with the suppression of autonomous working-class activity in industry, and the repressive measures against the professional classes, provided a framework which imposed the economic priorities of the party leaders on the whole of society. In this broader sense it formed part, though a costly part, of the Stalinist mechanism for industrialisation.

Further reading

The best general introduction to Soviet economic history is Alec Nove, *An Economic History of the USSR* (latest edition published by Penguin in 1989).
See also: R. W. Davies, 'Economic and Social Policy in the USSR, 1917–41,' *Cambridge Economic History of Europe*, viii (1989), 984–1047, and the Bibliography on pp. 1198–1203. Eugène Zaleski's two volumes (1971, 1980) listed in the Bibliography of the present volume provide a systematic comparison of plan and performance for the whole period.

2 The crooked mirror of Soviet economic statistics

S. G. Wheatcroft and R. W. Davies

Statistics have very seldom been collected for purely historical analysis. They have normally been collected to assist in such functions as administration, planning, and levying taxes. Historians by the very nature of their subject are forced to use other people's statistics. They cannot redesign the surveys and questionnaires that were used in the past, they cannot measure things that were not measured or affect the timing and location of those surveys, censuses, investigations and registrations that were carried out. They have to make the best use of what statistical data and accounts are available to them. Before they begin using these data, however, they should attempt to discover how the data were collected and calculated, and by whom these operations were carried out. They should attempt to see whether there are any reasons for doubting the reliability of these data. Where doubts do arise as to their reliability, they should attempt to make an assessment of the possible scale of the inaccuracy. It is extremely dangerous to accept figures on trust without understanding their origin and history.

These homilies apply to the study of the economic and social development of any country at any time. They are even more important in the case of Soviet history. It is true that Western historians working on the economic and social history of the USSR have the advantage of dealing with a country that had a well-developed central statistical agency and was gathering and publishing data on all sorts of social phenomena. This was unique for such a large and underdeveloped country. On the other hand, they have the disadvantage that political and ideological bias has distorted published Soviet government statistics to an exceptional extent. In the crucial period of Soviet development in the 1930s and 1940s the authorities selected for publication those statistics which would portray their activities in a favourable light. At the height of the Stalin period very few specific figures were published. In a number of important cases the authorities deliberately distorted the statistical record in order to conceal disasters and repressions.

Fortunately a great deal of information is available which enables us to examine actual statistical procedures and the contemporary debates among statisticians over these procedures. Many blanks in the record have been filled in since the death of Stalin by the release of previously unpublished data, and in the past few years a vast range of formerly secret archives has been made available to Western as well as Russian historians. The economic history of the Soviet Union can now be based on reasonably full and reasonably reliable data.

In this chapter we introduce the reader to the chequered history of Russian and Soviet statistics; and to the many Western studies which have sought to clarify and assess Soviet economic and social data.

(A) A brief history of Russian and Soviet statistics

A Statistical Department was established as early as 1811 by Alexander I, subordinate to the Ministry for Police. By 1857 this had been transformed into the Central Statistical Committee (Tsentral'nyi Statisticheskii Komitet – TsSK) attached to the Ministry for Internal Affairs. TsSK, and its associated provincial statistical committees, steadily expanded until the Bolshevik revolution of October 1917 brought them to an abrupt end. Among the most important achievements of TsSK was the preparation of national series on the harvest, using data on sown area and yield sampled from the millions of peasant households. It also collected population data, culminating in the first full population census in 1897.

From the end of the 1860s the new units of local government, elected on a restricted franchise – the *zemstva* – also began to establish their own statistical agencies. In their studies of peasant economy, including the budgets of peasant households, they were world pioneers. In 1916, the *zemstvo* statisticians were allowed to organise the first all-Russian agricultural census.[1]

Pre-revolutionary government departments also established their own statistical departments. Thus by the end of the 1890s the Ministry of Finance and the Ministry of Trade and Industry systematically collected data on industrial production and employment, which formed the basis for first-class studies of the factory industry of the Russian Empire published in the 1920s.[2]

Pre-revolutionary statistics were by no means free of bitter controversy. The *zemstva* were extremely hostile to the TsSK, which they regarded as a puppet of the tsarist government. Statistical reliability was not the prerogative of either camp. As we shall see in chapter 6, we have come to the conclusion that the grain harvest data of TsSK, much criticised for underestimating production, were reasonably reliable. On the other hand, we accept the view that its population data in the years following the 1897 population census were greatly overestimated.

After the October 1917 revolution, the new Bolshevik government under

Lenin sought to combine the traditions and activities of the TsSK and the *zemstva* in a unified hierarchy of statistical agencies. Lenin's own very serious attempts to study the pre-revolutionary economy convinced him of the importance of statistics for both analysis and policy-making. On 23 July 1918, the Central Statistical Administration (Tsentral'noe statisticheskoe upravlenie – TsSU) was established;[3] it has continued to exist, together with its local agencies, under various names and variations until the present day. Its first director was P. I. Popov, a prominent *zemstvo* statistician; it was Popov who organised the 1916 agricultural census.

Ministerial statistical departments also continued to exist. While in principle and to some extent in practice they coordinated their activities with TsSU, they always retained a considerable degree of autonomy. Perhaps the most important was the Central Statistical Department (Tsentral'nyi Otdel Statistiki – TsOS) of the Supreme Council of National Economy (Vesenkha or VSNKh), in practice responsible for industrial statistics.

With the restoration and expansion of the economy after the end of the Civil War, the 1920s was the decade in which statistics flourished, and a huge amount and variety of statistical data were published. Outstanding publications included: the balance of the national economy for the economic year 1923/24; the population census of 1926 (the first since 1897), the final results of which appeared in 56 volumes; and the 1929 census of small-scale industry.[4] A more detailed account of Soviet statistical publications in the 1920s and 1930s will be found in Wheatcroft's chapter in S. Fitzpatrick and L. Viola (eds.), *A Researcher's Guide to Sources on Soviet Social History in the 1930s* (1990), pp. 153–75.

In the 1920s the Soviet leaders insisted on the importance of objective statistical data. Even Stalin piously proclaimed in 1924:

no work of construction, no state work, no planning work is conceivable without correct *records* (*uchet*). And records are unthinkable without statistics ... In a bourgeois state a statistician has a certain minimum of professional honour. He is unable to lie. He may be of any political persuasion or outlook, but in relation to facts and figures, even if he is abused, he will not state an untruth. We should have more of such bourgeois statisticians.[5]

But during the course of the 1920s statistics in practice became increasingly subject to political control.

At the outset of the New Economic Policy, when Lenin presented harvest data to the X Party Congress, he used the uncorrected results of the 1920 agricultural census to claim that the harvest was low, and hence to justify a radical shift in policy towards a more flexible arrangement with the peasants. Popov, the head of TsSU, and Tsyurupa, the People's Commissar for Food, confirmed the accuracy of these low harvest figures. The radical shift in policy proposed by Lenin was undoubtedly necessary; but it is equally certain that the harvest figures for 1920 were underestimates, as TsSU itself later admitted. It is not clear how far Lenin deliberately presented figures which he knew were unreliable. But this incident was probably a major factor in lowering the credibility of the statisticians in the eyes of senior party officials such as Stalin. When Stalin later practised far greater statistical deceit, he could easily persuade himself that he was following a Leninist precedent.

A further dramatic incident followed in the autumn of 1925. TsSU had prepared figures showing, probably accurately, that a high proportion of grain surpluses came from peasant households with larger sown areas. These figures were used by a leading Bolshevik Lev Kamenev, in opposition to a party majority which included Stalin and Rykov, to argue that economic polarisation among the peasantry was increasing.

To investigate this incident the party set up a special commission which found against TsSU; and simultaneously TsSU proposals to increase expenditure on the collection of state statistics were rejected. In January 1926 Popov resigned, and he was replaced a month later by V. V. Osinskii, a quite prominent party member.[6] Osinskii's remit was to reorganise TsSU, and to cooperate more closely with Gosplan, the State Planning Commission. At this time, the period of recovery from war and civil war was coming to an end, and great attention was being devoted to state planning. With the twin aims of increasing the usefulness of statistics for planning purposes, and of increasing the influence of Gosplan over TsSU, Groman, a Gosplan official, was appointed a member of the collegium of TsSU and placed in charge of the planning of statistics.[7]

These developments did not mean the immediate collapse of statistical independence or objectivity. Osinskii had worked in a provincial statistical office before the First World War, and had a justified reputation in the party for his independent spirit. In general he defended the interests and objectivity of the statisticians. But two years after his appointment he was removed from office.[8] This was apparently because he was not prepared to accept the optimistic assessment of the 1927 harvest which formed part of Stalin's justification for the strong measures adopted to obtain grain from the peasants.[9] Osinskii was replaced by V. P. Milyutin, a prominent, colourless and amenable party member. In the period between the spring of 1928 and the summer of 1929 the dispute between Stalin and the Bukharinist 'Right Wing' was not finally resolved in Stalin's favour. For the moment statisticians were still able to put forward data which conflicted with the official conception of reality. But during 1928 and 1929 open discussion of economic matters was more and more restricted.

Among the statisticians matters came to a head in the course of the discussion about the size of the 1929 grain harvest. Ironically, it was Groman, formerly a critic of TsSU for its underestimation of the harvest, who now ran foul of the party authorities for underestimating the harvest prospects. At a party conference in September 1929 Molotov condemned 'Menshevik and Socialist Revolutionary influences' in grain statistics, and the pliable Milyutin obediently rejected Groman's 'bankrupt predictions' (Groman was an ex-Menshevik).[10] In the winter of 1929–30 a vigorous campaign brought charges of wrecking against non-party economists and statisticians of various persuasions. Prominent senior members of staff in Gosplan, TsSU and other government departments were arrested, and many of them perished in the camps.[11] In the course of this upheaval, on 30 January 1930, TsSU was amalgamated with Gosplan as its 'economic-statistical sector'.[12]

Henceforth it was much more difficult for a Soviet statistician to display that 'minimum of professional honour' which Stalin had claimed to advocate in 1924; and in 1930 and 1931 the scale of central statistical work was greatly reduced. No general statistical handbooks or journals were published. Many statistical series ceased to appear in the press, including all price indexes.

This was not, however, the end of the story. In December 1931, something like a new TsSU was established in the form of the Central Administration of National-Economic Records (Tsentral'noe upravlenie narodno-khozyaistvennogo ucheta – TsUNKhU).[13] The word 'records' was used in its title rather than 'statistics' because it was assumed that under socialism the study of probabilities associated with statistics was no longer necessary – planning would deal with firm records not statistical uncertainties. In spite of its inauspicious name, the establishment of TsUNKhU was a change for the better. TsUNKhU was a separate administration. Unlike the old TsSU, it was attached to Gosplan, but, unlike the 'economic-statistical sector', TsUNKhU was no longer directly subordinate to Gosplan. The enhanced authority of TsUNKhU was emphasised by the appointment of Osinskii as its director.[14] He immediately set about restoring statisticians to its staff. Within a few months of his appointment several statistical handbooks were published, and a preliminary and very elaborate balance of the national economy for the years 1928, 1929 and 1930 was completed and circulated for official use. This balance was the first since the 1923/24 balance. It has been translated and published in English as S. G. Wheatcroft and R. W. Davies (eds.), *Materials for a Balance of the National Economy, 1928–1930* (1985); and contains a very full account of the way in which individual series of statistics were compiled and collected at that time. A further development in the first few months after the appointment of Osinskii was that several important production figures, including those for the grain harvest, were revised downwards.[15]

This revival of more objective state statistics did not survive the next few years. In December 1932, a Politburo resolution prepared by Stalin, Molotov and Kaganovich criticised TsUNKhU for 'very crude political mistakes', due to the 'presence on the central staff of a bourgeois tendency concealed under the banner of "objective" statistics'. The alleged mistakes included the underestimation of both the grain yield for 1932 and the industrial results of the five year plan.[16] Osinskii received an official reproof, and his first deputy was dismissed, together with the eminent statistician Nemchinov. The status of TsUNKhU was reduced; henceforth it was not 'attached' to Gosplan but formed a subordinate part of it.[17] Kraval', a strong supporter of Stalin, was appointed as Osinskii's first deputy.[18]

In the next few months the control of the Politburo over statistics was further strengthened. In June 1933 Stalin and Molotov sent a telegram to the Odessa regional authorities claiming that 'reliable data' showed that the Odessa Grain Trust had deliberately underestimated their harvest.[19] This extraordinary intervention by the highest authorities resulted in widespread upward revision of the harvest estimates. Osinskii was finally forced to back down on his more objective evaluations of agricultural production. Two years later, in August 1935, Osinskii was dismissed and replaced by Kraval'.[20]

Even by 1935 professional statistics was not dead. In 1937, a further crisis occurred when the preliminary results of the 1937 population census, the first since 1926, showed that the population of the USSR was at least eight million less than had been officially anticipated (see chapter 4). The results of the census were suppressed, and Kraval' was accused of wrecking, and arrested.[21] TsUNKhU, like all other government departments, was engulfed in the 'Great Purge' of 1937–8.

Behind the scenes, however, a great deal of statistical material continued to be prepared and circulated within a narrow circle. An industrial census was carried out in 1938, and this was followed by a successful population census in 1939. Many of the older professional statisticians continued to work within TsUNKhU, including P. I. Popov, who had resigned from its leadership in January 1926.

In spite of this activity of statisticians behind the scenes, which continued throughout the Stalin period, very little statistical material was published in the USSR from 1937 until 1956, three years after Stalin's death. And in the later years of the Stalin period the figures which were published were often distorted or falsified. The Soviet economy was presented to the Soviet people and to the West in a crooked mirror. Some of these statistical practices continued until well after the launching of *perestroika* in 1985.[22]

(B) Distortions

The Soviet authorities pursued several different and often contradictory objectives in developing their elaborate arrangements for collecting statistics at a local, departmental and national level. They sought to know the truth about the economic situation in the country, particularly in relation to successes and failures in pursuing their key priorities. But they also sought to reward achievements and penalise failure with the aid of their knowledge of the quantitative results achieved by individual economic units, and by whole sectors of the economy. This gave strong incentives to participants in the system at every level to exaggerate their reported results; and the central authorities were not always able to correct this deficiency adequately. Moreover, the central authorities and the competing interests within the party, and within the state apparatus, were all willing to distort statistics in their own interests.

The authorities also used their statistics to publicise the achievements of the Soviet system to the world. Published statistics therefore suffered a further distortion as compared with internal statistics for official use: Soviet successes were exaggerated, and failures minimised or simply omitted from the published record. The published record was further complicated by the Soviet passion for secrecy. What constituted a state secret was far more broadly defined in Soviet practice than in the practice of other Great Powers. The relative unimportance of commercial secrecy in the Soviet Union mitigated this defect, but only to a relatively minor extent.

At worst, Soviet published statistics were deliberately falsified. We shall see in the course of this book that the published harvest data were falsified throughout the Stalin period from 1933 onwards. It is evident that the Soviet authorities, including Stalin, were tangled in their own distortions, and to some extent even deceived themselves about the size of the harvest. (See chapter 6.) Demographic data were also deliberately falsified; thus the size of the Soviet population was exaggerated in the published results of the 1939 population census. The official figure for deaths in the Second World War announced by Stalin was greatly underestimated, presumably with the intention of concealing Soviet weakness from the capitalist world. (See chapter 4.)

Apart from such cases of deliberate falsification, the authorities always adopted those statistical series which gave the most favourable presentation of the rate of growth. No unambiguously objective estimate of rates of growth is possible. The composition of output and relative prices of different kinds of output differ considerably over time, particularly in a fast-growing economy. The choice of base year when estimating *index numbers* can therefore make a considerable difference to the result. (For a more detailed discussion of index numbers, see Box.)

Index number problems

When the structure of prices and outputs is changing, it becomes impossible to measure changes in real output and the price level unambiguously.

Consider an index of the current, nominal value of GNP in 1937 expressed as a percentage of 1928 (we call 1928 the *base year*, and 1937 the *current year*; P_n is the set of prices, and Q_n the set of quantities produced, in year n):

$$\text{Nominal GNP index} = \Sigma P_{37} \cdot Q_{37} / \Sigma P_{28} \cdot Q_{28}$$

To find the change in real GNP in 1937 (the current year), compared with 1928 (the base year), this index must be divided by a price index. The price index can be weighted by the structure of output either in the base year (a *Laspeyres index*) or in the current year (a *Paasche index*). In conformity with the Gerschenkron effect, we expect the Laspeyres index to grow more rapidly, because the prices of food and consumer products grew rapidly over the period, and in 1928 agriculture and light industry had the largest weight in the structure of output. The Paasche price index will grow more slowly, because machinery prices were relatively stable, and the weight of machinery in the structure of output in 1937 was relatively large.

Real GNP, measured by the nominal value of output, deflated by the Laspeyres price index, will therefore appear to grow more slowly. In fact, it will form a Paasche index of volume, weighted in this case by the current (1937) structure of output, as the following expression shows:

$$(\Sigma P_{37} \cdot Q_{37} / \Sigma P_{28} \cdot Q_{28}) / (\Sigma P_{37} \cdot Q_{28} / \Sigma P_{28} \cdot Q_{28})$$
$$= \Sigma P_{37} \cdot Q_{37} / \Sigma P_{37} \cdot Q_{28})$$

Conversely, the nominal value of GNP, deflated by the Paasche price index, gives a Laspeyres index of real output:

$$(\Sigma P_{37} \cdot Q_{37} / \Sigma P_{28} \cdot Q_{28}) / (\Sigma P_{37} \cdot Q_{37} / \Sigma P_{28} \cdot Q_{37})$$
$$= \Sigma P_{28} \cdot Q_{37} / \Sigma P_{28} \cdot Q_{28}$$

More generally, the value of output
 = Paasche price index × Laspeyres volume index
 = Laspeyres price index × Paasche volume index.

This *index-number effect* is particularly important in the case of Soviet industrial production in the 1920s and 1930s. The Soviet series are calculated in terms of the initial-year prices of the economic year 1926/27. But the rate of growth of Soviet industrial production is much greater when it is measured in initial-year prices rather than prices of a later year (1937 or later). In the 1920s, machinery costs and prices were relatively high, because most machinery was produced on a small scale. At the same time food prices were relatively depressed. By 1937, the concentration of resources on the capital goods industries in general, and on the machine-building industry in particular, had led to a sharp fall in costs and prices relative to those of other products, especially industrial consumer goods and agricultural products. But the output of machinery and capital goods grew much more rapidly than the rest of the economy. This resulted in the 'Gerschenkron' effect, named after the American–Russian economist who first observed it. When Soviet goods and services are valued at 1926/27 prices, the growth of total output is dominated by high-priced machinery, and the rate of growth is exceptionally rapid. If 1937 prices are used, total output is dominated by consumer goods and agricultural products, which grew much more slowly. (See Box for further discussion of the Gerschenkron effect.)

These real changes in output and costs have a similar effect on price indexes. A price index weighted by the structure of output in the 1920s, when the economy was dominated by agriculture and light industry, shows

Gerschenkron effect

In the early 1950s, Alexander Gerschenkron identified a difficulty in making unambiguous comparisons of real output through time in the Soviet case, when the structure of prices and quantities was changing rapidly. Between 1928 and 1937, Soviet machinery output grew much faster than other branches, while machinery prices fell relative to prices of food and consumer goods. As a result, when Soviet goods and services are valued at constant prices of 1928, the growth of total output is dominated by high-value machinery, and grows with excep-tional rapidity. When 1937 prices are used, however, total output is dominated by more slowly growing food and consumer goods, and the index of real output grows more slowly.

By the same token, a price index covering all goods and services, weighted by the structure of output in 1928 (when the economy was still dominated by agriculture and light industry) would show much sharper increases over the period to 1937, in line with spiralling inflation in consumer markets. A price index weighted by the 1937 structure of output would be correspondingly more influenced by machinery prices, and would rise more slowly.

much sharper increases in the period up to 1937, when prices on consumer markets spiralled upwards. Price indexes weighted by the structure of output in later years are correspondingly more influenced by machinery prices, and rise more slowly.

The 'Gerschenkron effect' is also found in other countries at a similar stage of development, such as the United States in 1899–1939.[23] It is particularly marked in the Soviet Union because the pace of change was so precipitate. There is no methodological reason to prefer index numbers in initial-year prices ('Laspeyres' indices) to index numbers in end-year prices ('Paasche' indices): both provide 'true' if substantially different rates of growth. But the Soviet exclusive preference for the Laspeyres index, and the extreme difference in the two indices due to the rapid transformation in the Soviet machine-building industry, certainly resulted in a one-sided presentation of Soviet economic success.

Such distortions and ambiguities have greatly complicated the task of Western economic historians in our efforts to assess the Soviet economic effort. But as long as the reliability of different kinds of data published in different periods can be graded, and the methods used to distort and exaggerate can be identified, Western students of the Soviet economy have been able to take steps to check and correct the exaggerations. And our knowledge has been considerably extended by the publication, from 1956 onwards, of previously secret statistical data for the Stalin period, and the more recent availability of formerly secret publications and of statistical archives.

(C) Re-evaluations

Soviet official statistics were challenged as early as the 1930s by émigré economists and well-informed journalists; the exaggerated post-1932 harvest figures were particularly strongly criticised.[24] Aggregate statistics for the growth of industrial production and national income were also widely discounted. In 1939 Colin Clark, a Western statistician, attempted to estimate the order of magnitude of Soviet growth by evaluating a small group of commodities in United States' prices. He concluded that official index numbers for overall growth were greatly exaggerated.[25]

After the Second World War Soviet statistics were analysed carefully and systemically by a large number of Western scholars. The pioneer was the demographer Frank Lorimer, whose book *The Population of the Soviet Union*, published by the League of Nations in 1946, was primarily based on the 1926 and 1939 population censuses (only a few tables from the 1939 census had been published). We shall frequently refer to this brilliant study in our subsequent discussion.

Soviet military achievements during the Second World War appeared to demonstrate that the Soviet economy was much stronger than previously believed. With the growing tension between the Soviet Union and the West, an assessment of Soviet economic power became a major preoccupation. The pioneer was the émigré economist Naum Jasny, who, working on his own, attempted in a series of volumes published between 1949 and 1962 to estimate the growth of industry, agriculture and national income. His most important books, still relevant today, are: *The Socialized Agriculture of the USSR* (1949); and *Soviet Industrialization, 1928–52* (1961). His general quantitative results are conveniently summarised, and compared with those of other scholars, in his *Essays on the Soviet Economy* (1962), pp. 1–92. Jasny made many errors, both in arithmetic and in methodology, but – perhaps because of his wide-ranging knowledge of the Soviet economy – his estimates did not differ widely from those reached by large teams of American researchers.

The most important Western work on Soviet statistics was undertaken in 1946–55 by a United States team headed by Professor Abram Bergson, developing work undertaken by the Office of Strategic Services during the war, and financed by the United States' Air Force. They prepared a series of major sectoral studies which enabled Bergson to compute solidly-based national income statistics in fixed and current prices for the years 1928, 1937, 1940, 1950 and 1955. National income was primarily estimated in terms of end use, and the most important sectoral studies concerned consumption and investment. The statistics of consumption were primarily based on the work of Janet Chapman, published as: *Real Wages in Soviet Russia since 1928* (1963). Retail trade data in current prices were deflated by the use of retail price indices based on a large body of data on individual prices. The investment series in real terms combined separate series for capital equipment and construction, also published in large monographs: R. Moorsteen, *Prices and Production of Machinery in the Soviet Union, 1928–1958* (1962); and R. Moorsteen and R. Powell, *The Soviet Capital Stock, 1928–1962* (1966). The Moorsteen and Powell study also includes an annual series for Soviet national income (gross national product) by sector of origin; the authors compare this with capital and labour statistics to evaluate changing economic efficiency. The conclusions of Bergson and his team, with some international comparisons, are summarised in: A. Bergson, *The Real National Income of Soviet Russia since 1928* (1961), and in a collection of essays: A. Bergson and S. Kuznets (eds.), *Economic Trends in the Soviet Union* (1963).

The rival studies by Jasny and Bergson were the subject of much acid dispute at the time. Jasny believed that Bergson's team overestimated Soviet achievements and underestimated Soviet failures. Bergson originally merely undertook a series of studies of separate years in current prices, believing that available price data would not make possible a comparison in terms of constant prices. It was only after Jasny demonstrated that abundant price data were available, and published his own rough results in 1951–2, that Bergson embarked on his comparison of different years in constant prices, which was not published until 1961. Jasny claimed that his announcement that he had found several previously unused volumes of detailed price data for capital goods and industrial materials in the Library of Congress led the agitated American authorities to send a despatch rider round to Jasny's home to collect them.

In their turn, Bergson and his colleagues were irritated by the inaccuracies and wild guesses with which Jasny's work is peppered. A supporter of Bergson published an article critical of Jasny entitled 'Arithmancy, Theomancy and the Soviet Economy'.[26] Bergson pointed out, for example, that although Jasny's calculations for 1928–1937 are stated to be weighted by 1926/27 initial-year prices (a 'Laspeyres index'), in fact he inadvertently used the current prices for each year.[27] Jasny's estimated growth rate was therefore remarkably close to Bergson's when the latter used prices of 1937. In this unintended way, the two results actually confirmed each other, and served to cast doubt on Colin Clark's estimates, which were lower still. The average annual rate of growth of Gross National Product between 1928 and 1937 in the different estimates is as follows (in per cent):

Clark	3.2
Jasny	5.3
Bergson (1928 prices)	11.9
Bergson (1937 prices)	5.5

The difference between Bergson's two estimates is of course a result of the Gershenkron effect.

While we should acknowledge Jasny's outstanding work as a pioneer, it is the volumes of Bergson and his colleagues which must be on the desks of researchers in Soviet economic history, as their careful accuracy make it possible to use the detailed figures they cite from Soviet sources with confidence.

In the 1960s and 1970s individual scholars made further contributions to our knowledge of the quantitative aspects of Russian and Soviet development: Crisp and Gregory on the pre-revolutionary economy; Hodgman and Nutter on industrial production; Eason, Redding and Nimitz on employment; Hunter on transport; Gardner Clark on steel. The French economic historian Eugene Zaleski has carefully compared quantitative plan indicators with performance for the whole Stalin period. Their work will be discussed in the appropriate chapters below, and is listed in the Bibliography.

More recently, several of the authors of the present volume have under-taken further work on Soviet statistics. If the earlier studies were primarily concerned with assessing the growth of Soviet power, the main thrust of our studies, like Zaleski's, has been to relate the statistical data to policy changes and the operation of the Soviet system. Gatrell has examined heavy industry before and during the First World War, with special reference to armaments production. Wheatcroft has investigated agricultural production, building up a new index by combining revised indexes for individual product groups. He has also undertaken a great deal of work on population, including the controversial questions of the number of persons incarcerated in camps, and the number of excess deaths in this grim period of two world wars, civil war and Stalinist repression; he was the first Western scholar to use the pre-viously secret files of the 1939 population census. Lewis has estimated the size of Research and Development employment and expenditure during the industrialisation period. Cooper, Davies and Harrison have recalculated military production and military expenditure during the 1930s and the Second World War, showing that military expenditure was much more substantial in the early 1930s than was previously believed, and that military production during the Second World War was previously underestimated. We shall present our findings in the appropriate chapters, and compare them with those of other scholars.

In recent years, a fresh debate has broken out. Russian economists, critical of their past, have launched a series of attacks not only on Soviet official statistics, but also on Western estimates. They claim that Western economists, including the CIA, have given far too much credence to Soviet published statistics. The main thrust of their criticisms has been directed at Western estimates for the 1970s and 1980s. But the statistics of the 1930s and 1940s have also been re-examined.

The most detailed criticism of Western work appears in the ongoing publications of G. I. Khanin. Khanin claims that national income increased by only 3.2 per cent a year between 1928 and 1941 (50 per cent total growth). This is less than two-thirds of Bergson's estimated rate of increase, 5.0 per cent a year for 1928–40 at 1937 prices (79 per cent total growth). Unfortu-nately Khanin does not supply enough data to enable an independent assessment of his estimates. He does not differ substantially from his Western colleagues in the case of three of the four major production sectors – industry, agriculture and railway transport. Khanin estimates the rate of growth of industrial production at 10.9 per cent in 1928–41[28] (so 1941 is 384, with 1928 = 100). This may be compared with Moorsteen and Powell's 10.1 per cent in 1928–40 at 1937 prices (1940 is 318, with 1928 = 100).[29] For agriculture and railway transport, Khanin uses official figures. He rejects Powell's estimate of the rate of growth of construction as too high.[30] But construction amounted to a mere 5 per cent of GNP in 1937,[31] so cannot have made a substantial difference to the outcome.[32] The only possible explanation is that Khanin has given a higher weight than Bergson and Moorsteen/Powell to agriculture, which had a lower rate of growth than the other main sectors of the economy.

A further recent study by three Russian demographers, Andreev, Darskii and Khar'kova, who worked in the TsSU research institute, concerns the much-disputed estimates of excess deaths during the upheaval of collectivisation, famine and repression in 1928–37. Their estimates of excess deaths are discussed in chapter 4. They are considerably higher than Lorimer's estimates, or than those published in the West more recently by Wheatcroft and Maksudov. The main disagreement is about the number of infant deaths in the famine.

The Russian historians Zemskov and Dugin have used data in newly-opened archives to calculate the number of people imprisoned and sent to labour settlements and camps in 1928–40, and the total number in camps and in settlements in each year. Their estimates are lower than Wheatcroft's, and far lower than those by Robert Conquest and others.

In our discussion below we return in more detail to the recent work of Khanin, Zemskov and others. But many of these controversial issues – if they can be settled at all – must await the laborious processing of the archival data.

Further reading

A general guide to the problems of Soviet statistical sources is provided by S. G. Wheatcroft in S. Fitzpatrick and L. Viola (eds.), *A Researcher's Guide to Sources on Soviet Social History in the 1930s* (Armonk, NY, 1987), 153–75.
For a detailed discussion of Soviet statistical terminology see S. G. Wheatcroft and R. W. Davies (eds.), *Materials for a Balance of the Soviet Economy, 1928–1930* (Cambridge, 1985).

The major Western assessments of Soviet statistics are discussed and listed in chapter 2: Bergson (1961), Bergson and Kuznets (eds.) (1963), Chapman (1963), Jasny (1962), Moorsteen (1962), Moorsteen and Powell (1966).

3   National income

Mark Harrison

In 1913, Imperial Russia was the least developed of the European powers. By 1940 the USSR had become, to a large extent, a modern industrial state. The employment share of agriculture had declined from three quarters in 1913 to one half in 1940; its contribution to national income had shrunk from one half to a mere 30 per cent. The product of industry, construction, and transport had doubled and tripled. Most striking of all was the fact that these great changes had been compressed into a single decade of intense activity, under the first and second five-year plans (1928–37); in the same decade, the advanced capitalist economies had suffered the worst depression of modern times.

There was a debit side to the Soviet achievement. The era had begun with a catastrophic foreign war which had ripped apart the fabric of the old regime. World war (1914–7), the two revolutions of 1917, and civil war (1918–21) had merged into a single process which left Soviet Russia, in 1921, traumatised and exhausted from years of bloody fighting and institutional upheaval, now entering a disastrous famine. The economy was still recovering when Stalin's policies of mass collectivisation of peasant farming, forced industrialisation, and sweeping purges of government and society imposed fresh burdens. Inter-war economic development was crisis-ridden, not by the demand deficiency and trade wars which fettered the market economies at this time, but by periodic overcommitment and over-strain of supply, culminating in sharp slowdowns of economic expansion in 1931–2 and 1937–40.

How did these processes balance out in the behaviour of the Soviet gross national product (GNP), in total, and per head of the population? To what extent did forced march industrialisation add up to increased national income? By a GNP standard, to what degree had the Soviet economy advanced its position by 1940, both absolutely, and relative to its main competitors – the Soviet allies and enemies of two world wars, Germany, France, the United Kingdom and the United States, and Italy and Japan?

These are not idle questions. In 1931, Stalin had set before Soviet industrial leaders the scale of the development lag between the USSR and the west: 'We are fifty or a hundred years behind the advanced countries. We must make good this distance in ten years. Either we do it, or they crush us.'[1] The extent of 'catching up' achieved within the time limit set by Stalin (of course, in 1931 'ten years' was not an exact forecast, but just stood for a relatively compressed period of effort) is of intrinsic historical interest as a test of his regime and its policies.

This also suggests the more general historical significance of GNP relativities in 1913 and 1940. In both years, Russia (the USSR) stood on the edge of war. In these two Great Wars, among the ultimately decisive factors would be GNP and population. GNP and population measured the size of the economy, and sheer mass (of soldiers, weaponry and war materials) would weigh heavily on the battlefield. GNP per head – the proportion between GNP and population – measured the economy's development level. Development level would also be among the decisive factors permitting economic mass to be translated into military power. Additionally, the Soviet economy would show considerable advantages over other, wealthier powers when it came to raising the ratio of military spending to GNP.[2] For such reasons, Russian and Soviet GNP in the two benchmark years must remain an important object of research.

Making reliable GNP evaluations involving the Soviet economy has traditionally presented awesome difficulties. Official data are unsatisfactory for several reasons. One is that the Soviet statistical authorities followed the material product system of accounts; their national income concept, net material product (NMP) differed from the GNP concept followed in Western economies in the ways shown in the inset box.[3] But here is a technical difficulty at most, relatively easy to overcome, and not a source of major distortion or bias.

The more important difficulties arise from index number problems, hidden inflation, and the welfare evaluation of real output. Soviet measures of real product tended to take the form of index numbers based on the fixed prices of years in the distant past, giving rise to a large Gerschenkron effect (see chapter 2). Moreover, the official price index tended in practice to contain a great deal of hidden inflation – some of the growth of 'real' output shown in official data was just a rise in ruble values, without any increase in real output. In any case, the increase in welfare associated with an increase in real output was often difficult to evaluate without taking into account persistent shortfalls of quality and availability of goods and services. To make matters worse, none of these obstacles to comparability was ever more acute than in the inter-war period.

After the Second World War, considerable resources of western scholarship began to be invested in these tasks. The pioneering work of the first post-war years was led by Abram Bergson under the sponsorship of the

Definitions of national income, NMP, GNP/GDP, etc.

In the material product system (MPS) of accounts used in the USSR and other state socialist countries, national income was defined as the *net material product* (NMP): the value of final output of material goods (but not services, although intermediate services such as transport are included in this value), net of depreciation, valued at transfer prices which include net indirect taxes. From a *sector-of-origin* point of view, 'NMP produced' came from agriculture, industry, construction, transport, and trade. From an *end-use* standpoint, 'NMP utilised' was divided into material consumption and material accumulation (the latter included not only net investment in a western sense, but also other material non-consumption including outlays on defence stocks). NMP produced was converted into NMP utilised mainly by adding net imports.

In the Western system of national accounts (SNA), national income is most commonly defined as the *gross national product* (GNP): the final value of all goods and services, gross of depreciation, usually at factor cost (i.e. market prices less net indirect taxes). GNP includes net profits and interest earned abroad by nationals; subtracting the latter from GNP makes *gross domestic product* (GDP). In the case of the USSR, which neither earned nor paid foreign property income, GNP and GDP are interchangeable. The deduction of depreciation leaves net national or domestic product (NNP, NDP). By *sector of origin*, GNP is produced in agriculture, industry (including construction and transport), and services; by *end use* GNP is composed of outlays on household consumption, government consumption (including all defence outlays), gross investment, and net exports. Therefore:

Concept	GNP/GDP	NMP
Production	Final value of goods and services	Final value of goods, but not services (intermediate services included in final value of goods)
Value standard	Factor costs	Prevailing prices
Net indirect taxes	Excluded	Included
Capital depreciation	Included	Excluded

RAND Corporation.[4] But almost as soon as some Western economists began to demonstrate the necessary ingenuity, others began to raise less tractable issues of the reliability of Soviet price and production statistics, and the significance of restrictions on the quality, availability, and range of variety of Soviet products. If the ultimate goal was to measure 'the output of utility, not goods', it would be easy to overstate the welfare significance of Soviet output on the basis of conventional measures.[5] Right from the start, such issues of principle threatened to overshadow the technical details of accounting methodology, making divergent perceptions of Soviet economic progress impossible to reconcile on the basis of present knowledge.

(A) The growth of total output

Official data suggest that, in the quarter-century from 1913 to 1940, within constant (pre-1939) frontiers, Soviet national income expanded roughly sixfold. During the first 15 years of this period, national income at first collapsed, bottoming out at 40 per cent of the 1913 level in 1920; by 1926 it had recovered (by 1927, in per capita terms), and in 1928 exceeded the pre-war benchmark by about one-fifth. Then came 12 years of whirlwind transformation under Stalin's first three five-year plans, during which the Soviet economy shot to the top of the international growth league. The published index numbers, calculated in 1926/27 prices, and as percentages of 1913, are as follows.[6]

	1928	1932	1937	1940
Total	119	217	459	611
Per head	109	188	386	448

Western independent estimates testify to considerable elements of exaggeration in this account. First, as late as 1928, Soviet national income still fell short of the level previously attained in 1913; more controversially, it has been argued that this indicates an element of reserve capacity, which contributes to explaining the rapidity of economic growth after 1928. Secondly, Western studies have also been much more cautious in their evaluation of economic growth from 1928 to the outbreak of the Second World War.

(i) 1913–1928

Observers have criticised the Soviet official comparison of 1928 and 1913 national income on three grounds.[7]

First, it understates 1913 national income by including some elements which were averages for 1909–13, rather than for the year 1913 itself (M. E. Falkus). Secondly it exaggerates 1928 national income by neglecting a significant decline in product quality (the émigré Russian economist S. N. Prokopovich). Thirdly, it exaggerates 1928 national income by understating inflation, 1913–28; it implicitly assumes that all transactions in 1928 took place in state-controlled markets at relatively low prices, ignoring the higher prices in unregulated markets (Paul R. Gregory).

This has led Gregory to estimate 1928 national income as only 93 per cent of 1913, implying a still greater fall in income per head.[8] His figure carries important further implications: it suggests that NEP failed to achieve full economic recovery, and that a considerable part of the subsequent great leap forward can be attributed to taking up the productive capacity still left in reserve.

Not all Western observers agree with this pessimistic view of the results of economic recovery up to 1928. Davies and Wheatcroft have suggested two reservations. First, Gregory's low figure for 1928 national income assumes an unrealistic decline in peasant on-farm food consumption, so that 1928 national income is understated. Secondly, to use 1913 national income for the pre-war benchmark overstates the permanent income of the pre-revolutionary Russian Empire, because it includes a large transitory element – an unexpected bumper harvest. If GNP in 1928 fell short of 1913, it was not because NEP had failed to bring about complete recovery, but because the prosperity of 1913 was abnormal. Combining 1913 non-agricultural production with agricultural production averaged over 1909–13 would better represent the normal utilisation of pre-revolutionary capacity.[9]

Gregory himself has suggested a figure which takes into account the first of Davies and Wheatcroft's reservations. When this is further revised on the lines of their second proposition, 1928 national income emerges as roughly 111 per cent of 1913 permanent national income ('permanent' income = actual income, less transitory income).[10] This implies that income per head in 1928 had just barely recovered.

In summary, the range of Western estimates for national income in 1928, within constant pre-1939 frontiers, in 1913 prices and per cent of 1913, can be shown as follows, in comparison with the traditional Soviet official version:

	total	per head
TsSU (official)	119	109
Gregory	93	83
Davies, Wheatcroft	111	100

(ii) 1928–1940

The traditional view reported in Soviet official data suggests a five-fold increase in national income in a dozen years. This view has also been criticised by independent scholars as greatly exaggerated, for three reasons.

First, in 1926/27, the base year for Soviet official inter-war data, the relative price of capital goods was much higher than before (say, in 1913) or afterwards (in 1937 or subsequent years). This contributes to the rapid growth of the official index, because capital goods were the most rapidly growing component of material production (see chapters 2 and 7). In itself this does not make the official index wrong, but the relatively high value of capital goods makes its growth an upper limit on what would be reasonable. Moreover, if the relative price of capital goods was high in 1926/27 because administrative pressure was holding down the prices of food and consumer products relative to production costs and scarcity values, then we would be right to regard 1926/27 prices as distorted.

Secondly, official data claimed to measure the real output of later years at fixed prices of 1926/27, but in practice the 'unchanged' prices were changeable, and the volume estimates associated with them included an element of hidden inflation. Hidden inflation came from several sources – the introduction of new products at higher prices, the unacknowledged further deterioration of product quality, and the concealment of production shortfalls (see chapter 7).

Thirdly, at least one element in the official measure of material production was directly distorted as a result of deliberate high-level decisions. Agricultural output after 1932 was exaggerated by comparison with the late 1920s by means of an unacknowledged shift from reporting the harvest on the basis of the barn yield, net of harvest losses, to the 'biological' yield of the crop still standing in the fields (see chapter 6).

The American scholars who went to work under Bergson in the post-war years proceeded along two main avenues of inquiry. Bergson himself calculated Soviet GNP for various benchmark years (including 1928, 1937, and 1940) from the expenditure side, deflating expenditure from ruble prices prevailing in each year to constant factor costs. Subsequently, Richard Moorsteen and Raymond P. Powell calculated annual series for GNP from the physical output of goods and employment in services, at ruble factor costs of 1937. The results were to some extent interdependent, and coincided closely.

The most striking result was their agreement on growth estimates which were very rapid by international standards, but fell far short of the TsSU data. Thus, where official series showed a near quadrupling of national income under the decisive first and second five-year plans (1928–37),

Bergson found that Soviet GNP fell short of a three-fold increase, even at factor costs of 1928. When 1937 provided the standard of factor-cost valuation, the increase in GNP was just 62 per cent over 1928 (72 per cent when measured by Moorsteen and Powell from the output side).

Taking the story up to 1940 is complicated because in 1939–40 the USSR absorbed significant territory in Poland and the Baltic region, including more than 20 million people. The main Western estimates of Soviet GNP in 1940 cover the territory within contemporary frontiers, but we can make a rough adjustment to pre-1939 frontiers in proportion to the extra population.[11]

On this basis, the range of Soviet official and Western estimates for Soviet national income in 1937 and 1940, in constant prices, and as if within constant pre-1939 frontiers, can be summarised as follows (1928 = 100); the comparison includes estimates by Clark and Jasny already surveyed in chapter 2.[12]

		1937	1940
TsSU	NMP, at '1926/27' prices	386	513
Clark	Real product, in 'international units'	133	145
Jasny	NNP, at 'real' 1926/27 prices	172	189
Bergson	GNP, at 1928 factor costs	275	..
Bergson	GNP, at 1937 factor costs	162	179
Moorsteen and Powell	GNP, at 1937 factor costs	172	187

In 1987 the impatience with which Soviet unofficial analysts looked on traditional TsSU exaggerations finally boiled over into print. The Academy of Sciences Institute of World Economy and International Relations (IMEMO) was first to publish a wide ranging reevaluation of Soviet economic development in international comparison, based on deflating official national income data by means of an unofficial estimate of inflation. The result appeared broadly consistent with those of the Bergson project.[13] Another, more pessimistic view was soon published by the independent researcher, G. I. Khanin. On the basis of a more fundamental, methodologically rather original root-and-branch reappraisal of basic economic data, he found that Soviet national income increased by only 50 per cent, 1928–41, even within expanding contemporary frontiers, compared with the 79 or 87 per cent increase found by the RAND project researchers.[14] Khanin emphasised agricultural setbacks and the falsification of product growth as factors in poor Soviet inter-war economic performance, but it is not clear whether these justified such a depressing assessment of the achievements of the period.[15]

(B) The level of development

(i) GNP per head: its rate of growth

Reliable index numbers of total output are very necessary, and indeed they
formed one of the essential foundations for the Soviet economy's reputation
for rapid growth. But without adjustment for population changes, which in
the Soviet case were violent and not at all continuous, they tell us little about
change in the level of economic development. Here a further problem is that
Soviet demographic statistics of the 1930s were officially distorted or concealed. Only recently have underlying census data, and more reliable evaluations, become available (see chapter 4).

We can combine Moorsteen and Powell's annual series for GNP at 1937
factor costs, 1928–40, with new annual population series for the same years
from Andreev, Darskii, and Khar kova, and Davies and Wheatcroft's
assumption for 1928 of no change over permanent GNP per head of the
Russian Empire in 1913.[16] This gives us the following picture (Figure 1 and
Table 1). By 1928, Soviet GNP per head had recovered to the permanent
income of 1913. Under the first five-year plan there was a modest increase of
roughly 6 per cent up to 1931, after which industrial growth decelerated,
and was more than offset by agricultural setbacks; in 1932, GNP per head
fell slightly.

There was only a momentary breathing space. From 1933 onwards,
expansion was resumed. By 1937, the last year of the second five-year plan,
GNP per head stood 60 per cent above the level of 1928. But five years of
continuously rising output were followed by three years of stagnation.
Again, the economy had become overstretched, and economic coordination
was breaking down under the pressures of repressed inflation, emergency
rearmament against real enemies without, and political mobilisation against
the imaginary enemy within. While Europe rolled towards war, the Soviet
economic development process marked time.

In summary, by the outbreak of the Second World War, Soviet GNP per
head stood three-fifths higher than Russian GNP per head on the eve of the
First World War. This dramatic rise did not take place smoothly; the entire
increase was compressed into nine hectic years (1928–37). On either side of
this growth phase were two sub-periods of stagnation and setback (1913–28,
and 1937–40). Even the growth phase itself was not continuous, and suffered a break in 1931–2. Taking the long view, however, in spite of the
incidence of wars and revolutions, the annual average growth of 1.8 per cent
over the whole period from 1913 to 1940 exceeded the 1.6 per cent annual
average growth of national income per capita achieved by Tsarist Russia,
1885–9 to 1909–13.[17]

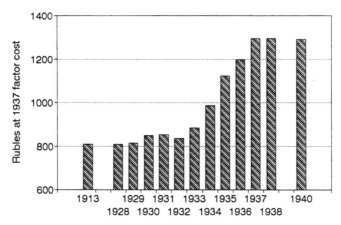

Figure 1   Gross National Product per head, 1913–1940. *Source:* table 1.

What were the implications for the relative standing of the Soviet economy in the world arena? Figure 2 compares Soviet growth with that of the other Great Powers. Over the whole period from one world war to the next, the Great Powers divided into two groups. The USA, UK, France, and Italy formed the slowly growing economies – by 1940, even under the impact of economic mobilisation for the Second World War, per capita GNPs of these countries had grown by no more than one-third over 1913. Amongst a more dynamic group, per capita GNPs had risen by three-fifths or more; the USSR belonged to this group, together with Germany and Japan.

In other respects, Soviet economic growth followed a pattern exactly converse to that of other countries, expanding when they stagnated, and faltering when they prospered. Thus for the capitalist industrial powers the years from the end of the First World War to the Wall Street Crash of 1929 were a time of considerable prosperity, with incomes rising above pre-1914 levels virtually everywhere; meanwhile the USSR struggled to achieve a bare recovery. Then, while the West plunged into a severe and prolonged depression of markets and demand, the Soviet economy mobilised for all-out industrialisation. In the years from 1928 to 1937 the 60 per cent increase in per capita GNP recorded by the Soviet economy exceeded the growth achieved elsewhere by several times; in the UK, Germany, Italy, and Japan, GNP per head rose by no more than 10–20 per cent, French incomes stagnated, and US incomes fell.

But the stagnation of the capitalist economies came to an end in the late 1930s with rearmament and war. War meant unlimited demands for food-stuffs, fuels, and industrial goods; with demand limitations removed, the market economies utilised their productive potential more fully. By 1940 per capita GNPs of the Great Powers were rising smartly – with two exceptions: in occupied France, and in the USSR, which was still locked into a persistent crisis of economic overcommitment and dislocation.

(ii) GNP per head: its relative level

What implications does all this have for the relative standing of the Soviet economy? Comparing development levels is difficult enough between countries which have good national income data to start with. To compare one economy with another, at the same point in time, we need to measure both national products in comparable currency units. Exchange rates are little help, even for convertible currencies, because they are known to distort the relative purchasing power of national currency units.[18] Since the Soviet Union lacked good national income data, and since the ruble was inconvertible at the time, its exchange rate being fixed arbitrarily by decree, valuing Soviet national income in dollars or sterling at the official rate would be simply pointless.

There are two main alternatives. In recent years much research effort has gone into revaluing the post-war GDPs of many countries at US dollar prices, or average prices expressed in 'international' dollars ($INT). A World Bank team led by Paul Marer valued Soviet GDP per head in 1980 at $INT 5550; this can be compared with the per capita GDPs of the market economies found for 1980 by Phase IV of the International Comparison Project, and amounts to 47 per cent of the US figure.[19] When these GDPs are extrapolated back to the inter-war period, using national growth rates of GDP and population, it emerges that Soviet GDP per head in 1938 was $INT 1826, 40 per cent of the United States' figure, and 50 per cent of the United Kingdom's.[20]

This method looks reliable, but everything depends on the reliability of the Marer study. Here there is a difficulty, because in recent years any scholarly consensus over the post-war Soviet development level has simply disintegrated. Serious estimates of the Soviet/US ratio of GNP per head in recent years range from the CIA's 57 per cent (for 1980, in US dollars – perhaps 54 per cent for 1987) to the Russian economist V. Belkin's 12–24 per cent (for 1987, also in US dollars); there are several intermediate estimates, most of them well above Belkin's basement figure, but also below Marer's estimate.[21] Given this kind of disagreement about very recent history, it is hard to have much confidence in the results implied for GNP relativities more than half a century removed.

An alternative method assumes that the results of backtracking from 1980 give reliable results for the inter-war period, at least for the economies with good national accounts. The author has estimated the multiple correlation between GDP per head in 1937 and indirect indicators of development such as the consumption of industrial materials and energy, transport and communications activity, the rate of infant mortality, and so on, for a sample of market economies with relatively good national accounts. Applying this relationship to the countries with poor national accounts (but relatively reliable indirect indicators) allows us to estimate their likely GDP per head indirectly. Although it is still difficult to obtain firm results, a lower estimate for Soviet pre-war GDP per head is suggested – not more than half that of the UK, and more likely two-fifths or one-third.[22]

For present purposes, I take 40 per cent as a reasonable figure for the ratio of Soviet GDP per head to the UK level in 1937 (one-third of the United States). On this basis, we can show Soviet inter-war GDP per head in units comparable with those of the other Great Powers (Table 2). Figure 2 shows that in 1913 Russian GDP per head was far below that of all the other Great Powers except Japan. By 1928, the USSR was lagging badly, and had probably been overtaken by Japan. The huge efforts of 1928–37 took the Soviet economy significantly closer to the development level of its main competitors, running neck and neck with Japan, although the gap with the western powers remained a daunting one. But as hostilities approached, the Soviet economy dropped back again; now that Japan had begun its extraordinary ascent, the USSR was entering the Second World War the poorest of the Great Powers.

(C) Investment and consumption

More detailed examination of the uses of national income for investment and consumption throws additional light on the nature of the Soviet economic development model.

(i) Investment

The Soviet economic transformation of 1928–40 was driven largely by investment, in several senses. Ambitious investment programmes fostered a sense of mission, and helped to mobilise supporters of the regime. In the process of implementation, these programmes strained the supply side of the economy, disrupted the market sector and the traditional agrarian economy, forced a transition away from the market towards comprehensive physical controls, and created widespread economic difficulties which the authorities used to justify widespread repression. Once accomplished, these same investment programmes also brought about a transformation of the capital stock which is still surprising in its scope.

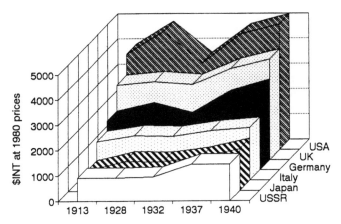

Figure 2   Gross Domestic Product per head in international
comparison, 1913–1940. *Source:* table 2.

Between 1 January 1928, and 1941, within constant pre-1939 frontiers,
the total net capital stock (measured by Moorsteen and Powell at 1937
prices) more than doubled; this was despite the collapse of livestock
numbers, which had formed almost a quarter of the capital stock in 1928.
The increase within actual frontiers of the time was significantly greater,
because the annexations of 1939–40 in Poland and the Baltic region
increased the 1940 capital stock by about 10 per cent; this brought the total
on 1 January 1941 to a multiple of 2.5 times 1928.[23]

The composition of the net capital stock also changed markedly. The
share of livestock fell from 24 per cent in 1928 to 8 per cent in 1933, and
remained at this low figure during the remainder of the inter-war period.
There was a corresponding rise in the share of 'non-agricultural, non-
residential' fixed capital – from 16 per cent in 1928 to 47 per cent in 1941.
The average age of fixed capital in operation also declined, from 17.6 years
to 13.8 years over the same period.

As a result of the growth in the capital stock, Moorsteen and Powell found
that the capital-labour ratio in the economy as a whole (measured by capital
per hour worked) had risen by almost one half, while the capital-output
ratio rose more gently, by 13 per cent over the period.[24] The implications of
these changing ratios are considered below in chapter 9.

The investment effort which brought all this about followed a pronounced fluctuation (Table 3). Soviet net investment was probably, in
1926/27, still slightly below the 1913 level, and, by 1927/28, significantly
above. Just as important was the change in its composition, which was to
prove permanent, away from residential and services construction towards

productive investment in industry and agriculture.[25] By 1928 a huge upsurge of investment effort was already under way. Between 1928 and 1932, gross investment (measured by Moorsteen and Powell at constant prices of 1937) doubled – half the increase took place in a single year, 1929/30 – and then fell back. In 1934 another surge of effort began, taking investment to four times the 1928 level by 1936. But in 1937 came another setback, and after that investment stagnated until the outbreak of war.

Both the investment upsurges (1928–31 and 1934–6) shared a common pattern. In the first phase, a large number of new projects was designated with the aim of accelerating the economic and social transformation. Since the economy was growing rapidly, construction materials and equipment were plentiful, and the general air of optimism encouraged all the projects designated and more to be begun.

Soon, however, the requirements of all the projects simultaneously in progress began to outrun the resources available. Not all projects could be supplied at once with materials, machinery, power, and building workers. Existing building sites were frozen, reduced to idleness, in order to divert supplies to new ones. At this point, policy sometimes made matters worse; identifying shortages of steel, cement, power, and machinery, the authorities imposed fresh lists of urgent new projects to create additional capacity in the 'bottleneck' sectors; this widened rather than reduced the excess of demand over supply. It became more and more difficult to finish off the projects begun and add to the capacity available for operation.

In each crisis an essential role was played by apparently extraneous factors – in 1931–2, food shortages, falling export values, rising industrial costs, and unforeseen military outlays; in 1936–7, internal and external security fears, purges, and accelerated rearmament. A common thread, however, was the inability of the planners to allow for the unexpected, and to adapt to unforeseen demands until such difficulties had coalesced into a crisis affecting the whole economy.

Ultimately, unfamiliar restraints on investment had to be reimposed from the centre. New projects had to be prohibited, and investment goods redirected to projects near completion. Only with the commissioning of new, finished capacity would new resources be created, allowing output and investment to grow again.

The year-on-year change in the backlog of unfinished construction thus provided a sensitive measure of the tendency to excessive mobilisation, since it rose sharply with overinvestment, then fell back again as the investment process was brought back under control.[26] Two alternatives to Moorsteen and Powell's measure of capital projects in progress have been offered by R. W. Davies on the basis of classified and archival sources not previously available; these are shown as series (A) and (B) in Table 3, after adjustment to 1937 prices. For the later 1930s series (B) is preferred to series (A) because the former may exclude (and, if so, the latter includes) defence industry construction.

Table 3 shows that there were two pronounced peaks in the share of investment absorbed by unfinished construction. In the first five-year plan, this share peaked at 19 per cent in 1931 (series A), then fell back to a negligible figure in the following recovery, and in 1935 the backlog of uncompleted projects actually fell. In fact, much of the very rapid economic growth of the mid-1930s is attributable to success in at last finishing off many of the big projects begun under the first five-year plan, but not completed on schedule. Shortly, however, a return to overinvestment and excessive mobilisation was signalled by the share of the increase in unfinished construction (series B), which again hit high levels – 16 per cent in 1936, 15 per cent again in 1937. This was the peak of the increase, but the total backlog of projects in progress continued to rise until 1941.

Failure to control this backlog was not accidental, and reflected an intrinsic bias in the economic system. Faced with shortages and other supply-side difficulties, the system was biassed towards solutions which involved widening the capital stock, and building and staffing new factories, on an 'extensive' model of economic growth, rather than following a more 'intensive' model towards resource-saving innovation, rationalising and deepening the existing capital stock, and reducing requirements on the demand side. Again, the implications are reviewed in chapter 9.

(ii) Consumption

In 1928, GNP per head of the population, in 1913 prices, probably stood at about the same level as in 1909–13. According to Gregory's comparison of 1928 and 1913, the share of personal consumption in national income may fallen slightly; if so, then living standards remained a little below the prewar norm.[27] (In the interval, marked by world war and civil war, they had collapsed, then recovered.) Beyond this, there are few safe generalisations. In 1928 the urban consumer probably still fared worse than before the First World War, certainly as far as diet was concerned. Evidence relating to the changing production and utilisation of food products also suggests that peasants had been substantial beneficiaries, since in 1928 they retained and consumed a much larger share of their own produce than before the revolution.[28] However, Paul Gregory has found it difficult to identify any increase in farm consumption in kind sufficient to allow for a rise in peasant living standards.[29]

After 1928, living standards followed another violent zigzag. The turn to non-market forms of food procurement stripped the countryside of food, as well as fodder, precipitating a disastrous decline in rural subsistence, which culminated in harvest failure and famine in Ukraine, North Caucasus and elsewhere in 1932–3. The demographic consequences are described in chapter 4. The burden was unevenly distributed and, since free market prices rose to very high levels, those peasants (mainly in other regions) with disposable food surpluses could acquire cash and prosper, at least relatively to their neighbours. However, the overall shortfall of farm consumption in kind was by no means compensated by peasant purchases of processed foods and manufactured consumer goods for cash; in 1934, when the post-famine recovery was under way, total peasant purchases of these goods in 'social-ised' retail outlets still fell short of the 1928 level by roughly 60 per cent.[30] After this, rural living standards continued their recovery, but Bergson found total farm consumption in kind in 1940 (at 1937 prices) to be still 15 per cent below 1928, and overall rural consumption per head must also have remained well below the level of the late 1920s.[31]

Living standards of the urban population after 1928 have been researched in some detail. Initially there was a sharp decline, accompanied by the introduction of consumer rationing which retained a wide scope until 1935. The emergence of the USSR from agrarian crisis was followed by de-rationing, but consumer shortages were never completely eliminated. After 1937 the Soviet consumer was squeezed again between the opposing pressures of accelerating rearmament and overall economic slowdown, so that the degree of shortage rose again. However, consumer rationing was not reimposed until the late summer of 1941, when the post-invasion crisis was nearing its height.

According to Janet Chapman's careful investigation, the real disposable income of wage and salary earners outside agriculture never fully recovered from the crisis of 1932–3; by 1937 they were still two-fifths below the 1928 level, when measured at 1937 prices. If the further deterioration of 1937–40 is taken into account, the decline compared with 1928 approached one-half.[32]

Urban living standards, however, fell by much less and, on some measures, even rose. Most important in explaining this were the decline in unemployment and the increased participation of family members in the workforce, which together reduced sharply the number of dependents per wage earner – from 2.46 in 1928 to 1.28 in 1940. In consequence, purchases of consumer goods per head of the urban population fell by only one-quarter, 1928–40, at 1937 prices (and at 1928 prices, they rose by one-eighth.)[33]

When we return to aggregate trends in living standards, we are left with Bergson's finding of a small decline in household consumption per head of the total population – by 3 per cent in 1937, compared with 1928, or by 7 per cent if we include the rearmament period of 1937–40. However, the picture changes to one of modest improvement (by 10 per cent over 1928–37) if we include the increase in communal services (health, education, etc.) supplied by the government free of charge.

Because of reduced unemployment and increased participation, the typical household had to supply much more labour than before to secure this standard of living, and household consumption per worker underwent sharp decline.[34] Since the decline in consumption per worker (27 per cent, 1928–40) fell well short of the decline in the real wage outside agriculture reported by Chapman (46 per cent), Bergson concluded that the industrial worker fared worse, relatively speaking, than the farmer.[35] If so, there was a further drawing together of real incomes in town and country. However, this generalisation is unlikely to have held much validity in the early 1930s, when significant regions of the countryside were deprived of essential food to guarantee urban workers' subsistence.

On the eve of rapid industrialisation, Soviet plans promised rapid improvement in living standards. This objective was based on overoptimistic assumptions, and in practice was easily overridden by other priorities of national economic development and defence. As a result, while their country became a significant industrial power, most Soviet peasants and workers remained no better off than in 1928 or 1913. Substantial elements became significantly worse off, and the deterioration was associated with abnormal rural mortality. There is inconclusive evidence of a long run convergence of rural and urban living standards; even if accepted, it is hard to see this as reflecting any advance of the rural population in general. The corollary of deterioration for some sub-groups, however, is that others did experience significant improvement, especially those peasants who escaped the hungry village for permanent urban employment, and workers promoted to skilled, supervisory, or administrative posts.

(D) The development model: a summary

The Soviet growth pattern involved violent structural change, clearly visible in the national accounts; the picture is only a little blurred by the difficulty of making an accurate comparison between the Soviet period and 1913. Making this comparison is complicated by lack of data in strictly comparable prices. We have Gregory's estimates for 1913 in the prices of that year, and Moorsteen and Powell for 1928–40 at 1937 factor costs; we also have the limited security of knowing that the structures of 1913 prices and 1937 factor costs were more nearly comparable than either was with prices of 1926/27 or factor costs of 1928.[36]

(i) The structure of GNP

Rapid industrialisation forcibly altered the distribution of national income by sector of origin (Table 4). The pattern of 1928 was rather like that of 1913 (except for a decline in the share of services output, in which military demobilisation played a part), while that of 1932 was closer to that of 1937 or 1940. Most of the change was compressed into four years, 1928–32; in this unbelievably short period, the share of industry, construction, and transport rose from 28 to 41 per cent of national income. Between these two dry numbers lay the first stage of 'building socialism in a single country', which converted the whole country into a huge building site almost overnight; peasants became labourers and factory workers, while power stations, steel mills, engineering works, new cities, roads, and railway lines were thrown up in a profusion of record breaking endeavours. The mushrooming apparatus of government planning and administration (including defence and security), and of health, education, and welfare services, ensured that the share of services also generally rose. At the same time the contribution of agriculture, which once exceeded half of national income, was diminished to less than one-third.

The bad news was that little economic growth was associated with the violent structural change of 1928–32. This structural change was brought about as much by the collapse of agriculture as by the rise of industry. After 1932, however, agriculture recovered, while non-agricultural production continued to expand. Now came the years up to 1937, when per capita incomes rose markedly. But Table 4 shows that from now on the makeup of national income on the output side was quite different from before, with much more of it originating in industry, construction, transport, and services – two-thirds in 1940, compared with two fifths in 1913.

Related pressures reallocated national income between alternative uses (Table 5). In 1928 the shares of national expenditure were similar to those of 1913. The main difference was that the burden of domestic investment now fell exclusively on domestic savings; before the First World War, a significant contribution had come from foreign capital. In 1937, by contrast with 1928, the share of net investment had more than doubled, rising from 10 to 23 per cent of national income. (Net investment and national product are shown here for the sake of comparability with prewar data, but the share of *gross* investment in GNP would peak in 1937 at a still higher figure of 26 per cent.) The share of government consumption (both military and civilian) had almost tripled, rising from 8 to 23 per cent. As a result, household consumption had suffered a terrific squeeze, its share falling from more than four-fifths of national income in 1928 to barely more than a half in 1937.

Worse followed in the short period remaining before war broke out. In just three years, 1937–40, rearmament swallowed up an additional 10 per cent of national income (which itself was no longer rising). Government non-defence consumption maintained its share. Household consumption gave further ground; just as significant, in view of government priorities, was a notable squeeze on net investment, which fell from 23 per cent of national income in 1937 to a bare 15 per cent in 1940. While the pressure on consumption could be expected, the failure of investment was an important measure of the severity of the crisis, as the logjammed supply side failed to meet the competing demands of national economic development and security.

(ii) GNP and industrialisation

The Soviet development model of the inter-war years presents an instructive case study in forced, rapid industrialisation. Stalin's regime had translated Bolshevik aspirations of sweeping social and economic reconstruction into a concerted effort to 'catch up and overtake' the leading capitalist industrial nations within a few years. Soviet leaders identified the key determinants of industrial wealth and power in the early twentieth century as steel, cement, electric power, and engineering and transport capacity. The chief means for acquiring these was to be the rebuilding of capital stock under public ownership and on large-scale, urban, industrial lines.

Thus, a low-income, agrarian country was subjected to radical and very rapid structural change, reflected in simultaneous shifts in the structure of national income by end use and sector of origin. On the expenditure side, investment was pushed up to the limit of society's tolerance – almost certainly, beyond this limit in the early and late 1930s. On the output side, industry, construction, and transport became the biggest production complex, while agriculture suffered from the alternating attentions and inattention of the regime, and stagnated as a result.

In the outcome, rapid structural change was accomplished; the country did in fact become much more industrialised and urbanised within a very short period of time. There was also a substantial increase in GNP per head, largely a result of the declining weight of agriculture. Thus, millions exchanged employment in the low productivity agrarian sector for somewhat more productive employment in factory industry and services. But the USSR remained a low income country in relative terms, and did not succeed in escaping from relative poverty. Many of the old agrarian work patterns and relations of authority and indiscipline were reproduced in the new, urban and industrial context, and the new industrial jobs still represented low productivity employment in international comparison. Low productivity also remained a characteristic of the millions left in agriculture.

Probably, the Stalinist concept of the economic development process was seriously oversimplified. The high per capita GNPs of the western capitalist economies were based on more than heavy industrialisation. There, investment in human capital, rising living standards for a widening labour aristocracy, and the spread of new technologies for communications and information, all complemented the rising productive capacities of established industries, and gave the market economies a resilience which Soviet leaders of the Stalin generation failed to foresee. As a result, despite the Soviet great leap forward of 1928–37, which coincided with the destabilisation and breakup of the international market economy, the USSR did not win the expected decisive victory in the economic race with the capitalist powers. This makes the Soviet victory in the Second World War, perhaps, still more remarkable.

Further reading

P. R. Gregory, *Russian National Income, 1885–1913* (Cambridge, 1982) is a standard work on the growth of pre-revolutionary national income; on the Tsarist legacy and the economic foundations of economic growth in the Soviet period, see also P. R. Gregory, 'National Income', in R. W. Davies (ed.) *From Tsarism to the New Economic Policy: Continuity and Change in the Economy of the USSR* (1990), and S. G. Wheatcroft, R. W. Davies and J. M. Cooper, 'Soviet Industrialization Reconsidered', *Economic History Review*, 2nd series, xxxix (1986). On the long-term growth of national income in the Soviet period, Bergson's results were summarised in A. Bergson, 'National Income', in A. Bergson and S. Kuznets (eds.), *Economic Trends in the USSR* (Cambridge, Mass., 1963), and are updated and set in a wider context by G. Ofer, 'Soviet Economic Growth: 1928–1985', *Journal of Economic Literature*, xxv (1987).

An original study of 'what might have been' in Soviet economic growth is provided by H. Hunter and J. M. Szyrmer, *Faulty Foundations: Soviet Economic Policies, 1928–1940* (Princeton, NJ, 1992).

For international context see P. Bairoch, 'Europe's Gross National Product: 1800–1975', *Journal of European Economic History*, v (1976), and A. Maddison, *The World Economy in the 20th Century* (Paris, 1989).

4   Population

S. G. Wheatcroft and R. W. Davies

The tumultuous and agonising transformation of the Russian Empire and the Soviet Union in the first half of this century brought about dramatic changes in the size and structure of the population.

On the one hand, broadly in common with other industrialising countries – at first in Europe and then elsewhere – there was a long-term improvement in prosperity, living conditions and health provision affecting a large number of the population. In the mid-nineteenth century, birth rates and death rates were extremely high. But from the 1880s onwards both the death rate (CDR – crude death rate) and the birth rate (CBR – crude birth rate) in the Russian Empire as a whole steadily declined. This decline continued with interruptions through all the upheavals of the next eighty years, and by the 1960s the Soviet Union was already a society with the low birth rate and the low death rate characteristic of most industrialised countries. Simultaneously, the proportion of the population living in the towns greatly increased, from a mere 12–15 per cent in the 1890s to 33 per cent on the eve of the Second World War and over fifty per cent by the 1960s.

Our three decades were dominated, however, by three unprecedented demographic convulsions which distorted and disguised the long-term trends. In each case a large number of people died from violence, famine or epidemics; in the discussion which follows we shall refer to these premature deaths as 'excess deaths'. In addition, during each demographic crisis the birth rate temporarily fell substantially. We shall refer to the total of excess deaths plus the loss of population due to the fall in the birth rate as 'the population deficit'.

In the account which follows, we begin by summarising the main trends for the whole period, and then consider developments chronologically in more detail.

The first demographic convulsion, in 1914–1922, was the result of the First World War and the succeeding civil war, epidemics and famine. Excess deaths amounted to about sixteen million – soldiers and civilians who were killed, or who died prematurely. Simultaneously, the birth rate temporarily declined, and as a result the number of children born in this period was ten million less than normal. At the beginning of 1923, the population was 4 – 6 million smaller than in 1914, and some 28 million smaller than it would have been if pre-war death and birth trends had continued.

The second demographic convulsion, in the 1930s, resulted from the famine and repressions which accompanied the industrialisation drive and the collectivisation of agriculture. Estimates of the number of excess deaths vary widely, particularly because there is no agreement on the number of births which took place between the population censuses of 1926 and 1939. On present evidence, some ten million excess deaths occurred between these dates, most of them during the 1933 famine. But if the birth rate remained at a 'normal' level in 1933, as some Soviet demographers have argued, and infant mortality rose to an unprecedented level in that year, the number of excess deaths during the famine would have been several million greater. In the 1930s as a whole, in contrast to the crises brought about by world war and civil war, the population continued to increase (except during the famine year 1933). The population rose by about twenty million during the twelve inter-censal years 1927–38. The total population deficit in this period, including both excess deaths and children not born owing to the temporary decline in the birth rate, may have amounted to some twenty million. And infant mortality almost ceased its long-term decline, so that in 1938 it was only 12 per cent lower than in 1926.

The third demographic crisis, in 1941–5, was primarily a consequence of the German invasion during the Second World War, and was by far the most profound. The number of excess deaths among soldiers and civilians between the German invasion of June 1941 and the end of 1945 amounted to some 25 million, and in addition some ten–fifteen million children were not born owing to the fall in the birth rate, so the total population deficit in these 4 1/2 years amounted to 35–40 millions. In consequence, between mid-1941 and the end of 1945 the population declined by as much as 25 million; it did not recover to the mid-1941 level until 1955, ten years after the end of the war.

In the post-war period the long-term trends almost immediately resumed. By 1950 the birth rate was substantially lower than on the eve of the Second World War, and the crude death rate had almost halved; as part of this decline infant mortality had fallen to less than half the 1938–9 level.

(A) The eve of the First World War

The only full population census before 1914 was held on 28 January 1897. It revealed that the population of the Russian Empire (excluding Finland and the Kingdom of Poland) amounted to 127.8 million, about 106.1 million of which were located within the pre-1939 frontiers of the USSR.[1] In the absence of a later pre-war census, the population on the eve of the First World War has to be estimated primarily by using data from the registration of births and deaths for the years 1897–1914. Before the revolution annual estimates of the population were made both by the Central Statistical Committee (TsSK) and the Chief Medical Inspectorate of the Ministry of Internal Affairs. In the 1920s these figures were corrected by Soviet statisticians working in the Central Statistical Administration (TsSU) and in the State Planning Commission (Gosplan); they demonstrated that the TsSK had overestimated the annual growth of the population and in consequence had overestimated the total population in 1914 by 5 or 6 per cent.[2]

Throughout the period between 1897 and 1914 the population had continued to increase rapidly, by 2.5 – 3 million per year; even on the lower estimates the total population of the Russian Empire in 1914 exceeded that of 1897 by over 30 per cent, with no increase in territory. Against this background of an expanding population, all authorities agreed that the CDR and CBR had both declined steadily since the 1880s. However, the CDR and in particular infant mortality remained very high by the standards of Western Europe. Even in 1914 infant mortality amounted to 273 (that is, of every one thousand children born, 273 died before the age of one). This figure was much closer to the rate in India at the same time than to those prevailing in Western Europe or even Japan.[3] It was close to the estimated 255 for Western Europe at the beginning of the nineteenth Century.[4]

The best estimate available of the population on the pre-1939 territory of the USSR is 139.9 million in mid-1913 and 141 million on 1 January 1914; the equivalent figure for the Russian Empire on 1 January 1914 is 167.5 million.[5]

This was a population in movement, undergoing a quite rapid change in its structure. Throughout the nineteenth Century the urban population increased more rapidly than the population as a whole, and the increase accelerated in the second half of the century. Between 1897 and 1914 urban population rose from 15.0 to 17.5 per cent of the total population, using the definition of 'urban' in the 1926 census (using the 1897 definition, it increased from 12.4 to 14.6 per cent).[6] The degree of urbanisation was of course substantially lower in Siberia and Central Asia than in most of the European provinces of the Russian Empire. It was substantially higher in the main industrial regions: the St Petersburg region, the central industrial region round Moscow, and the mining areas of the Urals and Ukraine. But it rose above 30 per cent in only half-a-dozen of the fifty provinces of the European Russian Empire.

The CDR and CBR of the towns and urban settlements on average were both lower than in the countryside. But this did not indicate that living conditions were healthier. As is normally the case in industrialising countries, the proportion of adult males of working age was substantially higher in the towns, and the proportion of women, children and older males was lower. This was primarily because young men tended, to a greater extent than women, to move from countryside to town in search of better opportunities; and then to return to the countryside in middle age. The lower CDR and CBR in the towns is entirely explained by this age and sex structure. Age-specific mortality data indicate that, age for age, mortality was lower in the countryside than in the overcrowded unhygienic towns, where elementary sewage facilities and clean water were a rarity.[7]

The decades before the First World War were also a period of large-scale migration. Between 1897 and 1914, an estimated 3,407,000 people migrated from European Russia (USSR pre-1939 frontiers) to Siberia and Central Asia, continuing the trend of previous decades and centuries. By 1914, Russians constituted 85 per cent of the Siberian population, and 19 per cent of the more recently-colonised Kazakhstan and Central Asia. The pre-war decades also saw a greatly accelerated emigration abroad, mainly to the United States and Canada; emigration in 1897–1914 was estimated at 875000 persons over the whole period. The total migration from European Russia in this period, 4,282,000 persons, amounted to 14.7 per cent of the natural increase of the population.[8]

(B) World War and Civil War, 1914–1922

In the years of world war and civil war the population of the former Russian Empire suffered disturbance and destruction on a huge scale. 'During the years 1915–1923', wrote Lorimer, 'the Russian people underwent the most cataclysmic changes since the Mongol invasion in the early thirteenth century'.[9] Immense population losses accompanied or followed the uprooting or temporary displacement of the population.

(i) Population displacement, 1914–22

The *first wave of population displacement occurred* during the First World War, between *July 1914 and the autumn of 1917*. A huge Tsarist army was mobilised; by the end of 1917 this had involved in all some 15.7 million people. Of these, 13.7 million saw active service, and before the end of 1917 the vast majority of these had been captured, killed or wounded, or had suffered from some disease. The best available estimate is as follows (million):[10]

Killed or died in action	
(including those dying from wounds)	0.7
Wounded (2.7) or sick (2.4)	5.1*
Prisoners of war or missing	5.1+
Deserted (0.47) or demobilised (0.58)	1.0
Other	(1.8)
Total	13.7

* Of these, 1.1 subsequently died of wounds or sickness; 3.2 million returned to active service.
+0.18 million died in captivity. Of the remainder, 4.13 million were estimated to have lived on Soviet pre-1939 territory.

In the course of the battles on the Eastern front, in addition to the large number of Russian prisoners of war captured by Germany and the other Central Powers, there was also a substantial inflow of enemy prisoners of war captured by the Tsarist army. Refugees fled to the interior of Russia in large numbers from areas occupied by the enemy; others fled to Russia from pogroms and brutal attacks taking place on enemy territory (notably the Armenians fleeing across the Southern front from the Turkish massacres).

According to Volkov, at the end of 1917, immediately after the Bolshevik revolution of October/November, the total population still unsettled at that time amounted to 17.5 million persons, 12.4 per cent of the total population. This included the military (7.8 million), and refugees and foreign prisoners of war (together amounting to 9.7 million). The total of 17.5 million included 6.3 million displaced persons who were now living in the towns – 24.6 per cent of the urban population.[11] This was the explosive mixture that had its dramatic outcome in the social unrest of the revolution and its aftermath.

The *second wave of population displacement in 1917–20*, following the October revolution, was equally dramatic. It consisted of several different sub-waves. *First*, the remainder of the Tsarist army was rapidly demobilised; and in its place by the summer of 1918 the Red Army and numerous anti-Bolshevik armies had already been brought into being. The civil war armies were smaller than the Tsarist army. The Red Army increased to a maximum of 3.5 million people in September 1920; the peak size of the White Armies in May 1919 has been estimated at just over one million.[12]

Secondly, the bitter civil war in which these rival armies fought to and fro across the vast territory of the former Empire was accompanied by flows and counter-flows of refugees. Reliable estimates of the number of refugees involved in this second wave have not been made; there were certainly many millions.

Thirdly, many people left the towns in 1918–20, particularly the large Northern towns. The pattern of movement out of the towns was complicated, and imperfectly recorded. The population of Moscow and Petrograd taken together fell dramatically from 4.30 million at the beginning of 1917 to a mere 1.86 million in July 1920, and the population of some larger towns like Kiev and Odessa also declined substantially.[13] But the decline was less dramatic for the urban population as a whole than for the largest towns; the number of people living in small urban settlements apparently even remained constant.[14]

Fourthly, with Bolshevik victory many defeated White officers and soldiers and many members of the old wealthy classes fled abroad, as did many professional people. The number emigrating has usually been estimated at approximately two million, though some estimates place it as high as 3.5 million.[15]

The third wave of population displacement took place in *1921–2,* with the flight of refugees from the famine in the Volga region, the North Caucasus and Ukraine, following the drought and harvest failure of 1921. This was possibly the largest of all movements of refugees; it certainly involved the most suffering. Millions of refugees set off in different directions. Initially peasants set off from the Volga heading West to Ukraine, where they wrongly believed food to be plentiful. Others moved from west to east heading towards Tashkent; yet others moved to the north.

(ii) Population losses, 1914–22

These successive population upheavals of 1914–22 involved human privation, suffering and misery on an enormous scale. The number of people who died prematurely in these years can only be roughly estimated.

We shall first consider *the years of the First World War, 1914–7.* The number of soldiers who were killed , or died of wounds or disease, is known only approximately. Estimates vary from 1.6 to 2 million, and this excludes many soldiers who were sent back from the front wounded or sick but still alive, and whose lives were shortened.[16] Some increase in deaths among the civilian population no doubt also occurred in 1914–7, though in those towns away from the front for which data are available the CDR did not increase substantially.[17]

During the civil war of 1918–20, the vast majority of deaths resulted from disease. Estimates of the number of soldiers who died in 1918–20 are in the range 0.8–1.2 million; the lower estimate seems more probable.[18] This was a small fraction of the total number of deaths. During the years of the world war, food shortages, overcrowding and insanitary conditions among refugees undoubtedly weakened resistance to disease, and from the summer of 1918 a series of epidemics spread rapidly, reaching a peak in 1920. In European Russia alone deaths from typhus, typhoid, dysentery and cholera amounted to two million in 1918–20, the majority from typhus, as compared with 257,000 in the previous three years.[19]

After the end of the civil war, *the famine of 1921–2* resulted in large numbers of deaths from hunger in the Volga regions and Ukraine, and in an accompanying increase in deaths from infectious disease among people suffering from severe malnutrition. Epidemics also spread in areas outside the famine regions, so that in Petrograd, for example, the CDR in December 1921 was twice as high as in December 1920.[20] In European Russia 858,000 people died in 1921–2 from the four diseases referred to above, nearly five times the normal number. These were also the years in which a devastating influenza epidemic swept through Europe. Total premature deaths from famine and disease may have amounted to over five million.

Surveying the whole period between the outbreak of the First World War in 1914 and the population census of December 1926 Lorimer estimates that the total population deficit arising from the war and civil war amounted to 28 million, subdivided as follows:

Military deaths	2
Civilian deaths	14
Emigration	2
Birth deficit	10

The total figure of 28 million was obtained by comparing the actual population at the time of the population census of December 1926 (this was recorded as 147 million) with the hypothetical population in December 1926 estimated by extrapolating from the rate of natural increase of population in 1897–1914 (this worked out at 175 million). We have already discussed military deaths and emigration, for which Lorimer's figures are fairly conservative. Lorimer estimated the birth deficit on the basis of the age cohorts of the 1926 census; he concluded that the number of children not born through the decline in the birth rate was a maximum of ten million. The figure of 14 million civilian deaths was obtained as a residual. Checking it against the 1926 census, Lorimer came to the conclusion that it included 3 million premature deaths of children born since 1912 and 11 million premature deaths of men and women already born by that year.

Lorimer's figure for the number of military deaths should be increased to about 3 million to include military deaths during the civil war. If the higher figure for emigration (3.5 million) were also accepted, the number of civilian losses would fall to 11.5 million.

Alternative estimates have been made by Soviet historians comparing the pre-war population not with the population at the time of the December 1926 census but with the population at the lowest point, immediately following the famine of 1921–2. In his study undertaken in the 1920s Volkov concluded that there was an absolute decline in the population of 6.3 million between January 1914 and January 1923. In more recent estimates the equivalent decline is given as 7.3 million by Danilov and 9.6 million by Polyakov. These figures imply a population deficit, including the deficit from the decline in CBR, of 30 million or more between the two dates.[21]

The annual estimates of total population show clearly that the population deficit was concentrated into the years after 1917. In spite of the military losses, the total population continued to increase in 1914 and 1915, though much more slowly than in the pre-war years. The increase in population between the beginning of 1914 and the beginning of 1917, as estimated by our different authors, ranges from 2.6 to 4.7 million. This may be compared with the normal pre-war increase over three years of about 7.5 million (2.5 million a year).[22]

In the ensuing six years 1917–22 the population fell sharply; the different estimates range from 9 to 14.3 million. According to Danilov, excess deaths from famine and disease amounted to eight million persons in 1918–20.[23] This implies that a further six million people may have died prematurely in 1921 and 1922 from famine and disease.

The fairly large differences between the various estimates arise from the gaps and uncertainties in the statistics at this time of demographic catastrophe, when birth and death registrations were inadequately kept. The total population deficit is extremely sensitive to variations in the assumed 'normal' birth and death rates; and it is even more difficult to assess how far the deficit of young children in the years after the demographic catastrophe is due to a drop in the birth rate, and how far to the death of babies whose birth had not been registered. We shall see that these problems cause us great difficulty when we turn to the demographic crisis of the 1930s.

(C) The mid-1920s

The country soon emerged from the crisis. By 1924 the pre-war pattern of population growth had been approximately restored. In each of the two years before the population census of 17 December 1926 (1925 and 1926) the net increase in the population was well over three million, a larger annual increase than before the war.

The size of this increase was not the result of an increase in the birth rate as compared with the immediate pre-war years. In 1923–6, the birth rate did increase rapidly from the low level of 1922. Nevertheless, in the mid-1920s it was probably somewhat lower than on the eve of the war. This was partly because the age at which women married was higher than before the war: in European Russia/USSR the percentage of women who were under twenty when they married was 55 per cent in 1910 but only 34 per cent in 1927.[24] A further factor in the probable slight decline in the birth rate was the incidence of abortion, which had been legalised after the revolution.[25]

In contrast the death rate had fallen substantially. The decline in CDR may have affected a wide range of age-groups; but it was primarily due to a decline in infant mortality from 273 in 1913 to 174 in 1926.[26] This decline was part of a general European trend: in Germany and Austria infant mortality declined by over 40 per cent in the same period. But the improvement in the USSR was remarkable in view of the turmoil in the intervening years.[27] It was this fall in CDR which accounted for the rapid annual increase in population just before the 1926 census.

As a result of the expansion of population in 1924–5, the population census of 17 December 1926 recorded a total population higher than that on the same territory on 1 January 1914. Some authorities have suggested that there was some undercounting in the 1926 census: the official figure was 147.0 million. A recent Soviet estimate, by Andreev, Darskii and Khar'kova (referred to henceforth as ADK) raises this figure to 148.5 to allow for underrecording of children under three years of age (see Figure 3 and Table 6).[28] Estimates of the pre-war population vary between 139.7 and 142.4 million (see p. 335 note 5 below), so the increase between 1 January 1914 and the end of 1926 is within the limits 3.2 and 6.1 per cent.

The urban population also somewhat exceeded the pre-war level in absolute terms, and thus remained almost exactly the same proportion of the total population; it amounted to 26.3 million at the time of the 1926 census (17.7–17.9 per cent of total population) against 24.9 million in 1914 (17.5–17.8 per cent) (the same list of towns has been used in each case).[29]

Although the population had recovered to its pre-war level, the consequences of the upheavals of war and civil war continued to be felt. The extent of the recovery varied considerably between different regions. Broadly speaking, the areas in which recovery was slowest were those in which civil war and famine had caused the greatest harm to agriculture and agricultural capital. The population was still 5 per cent below its pre-war level in the Central Producer Region, and in this region the urban population had also failed to recover to the pre-war level. But in the Eastern Producer Region and the Southern Consumer Region, which were least affected by civil war and famine, the population was as much as 10 per cent larger than in 1914.

As a result of the ravages of war and famine, the structure of the population in December 1926 was far from the pre-war norm. There was a large deficit in the age group 5–9 (children born in 1917–21), reflecting the lower fertility and higher infant mortality during those years. There was also a quite substantial deficit in the age group 10–14, born in 1912–6; this group includes the years of very low birth rate 1915–6. Among adults, the most striking feature is the consistently lower number of males than females in every age group, reflecting military losses and the greater susceptibility of males to infectious disease.[30] In 1926 the total number of females in the population exceeded the total number of males by 4.9 million, as compared with less than one million in 1914.

The absolute level of the CBR and CDR in the first post-census year 1927 are extremely controversial. They are important not only as an indication of the demographic situation in the last full year of the New Economic Policy, but also because they form the starting point for all estimates of the fate of the population during the tumultuous years of the 1930s. The only reliable data available on the size and structure of the population are for the census years 1926, 1937 and 1939. What happened in the intervening years has to be estimated, and an important element in any estimate is the estimated CBR and CDR. If the normal CBR was high and the normal CDR was low in the intervening years, then the number of excess deaths from the famine and from violence against the population would be larger; if normal CBR was low and normal CDR was high, then the number of excess deaths would be smaller.

Here are three substantially different estimates for 1927 (per thousand population); NRR (net reproduction rate) = CBR − CDR):

	CBR	CDR	NRR
Registration data[a]	43.7	21.0	22.7
Lorimer estimate[b]	45.0	26.0	19.0
ADK estimate[c]	46.3	26.5	19.7

[a] CBR as given by Urlanis (1977), 11–12; CDR estimated from this figure and registration data for net increase in population in 1927 (3,339,000) (RGAE, 105/1/10, 16–7). Note that *Stat. spr. 1928* (1929), 76–9, gives CBR and CDR for European USSR as 43.0 and 20.8 (i.e. NRR was 22.2).
[b] Lorimer (1946), 134; he discusses how he obtained these figures on pp. 113–133 (see our text).
[c] ADK (1990a), 41. The authors state that these figures were derived 'on the basis of the age and sex structure of the population in each year', but give no further details. On p. 43 they give an alternative NRR for 1927 of 17.55; and in their estimates on p.41 they appear in practice to use an NRR of 19.95.

On the birth rate, Lorimer believes that the registration data for the European USSR were 'reasonably complete'. He then assumes that the demographic characteristics of the remaining area were similar to those of the Ural and Vyatka regions, where the CBR was higher than elsewhere in European Russia.[31]

Lorimer's upward revision of the CDR was more substantial. He argues that there are several reasons for supposing that the CDR based on the registration data is too low. The most important of these for the European USSR was the abnormal structure of tables for the European USSR showing the expectation of life at various ages (life tables). In these life tables for 1927 mortality rates rise only slowly in moving from early adult years to later years, especially in the case of females. Lorimer attributes this abnormality to the incomplete registration of deaths among the higher age groups. For that part of the Soviet Union where deaths were not registered, Lorimer follows the procedure he used for the CBR, and assumes a higher CDR comparable to that in the Vyatka and Ural regions (where it was 50 per cent higher than in the rest of the European USSR). This gives him 'a hypothetical death rate' for the whole USSR of 26.0.[32]

Maksudov rejects Lorimer's proposal to increase the CDR for the European USSR on the grounds that burials took place in a small number of cemeteries, which were firmly under state control; moreover, the local statistical bureaux were able to check death registrations against medical records of deaths. While Maksudov accepts that the CDR for the European USSR should be increased when estimating CDR for the USSR as a whole, he argues that Lorimer's increase was too large.[33]

Unfortunately the recent article by ADK (1990a) does not explain clearly how their estimates were derived; for 1927 (unlike later years) they are close to Lorimer's. The Lorimer and ADK estimates result in estimates of the net increase of population in 1927 which are substantially different from the earlier estimates based on the registration data. According to Lorimer, the net increase in the population in 1927 was 2,869,000;[34] according to ADK, it was 2,965,000;[35] but according to the earlier estimates based on the registration data it was as much as 3,339,000.[36] The discrepancy persists for the following two years 1928 and 1929. While Lorimer estimates that the population on 1 January 1930 was about 155.5 million, the registration data gave a figure of 157.4 – 157.7 million; the prevalence of this higher and possibly exaggerated figure played a significant role in the bitter disputes about the size of the population in 1937.[37]

(D) Years of tumult and disaster, 1929–1939

The years of forced-march industrialisation were also years of a social upheaval far greater than had occurred elsewhere in peace-time Europe in the modern era.

The disruption of the lives of the peasant population which accompanied industrialisation has a certain analogy with the enclosure movement in Britain. But it was an upheaval compressed into a few years instead of decades or centuries. In the simultaneous 'elimination of the kulaks as a class', something like the treatment of the Scottish highlanders was extended to a minority of peasants in every village in the whole USSR, while simultaneously most peasants were required to change drastically their methods of earning their living. The Soviet peasantry was at one and the same moment hurled into a much more mechanised agriculture and into a social system analogous with serfdom.

Perhaps five or six million peasants, over one million of the 25 million peasant households, were direct victims of dekulakisation in the years 1930–3. They were subdivided approximately as follows (million persons):

(1) Exiled outside their own region   2.1
(2) Exiled within their own region   2 – 2.5
(3) 'Dekulakised themselves'   1 – 1.25

The first group, an estimated 2,142,719 peasants, were exiled from their villages to other regions, usually in remote parts of the country, where they became 'special settlers (spetsposelentsy)' in work camps or settlements under the control of the OGPU (later NKVD).[38] The second group includes peasants removed from their lands to the outskirts of their village or to elsewhere in their district or region. The precise number is not known. According to Danilov, the number exiled within their own region in 1930–1 alone amounted to 400000 or 450000 families, 2–2.5 million persons. Some of those exiled within their own region were subsequently exiled to remote regions; they are apparently included within the total of 2.1 million above.[39] A third group, comprising a further 200000 to 250000 households, 1 – 1.25 million persons, 'dekulakised themselves (samoraskulachilis')' by leaving their land and cottages and fleeing to the towns or other regions.

The former kulaks did not simply remain where they were. Several hundred thousand died: according to the official records, 241355 died in exile in 1932–3 alone. These figures exclude an unknown number of peasants who died in the often appalling conditions in which they were transported from their villages to exile; they also exclude those who were executed. According to the official records, even larger numbers escaped from exile: in 1932–3 alone 330677 escaped and were not recaptured (it seems quite possible, however, that some of those recorded as escaping in fact died or were killed in the course of attempting to escape).[40]

Collectivisation and the forced requisitioning of agricultural products which accompanied it also had frightful consequences for many peasants who were not classified as kulaks. In Kazakhstan, the attempt to settle nomad farmers in collective farms led to the death of most of their animals, the main source of food in this region. A large number of Kazakhs died of starvation in 1931–3, and others fled abroad.[41] In 1933, a devastating famine affected most of Ukraine, and large areas of the Volga regions and the North Caucasus; several million peasants died.

Against this sombre background in the countryside the towns expanded extremely rapidly, largely because millions of peasants moved to the towns in search of a better life. Even in 1928, before collectivisation, as many as 6,477,000 peasants were recorded as moving temporarily to the towns and urban settlements, and 1,062,000 as settling permanently. In the 1930s the numbers greatly increased:[42]

Migration (in thousands)

	to town	away from town	settlement in town
1928	6477	5415	1062
1929	6958	5566	1392
1930	9534	6901	2633
1931	10810	6710	4100
1932	10605	7886	2719
1933	7416	6644	772
1934	11856	9404	2452
1935	13732	11176	2556
Total			17686

The annual migration figures suffer from double-counting, and show a substantially larger settlement in the towns than in fact occurred. But the proportions between years are no doubt approximately correct; they show that settlement was concentrated into the three years 1930–2. In the course of 1933 internal passports or identity cards were introduced for the urban population in order to control movement into the towns; but the movement into the towns resumed in 1934. More reliable figures covering the whole inter-censal period between 1926 and 1939 show that the urban population increased from 26.3 to 56.1 million persons. Of this increase of 29.8 million, 5.5 million were due to natural growth, 5.8 million to the reclassification of former rural areas as urban areas; the remainder, 18.5 million or 62 per cent of the total increase, were peasants and other rural inhabitants who migrated to the towns.[43]

There were other subsidiary movements of the population. Particularly in the early 1930s, labour turnover was extremely high. Workers, particularly those who had recently ceased to be peasants, roamed from factory to factory and building site to building site in search of better food, accommodation and working conditions.

It was not only 'kulaks' who suffered exile and imprisonment. In the first half of the 1930s smaller numbers of former private traders, 'bourgeois specialists' accused of sabotage, and others, were arrested or exiled. In 1933, members of the families of former nobles, merchants and other classes were

exiled from the major towns. Then in 1936–8 in the 'Great Purge' members
of the party and professional elite were arrested in large numbers; many of
them were executed. The 'Great Purge' did not merely affect the professional classes. For example, an NKVD order of 30 July 1937, following a
Politburo decision of 2 July, instructed local NKVDs to execute and exile
'former *kulaks*, active anti-Soviet elements and criminals'; execution and
exiling were to begin on 5 August and to be completed within four months
of that date. The numbers allocated 'for guidance' to regions in the RSFSR,
Ukraine and Kazakhstan totalled 72950 persons to be executed and 186500
to be sentenced to confinement in camps or prisons for 8–10 years.[44]

At the time of the population censuses of 1937 and 1939 the total number
of prisoners and exiles managed by the NKVD was comprised as follows
(thousands):[45]

Location	1937	1939
Camps	821	1317
Colonies	375	355
Prisons	545	351
Labour settlements	917	939
Total	2658	2962

Persons with sentences less than three years were sent to colonies; persons
with sentences of three years or more were allocated to 'corrective-labour
camps' (earlier known as 'concentration camps'). 'Special settlers (*spetspereselentsy*)' were exiles compelled to live in fenced-in settlements and undertake work on the instructions of the NKVD; the *spetspereselentsy* were
known as 'labour settlers (*trudposelentsy*)' between 1934 and 1944, and as
spetsposelentsy from 1944 onwards. In the early 1930s the *spetspereselentsy*
were mainly exiled '*kulaks*'. From 1934, camps, colonies, settlements and
prisons were all subordinate to the Chief Administration for Camps
(GULAG) of the NKVD. These figures do not include persons sent into
exile without confinement in a camp or settlement (known as *ssyl'nye*).[46]
Nor do they include an unknown but large number of former prisoners and
exiles of various kinds who had been freed from their places of confinement
but were excluded by a note in their internal passport from living in certain
cities. No statistical information has yet been published about this important category of people whose movement was restricted, or about other
ssyl'nye. Police and free personnel working in places of confinement are not
included in these figures; they probably amounted to 143000 persons in
1937 and 189000 in 1939.[47] They also exclude NKVD personnel themselves, amounting to an additional 271000 in 1937 and 366000 in 1939.[48]

While we now have fairly precise figures about the number of people

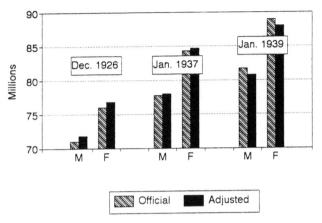

Figure 3   The census of population, 1926, 1937 and 1939. *Source:* table 6.

incarcerated in prisons, camps and colonies in the 1930s, our knowledge about the number of normal or excess deaths during the demographic catastrophe of the 1930s, and about when these deaths occurred, remains extremely uncertain. Before *perestroika*, Western scholars sought to estimate excess deaths with the small amount of data then available; the most important and careful analysis was undertaken by Lorimer in 1946. In 1990, the results of the 1937 census were published in some detail, and much more information has become available about the 1939 census. In addition, national and regional data on birth and death registrations have been made accessible to Western as well as Soviet historians. In consequence our estimates are now much better informed; but a very wide margin of error remains.

The results of the three censuses provide the starting point for analysis (see Figure 3 and Table 6). As we have seen, the figure for the 1926 census is *relatively* uncontroversial, varying between 145.5 and 148.5 million.

The population revealed by the preliminary returns of the 1937 census was far smaller than the political leaders or the statisticians anticipated. Gosplan had predicted in the late 1920s that the population would continue to increase at the high rate which it had estimated for 1927, and would reach 180.7 million by 1937. Even as late as 1936, a few months before the census, the official estimate of the population at the beginning of 1933 was as high as 165.7 millions.[49] But the actual census figure four years later at the beginning of 1937 was only 162 millions, at least eight million less than the 1933 figure implied. In March 1937 the TsUNKhU official Kurman proposed to increase this figure by one million to allow for undercounting, and then his superiors in TsUNKhU claimed that undercounting amounted to as much as 6.5 million, so that the population was not 162 but 168.5 million.[50] This proposal, made in a desperate effort to reconcile the census data with the previous estimates, had no serious foundation.[51] The census was cancelled and leading statistical officials, including both the head of TsSU and Kurman himself, were arrested. With the publication of the census results over half a century later in 1990, ADK, on the basis of a comparison of the age and sex cohorts of the 1937 and 1939 censuses, have proposed a small increase by 0.7 million, raising the total to 162.7 million.[52]

In the case of the 1939 census, Western writers have long suggested that the official figure, variously given as 170.1 and 170.5 millions, should be reduced.[53] Recent data from the archives have revealed that the figure was deliberately exaggerated. The total number of people recorded in the census was in fact 167.3 million, comprising a basic return of the civilian population amounting to 159.1 million, plus 2.3 million for the population in distant regions, 2.1 million recorded by the military and a 'special contingent' of 3.7 million recorded by the NKVD.[54] The Soviet authorities more or less arbitrarily increased the total figure by 2.82 million: 1.14 million to allow for persons temporarily away from home and not recorded elsewhere, and a further 1 per cent (1.68 million) to allow for undercounting. This brought the total to 170.1 million.[55] Both these increases were obviously far too great; ADK suggest a total increase of 1.6 million to 168.9 million, to allow for undercounting. Other authorities believe this increase is too large, and accept the raw figure, 167.3 million.[56] The higher figure is consistent with the treatment of the previous censuses by ADK: they increased the 1926 census by 1.5 million and the 1937 census by 0.7 million.

On the basis of the data of the 1926 and 1939 censuses, serious estimates of the number of excess deaths between 1926 and 1939 have ranged from 5½ million to 10–14 million. The American demographers Anderson and Silver have shown that alternative assumptions about the 'normal' level of fertility and mortality can produce a total population deficit as compared with normal expectations ranging from zero to 24 millions, including a deficit among those already born at the time of the 1926 census ranging from 0.5–5.5 million. The lowest figure assumes low normal fertility and high normal mortality, while the highest figure assumes high normal fertility and low normal mortality.[57] If the entire population deficit was due to mortality higher than normal, the figure for population deficit would be equal to the number of excess deaths; for those already born in 1926, the population deficit is of course in any case identical with the number of excess deaths.

The earliest attempt to measure population deficit and excess deaths in the inter-censal years 1927–1938 was made by Lorimer in 1946. He presented two estimates (see Box). The first gave the total deficit in the inter-censal years as 5.5 million, the second, obtained from life-tables, gave a deficit of 4.8 million for those already born at the time of the 1926 census.

Lorimer's and Maksudov's estimates of excess deaths between the 1926 and 1939 census

Lorimer's first estimate (made in 1946) This assumed that (i) CDR declined steadily between Lorimer's estimated rate for 1926–7 (26 per 1,000) and the reported rate for 1938 (17.8 per 1,000); (ii) CBR declined until 1934, and then increased in 1936–8 following the anti-abortion decree of 1935. This yielded what he called a *'discrepancy' (or population deficit) of 5.5 million* (see Columns 2, 5, 8 and 11 of Table 7). Lorimer believed that this deficit was likely to have been due to excess deaths above the normal mortality trend, rather than to a CBR lower than in his estimates. In his 'adjusted' figures (see Columns 3, 5, 8 and 12 of Table 7) Lorimer absorbed the deficit into a hypothetical annual series showing the likely actual size of the population; he assigned one-third of the 5.5 million deficit to the single famine year 1932.

Lorimer's second estimate (also made in 1946) (not shown in Table 7). Together with Ansley Coale, Lorimer also undertook a second more elaborate estimate of excess deaths in 1926–39, confined to those already born at the time of the 1926 census; i.e. aged 12 or over at the time of the 1939 census. The expected population in December 1938 was estimated by applying twelve-year survival ratios to each age-group in December 1926. These ratios were derived by Coale from 1926–7 life-tables for the European USSR adjusted by Coale to allow for the presumed under-registration of mortality in higher age groups (see p. 67 above). This produced a substantially higher figure for excess deaths: *4.8 million for those already born in December 1926.*

Maksudov's estimate (1982). Many years after Lorimer published his estimates, but before substantially new data became available, similar calculations were made by the French demographer J. N.Biraben (in 1958) and the Russian émigré S. Maksudov (in the early 1980s). Biraben does not explain his method of calculation; his estimates imply a total population deficit of 9.8 million, including excess deaths of persons already born at the time of the 1926 census of 5.7 millions. Maksudov's equivalent figures, for which he explains the derivation in some detail, are almost exactly the same as Biraben's, but he more realistically suggests a margin of error of ± 3 millions for the total deficit. In the light of the results of the 1937 census, Maksudov increased his estimate as explained in the text of this chapter. (Maksudov (1989), 145–7; and Maksudov in *Zven'ya*, I (1991), 65–110.)

Many years later, Maksudov, on the basis of somewhat similar calcula-tions, reached a substantially higher figure, or rather range of figures, for excess deaths, a total of 9.8 million ± 3 million, of which 5.7 million were already born in December 1926 (see Box on p. 73).

When Lorimer and Maksudov prepared their estimates, the results of the 1937 census were not available. Lorimer's rough guess that the population at the beginning of 1937 was 163.4 million (see Table 7) was remarkably accurate; it exceeds the census figure by at most one million. Lorimer correctly supposed that excess deaths were concentrated into the period 1930–5, though he wrongly placed the peak in 1932 instead of 1933. He was also unaware that the published figure for the 1939 census was exaggerated by 1.6–3.2 million. The total deficit between 1926 and 1939, using Lorimer's own methods, therefore amounted not to his estimated 5.5 million, but to 7.1–8.7 million. Maksudov's estimate of total excess deaths should similarly be moved to the upper margin of error. Maksudov stated in 1991 that the disclosure that the population was only 162 million at the beginning of 1937 'probably allows one to speak of losses [i.e. excess deaths] of 11.5 million persons with a margin of error of + 3 millions and − 1.5 millions'.[58]

The births and deaths registration data for 1927–37 also became available (in part) in 1989–90, and together with the results of the 1937 census they modify Lorimer's conclusion that the total deficit was 5.5 million in at least two ways (see Box on pp. 75–6). First, the registration data show that the number of excess deaths in 1932–3 was considerably greater than Lorimer supposed, amounting to 3.4 million excess registered deaths, as compared with Lorimer's 1,135,000 in his peak year 1932.

Secondly, these registration data did not incorporate the total number of deaths. When the results of the 1937 census were first obtained, Kurman prepared a memorandum which showed that the 1937 population was some eight million smaller than the figure obtained from births and deaths registrations. The Kurman gap has been widely discussed. On present evidence, it includes some five million excess deaths; together with the registered excess deaths in 1932–3, the total number of excess deaths in 1927–1936 may amount to as many as 8.5 million.

In 1990 a further estimate of births and deaths in 1927–36 was made by the Soviet statisticians Andreev, Darskii and Khar'kova (referred to here as ADK). They assumed that the birth rate in 1933 was substantially higher than the numbers registered, and concluded that excess deaths, registered and unregistered in 1932–3 alone, were as high as eight million. The discrepancy between this figure and the number of famine deaths estimated by Wheatcroft (1990, p. 358) – four to five million – is due to

**Excess deaths between 1926 and 1937 censuses
(December 1926–January 1937)**

(1) The births and deaths registration data show excess deaths in 1932–3 amounting to at least 0.24 million in 1932 and 3.12 million in 1933, *3.36 million in all* (taking 1930 as a normal year)

(registered deaths in 1930:	3.101
1931:	3.144
1932:	3.344
1933:	6.217

derived from CDR for 1930–3, given in RGAE, 1562/20/42, 76).
(2) In addition the *'Kurman gap'* reveals *8 million unregistered deaths* between December 1926 and January 1937 (see Table 8).
According to the two censuses, the population increased by *15 million*.
According to the registration data (total births minus total deaths), as adjusted for territory, *it increased by as much as 23 million*.
Kurman explained the gap as follows:

1 emigration	2.0
2 over-estimate of 1926 population	1.5
3 under-estimate of 1937 population	1.0
4 unregistered deaths in 1933	1.0
5 unregistered deaths in NKVD system	1.0–1.5
6 deaths not registered by ZAGS in other years	1.0–1.5
Total	8.0

His first three items can almost certainly be discounted; some emigration occurred, but it was much less than 2 million. The bulk of his 8-million gap must therefore be attributed to items 4–6.

Tsaplin suggests: unregistered deaths from famine	1.0
unregistered deaths in NKVD system	2.8
Estimate of Kazakh deaths during collectivisation (see chapter 4, note 41)	1.3
Total	5.1

If these figures are correct, 2.9 million 'normal deaths' remained unregistered over the whole period 1927–36. This would increase the CDR in each year by about 2 per 1,000 above the registered deaths. The total number of excess deaths in 1927–36 would amount to

3.4 million registered in 1932–3 and

5.1 million unregistered

8.5 million in 1927–36

(3) *Andreev, Darskii and Khar'kova* (ADK) (see Table 7, Columns 4, 6, 9 and 13). ADK argue that the number of births during the famine was much greater than the number registered. Kurman allowed for under-registration by increasing the number of births by 1.7 million above the total registered for the whole period 1927–36. But ADK assume that there were 5½ million more births than in the registration data presented by Kurman, so that deaths were not eight million but about 12½ million higher than the number of registered deaths.

In particular, they argue that the CBR declined only slightly in 1933. According to the registration data, it fell from 31.9 to 25.3 per thousand. According to ADK, it fell only from 35.9 to 34.7. Using the age-cohorts in the 1926 and 1927 censuses, they therefore estimate a much larger number of famine deaths than are suggested by Tsaplin or others. Taking their estimate for 1929 as a 'normal' number of deaths, excess deaths in 1932–3 amounted to 7,966,000 of which 7,312,000 occurred in 1933 alone (estimated from data in Table 7).

their assumption that birth rates declined only slightly in 1932, and is entirely attributable to babies which died shortly after birth.[59]

The two years between the 1937 and 1939 censuses, 1937 and 1938, are somewhat less controversial, now that total populations at the beginning of 1937 and 1939 are reasonably well known. Even so, we have a population increase in the two years which varies between 4.6 and 6.9 million, according to the population estimate used (taking either the higher or the lower estimate of the census figure in each case, which is more reasonable, the range of the increase falls to 5.3–6.2 million). According to the registration data, however, the net growth in population in these two years amounted to some 6.8 millions.[60] Unregistered deaths in 1937–8 may therefore have amounted to between 0.6 and 1.5 million persons. These unregistered deaths presumably included persons executed by the NKVD during the Great Purge, and deaths in NKVD camps and colonies. At the June 1957 plenum of the party central committee, it was stated that 681692 persons were executed in 1937–8. This is entirely compatible with the figures for unregistered deaths, as is Tsaplin's estimate that unregistered deaths in places of confinement in 1937–8, including executions, may have amounted to 1.3 million.[61]

In summary, the total number of excess deaths in 1927–38 may have amounted to some 10 million persons, 8.5 million in 1927–36, and about 1–1½ million in 1937–8. On all estimates, most of the deaths took place during the 1933 famine. The estimate of 10 million would be substantially increased if the number of babies born in 1933 was as high as ADK suggest.

Apart from their tragic results in the deaths of large numbers of the population, the repressive policies and social upheaval also postponed the long-term trend towards the improvement of the health and expectation of life of the Soviet population. Substantial resources were invested in the health services in the 1930s, particularly by increasing the number of doctors, nurses and others working in the health services. But these increases hardly kept pace with the deteriorating conditions resulting from forced industrialisation. While the CDR declined between 1927 and 1939, the child mortality rate remained high. Infant mortality (deaths between 0 and 1 year of age) declined only slightly from 174 to 161 per thousand.[62] (See Table 9.)

(E) The Second World War, 1939–1945

The Soviet Union was not invaded until 22 June 1941, but the outbreak of the European war in September 1939 provided the opportunity to annex territories from Eastern Poland and Romania, and the three Baltic republics; these territories had almost all formed part of the Tsarist Empire in 1917. The exact population of these areas is not known, but is estimated at 20.3 millions at the beginning of 1939, bringing the total population to 188.8 millions (168.5 + 20.3), using the ADK figure for the 1939 census. On this basis it was estimated that the total population in mid-1941 amounted to 196.7 millions.[63]

The upheaval of 1941–5 involved far greater destruction of human lives and greater movements of population than the previous two demographic catastrophes. Millions of Soviet soldiers were killed or died in captivity. Most of the European USSR was occupied by Nazi Germany and its allies, and millions of civilians were transferred to work in Germany and German-controlled Europe. Millions more were evacuated or fled to the interior in face of the advancing German armies. With the liberation of occupied territory by the Soviet army, many civilians returned to their homes; a far smaller number departed westwards with the German armies. The Soviet government itself, from 1940 onwards, deported to the interior millions of civilians from national minorities, first from the newly-annexed areas in the West, and then from Soviet pre-1939 territory. All these vast movements of population took place in insanitary conditions, and with inadequate nourishment of the victims.

The number of excess wartime deaths due to military action, malnutrition, disease and repression was concealed while Stalin was alive, presumably in the hope of concealing Soviet weakness as a result of the war. Stalin admitted a mere 7 million war deaths. When the Soviet population was officially reported as amounting to only 200.2 million in April 1956,[64] this figure was 20 million less than some Western observers had anticipated. Khrushchev in 1961 stated that military and civilian deaths amounted to 'more than 20 million persons'.[65]

In recent years, more reliable attempts have been made to estimate war-time deaths. The most careful is by ADK.[66] On the basis of registration data and the results of the 1959 census they conclude that the total population at the end of 1945 was only 170.5 millions, 26 million less than at the time of the German invasion.

From this starting point the authors estimate separately the number of deaths among the population already born in 22 June 1941, and the number of deaths among children born after that date. Of the total population at the end of 1945, 159.5 millions were already born before 22 June 1941, so that the number of deaths in 4½ years was 37.2 millions (196.7–159.5). If the CDR had remained at the level of 1940, only 11.9 million people already alive in June 1941 would have died in this period; the number of excess deaths was therefore 25.3 millions (37.2–11.9).

The number of children born in the 4½ years is estimated by ADK at 15.7–16.4 millions, of which 4.6 million died by the end of 1945. If the death rate for these children had remained at the level of 1940, only 3.3 million would have died, so excess deaths among children amounted to 1.3 million. Hence the total number of excess deaths in 1941–5 amounted to 26.6 millions (25.3 + 1.3). This included 19 million males and only 7 million females; the number of females in the population at the end of the war exceeded the number of men by some 20 million, as compared with 7.2 million in 1939 and 5 million in 1926. This figure does not make any allowance for net emigration from the USSR, which must be deducted from the total number of excess deaths. The population deficit, including children not born as a result of the decline in the birth rate, may be estimated at nearly 40 million.

Other estimates of excess deaths are even higher. V. I. Kozlov claims that the population amounted to only 167 million at the end of 1945, as compared with an expected population, given normal CBR and CDR, of between 212 and 215 millions. The total population deficit was therefore 45–8 million. About ten million of this total was due to the decline in birth rate, so the number of excess deaths was 35–8 million. Kozlov even advocates increasing this figure to 40 million on the grounds that the size of the population in 1940 was underestimated.[67] Kozlov's estimates are much cruder than those by ADK.

Our knowledge of the breakdown of the 26 million excess deaths estimated by ADK is extremely limited. An army commission was established to estimate military losses, and early in 1990 M. A. Moiseev, then head of the General Staff, announced that the total number 'killed and missing, plus prisoners who did not return, plus those military who died from wounds, illness and accident' amounted to 8,668,400; an unknown number of these were prisoners and missing persons who did not return to the USSR.[68] Several Soviet commentators have suggested that this figure is too low, and that in reaching it the military were influenced by their wish not to admit that far more Soviet than German soldiers were killed.[69] V. I. Kozlov claims, or guesses, that there were as many as 15–20 million military losses, including 11–13 million in the army.[70] Volkogonov suggests an intermediate figure of 10 million.[71] The deaths among prisoners of war have been estimated at at least 3.3 million. If the Moiseev estimate were true, the number of military fatalities in combat and in the rear would be only 5 million.[72]

All sources agree that the number of excess deaths among civilians must have amounted to 15 million or more. How this figure is made up is not known. Deaths among certain specific groups were very high: over 2½ million Jews were murdered by the exterminators of Nazi Germany and its allies; 0.8 million civilians died in the seige of Leningrad. According to one estimate, total deaths of civilians from territory occupied by the enemy amounted to 11 million, of which 5 million died in captivity.[73] In the Soviet rear, many deaths occurred among prisoners of the NKVD. According to NKVD statistics 622000 died in labour camps alone in 1941–5, at least 400000 in excess of the normal death rate. A substantial number of the various nationalities deported in 1940–5 died en route or while in exile; the total number deported amounted to over 3 million, including 1.1 million Soviet Germans, 1.2 million from Western Ukraine and Western Belorussia, and some 0.6 million from the Caucasus.[74] But the overwhelming majority of civilian deaths, over 10 million of the total of 15 million, must have occurred from illness, malnourishment and ill-treatment on occupied territory and in captivity in German-occupied Europe, and in the harsh conditions of the Soviet civilian rear, where food was in extremely short supply and sickness was rife.

Further reading

No systematic study of population comparable with F. Lorimer, *The Population of the Soviet Union* (Geneva, 1946) has yet been published; and Lorimer did not have access to the results of the 1937 census or to other archival material. The basic materials of the 1937 census are presented in articles by Yu. A. Polyakov, V. B. Zhiromskaya and I. N. Kiselev, translated and introduced by R. E. Johnson, in *Russian Studies in History*, Summer 1992. Recently available statistical material on excess mortality and repression is presented in S. G. Wheatcroft, 'More Light on the Scale of Repression and Excess Mortality in the Soviet Union', *Soviet Studies*, xlii (1990), 355–67, and in two Notes by A. Nove, 'How Many Victims in the 1930s?', in *Soviet Studies*, xlii (1990), 369–73 and 811–4, and two further Notes by M. Ellman in the same journal, xliii (1991), 375–9 and xliv (1992), 913–5.

For a systematic presentation of archival data on forced labour, see E. Bacon, 'Forced Labour in the Soviet Union: New Information on the Gulag before and during World War Two', *Soviet Studies*, xliii (1992).

5   Employment and industrial labour

J. D. Barber and R. W. Davies*

The 1917 revolution destroyed the economic power of the landowners, the industrial capitalists and the large merchants. But at the end of the first decade after the revolution the occupational structure of the population as a whole was little changed from before the First World War. Over 80 per cent of the population were engaged in agriculture both in 1914 and in 1926. Among the 20 per cent outside the agricultural sector, the main changes were a precipitate decline in the number of domestic servants, the reduction in the size of the armed forces by 50 per cent, and a substantial growth in unemployment.

Between the two population censuses of 1926 and 1939, an occupational revolution took place. The number of persons working in the agricultural sector declined considerably, while the number engaged in all kinds of non-agricultural activities more than trebled. This included a trebling of the number employed in the education and health services as well as in industry. Educational levels rose sharply. The number of schoolchildren increased by over 150 per cent, so that by the end of the 1930s two-thirds of all children were attending school for seven years. The number of graduates increased from less than a quarter of a million in 1928 to nearly a million by the eve of the Second World War, though they still amounted to only just over one per cent of the labour force.

The core of the process of industrialisation was the expansion in the number of industrial workers, particularly those employed in the capital goods industries. Millions of new workers poured into factories and building sites from the countryside, and simultaneously the number of women employed in industry and related occupations greatly increased. The account which follows first outlines the general changes in employment, and then looks more closely at the expansion of the industrial labour force, and at its working and living conditions.

* Section I and Sections II (A) and (B) were primarily written by Davies, Section II (C) by Barber.

I Employment[1]

(A) Eve of War

On the eve of the First World War the vast majority of the gainfully-occupied population were engaged in agriculture. No accurate measurement of the numbers engaged in peasant farming is possible. On one estimate, they amounted to over 55 million adults. An alternative estimate, which includes children and senior citizens still engaged in agriculture, suggests that the true figure is over 70 million (see Table below). This compares with a gainfully-occupied population in all other categories (including pensioners etc.) amounting to some 17 million persons. This figure includes some five million persons self-employed as artisans of various kinds, or as traders. The number of persons employed in non-agricultural occupations by the state, and by private companies and individuals, probably amounted to no more than 10 millions, including 3½ million in large-scale industry and in building work, and nearly a million in transport and communications.

Number of gainfully-occupied persons in Russian Empire, 1913
and in Soviet Union, 1926
(approximate figures, millions)

	1913	December 1926
Self-employed		
Agriculture	53–70	70.5
Small-scale industry	2.7	1.6
Building	0.5	0.2
Trade	1.2	0.5
Employed		
Agriculture	3.	1.2
Industry	3.6	3.1
Building	0.5	0.2
Railways	0.7	0.9
Trade	0.5	0.7
Army	1.2	0.6
Other	4.7	6.6
Total	71.6–88.6	86.2

The ruling classes or ruling élites on the eve of the war may be crudely divided into two main segments: the noble landowners and the bourgeoisie. The American historian Seymour Becker estimates that there were some 95000 noble landowning families in 1912.[2] The connection between landownership and noble status declined in the last years of Tsarism; the amount of land owned by nobles in European Russia fell by over 40 per cent between 1877 and 1914.[3]

Simultaneously with the decline of the landowning nobility, the expansion of industry, trade and finance led to the growth of owners of capital, in Soviet terminology the 'big' and 'middle' bourgeoisie. (The Soviet term 'petty bourgeoisie' referred to peasants, artisans and small traders who owned their own means of production; this group has been included with the appropriate categories of the gainfully-occupied population.) On a rough estimate, there were approximately 213000 enterprises belonging to the bourgeoisie in 1912, including some 13000 large industrial enterprises and wholesale businesses.

The pre-revolutionary élite in terms of educational attainments constituted an even smaller proportion of the population. Only 136000 persons out of a gainfully-occupied population of over 70 million had completed higher education by 1914. But higher education was expanding rapidly, and at the outbreak of the First World War 127,000 students were enrolled in higher education. (Changes in employment during the first world war are discussed in chapter 11.)

(B) From Tsarism To NEP

The upheaval of the 1917 revolutions and civil war led to the disappearance of the landowning class and the 'big' bourgeoisie. A large proportion of these may have emigrated or been killed by 1921, together with a smaller proportion of the 'middle' bourgeoisie. In the 1920s, all private ownership of land continued to be banned. Private trade and industry were permitted a grudging existence. But, even at the peak of NEP in 1926/27, only 76000 persons were recorded as employing any kind of hired labour in the non-agricultural sector (apart from domestic labour) and only 30000 of these were classified as 'middle and large capitalists'.

Of the 'educational élite' with higher education, many emigrated after the revolution; but, judging by detailed figures available for the medical profession, most probably remained. The number of students in the 1920s was substantially greater than before the revolution; the total number of graduates by 1928 consequently increased to 233000, 70 per cent more than in 1914.

The new regime established a new ruling élite. According to the 1926 census, the number of senior administrators, managers and specialists amounted to about half a million persons out of the total gainfully-occupied population of 86.2 million. At the highest level, personnel employed in the administration before the revolution had largely been eliminated; and a substantial proportion of the administration consisted of ex-workers and peasants. But at the higher levels most of those who replaced the pre-revolutionary staff came from the middle classes; and the proportion of women in leading posts, while higher than before the revolution, remained extremely low.

In spite of the social upheaval of revolution and civil war, by the mid-1920s the occupational structure of the population was very similar to its structure before the revolution. In the countryside, with the post-revolutionary division of peasant households, the number of households increased from some 18.7 million in 1914 to about 24 million in the spring of 1927.[4] But the number engaged in agricultural activities remained approximately the same; the most significant change was the decline in agricultural labourers from 3 million in 1913 to 1.2 million in 1926.

In the non-agricultural sector, at the time of the December 1926 census, the number employed in large-scale industry was approximately the same as in 1913, and the number employed on the railways had substantially increased. But the number engaged in artisan industry and construction had substantially declined, and the number of servicemen was about half the 1914 level. Perhaps the most striking change was the decline in the number of persons employed in domestic labour from 1.6 million to only 317000.[5]

The 1920s also saw the growth of unemployment. The number of unemployed recorded in the 1926 census was 1.0 million; the true figure is closer to 1.4 million, over 14 per cent of the employed population. The precise number unemployed in 1913 was not recorded; it was probably no higher than 500000.[6]

In contrast to the situation in Western Europe and the United States, the prime cause of unemployment in the USSR was not economic depression. The number of employed persons increased from 6.7 to 10.4 millions between 1924/25 and 1929, sufficient to absorb more than the natural increase in the able-bodied urban population.[7] But the growth in employment was outweighed by the continuous pressure of the migration of adult labour from country to town; according to Soviet estimates, annual net migration increased from one-third of a million to nearly one million people a year during 1923–6.[8] The reasons for the huge increase in rural-urban migration compared with the pre-revolutionary period have not yet been satisfactorily elucidated. But the growth of job opportunities, and the high prestige of the towns, and of urban labour, must have played a major part.

Unemployment was a constant reproach to the authorities, an urgent reminder that the New Economic Policy was grounded in the capitalist economics of the market. It provided one of the most telling Left Opposition criticisms of official policies. The attempt to support industrialisation by economy measures and by rationalisation resulted in increased productivity, reduced employment possibilities, and sometimes led to an increase

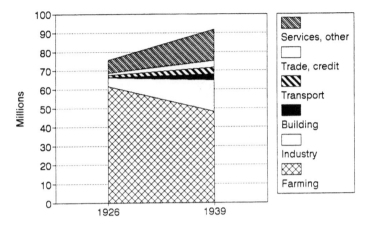

Figure 4   Gainfully occupied population, by branch, 1926 and 1939.
Source: table 11.

in unemployment. Until the very end of the 1920s it seemed to all concerned that the early stages of Soviet industrialisation might alleviate, but could not eliminate, mass unemployment.

(C) The impact of industrialisation

The precipitate growth in the number of persons working outside agriculture in the Soviet Union was a striking manifestation of the transformation of Soviet society which took place in the 1930s. Between the 1926 and 1939 population censuses, a period of just over twelve years, the number of persons engaged in all kinds of non-agricultural activities, both employed and self-employed, more than trebled, from 11.6 to 38.9 million. Lorimer commented about this transformation that 'these figures undoubtedly represent the most remarkable expansion of mechanical, technical and administrative activity ever achieved in any nation in so short a time'.[9] Simultaneously, the number working in the agricultural sector declined considerably, from some 62 to some 48 million (see Figure 4, Table 10; these figures are further discussed in the text below and in the footnotes to the Tables).

(i) Non-agricultural activities

The data are available from two major sources: the population censuses, which took place in December 1926 and January 1939 (see Tables 10 and 11), and the annual employment data (see Table 12). The main differences between the two series are set out in the Box.

Two sources of employment data

	Population censuses	Annual employment data
State enterprises	Included	Included
Cooperative enterprises	Included	Included
Private enterprises	Included	Included
Members of cooperatives	Included	Included
Self-employed	Included	Excluded
Those confined in labour camps, prisons etc.	Included	Excluded
Part-time work	Excluded	Included on full-time equivalent basis

Thus the employment data are less complete than the population data in two major respects. First, the population censuses include the self-employed, while the employment data broadly speaking include only those working for state, cooperative or private enterprises as employed persons or as members of cooperatives. Secondly, the population census includes persons confined in labour camps, prisons and other organisations controlled by the OGPU/NKVD. In 1926 the numbers were quite small, but in 1939 they were substantial but were concealed, probably simply by adding them to the total for each branch of the economy. The employment series omits this unfree labour.

These differences between the two series are quite large. Thus in the 1926 census the number recorded as engaged as private employers and self-employed in small-scale industry was 1,565,000 as compared with the 974000 recorded as employed in small-scale industry in 1928 (this includes members of industrial cooperatives). In trade, the 1926 census includes 23000 private employers and 456000 individuals and members of their families working on their own account who do not appear in the employment data. (The 1926 census data are in *Vsesoyuznaya perepis'*, xxxiv (1930); for 1928 employment see Table 13.)

It is worth noting, however, that the data for the building industry in the 1926 population census are incomplete. They exclude as many as 178000 persons who were engaged in building activities in industry and other branches of the economy, and the many seasonal workers who recorded building as a *secondary* occupation (482000); those in the former category appear under other headings in Table 11, but those in the latter category, like all other secondary occupations, do not appear at all in the census data we have used here. The inclusion of both these items would increase the number of persons engaged in building in 1926 to 1,024,000.

Thus the higher figures for industry and trade in the 1926 census as compared with the 1928 employment data were partly counteracted by the lower figure for building: in all, non-agricultural occupations in the 1926 census amounted to 10,840,000, as compared with 10,518,000 in 1928 (in the eighteen months between the population census at the end of 1926 and the employment data for 1928, which roughly correspond to mid-year, non-agricultural employment increased by about 750000). In addition, the 1926 census included 137000 members of 'free professions' (mainly priests), and a total of 3,500,000 in such varied categories as armed services; students; pensioners; rentiers; and unemployed. None of these is included in the data for employment. All these items together increase the non-agricultural total in the census figures for 1926 in Table 11 to 14.5 million as compared with 10.5 million employed persons in 1928 in Table 12.

The 1939 population census describes the new social order in which private employers no longer existed and the number of self-employed artisans and family members working with them had fallen to 638000. Moreover, occupations which were previously mainly seasonal had now normally become full-time activities, notably the building industry. So in these respects the census and employment data correspond more closely than in 1926. But the employment data for 1940 were incomplete in other significant ways. First, in the case of industry both auxiliary enterprises of non-industrial organisations (664000 in 1938) and the industrial enterprises of collective farms (perhaps 500000) were apparently excluded. Also excluded are the 638000 individual artisans and family members already mentioned. But if we exclude all these categories from the census data for 1939 – 1,782,000 in all – the census figure still exceeds the figure for industrial employment by 2,059,000. There is a similar excess for building of 1,239,000. The discrepancy may be partly because the 1940 employment data are average annual data (i.e. full- time equivalents), whereas the census data are for the main occupation irrespective of the length of employment in the year. But the main explanation for these discrepancies is that the population data for 1939 include forced labour, whereas the employment data for 1940 do not.

A further complication is that data for the first half of the 1930s were collected on a somewhat different basis by the People's Commissariat for Labour and by the trade unions. The two series are carefully compared and explained in a neglected but extremely valuable Ph.D dissertation: Redding (1958).

The vast expansion of non-agricultural employment shown in the Tables was primarily achieved by the increase in the urban population from 26 million in 1926 to 56 million in 1939 – in 1939 63 per cent of all non-agricultural employment was located in the towns; this compares with about 74 per cent in 1926.[10] Part of the increase in urban population was due to net additions to the population which was already living in the towns in 1926; but over 75 per cent of the increase was due to migration from the countryside to the town.[11]

But the gainfully-occupied population grew even more rapidly than the urban population as a whole. This increase in the participation rate (the proportion of the urban population who were working) was due to two major factors. First, the unemployed, recorded as 1,014,000 in the 1926 census, and largely located in the towns, were almost all absorbed into the labour force as early as 1931. Secondly, a substantial number of women previously engaged solely in housework took up gainful employment. In 1928 women amounted to 28.6 per cent of all the employed persons shown in Table 12, and this had increased to 40 per cent by 1940. This increase took place primarily in the middle and late 1930s, years in which the shortage of male labour was particularly acute. The purges of 1936–8 primarily affected men, and in the later 1930s the number of men called up for the armed services greatly increased. Between 1935 and 1940, women accounted for more than half of the total increase in employment. In all, between 1928 and 1940, the numbers employed in non-agricultural activities increased by twenty millions; of this one million was a result of the absorption of the unemployed and 3.5 million was due to the more rapid increase in female than male employment.

At the core of the expansion in non-agricultural employment was the huge expansion of heavy industry, and the vast construction programme associated with this expansion. The number employed in industry trebled between 1928 and 1940, and the proportion of the total employed in heavy industry greatly increased. The number employed in building increased at a similar rate, if we include forced labour, which was substantial by the end of the 1930s. Industrial labour is discussed further in Part II, p. 92 below.

An equally rapid expansion took place in the numbers employed in the education and health services. Substantial growth of the social infrastructure distinguishes industrialisation in the twentieth century from its classic predecessors; but the increase in the case of the USSR was particularly rapid. The rise in numbers employed in the education services was primarily due to the huge expansion in childrens' education in the 1930s; this continued at an even faster rate the process of bringing literacy and elementary education to the mass of the people which was already well under way before 1914. Between the 1927/28 and 1940/41 school years the number of children at school increased from 12 to 35 millions. In 1927/28 most children, including those in rural areas, were already attending school for four years, usually from seven to ten. But only a small proportion remained at school after the age of ten, and the number of children attending school above the age of fourteen was minute, and they were virtually all urban children. By 1940/41 the situation was transformed. Two-thirds of all children attended the top three forms of seven-year school, from eleven to thirteen; this included nearly all the urban children, and about half the rural children. Furthermore, about one-third of urban children aged fourteen to seventeen attended school (as against one-tenth of rural children).[12]

In the case of higher educational establishments the increase in staff was even more rapid, owing to the huge rise in the number of students. As a result of this expansion, the total number of specialists with a higher education more than quadrupled between 1928 and 1940. This increase was more rapid than that of the labour force as a whole: in non-agricultural subjects the number of specialists increased from 1.9 per cent of the employed labour force in 1928 to 2.7 per cent on 1 January 1941.[13] According to official figures, the number of specialists with a secondary specialised education (technicians, midwives, etc.) increased even more rapidly; but the figures for 1928 may be incomplete, so the rate of increase may be exaggerated.

The teacher-pupil ratio substantially *increased* between 1927/28 and 1940/41: the number of pupils increased by 203 per cent, the number of teachers by 251 per cent.[14] The abundance of teaching staff – often hastily trained – partly compensated for the inadequate buildings and equipment. Little new building took place; most schools worked two shifts, some even three shifts.

In important respects the quality of education deteriorated in the 1930s. In higher education, a broader technical education gave way to narrow specialisation, and history and the social sciences were confined in the straight jacket of ideological conformity and falsification. Both higher and school education abandoned the experimentation of the 1920s in favour of formal methods of education. Nevertheless, this was an educational revolution. It raised the skills and knowledge of Soviet young people and in important respects provided the preconditions for *perestroika*.

A similar expansion in employment took place in the health services: the number of doctors increased from 51000 in 1927 to 139000 in 1939, and auxiliary medical personnel increased even more rapidly. As in the case of education, the supply of facilities (including in the case of the health services medicines and medical equipment as well as buildings) increased far less rapidly; and the consequences were far more serious. In the 1930s the population had to endure poor working and living conditions. Most of the industrial population was crowded into existing towns, or lived in makeshift accommodation in very unhealthy conditions in the new towns and settlements. A significant minority of the population suffered the harsh conditions of labour camp and exile; a substantial number of people were executed.[15] But the most important factor making for poor health was malnutrition. Several million people died in the famine of 1932–3 (see chapter 4). Even by the end of the 1930s the amount of protein, especially animal protein, consumed per head of population was less than in 1926. In spite of the great increase in the number of health personnel, the crude death rate fell quite slowly (see Table 9). At the time of the 1939 population census a mere 6.8 per cent of the population were over the age of sixty, the same proportion as in 1926.[16] And infant mortality (deaths before the age of one, per thousand births) actually increased from 174 in 1926 to 182 in 1940; junior mortality (deaths before the age of five) also remained high. A rapid improvement in infant mortality and in other health indicators did not occur until after the Second World War, when the harsh conditions of the 1930s were somewhat mitigated.

The number employed under the heading 'Administration' grew far more slowly than any of the sectors we have discussed so far, increasing by a mere 80 per cent between 1928 and 1940. This is a strange paradox: although the Soviet Union may reasonably be described as a bureaucratic society, the number of bureaucrats apparently increased relatively slowly.

This slow rate of growth was partly a statistical distortion, due to the narrow definition of this sector. The full heading is 'Apparat of organs of state and economic administration; organs of administration of cooperative and voluntary organisations'. This accordingly covers the staff of the state and economic administration both in central and local government, and the staff of voluntary bodies which do not legally form part of the state structure such as the Communist Party and the trade unions. But it excludes the staff of primary eonomic and other organisations, including the administrative and managerial staff of industrial and other enterprises, and of schools, hospitals and other establishments. These very large staffs appear under the appropriate branch sector concerned (see Table 12, note j). Administrative staffs were the object of periodic campaigns to reduce numbers in the 1920s and 1930s (and these campaigns have continued ever since). In the case of the central and local organs of administration which are included in the Administration sector of Table 12, these campaigns were quite effective. But the administrative personnel of enterprises and establishments were not controlled so stringently: it may be significant that white-collar personnel (*sluzhashchie*) as a proportion of total employment increased from 26 per cent in 1928 to 33 per cent in 1940.[17]

In spite of these qualifications, there is no doubt that one of the factors – though not the most important – resulting in bureaucratic behaviour in the 1930s was a lack rather than an excess of administrative personnel. The lack of staff in Soviet offices, particularly of secretarial staff, meant that paper flowed more slowly and the public had to queue longer. The concentration of the labour force on the capital goods industries was partly secured by restricting the expansion of the administrative and other services.

(ii) Agricultural activities

While all other sectors expanded, the number of persons engaged in agricultural activities declined by some 20 per cent (see Box). This decline in the number of persons engaged in agriculture was associated with the absolute decline in the rural population from 121 to 115 millions. The number engaged in agriculture declined more sharply than the rural population partly because the proportion of the rural population engaged in non-agricultural activities increased (see note 10, pp. 338–9 below), and partly because of the decline in the number of children working in agriculture.

Measuring the number engaged in agricultural activity

The raw data of the two population censuses show a decline from 71.7 millions in 1926 to 48.2 millions in 1939 (see Table 10). But this exaggerates the decline. The definition of those engaged in agriculture was wider in 1926 than in 1939. It included all children from the age of ten and a substantial number of men and women over the formal retirement age (which was 55 for women and 60 for men). The 1939 census excluded both children under the age of sixteen and all persons above the formal retirement age. There is no doubt that children aged 10 – 15 worked less in 1939 than in 1926, owing to increased school attendance; but it is unrealistic to assume that no children of this age were working in agriculture in 1939. Nor is there any reason to suppose that in 1939 men and women had ceased to work after the formal retirement age. We have therefore tried to make the two census years comparable by reducing the 1926 data by about ten million persons (for details, see Note 1 to Table 10). (It would obviously have been better to increase the 1939 data by the number of children and retired people who were working in agriculture in 1939 but had not been counted; but the data are inadequate. It should therefore be borne in mind that both the 1926 and the 1939 data underestimate the true figure by about ten million persons.)

Such an absolute decline in the rural population is unusual in the history of industrialisation: elsewhere the normal pattern has been that the rural population declined in relative terms, but a decline in absolute terms, if it occurred at all, took place very slowly. The Soviet decline was largely a result of the huge expansion of occupations in the towns, to which as we have seen the rural population moved in large numbers. The migration from the countryside was accelerated by the serious deterioration of rural conditions following collectivisation. A significant part of this migration was compulsory or quasi-compulsory. Over one million 'kulak' families, six or seven million people in all, were exiled from their villages (see chapter 4). Some of these continued agricultural work in grim conditions elsewhere; but many former agriculturalists were now engaged in non-agricultural occupations in the camps or in exile, or in the town to which they had fled to escape expropriation. And the rural population was further reduced by the premature deaths during the famine of 1932–3.

Agricultural production was a few per cent higher in 1939 than in 1926, as will be shown in chapter 6. Accordingly, the decline in the population engaged in agriculture by over 20 per cent means that the productivity of agricultural labour increased by about one quarter. This does not seem to have been a result of the increase in hours worked; peasants, except on their household plots, tended to work less hours in the conditions of collectivisation. The main factor leading to this rise in productivity must be the large investment in machinery and other facilities, which not merely replaced the animal traction-power destroyed during collectivisation but also enabled some agricultural processes to be carried out with less labour. To this extent the industrialisation of agriculture replaced the labour which had moved into industry-related activities.

II Industrial Labour

(A) Eve of War

By 1914, approximately 2.5 million people worked in large-scale industry within the pre-1939 frontiers of the USSR, including both mining and manufacture. The industrial labour force had increased by about 2.5 per cent a year since 1860, when industry had employed a mere 800000 persons. Nevertheless, fewer persons were engaged in large-scale industry than in small-scale rural and urban industry and handicrafts, though many of these craftsmen worked in industry for only part of the year (see p. 134 below). Only 27 per cent of the industrial labour-force were women, and women outnumbered men only in the cotton textile industry. But the share of women had increased from a mere 18 per cent in 1900. Women were beginning to be engaged in traditionally male industries such as the metal trades.[18]

In the course of the previous decades the industrial labour force had gradually established itself as a distinct and relatively permanent section of the population. The level of literacy among industrial workers had increased considerably, and by the eve of the First World War had reached about 64 per cent, as compared with less than 40 per cent in the adult population at large.[19]

The labour force in large-scale industry had gradually broken its ties with the countryside. Most workers were employed in industry throughout the year, and did not return to the countryside during the harvest season – the coal industry was a significant exception. According to a survey carried out at the end of the 1920s, 59 per cent of workers who began employment in industry in 1906–13 were children of workers, only 35 per cent were children of peasants.[20] This figure may be exaggerated, because at the end of the 1920s it was advantageous to claim to be an 'hereditary proletarian'. A substantial proportion of workers retained close links with the countryside. The partial industrial census of 1918 showed that as many as one-third of all workers owned land before the revolution. Many workers aged 40–50 returned to the countryside to live.[21] A high proportion of workers – perhaps as much as 50 per cent in St Petersburg – regularly sent remittances to the countryside.[22] But more than one-half of all workers – more in the larger towns – were probably stable members of the industrial labour force, with only vestigial connections with the countryside.

We show elsewhere that labour productivity was lower than in Western Europe, and far lower than in the United States. Conditions of life and work for the Russian industrial worker were also far inferior. According to one estimate, 'the wages the workers received were only between one-quarter and one-third of the average in Western Europe'.[23] Living conditions were poor: many workers lived in barracks, all in overcrowded and insanitary conditions. Even in St Petersburg, the number of people living in each room or cellar was double the average for Berlin, Vienna or Paris.[24] Infant mortality in the large towns was as high as, or higher than, in the country as a whole.[25] The workers' lot was mitigated by Factory Acts, and by welfare provisions in large firms. Nevertheless, the working day, excluding overtime, amounted on average to 9.7 hours, longer than in most of Western Europe.[26] In spite of the Factory Acts, in most factories safety conditions were poor. An oppressive factory hierarchy treated the workers despotically. According to Leopold Haimson, this issue of 'human dignity' was a crucial aspect of the workers' hostility to the old regime.[27]

(B) In transition, 1914–1927

With the rapid recovery of industry, the numbers employed expanded rapidly from the low level of 1920–1. Many, perhaps most, of those recruited in 1922–5 had worked there before the revolution. This was in considerable part a second-generation working class, and a working class which had lost close connections with the countryside in the form of land holding.[28] In the largely seasonal building industry, however, as before the revolution, workers were closely tied to the land.[29]

The industrial workers were the heroes of the October revolution and its major beneficiaries. Between 1917 and the mid-1920s their political strength greatly diminished. The workers had effectively lost their hard-won right to strike; the penalties against strikers were already more severe than before the revolution. But in other respects the revolution had brought a vast enhancement in the status of the industrial workers, in their rights and privileges, and in their material position relative to the peasants, the professional classes and the minor officials.

The trade unions and the party cells drew factory personnel closely into the political and administrative system, acting both as agents of higher authority and, to a diminishing extent, as representatives of the workers. As compared with pre-revolutionary times, the authority over the worker of the factory engineer and the foreman, if not of the factory manager, had considerably diminished.[30]

The enhanced status of the worker brought important material changes, including greater equality of income not only between masses and rulers but also within the industrial working class itself. The differentiation in earnings between higher-paid and lower-paid workers declined substantially between 1914 and 1928.[31] This was the result of deliberate policy.

War and revolution also brought wider job opportunities and less economic inequality to women workers. As in other belligerent countries, the war considerably widened the range of jobs accessible to women, and in 1914–8 female employment increased rapidly as a percentage of all workers in census industry. After declining in the first two years of NEP, it then increased steadily between 1923/24 and 1926/27, but did not recover to its wartime peak.[32] Simultaneously, the wage gap tended to narrow between industries dominated by men, such as metalworking and mining, and industries in which the percentage of women was substantial, such as tex-

was easier in conditions of NEP to raise prices and pay higher wages in the consumer industries, where most women worked.[35]

Perhaps the most important reform in working conditions for everyone employed by the state was the introduction of the eight-hour day, the call for which was emblazoned on the banners of every European socialist party.[36] The normal length of the working day declined by over 20 per cent from 9.9 hours in 1913 to 7.8 hours in 1928.[37] On the occasion of the tenth anniversary of the revolution in 1927 further legislation authorised the gradual introduction of the seven-hour day.[38]

(C) 1928–1941

As the section of the population at the very centre of the drive to achieve rapid economic growth, the industrial working class was deeply affected by the policies implemented from the late 1920s onwards. Its size, composition and conditions changed radically between the launching of the first five-year plan in 1928 and the German invasion of 1941. In effect a new working class was created.

The most striking change was the huge increase in the number of manual workers employed in industry. Like the expansion of the Soviet economy as a whole, the rate of growth in the size of the industrial workforce was uneven. It was much greater in the first five-year plan than in the second and third, rising from 3.12 million in 1928 to 6.01 million in 1932, 7.92 million in 1937 and 8.29 million in 1940.[39] Even in the first five-year plan, however, much of the increase was concentrated in two years, from late 1929 to late 1931, when the number of workers in large-scale industry grew by over two million. (In 1932, by contrast, it fell slightly, as pressure was put on enterprises to shed surplus labour.[40]) During the second five-year plan (1933–7), the number, which was planned to rise by 47 per cent, in fact grew by only 32 per cent,[41] partly due to improved productivity and perhaps partly to the greater use of forced labour. Similarly, while the third five-year plan envisaged a rise of 17 per cent,[42] the increase during the three completed years of the Plan (1938–40) was only 4.6 per cent. In 1939, the number actually fell, probably as a result of increased conscription into the armed forces and the impact of the purges. 1940 saw the trend reversed, though some of the increase that year resulted from the acquisition of new territories following the Nazi-Soviet Pact.

The absolute increase in the number of industrial workers only partly reflects the scale of the influx of new workers into the labour force. The latter also had to compensate for the decrease in the number of workers, a result both of natural factors (such as illness, disability, child-bearing, old age, death), and of government policy (the promotion of workers to managerial posts, their secondment to full-time education, the return of newly recruited workers to the countryside during collectivisation, the arrest of workers followed by imprisonment or exile, and so on). The natural decrease in the number of workers in this period has been put at 4–5 per cent per annum;[43] but additional factors may have had at least as large an impact in some years. Even allowing for only the natural decrease, however, it is clear that the proportion of the workforce composed of new workers was significantly higher than the numerical increase suggests. In 1931 alone around 1.3 million new recruits entered Soviet industry; they comprised some 30 per cent of the total number of industrial workers.[44]

The pattern and priorities of Stalinist industrialisation were clearly reflected in the relative expansion of the workforce in different branches of industry and in different regions of the country. While the proportion of all workers in the national economy employed in Group A industries (producing capital goods) rose from 28.3 per cent to 43.5 per cent between 1928 and 1940, the proportion employed in Group B industries (producing consumer goods) fell from 26.6 per cent to 17.7 per cent.[45] The less developed regions of the USSR saw particularly rapid growth in the size of their industrial workforce. While the number of manual and white-collar workers in large-scale industry in the country as a whole grew by 83 per cent between 1929 and 1933, it rose by 179 per cent in eastern Siberia, 190 per cent in the Far Eastern region, 201 per cent in the Central Asian republics, 223 per cent in western Siberia, and 248 per cent in the Kazakh autonomous republic. Between 1928 and 1940 the largest increases in the size of the industrial workforce occurred in Uzbekistan (403 per cent), Kazakhstan (536 per cent), Kirgizia (620 per cent) and Tadjikistan (1140 per cent).[46]

But these were increases from a low base. Throughout the 1930s, the great majority of workers in large-scale industry continued to be located in the old industrial areas of the European part of the country: in the Moscow and Leningrad regions, in Ivanovo region, Gorkii (Nizhnii Novgorod) krai, Ukraine, the Urals and the North Caucasus. It was here that most of the examples of spectacular urban growth resulting from industrialisation took place in the 1930s. Completely new industrial towns were created, such as Stalinsk (with a population of 169,500 by 1939) and Magnitogorsk (145900); while other towns underwent a huge expansion, such as Chelyabinsk (from 59300 in 1926 to 273100 in 1939), Nizhnii Tagil (38800 to 159900), Sverdlovsk (140300 to 426500), Krivoi Rog (38200 to 197600) and Stalingrad (151500 to 446500).[47] In 1940, a third of all Soviet industrial workers were to be found in the Central Industrial region alone; the latter together with the North-Western region and Ukraine accounted for nearly two-thirds of the total. By contrast, the regions to the east and south of the Urals contained only 7.8 per cent.[48] The continued concentration of Soviet industry and its workforce in the western areas of the country was to result in great problems for the economy and the war effort following the invasion of the Soviet Union by Nazi Germany in June 1941.

(i) Length of employment

A corollary of the large influx of new recruits into the industrial workforce was a sharp decline in the average *stazh* (length of employment) of industrial workers. This had important economic and social consequences. While not the sole determinant of skill and productivity, *stazh* was seen as a key factor in producing a reliable workforce. The criterion for an experienced, 'cadre' worker is a matter of debate. In the late 1920s, the term was generally used to describe a worker who had first entered employment before the revolution, who thus had over a decade's work experience. More recently Russian historians have argued that in a modern factory environment five years are sufficient to produce a cadre worker.[49] Whatever the case, when the industrialisation drive began Soviet industry contained a large proportion of cadre workers. In 1929 the average *stazh* of workers in large-scale industry was around twelve years. Textile workers had the highest, coal miners the lowest; but even the latter had an average of eight years' employment. Over half of all industrial workers had begun work before the 1917 Revolution, and more than a fifth had been employed since before the 1905 revolution. If the five-year criterion is used, cadre workers constituted a substantial majority of workers in Soviet industry, including some 70 per cent of textile workers, 60 per cent of metal industry workers, and over 50 per cent of coal miners (see Table 14).

The entry of millions of new people into the industrial workforce transformed this situation. At the beginning of 1931, nearly a third of all industrial workers had been employed for less than a year. By the end of the first five-year plan, the average worker had two to three years work experience as compared with eight in 1929.[50] The proportion of workers with five or more years' *stazh* had fallen to around a third.[51] The experienced section of the workforce was now clearly in the minority.

After the first five-year plan the slower rate of growth of the industrial workforce produced an increase in the average *stazh* and a decline in the proportion of new workers. In 1934 manual and white-collar workers with less than a year's *stazh* comprised 10 per cent of the total employed in the national economy, and this level remained largely unchanged for the rest of the decade. The proportion with more than five years' *stazh* reached 44.6 per cent in 1935, and from 1935–40 averaged 58 per cent.[52]

While the industrial workforce thus became more stable and more experienced in the latter part of the period, it was by then to a large degree the product of the industrialisation drive. Allowing for a natural decrease of around 4 per cent in the number who had been industrial workers in 1928 (since most, though not all of the decrease would have come from older workers) and an equivalent decrease due to promotion and other contingent factors, the following picture emerges. Already in 1932, the proportion of industrial workers of pre-first five-year-plan *stazh* was 44 per cent. By the end of the second five-year-plan it had fallen to 27 per cent, and by 1940 it was a mere 23 per cent.[53] The great majority of workers who transformed the USSR into an major industrial economy were thus themselves the product of this transformation.

(ii) Young workers

One of the most striking features of the new recruits to industry was their youth. During the two years of the most intensive growth in the manual workforce, 1930 and 1931, one and a quarter million people under 23 years of age – more than two-thirds of the total increase – began work (see Figure 5 and Table 15).

Young workers were above all drawn into the most rapidly expanding branches of industry: engineering and metal work, iron and steel, chemical and mining. In 1928–30 some 40 per cent of new workers under the age of 23 went into engineering plants and 20 per cent to iron and steel plants.[54] The youngest workforce was to be found in coal mining; 40 per cent of the workers were under 23 in 1932.[55] The oldest was to be found in the textile industry.[56] Young workers were particularly numerous at the largest industrial plants. Workers under 23 were 60 per cent of the manual workforce at the Stalingrad tractor factory and 70 per cent at the Kharkov tractor factory in April 1932, while in Moscow they comprised 68 per cent of workers at the Stalin automobile plant and 73 per cent at the Serp i Molot metallurgical plant.[57]

As the rate of growth of the workforce slowed and the lower birth-rate of the post-revolutionary period took effect, the proportion of youth in the workforce declined. In the RSFSR the proportion of workers in large-scale industry aged under 23 fell from 35.7 per cent in July 1932 to 29.3 per cent in July 1936.[58] At some major new plants, youth was still conspicuous in the workforce. In 1935 July 47.1 per cent of workers at the Chelyabinsk tractor factory and 59.6 per cent of workers at the Stalinogorsk chemical combine were under 23.[59] But the trend was towards an older workforce. By the end of 1939, only 17 per cent of workers in large-scale industry were 25 or under.[60]

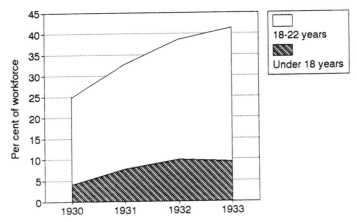

Figure 5   Young workers in large-scale industry, 1930–1933. *Source:*
table 15.

(iii) Female workers

The increase in the proportion of the industrial workforce composed of
women (see p. 94 above) was accelerated by the industrialisation drive.
From management's point of view, employing women had two particular
advantages. Many already lived in towns and did not have to be provided
with scarce accommodation; and they were less likely than men to change
their jobs, at least if they were married. Women thus figured increasingly
among recruits to industry. Between 1926 and 1930 they comprised 29 per
cent of new manual and white-collar workers in large-scale industry;[61] in
1931 they were 41 per cent of new members of industrial trade unions; and
in 1934 they were 43 per cent of all new industrial manual and white-collar
workers. During the second five-year-plan half of all new manual and
white-collar workers were women.[62] By 1937 the female proportion of
industrial workers had surpassed the First World War level of 40 per cent.
In Moscow women workers were by then already in the majority (51.4 per
cent).[63] In the USSR as a whole in 1939 women comprised 43.3 per cent of
all industrial workers.[64] (See Figure 6 and Table 16.)

   The most novel feature of female employment in the 1930s was the mass
entry of women into hitherto almost exclusively male branches of industry.
Traditionally, female labour had been concentrated in light industry, particularly textiles. In 1928, the latter accounted for 480000 women workers
out of a total of 700000 in all large-scale industry. The female proportion of
the manual labour force in the textile industry rose during the first five-year
plan, from 43.3 per cent to 57.2 per cent. But in capital goods (Group A)

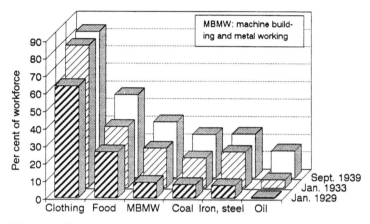

Figure 6   Women workers in large-scale industry, 1929–1939. *Source:* table 16.

industries it more than doubled, from 11.1 per cent to 24 per cent.[65] In some industries it more than trebled between 1929 and 1935, with the growth rate fastest in mining, iron and steel, engineering and metal work industries. It continued to rise up to the end of the 1930s in most industries, though in textiles it fell slightly.

The structure of female employment in the USSR in the 1930s contrasted sharply with that in a traditional industrial country like Britain. In 1935 the female proportion of the labour force in major British and Soviet industries was respectively 0. 6 and 24.1 per cent in coal mining, 5.4 per cent and 23.4 per cent in engineering and metal work, 54.2 per cent and 70.1 per cent in textiles, and 1.2 per cent and 19 per cent in building.[66]

Women workers in the USSR in the 1930s differed from their male counterparts in two significant social respects. First, the proportion of new workers from an urban (and probably proletarian) background was higher among women than men. In 1931 45.1 per cent of new female industrial trade-union members were of urban origin compared with 31.1 per cent of new male members. In 1932–4 the number of women of working age who moved to the towns was only 50–60 per cent of the comparable number of men.[67] Secondly, women workers were younger and less experienced. Well over half the women in the industries surveyed in the 1932–3 trade-union census were under 23. On average they were three to five years younger than male workers; and between a quarter and a third, depending on the industry, had a *stazh* of less than a year.

(iv) Social composition

A conspicuous feature of the Soviet working class up until the end of the 1920s was its large core of 'hereditary proletarians', the sons and daughters of manual workers. According to the trade-union census of April–May 1929 they amounted to more than half of all industrial workers: the remainder came mostly from the peasantry, with small percentages from the families of artisans, merchants and white-collar workers. The proportion of 'hereditary proletarians' varied considerably between industries and regions (see Table 17). It tended to be highest in the engineering, metalworking and textile industries, and lowest in mining, where the majority of workers were peasants by social origin. The Urals, the oldest centre of Russian heavy industry, had the highest proportions of hereditary proletarians, the Ivanovo region and Ukraine the lowest.

By the end of the 1920s the trend in some industries, such as engineering and metalworking was towards a decline in the proportion of workers by social origin. In 1929, among iron and steel workers who had begun work after 1925, 52 per cent were of peasant origin; in mining it was 69 per cent. In the textile industry, on the other hand, the trend was in the opposite direction.[68] In Leningrad and the Ivanovo region, the proportion of workers by social origin was higher, at 67 per cent and 62 per cent respectively, among the newest recruits than among any other group of workers. There had also been a small increase in the proportion of workers by social origin in the iron and steel industry of Ukraine and the Urals, and in the oil industry.[69]

This position changed sharply during the first five-year plan. It was far beyond the capacity of the towns to satisfy the demand for new workers. Until 1930 urban sources (the unemployed, members of manual and white-collar workers' families, artisans and craftsmen and déclassé elements) provided the majority of new workers for industry. According to Gosplan figures, only 40 per cent of new recruits to the urban workforce came from the peasantry between 1927 and 1930.[70] But from 1930 onwards the countryside was by far the largest supplier of recruits to industry. The trade-union census of 1931 summarised the position succinctly. 'From 1929 the role of the countryside in providing labour began to strengthen noticeably. In 1930 and especially in 1931, collective farmers and the poor and middle peasant groups of the countryside began to occupy the dominant place among the new recruits.'[71] At the end of the first five-year plan, Gosplan estimated that over two-thirds (8.6 million out of 12.6 million) of the manual and white-collar workers who had begun work during the period were peasants.[72] The proportion of ex-peasants among new manual workers alone must have been even higher, since relatively few peasants would have become white-collar workers.

The changing pattern of recruitment into the industrial workforce was clearly reflected in contemporary surveys. A survey of industrial workers joining trade unions in the latter part of 1931 showed that those of peasant origin outnumbered hereditary workers by 56.7 per cent to 34.7 per cent.[73] Since some 15 per cent of manual and white-collar workers did not at this time belong to trade unions,[74] and since former members of 'alien' classes (such as ex-kulaks) were excluded from membership, the peasant proportion of the workforce may have been still higher.

The change in recruitment into the working class during the first five-year plan radically changed its overall social composition. In a few branches of industry, hereditary proletarians continued to constitute the largest social category of workers. But in industry as a whole, ex-peasants predominated. In 1929 43 per cent of workers in large-scale industry were peasants by social origin,[75] and by the end of the first five-year plan the number of workers had approximately doubled, with the peasantry providing at least two-thirds of the new recruits. Former peasants must therefore now have predominated among workers in large-scale industry.

With the slower rate of growth of the workforce in the mid and late 1930s, the proportion of new workers who came from the countryside fell somewhat. But they still constituted the majority of recruits. According to Gosplan, 1.4 million new workers during the second five-year plan came from factory schools, 1 million from the urban labour reserve, and an estimated 2.5 million from the countryside.[76] Since around 40 per cent of students at factory schools between 1932 and 1935 (and 50 per cent of those admitted in October 1935)[77] were peasants by origin, some 60 per cent of new workers during the second five-year plan must have come from the peasantry. For the last three-and-a-half pre-war years, comparable figures are not available, although it has been estimated that 40 per cent of new manual and white-collar workers came from collective farms;[78] but in any case the total increase in the number of workers at that time was small. The overall picture, however, is quite clear: throughout the 1930s the industrial workforce was primarily composed of ex-peasants.

(v) Living conditions

While industrialisation of the USSR differed in many respects from that of capitalist countries, the two processes had at least one major feature in common: an immediate decline in the standard of living of the working class. Despite the promises and expectations of a rapid improvement in material conditions when the first five-year plan was launched, the opposite happened. Workers' living conditions rapidly deteriorated from 1928 onwards. Not until 1934 was the decline halted. From then until 1938, conditions improved, only to fall again as war approached. At no point, however, did they regain, let alone surpass, the level of the 1920s.

Real wages had risen steadily during NEP, and the expectation of the five-year plan was that they would continue to do so, by at least 53 per cent, during the period of the plan.[79] In the event, an increase in nominal wages was heavily outweighed by rising prices. Moscow workers' real wages were 52 per cent of their 1928 level in 1932, and still only 63.5 per cent in 1937.[80] The picture for the country as a whole is similar.[81]

To some extent, the fall in workers' real wages was offset by an rise in the 'social wage'. Increased provision of services such as education and health-care undoubtedly had a positive impact on the standard of living in the 1930s. On the other hand, the social wage had little effect on incomes, since the proportion of it provided as cash benefits, such as pensions or welfare allowances, sharply declined. More important factors affecting workers' incomes were the end of unemployment and an increase in the number of employed members of working-class families. The ratio of dependents to wage-earners changed from 2.26 in 1927 to 1.59 in 1935.[82] This compensated to a significant extent for the fall in real wages.

In other basic respects, however, there was little to mitigate the decline in living standards. Workers' housing conditions were already notoriously poor during NEP. References to the 'housing crisis' were common. The average living space for members of working-class families in the RSFSR excluding Moscow and Leningrad in 1928 was 4.8 square metres; in Moscow it was 4.34, in Leningrad 5.91.[83] But many people had much less than this. A 1929 survey of Donbass miners and iron and steel workers in 1929 found that 40 per cent had less than 2 square metres.[84]

The mass influx of migrants into the towns from 1928 onwards combined with the inability or unwillingness of the authorities to allocate sufficient investment to the construction of new housing produced a sharp decline in workers' living conditions. In Moscow the per capita norm for all groups of the population fell from 5.44 m^2 (square metres) in January 1929 to 3.94 m^2 (square metres) in 1931.[85] The national norm was a mere 3.77 m^2 in 1937.[86] Workers' norms were consistently below these averages, with many living in very inferior conditions – in barracks, mud-huts, in the corridors, halls or kitchens of communal apartments, even in the factories or mines where they worked.

Even housing problems, however, took second place in the early years of the industrialisation drive to those of obtaining food. Here the decline in workers' living conditions was most marked of all. During the latter part of NEP Soviet workers' diet was probably better than at any previous time before or after 1917. In 1925 the average Moscow worker was said to consume 3819 calories daily, comfortably in excess of the daily norm of 3400

for a man engaged in heavy physical work.[87] As the tempo of industrialisation quickened, however, the food situation deteriorated. Bread rationing
was introduced in the main cities in January 1929 and in other urban centres
soon after. Rationing of other foodstuffs followed.

To some extent, the rationing system made workers a privileged group.
Compared with low-paid white-collar workers, and still more with peasants,
they were protected from the harshest effects of the food supply crisis and
were guaranteed at least a subsistence diet. At the same time, it is clear that
their diet declined sharply in both quantity and quality during the first
phase of the industrialisation drive. In Moscow, working class consumption
of meat fell by 60 per cent and dairy products by 50 per cent between 1928
and 1932.[88] The average worker's diet during the first five-year plan was to a
large extent one of enforced vegetarianism, the bulk of it consisting of rye
bread, potatoes and cabbage. Rations, even bread, were not always issued in
full to all workers. Increasingly they were used as incentives, with shock
workers receiving several times the basic norm.

Rationing ended in 1935, by which time the food situation for workers
had improved considerably, at least in quantitative terms. But two qualifications must be made. In terms of consumption of meat and dairy products, workers' diet remained inferior to that of the NEP years for another
two decades. And the marked increase in wage differentials associated with
the industrialisation drive produced substantial variations in food consumption between the highest and lowest income groups.

Although workers' living conditions undoubtedly deteriorated after 1928,
it would misleading to exaggerate the impact of this decline. They had
known worse conditions both under Tsarism and during the civil war. A
foreign observer in 1936 produced a succinct answer to the question 'how,
granted these low wage rates and these high prices, the Soviet workman
manages to survive at all?':

The explanation involves a number of factors: cheap dinners at factories, the fact
that husband and wife are both wage-earners in most families, free medical attention, a largely bread diet and the free supply to workers of trade clothing . . . The fact
remains that the Soviet worker not only survives, but appears to be on the whole not
undernourished and at least adequately clothed.[89]

Workers had enough to live on; they could manage. The more important
consequence of their low standard of living during the years of Stalinist
industrialisation was that like other features of Soviet society then it was
tacitly accepted as normal. The low priority accorded to satisying the
material needs of the working class would thus survive long after the initial
period of rapid economic growth had passed.

Further reading

No general study of employment is available. For data on the technical intelligentsia, see N. Lampert, *The Technical Intelligentsia and the Soviet State* (London and Basingstoke, 1979), especially Chapters 4 and 7.

For industrial workers, see J. D. Barber, 'The Development of Soviet Labour and Employment Policy', in D. S. Lane (ed.), *Labour and Employment in the USSR* (Brighton, 1986), 50–65, and also Barber, 'The Standard of Living of Soviet Industrial Workers, 1928–1941' (in English) in C. Bettelheim (ed.), *L'industrialisation de l'URSS dans les années trente* (Paris, 1982), 109–22.

6   Agriculture

S. G. Wheatcroft and R. W. Davies

In the quarter of a century between the outbreak of the First and Second World Wars – normally a brief period in agricultural history – the agricultural economy of the Russian Empire/Soviet Union suffered a series of shocks and convulsive changes.

During the agrarian revolution of 1917–18 the peasants seized the estates of the landowners, for centuries masters of the Russian land; nearly all private land and agricultural property were distributed among the peasants. Until the end of the 1920s almost all agriculture on Soviet territory was carried on by over twenty million peasant households, largely organised in traditional village communes. But in the early 1930s the collectivisation of agriculture was imposed from above. Better-off or recalcitrant peasants were expelled from their farms, and collective or state farms, controlled by the state, were everywhere established. The collective-farm system still dominates in most former Soviet territory today.

Agriculture experienced two periods of crisis (1916–21 and 1930–3) and two periods of recovery and growth (1921–8 and 1934–40). During the first crisis, world war, revolution and civil war were accompanied by the huge population movements described in chapter 4. During the civil war food requisitioning was imposed on the countryside by both Bolshevik and anti-Communist governments. By 1920 grain production had fallen to a mere two-thirds of the 1909–13 level. Following the introduction of the New Economic Policy, the restoration of a market relation between the state and the peasants enabled rapid recovery, and by 1928 production exceeded the pre-war level.

The mass collectivisation of agriculture, launched at the end of 1929, was accompanied by the breakdown of the market and the remorseless exaction of grain and other products from agriculture in order to feed the growing industrial population, and for export. By 1932 agricultural production had fallen to 73 per cent of the 1928 level. From 1933 onwards, the relative stabilisation of the collective-farm system, and the greatly increased supply of machinery, resulted in a rapid recovery. But agricultural production in the later 1930s only slightly exceeded the 1928 level, and had declined in terms of output per head of population.

The two periods of crisis culminated in the disastrous famines of 1921–2 and 1932–3, each of which resulted in the death of millions of peasants from malnutrition and disease.

(A) Before the First World War

Although the 100000 noble landowners were the principal actors on the pre-revolutionary political stage, and derived most of their wealth from the land, they played a relatively minor part in agricultural production. An increasing number of estates were owned by 'bourgeois' landowners who did not have the status of nobles; and part of the land owned by the nobles was rented out to peasants. By 1916 less than 10 per cent of the total sown area of the Russian Empire was directly cultivated as landowners' estates.[1] The share of horses and cattle owned by landowners was even smaller.[2] The vast majority of agricultural production was the responsibility of the twenty million peasant households which constituted five-sixths of the total population living in the countryside in 1913.

Most peasant households were organised into rural communes. The bulk of the land in the main fields of the commune was divided into strips, and each household cultivated a number of strips; these fields were known as the *nadel*. In many communes the land in the *nadel* was periodically redistributed. Each peasant household also cultivated a permanent small household plot (*usad'ba*) located next to its cottage.

In spite of these traditional agricultural arrangements, the majority of peasant households were involved to a greater or lesser extent in the market economy. While the households consumed much of their own produce, a substantial part was sold on the market – over 40 per cent of grain production net of seed, for example. Moreover, many peasants also took part in economic activities outside their own farm, usually on a part-time basis. Over four million peasants worked seasonally outside their own village or rural district as agricultural labourers, and at least five million worked in building, forestry and various other nonagricultural occupations.

The agrarian reforms of Prime Minister Stolypin in 1907–10 sought to replace the village commune by independent peasant households each with their own permanent allocation of land. But by 1914 only about 10 per cent of households in European Russia lived on farms separated from the commune. Only a minority of this minority lived in 'farms' in the West European sense of the term, with the cottages and fields separated from their neighbours as single fenced-in units.

Grain was by far the most important product of Russian agriculture – and of the Russian economy as a whole. It covered about 90 per cent of all sown area and accounted for some 40 per cent of all agricultural production by value. It supplied about 70 per cent of all human calories in a direct form, and also provided over half the livestock feed stuffs. It also supplied industry with a large volume of raw materials. It provided about 35 per cent by value of all exports.

The absolute level attained by pre-war grain production has been the subject of fierce debate throughout this century. Both before the First World War and in the 1920s many economists and statisticians argued that the official statistics prepared by the Tsarist Central Statistical Committee (TsSK) were considerably underestimated. In the 1920s the State Planning Commission (Gosplan) claimed that the pre-war harvest figures should be increased by 19 per cent because both yield and sown area were underestimated. In 1925 a large correction coefficient was accordingly applied to the official pre-war figures. In the 1930s the coefficient was drastically reduced, evidently in order to present a more favourable picture of Soviet agricultural performance in comparison with that of Tsarism. From 1960 onwards Soviet official statistics reduced the pre-war harvest figure to 5 per cent *below* the uncorrected TsSK estimate!

The removal of the upward correction of the 1920s, while undertaken for political rather than scientific reasons, appears to have been justified.[3] (However, as we shall see later, the current official harvest figures for the 1920s and 1930s are not compatible with the uncorrected pre-revolutionary data.)

While the absolute level of grain production is controversial, it is certain that grain production rose substantially in the last twenty years before the First World War. The very high level of grain production in the single year 1913 was due to exceptionally favourable weather. In this book we shall therefore normally compare post-revolutionary harvests with the average harvest in the last five years before the First World War (1909–13); but it should be borne in mind that weather conditions which were better than average also imparted an upward bias to the average harvest in 1909–13.

Historians often claim that it was the Stolypin reforms which resulted in the sharply increased agricultural and particularly grain production of 1909–13; in view of the very large role of the favourable weather in this result, this assumption is extremely rash. But there was certainly a long-term improvement. Over the whole period 1895–1914 grain production grew by some 2.1–2.4 per cent a year, an increase of 0.5–0.8 per cent a year per head of total population.[4]

Long-established regional differences in grain production were of great significance in economic development. The Russian Empire was conventionally divided into grain-surplus and grain-deficit regions, generally known as 'producer' and 'consumer' regions. The Russian Empire on the eve of the war may be classified into five main agricultural regions. The principal Consumer Regions were the Northern Consumer Region (NCR), which incorporated the Northern, North-Western, Western and Central Non-Black-Earth Regions, and the Southern Consumer Region (SCR), incorporating the Transcaucasus and Central Asia. About 30 per cent of the population of the Russian Empire lived in these regions. The remaining 70 per cent lived in the three Producer Regions: the Central (CPR), incorporating the Central Black Earth, the Volga and the South-Eastern regions; the Southern (SPR), incorporating Ukraine and the Southern Steppe, and the Eastern (EPR), incorporating Urals and Siberia. The NCR and SCR produced some 17 per cent of the total production of grain and imported a further 6–7 per cent from the producer regions. The CPR, SPR and EPR together produced the remaining 83 per cent of the grain, exporting abroad some 16 per cent of all grain production and selling a further 6–7 per cent to the consumer regions. These three producer-regions therefore retained 60–61 per cent of the total production of the Russian Empire for consumption within the three regions.

The relation between the regions slowly shifted in the prewar decades. Production per head of population declined in the NCR; the share of total grain produced in the SPR increased; production per head of population in the CPR stagnated; the role of the SCR and the EPR remained roughly constant.

Livestock farming was the second most important sector, providing some 34 per cent of gross agricultural production. Our knowledge of its rate of growth in pre-war decades is frustratingly imperfect. Neither the absolute numbers of livestock nor their rate of increase are known with certainty; and no data are available about changes in the average weight of farm animals in this period. We have provisionally concluded that livestock numbers increased by only about one per cent a year between 1900 and 1914, or more slowly than the growth of population.[5]

The importance of *industrial crops* increased steadily during the pre-war decades. By 1913 they provided only about 4 per cent of gross agricultural production, but a very high proportion of this output was marketed for use by industry. Cotton, oilseeds and hemp were largely grown by individual peasants; sugar-beet, tea and tobacco largely on landowners' estates. In spite of substantial increases in production, most cotton was still imported on the eve of the First World War.

Potatoes, vegetables and fruit received far less attention from the statisticians – and the Tsarist authorities generally. This was because almost all fruit and vegetables and about one-third of the potato crop were grown not in the main village fields (*nadely*) but on the household plots (*usad'by*). They probably accounted for about 10 per cent of all agricultural production, though they were not included in the regular statistical records.

Meadow and pasture, the produce of which was almost entirely consumed by livestock as fodder, also received little attention in the statistics in spite of their importance for livestock production. They are roughly estimated to have supplied about 17 per cent of gross agricultural production, almost half the value of livestock production.

(B) War and reconstruction, 1914–1927

War, revolution and civil war saw a catastrophic decline in agricultural production and fundamental changes in its structure.

During the world war and civil war, grain production declined from 1916 onwards, but disaster was averted because the cessation of grain exports released some 10 million tons annually for internal consumption. By 1920 grain production had fallen to about 66 per cent of the 1909–13 (average) level, owing to a decline in both sown area and yields. The economic and social effects of this decline are discussed in chapter 11.

From 1916 onwards there was also a very rapid decline in livestock numbers; by 1922 the number of cattle had fallen by 30 per cent and the number of pigs by about one-half.[6] Industrial crops declined even more precipitately, particularly in the case of cotton and sugar-beet, which were almost entirely produced for the market. On the other hand, while comprehensive records are not available, it is certain that the production of potatoes, fruit and vegetables held up much better. These crops were largely consumed by the peasants themselves, and less subject to the depredations of the state requisition agencies than grain or livestock.

The landowners' estates tended to deteriorate in 1914–16 owing to the labour shortage resulting from war-time mobilisation. In 1917–18 this sector was altogether eliminated in the course of the agrarian revolution. Private land ownership was abolished. Most of the former private land (including the private land rented to individual peasants and peasant communes) was seized by or distributed among the peasants, together with the animals, agricultural implements and other property of the landowners. The livestock herds of the landowners, though relatively small, often contained the best pure-bred stock, and attempts by the local authorities to preserve this stock were rarely successful. The agrarian revolution also involved the restoration of the commune and of the periodical redistribution of strips where these had lapsed, or had been brought to an end by the Stolypin reform. Nearly all separate peasant farms were eliminated. Within the village, some equalisation or 'middlepeasantisation' (*oserednyachenie*) took place: the landowners' land, including land previously rented to more prosperous peasants, tended to be acquired by the poorer households, including previously landless peasants.

With the introduction of NEP, after the disastrous famine of 1921–2, agricultural production began to recover, and by 1926 it had reached the pre-war level. In 1926 grain production was just below the 1909–13 (average) level; this meant that production per head of total population had declined by some 3–6 per cent. The two main producer regions, SPR and CPR, lagged in their recovery, mainly owing to the loss of horses and hence of draught power during the 1921–2 famine. On the other hand, by the mid-1920s the EPR was producing substantially more grain than before the war. This was also true of the NCR, which in consequence became less reliant on grain purchased from the producer regions.

While gross agricultural production had reached the pre-war level, a smaller proportion of total agricultural production was marketed than before the war throughout the 1920s.

According to Gosplan estimates, marketed production in 1926/27 amounted to only 17 per cent of gross production, as compared with 22–5 per cent in 1913. The proportion of grain production sold outside the villages was only just over 50 per cent of the pre-war level. The reasons for the general decline in agricultural marketings, which had repercussions throughout the economy, are discussed in chapter 1 above.

One important consequence of the decline in grain marketings was that in the 1920s the export of grain abroad amounted to only a quarter of the pre-war quantity, even in the most favourable years. This was partly because less total grain per head of population was available, but mainly because of the increased consumption of grain within the peasant economy by the livestock sector. By 1926 the number of cattle already almost equalled the 1914 level, and continued to rise in 1927 and 1928, and the average weight of cattle, which partly depended on the supply of grain as fodder, was apparently substantially higher than in 1913.[7] The principal economic reason for this success was that meat and dairy products, unlike grain, were mainly sold on the free market, so that their prices were outside state control. Grain, seen as the crucial crop, was closely under state control and the price paid to the peasants tended to be kept relatively low.

The other agricultural sectors also recovered to higher levels of production than before the war. The total production of industrial crops is estimated to have exceeded the pre-war level as early as 1925; after a decline in 1926, by 1928 it reached 23 per cent above the 1913 level (see Table 18). While most sugar-beet had been grown on estates before the war, in the mid-1920s as many as 1,200,000 peasant farms grew sugar-beet, mainly on very small areas. Even so, by 1927 sugar-beet production had recovered to the 1913 level. Cotton growing, in contrast, was always mainly a peasant crop, but in the 1920s it was re-established on even smaller units. In 1927 the output of raw cotton also exceeded the 1913 level. The yield of both cotton and sugar-beet was substantially lower than in 1913; but the decline in yield was compensated by substantial increases in sown area.

By 1928, the production of potatoes, fruit and vegetables was as much as 42 per cent higher than in 1913 (see Figure 7 and Table 18). Though the statistics for these crops are very crude, the general trend seems certain. The 1928 harvest of potatoes was as much as 50 per cent higher than in 1913. There was probably a decline in fruit and vinegrowing owing to the destruction of landowner orchards and vineyards, but peasant vegetable production almost certainly increased.

On the eve of the enforced collectivisation of agriculture, as in 1914, over four-fifths of the population lived in the countryside – 120 million people divided into 25 or 26 million peasant households. The vast majority of households, some 23 million in 1926, were primarily engaged in farming. As before the revolution, each household cultivated its *nadel* in the main fields and its auxiliary *usad'ba* round the cottage. In the vast majority of villages, the strip system, and a simple three-field crop rotation still predominated. The commune, to which peasant households in most regions belonged, was usually responsible for distributing and redistributing arable land among the households, and also normally determined which crops should be grown on each field and when the ploughing, sowing and harvesting should take place. In the 1920s, as before the war, a substantial minority of peasant households, 6.7 million by 1926, were members of agricultural marketing or credit cooperatives. Informal forms of collaboration between families in the use of animals, implements and land were also frequent.

In spite of the various communal and cooperative arrangements, peasant households were independent economic actors. They took their own decisions about what equipment and animals to purchase, and what proportion of their production to take to market, or sell to state agencies. Land and implements could be leased to or rented from other peasants, and peasants could at their own discretion hire their labour out to other peasants, and engage in non-agricultural occupations. This was then a market economy, though one in which most peasant households grew most of their own food for personal consumption.

Even at the end of the 1920s peasant farming was largely non-mechanised, cultivating the soil by horse-drawn implements. Within this framework, agricultural techniques improved considerably during the 1920s. By 1928, over nine-tenths of the land area, the metal plough had replaced the primitive sokha (the ard or scratch-plough); and grain from more than half the land area was harvested and threshed mechanically by horse-drawn implements. Nevertheless, in 1928 as much as 44 per cent of the grain area was still harvested by sickles and scythes, and as much as 74 per cent was sown by hand.[8]

(C) The transformation of agriculture, 1928–1941: production

The economic and social transformation of peasant agriculture, launched precipitately by the Soviet government at the end of the 1920s, was the most ambitious of all Soviet economic projects – and the most unsuccessful. It sought to replace small-scale individual peasant farming based on animal power and physical human effort by large-scale mechanised socialist farming. The transformation was undertaken with extraordinary speed and ruthlessness. Stalin and his supporters believed that the towns could be fed and industry supplied with raw materials only if distribution of agricultural production were brought firmly under the control of the state, and farm technology and organisation emulated the most advanced large-scale American farms. The Soviet leaders were confident that the collectivisation and mechanisation would make it possible to 'catch up and surpass' the agricultural output of the United States in the course of a decade or so. 'When we have seated the USSR on an automobile and the peasant on a tractor', Stalin wrote on the occasion of the twelfth anniversary of the Bolshevik revolution, '– let the esteemed capitalists, who boast about their "civilisation", try to catch us up then.'[9]

These bright hopes soon faded. Agricultural production – and particularly production used for human food and animal fodder – declined very substantially in 1928–32. Even by the end of the 1930s gross agricultural production had barely recovered to the level of the mid-1920s. According to the official figures, as estimated in the 1960s, in 1940 it exceeded the 1928 level by a mere 2.5 per cent. Our provisional estimates reach similar conclusions (see Figure 7 and Table 18). Agricultural production increased less rapidly than population growth, which was about 12 per cent in this period.

(i) Livestock (Tables 20 and 21)

Livestock suffered the most precipitate decline. Between 1928 and 1933 the number of cattle fell by 44 per cent, of pigs by 55 per cent, and of sheep and goats by as much as 65 per cent. This decline – except in the case of pigs – was far greater than that which had occurred as a result of the six years of world war and civil war between 1914 and 1921. And these figures do not reflect the full extent of the calamity; animals after collectivisation were smaller and weaker than they had been in the 1920s.[10]

The slaughter of animals resulted in a very temporary increase in the consumption of meat in the countryside; but, with this exception, throughout the 1930s far less meat and dairy products were available per

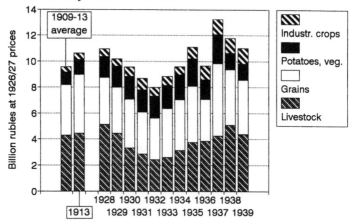

Figure 7   Gross agricultural production, 1909–13 to 1939. *Source:*
table 18.

head of population than in the late 1920s. The decline in the number of
animals also resulted in a proportionate reduction in the supply of hides for
the leather and footwear industries, and of raw wool for the textile industry.

Equally harmful was the decline in the number of horses, the main
work-force in agriculture apart from human labour; the number fell by 1933
to less than half the 1928 level.

As the total of all livestock in 1928 amounted to about half the total value
of means of production in Soviet agriculture,[11] so the destruction of livestock removed about a quarter of all existing capital – more if the decline in
the quality of the animals which remained alive is taken into account.

From 1934 onwards, the livestock sector began to recover, but only in the
case of pigs was the 1928 level exceeded by the end of the 1930s.

(ii) Grain and other food crops (Tables 19(a) and (b))

In the Soviet Union before the Second World War, as in Imperial Russia,
the level of grain production was the most crucial economic magnitude.
Bread was the main item providing both calories and protein in the diet of
the vast majority of urban and rural citizens.[12] Grain was also the main
fodder for horses and an important item in cattle fodder. In the 1920s, the
failure of grain production to recover to the pre-war level was the main
agricultural problem confronting the state; and very little grain was available for export. In these circumstances, a decline in grain production would
mean that the number of farm animals would have to be reduced, or even
that the population would go hungry. And a substantial increase in grain

production was essential if grain exports were to provide the foreign currency needed for the purchase of machinery. Some increase in production was also required merely to feed the growing Soviet population.

In the 1930s the authorities frequently announced that the 'problem of grain' had been solved. The official figures published at that time purported to show that, after a couple of poor harvests in 1931 and 1932, grain output rose by 1937 to a record 120 million tons, 64 per cent above the 1928 level and 50 per cent higher than the highest pre-revolutionary harvest in 1913. But these figures involved a deliberate distortion of the statistics. In official Soviet statistics from 1933 onwards grain output was measured – without any indication that this was the case – not as the harvest which reached the barns but in terms of 'biological' yield. This was the maximum possible yield of the standing crop in the field at time of maximum ripeness. It was estimated by taking samples from a variety of fields using a metrovka (a one-metre square device); the samples were threshed and the grain obtained was weighed. The total harvest was measured by multiplying this measured yield per square metre by the estimated sown area. Thus the 'biological' harvest made no allowance for losses between field and barn. But in reality losses amounted to 15 per cent or so at best; they rose to over 30 per cent in some years. Until 1936 some allowance was made for losses, though an inadequate one; from 1937 no harvest losses at all were deducted. It was not until 1956, three years after Stalin's death, that the Soviet authorities admitted that the harvest figure as published was measured without deduction of losses. The new series for 1933–40 which has since been published is probably a reasonably accurate measurement of the barn harvest in 1933–6, but it is likely that the harvests for 1937–40 are still exaggerated in the new series (see Table 19, note f).

But the distortions from 1933 onwards are not the whole story. In the 1920s the statisticians preparing the grain data attempted to obtain an accurate figure for the barn harvest. The raw data obtained from the peasants were certainly underestimated, so 'correction coefficients' were applied, increasing the harvest as measured by the raw data from the peasants. From 1926 onwards these correction coefficients were almost certainly too large. They were estimated under the influence of Gosplan, which believed that both pre-revolutionary and post-revolutionary grain output were higher than the estimates made by the rival Central Statistical Administration. And from 1929 onwards strong political pressure was brought to bear on the statisticians to 'improve' grain production by increasing the correction coefficients still further. In our opinion all the grain figures for 1926–1932 therefore need to be reduced by an annual percentage which systematically increases over the period. Data in the archives for the harvest of 1932 reveal that both the yield per hectare in kolkhozy and the sown area actually harvested were substantially below the figures used to estimate grain production; the 1932 harvest probably amounted to only 50–55 million tons, a mere 72–9 per cent of the official figure.[13] On our provisional estimate the exaggeration of grain production in 1930–2 had already reached some 20–30 per cent, so that the harvests in 1931 and 1932 were lower than in any post-revolutionary year except the famine year 1921. These reductions in the published figures have not been made in Soviet published data, but we have made them in our own estimates.

In the case of other food crops, the published figures were also exaggerated in 1934–40 by the silent replacement of barn yield by biological yield. In the case of both potatoes and sugar beet, recent Soviet publications indicate that the overestimate was relatively small in 1933–8 (11–9 per cent for potatoes, a mere 2–11 per cent in the case of sugar beet). But in each case the overestimate was as much as 45–50 per cent in 1939. This was evidently a result of the application of an unpublished instruction of 21 July 1939, requiring the harvests of potatoes and industrial crops to be recorded in terms of the 'actual' harvest, before deducting losses in both sown area and yield.[14] We have also assumed that, following the pattern in grain statistics, the 1926–32 harvest figures should be reduced. When these various adjustments have been made it emerges that the production of potatoes increased by only 4 per cent between 1928 and 1936–8. The increase in production of potatoes per head of population was substantial only in the two years 1935 and 1937, and the increase in 1935 may be the result of a change in the basis of measurement. However, if these revised statistics are reliable, production of vegetables, particularly cabbage, and of sugar beet, outstripped the growth of the population. Even with these crops, however, this improvement was offset by the bad harvests of 1936 and 1938.

(iii) Industrial crops (Table 19(c))

The greatest Soviet agricultural success was achieved in the case of certain industrial crops. In particular, the production of raw cotton in 1937–39 (average) was over three times as great as in 1928. This increase was more than sufficient to replace imports, which declined from 45 per cent of cotton consumption in 1926/27 to 2.6 per cent in 1933, even though total cotton consumed rose by nearly one-third in the same period.[15] But cotton was almost wholly exceptional even among raw materials for the textile industry. Flax production for the manufacture of linen textiles, after some increase in the early 1930s, declined to the 1928 level. And, as we have seen, as a result of the continuing lower number and poor quality of livestock, the supply of animal products to industry, including wool and leather, failed to recover to the 1928 level after the precipitate decline in the early 1930s.

(D) Factors influencing production, 1928–1941

Why did the Soviet agricultural programme fail? In launching the transformation of agriculture, the Soviet leaders assumed that the advantages of modern machinery and economies of scale would overcome any minor losses due to the disruption of peasant agriculture and the replacement of commercial exchange between state and peasant by compulsory state exactions. But the hopes that the losses would be minor proved to be entirely in vain. We consider below the main factors, favourable and unfavourable, which influenced production in the aftermath of collectivisation.

(i) State exactions (Table 22)

The relentless pressure of the state for grain and other products played a major and perhaps crucial part in the general deterioration of agriculture. The expansion of the towns and the urgent need of grain for export increased the requirements of the state for grain; the huge increase in price of the declining proportion of grain which was sold on the market impelled the state to increase its exactions of grain still further. In consequence, the amount of grain retained in the village for food, fodder and seed, and for sale on the market, was drastically reduced; it was on average 7 or 8 million tons per year below the level of 1927 or 1928. This was a decline of about 15 per cent in the grain retained in the countryside.

The decline in retained grain was a major factor in the disastrous collapse of the livestock sector in 1929–33. We estimate that in 1928–41 as a whole about 100 million additional tons of grain would have been required to maintain fodder for livestock at the level of 1928. The decline in the number of livestock meant that both urban and rural population obtained a much higher proportion of their nutrition from grain than from meat and dairy products. Grain used directly for human consumption yields far more carbohydrate per ton of grain than grain fed to animals. But in 1931–3 the pressure on the peasants to surrender their grain, accompanied by poor harvests, was so great that there was a decline in the amount of grain available as food for the population as well as for animal fodder. Malnutrition over wide areas in 1931 and 1932 was followed by the death of millions of peasants in the famine of 1932–3 (see chapter 4).

The remorseless efforts of the state to obtain grain and industrial crops led to an increase in the sown area. Consequently, the amount of wild hay and other natural fodder was reduced. In compensation, the area sown to fodder crops increased, but this was probably insufficient to compensate for the decline in natural fodder. The decline in fodder was the most important factor in the huge decline in the number of livestock and in the deterioration in animal quality.

The unremitting pressure to exact grain and other supplies from the collective farms meant that in most years and in most areas very little remained for distribution to collective farmers. Economic incentives to work on the collective land were small, or absent altogether. Attempts were made to design adequate economic incentives during the course of the 1930s, particularly after the regularisation of compulsory state deliveries in 1933. But the fundamental problem was the general lack of produce to distribute. The peasants were persuaded to work on the socialised land not by economic levers but from fear of not receiving the grain for bread on which their survival depended.

The excessive state procurement of grain harmed the agricultural economy in other ways. During the collectivisation drive, the system of crop rotation was thoroughly disrupted. But satisfactory rotations were not introduced even in the more stable years of the mid-1930s. This was primarily because pressure from the authorities to increase the crop sown to grain undermined the efforts at rational rotation. Even in 1935, according to a contemporary Soviet account, crop rotation operated on no more than 40 per cent of the sown area.[16]

The chain of disruption, originating in excessive procurements, spread through agriculture. As we have seen, the decline in fodder led to a livestock crisis. The reduction in the number of horses drastically reduced the draught power available in the arable sector (see sub-section (iii) below). The decline in livestock in turn resulted in a considerable reduction in the quantity of manure applied to the soil, owing partly to the decline in the number of animals, partly to the carelessness with which manure was handled. In 1932 the amount of manure applied to the soil had fallen to a fraction of its normal level. While the quantity used greatly increased in subsequent years, the failure to apply manure over a number of years considerably impoverished the soil. The use of artificial fertilisers was almost entirely confined to industrial crops.[17]

(ii) Dekulakisation

The decline in both arable cultivation and livestock breeding was partly due to the disruption caused by the process of collectivisation. The 'dekulakisation' campaign of 1929–31 expelled kulaks from their farms, despatching some to the outskirts of their villages and others to remote parts of the

USSR; a minority of male heads of households were summarily executed. (See Chapter 4.)

The authorities attempted to win over the mass of the peasants by encouraging class struggle within the village. In the towns, the grievances of the industrial working class, and of the urban poor generally, had provided a basis of support for the regime during revolution and civil war. Throughout the inter-war years 'class-conscious' industrial workers were inspired by their recollection of the injustices of private capitalism and their belief that the proletariat was a new ruling class. They provided an important segment of the cadres and activists who managed and supported the expansion of industry. But the rural capitalists – the *kulaks* – insofar as they existed, were not separated from and did not stand above the mass of the peasantry. It is true that the richer peasants owned substantially more capital than the average peasant. But even the top 3.2 per cent of peasant households owned on average a mere 2.3 draught animals and 2.5 cows, as compared with the average of 1.0 and 1.1 for all households. And within this group, only 0.6 per cent of all households were exploiters in the marxist sense that they employed an appreciable amount of hired labour (75 working days or more a year); a further 0.14 per cent were registered as engaged in 'entrepreneurial non-agricultural occupations'.[18] Moreover, while these '*kulaks*' did profit from the labour and poverty of their fellow-peasants, they were simultaneously working peasants who were members of the village community. And many peasants changed their economic group in the course of a lifetime, blurring the boundaries between classes within the village.

This ruthless campaign had little support from the mass of the peasants. While a minority of the poorer peasants supported and at first benefitted from dekulakisation, many peasants sympathised with their richer neighbours. In practice, dekulakisation was fundamentally a means not for inspiring class consciousness of the mass of the peasants but for frightening them into submission to collectivisation; its crucial role in this respect was recognised in the private communications between the rulers. Dekulakisation removed from the village the most successful and technically knowledgeable peasants; an unknown number of these were elders in charge of the village commune.

(iii) Decline and restoration of agricultural capital

During the collectivisation drive and the subsequent famine, as we have seen, livestock – the main item of agricultural capital – drastically declined; agricultural capital was then gradually restored as livestock farming recovered and the capital stock was augmented with the great increase in the supply of agricultural machinery to MTS and collective farms. According to Moorsteen and Powell, the total value of agricultural capital in 1937 prices declined from 61.7 billion rubles on 1 January 1928 to 39.3 billion on 1 January 1933; even on 1 January 1937 its value had only just reached the 1928 level.[19]

From the point of view of arable farming, the most damaging consequence of the decline in livestock was the decline in the number of work horses. The availability of animal or mechanical power to draw the ploughs and harvest the crop was the main physical constraint on grain cultivation.

The number of work horses declined from 23.4 million in the spring of 1929 to a mere 12.8 million on 1 July 1934.[20] This resulted in an unprecedented reduction in draught power for ploughing and other agricultural operations. The decline in the number of horses was most severe in the main grain-growing areas, and it was some years before the decline was fully compensated by the increase in the stock of tractors. In the worst year, 1933, traction power fell to 70–75 per cent of 1929, and in some areas cows were extensively used as a substitute for horses. Even though the Eastern and Southern Producer Regions were afforded priority in the allocation of tractors, the overall decline in draught power in 1929–32 was most severe in these major grain-growing regions,[21] and this in turn led until 1933 to a further worsening of grain production.

The mechanisation of agriculture was the main means by which the authorities sought to counteract the grave negative consequences of collectivisation and industrialisation, and was afforded very high priority in principle as well as in practice. How far was it successful? At first, in 1927 and 1928, the authorities proposed to expand the socialisation and mechanisation of agriculture in tandem: the availability of tractors and other agricultural machinery would encourage peasants to join the collective farms and simultaneously would enable the establishment of large state farms. But even on the most wildly optimistic estimate this meant that the process of collectivisation could not be completed in less than five or six years. At the end of 1929, committed to very rapid collectivisation in the interests of industrialisation, Stalin announced that for a transition period 'primary collective farms' would be established based on a 'simple putting together of peasant tools of production'.[22] But collectivisation without mechanisation did not work. The agricultural difficulties of the early 1930s, and in particular the rapid decline in the number of horses, eloquently demonstrated that widespread mechanisation was essential even if the level of production reached in the 1920s was merely to be maintained.

The tractor plan approved at the end of 1929, if successful, would have

swept away all difficulties within a few years. It envisaged that tractors with
a capacity of 9.5 million hp would be produced during the first five-year
plan;[24] together with imports, this assumed a total capacity of something
like 12 million hp in 1933. As tractors would be used more intensively in
the Soviet Union, the tractor horse-power hours per year would be greater
than in the United States.[25] In the first half of the 1930s, the tractor and
agricultural engineering industries received very high priority, and three
major tractor factories, a combine-harvester factory and a large machinery
factory were all completed in 1930–3. But, as with all other industrial
plans, the ambitious targets were not reached. Total tractor hp reached
only 3.2 million by the end of 1933, and 8 million by the end of 1936; and,
as a result of the switch of tractor factories to military production, total
tractor capacity available in agriculture rose only to 10.3 million hp by the
end of 1940.[26] While tractors were used for substantially more hours per
year than in the United States, the level of mechanisation remained much
lower. In the cultivation of grain, 95 per cent of threshing, 72 per cent of
ploughing, 57 per cent of spring sowing and 48 per cent of harvesting were
carried out mechanically in 1938.[27] But other farm operations were far less
mechanised, including the cultivation of row crops such as sunflower and
sugar beet, and all operations with hay.[28] Moreover, all operations with
machinery, in agriculture as in industry, required the use of much more
manual labour than in the United States. Thus in harvesting reapers
merely cut the grain; it was removed from the reaper platform and bound
mainly by hand, and weeding was very largely carried out by hand.[29] As
capital was scarcer and labour cheaper and more abundant than in the
United States, these arrangements were appropriate – but they reflected
the failure of the original objective to overtake the United States in the
level of mechanisation.

For most of the 1930s the level of mechanisation was even inadequate to
compensate for the loss of the draught power of work horses and oxen. In
July 1928 total animal draught power amounted to 27 million horsepower,
and the contribution of tractors to total draught power was insignificant. In
the course of the next five years, animal draught power fell to a mere 16
million horsepower in July 1933, but tractor horse power increased to only
some 3.6–5.4 million (in horse equivalent), depending on the measure
used.[29] Even by the end of 1938, combined tractor and animal horse power
had reached only 26–32 million hp.[30] Moreover, tractors and horses had to
undertake much of the transport within the village, and between the village
and the state collection points and urban markets. By the end of 1938, some
196000 lorries were used in Soviet agriculture; this compares with over one
million lorries in US agriculture in the same period.[31] It was only at the end

of the 1930s that total mechanical and animal power substantially exceeded the level of 1928.

(iv) Skills and technical training

As we have seen, dekulakisation removed many of the most competent peasants from the villages. Simultaneously, in the course of the collectivisation drive many of the fairly small number of trained agronomists and rural land surveyors were dismissed or exiled on grounds of insufficient loyalty. The countryside was denuded of much of its successful agricultural experience.

Neither the rural population nor their political masters, both local and national, had any experience of the collective agriculture and large-scale mechanised farming which replaced peasant agriculture. As we have seen, collectivisation involved the ploughing up of the boundaries between strips in the arable fields, and the collecting together of horses and ploughs into a common pool (sometimes located in the cottage of an exiled *kulak*, or the church of an exiled priest). It also involved the introduction into the villages for the first time of tractors, and later of combine harvesters; but in 1929 nearly all villages lacked even a single peasant who could drive a tractor or a lorry.

In the early 1930s, the state attempted to fill the gap by sending in tens of thousands of urban workers and others to assist in the running of the collective farms. But they had been hastily trained, and often lacked all experience of any kind of farming.

During the 1930s substantial resources were devoted both to the training of skilled workers to operate the new agricultural machinery and to the education of specialists who would provide the expertise required for large-scale mechanised agriculture. In the course of the 1930s some three million tractor drivers, combine-harvester operators and lorry drivers were trained: these included, in 1930–6 alone, 1,900,000 tractor drivers, over 240,000 combine-harvester operators and 100,000 lorry drivers.[32] These workers received far greater remuneration than the ordinary collective farmer. Labour turnover was not as high as in most industries, and far lower than in building.[33] Nevertheless, more than half the trained drivers left their jobs in agriculture in the course of the 1930s: in 1940 the total number of tractor drivers, combine operators and lorry drivers in collective farms, state farms and machine-tractor stations amounted to only 1.4 millions.[34]

Agricultural specialists were also trained in large numbers, and the total number nearly trebled between 1928 and 1941 (thousands):[35]

	1928	1 January 1941
Agronomists, zootechnicians and veterinary surgeons with higher education	27.1	64.7
Agronomists, zootechnicians, veterinary assistants (Fel'dshers) and technicians with secondary specialised education	31.3	88.7
Total	58.4	153.4

But many of these specialists had little practical influence on agriculture. In 1941 only a minority worked in collective farms, state farms and organisations directly serving agriculture – a mere 12.8 thousand specialists with higher education (19.8 per cent of the total number in this category), and 32.5 thousand with secondary specialised education (36.6 per cent). The overwhelming majority of agricultural specialists worked in research, administration, teaching or other branches of the economy.[36] In spite of all the resources devoted to technical training at all levels, shortage of expertise remained a chronic problem for Soviet agriculture.

(v) Central control and planning

The success of centralised plans obviously depends on the competence of the policies adopted; wrong decisions reverberate throughout the system. Central planning could claim one substantial success in agriculture: it brought about economies of scale from the production of large numbers of standardised tractors and combine-harvesters. But the Soviet leaders, from Stalin to the party secretaries in the rural districts, almost all lacked any experience of farming, whether mechanised or nonmechanised, as did the party cadres sent into the countryside. Policies were improvised, including the fundamental decisions about collective-farm structure. In the course of the great shifts in boundaries which accompanied the advance, retreat and renewed advance of collectivisation in 1929–32, much of the improvement in crop rotations and methods of cultivation characteristic of the 1920s was undone. The official prescription for the appropriate size of farm, and the organisation of the basic work units, changed several times during these years of confusion. Even when the system had acquired greater stability in the mid-1930s, unwise agricultural policies were imposed throughout agriculture by vigorous campaigns managed in detail from the centre.[37]

Within this unpropitious framework, considerable efforts were made by agricultural specialists to use the possibilities provided by coordinated planning to improve the conditions of agriculture; and they not infrequently managed to persuade the political authorities to adopt sensible policies.

The efforts to secure the effective use of mechanisation, and the vast training programme, have already been discussed in sections (iii) and (iv). Less well-known are the attempts to improve the quality of grain and livestock. Throughout the 1930s, Academician N. I. Vavilov and his colleagues endeavoured to build up a seed bank and develop better seed stock; and intermittent success in improving the quality of seed partly counteracted the disasters brought about by other aspects of agricultural policy.

In the livestock sector, against the background of the immense losses of the early 1930s, the authorities sought to preserve the more valuable thoroughbred stock. Artificial insemination was widely used to improve stock before it became a general practice elsewhere. In consequence, after collectivisation and famine the proportion of thoroughbred animals was higher than before.

These efforts, and the advantages of rapid technological change were, however, outweighed by the great disadvantages stemming from the ignorance of the politicians and the inherent tendency of a vast centralised bureaucracy to adopt over-simple decisions. Even if the party leaders and their agents had been extremely competent and knowledgeable, detailed control from the centre was particularly inappropriate in the case of agriculture, where great flexibility in farming techniques is required between different regions and sub-regions.

Over and above the general disadvantages of central regulation of agricultural technology and farming practices, the factor which outweighed all others was the squeeze imposed on agricultural output. As Jasny put it, 'collective farming was introduced and has developed under such unfavourable conditions in the Soviet Union that it would have failed even if it were, per se, a perfectly sound undertaking'.[38] It was only after the death of Stalin in 1953 and the subsequent reduction of compulsory deliveries that the permanent weaknesses of the centralised control of agriculture eventually became clearly visible.

(vi) The weather[39] (Table 23)

The fluctuations in the annual level of temperature and rainfall in the territory of the USSR are greater than in major grain-producing areas elsewhere in the world. The weather pattern is highly continental, and is complicated by the frequent but irregular dry hot winds (the *sukhovei*) which blow from Central Asia across the Volga region, North Caucasus and Ukraine in the critical growing months of late spring and early summer. These are the main grain-producing regions of the USSR, and over a large territory the critical insufficiency of humidity makes them particularly susceptible to drought resulting in high temperature and low rainfall. In normal times changes in the weather are the main cause of the large annual fluctuations in yield per hectare.

Was the weather a significant factor in the low grain yields which predominated in the 1930s, or were these entirely due to the technical and political factors which we have already discussed? In a preliminary attempt to answer this question, Wheatcroft has constructed a 'drought index' from data for 1883–1915, which assesses how far the annual fluctuation in the degree of drought in late spring and early summer might be expected to affect the grain yield. This estimate of annual fluctuation in yield due to the weather was then compared with the extent to which the actual yield in each year differed from long-term expected trend in yield.

The results are presented in Table 23. It is often assumed that good-weather years tend to cancel out bad-weather years, so that over a five-year period fluctuations can be ignored. This is demonstrably not the case. As we have already noted, the weather was largely responsible for the above-average yield over the whole five years, 1909–13, not only in the bumper harvest year 1913. In contrast, weather conditions were markedly less favourable in 1920–4 than in 1909–13. In 1925–9, however, the weather was only slightly worse than average. It should be noted that the lower yield in the crucial year 1927 was primarily due to the weather.[40]

In the 1930s, bad weather also played a significant role, particularly in the crucial years of the collectivisation drive of the early 1930s. Our index of the predicted agrometereological deviation from normal grain yield shows below-average conditions in both 1930–4 and 1935–9 (measured in tsentners per hectare):

1904–8	− 0.13
1909–13	+ 0.31
1920–4	− 0.82
1925–9	− 0.10
1930–4	− 0.37
1935–9	− 0.22

The year-to-year changes are also very relevant to our understanding of agricultural processes in the 1930s (see Table 23). In 1930, the year in which collectivisation was launched, the weather – and the harvest – were particularly favourable. The good harvest in a year of turmoil undoubtedly strengthened the illusion among the political leaders that agricultural difficulties would easily be overcome. But the drought in 1931 was particularly severe, and drought conditions continued in 1932. This certainly exacerbated the crisis of grain supply in 1931–2, which resulted in the famine in the following year. Four years later, in 1936, the weather was again extremely bad, and the harvest was low; but by this time the authorities were better able to manoeuvre stocks and grain collections, and famine was averted.

While our estimates indicate that the weather played a significant role in the poor grain harvests of the 1930s, they also confirm the commonsense view that this was not the major factor in the fairly low yields which characterised these years. After the mid-1920s the long-term trend for grain yields to rise was reversed; and the reduction in yield was far too large to be explained by the weather. In the ten years 1930–39, the average annual deviation of the grain yield from trend as predicted by our weather indicator was − 0.30 tsentners, but the actual deviation was as much as − 1.78 tsentners (see data in Table 23).

It is also worth noting that the Soviet Union was favoured by an exceptionally long drought-free period between 1937 and 1945. A drought during the Second World War could have had disastrous consequences – when a drought occurred in 1946, famine resulted.

In Soviet conditions weather fluctuations were particularly damaging to agricultural developments because the Soviet leaders, especially from the mid-1920s onwards, attached very little importance to fluctuations in the weather. In 1926 the agrarian economist Chayanov mildly commented that the 'continental climate and all the inconsistent meteorological factors' led to annual variations in what he described as '"Monsieur" yield'. His editor sharply reproved him, asserting that '"Monsieur" yield will become "Comrade" yield – the object of the planned action of the productive forces of the socialist state'.[41] Throughout the 1930s, the Soviet government gambled every year on good weather – and was often unlucky.

(vii) Household plot and free market

The disastrous decline in agricultural production in 1931–2, together with the continued resistance of the peasants to full-scale socialisation, impelled the state to approve a compromise in agricultural organisation. In practice, both the free market (the so-called 'collective-farm market') and the household plots of collective farmers and state farmers continued to exist in the early 1930s. In 1932 they were legalised, and became indispensable features of the agricultural economy. Every peasant household had the right to cultivate a small plot (*usad'ba*) around its cottage; both collective farms and individual collective farmers had the right to sell their produce on the free market, at prices formed by supply and demand, once their obligations to the state had been met. In 1938, the sown area of household plots of collective farmers amounted to 5.34 million hectares, or on average 0.28

hectares for each of the 18.8 million households; the plots amounted to a mere 4.6 per cent of the total sown area of collective farms.[42]

Of the total sown area of household plots (including the plots of state farmers, and the allotments of the urban population), 55.8 per cent was sown to potatoes, 31.2 per cent to other vegetables, and 21.8 per cent to grain.[43] The household plots were cultivated very intensively. In 1937 the household plots of collective farmers were responsible even on an official Soviet estimate for 25.4 per cent of total collective-farm production. They produced only 1.1 per cent of grain, but as much as 38.4 per cent of vegetables and potatoes and 67.9 per cent of meat and dairy produce.[44] On 1 January 1938, collective farmers and other individuals owned 64.6 per cent of all cattle, 75.1 per cent of all pigs and 56.0 per cent of all sheep and goats (see Table 21), and nearly all the poultry; the average collective-farm household owned 1.38 head of cattle.[45]

In general, collective farmers depended on the collective farm for their food grain, which they received as payment for their work on the collective land. But they obtained most of the other food products consumed by the household from their household plots; and most of the products sold on the free market came from the household plots. Collective farmers obtained most of their money income from their sales on the free market. Precise figures are not available, but the sources of the money incomes of collective farmers in 1937 were very roughly as follows (million rubles at current prices):

From collective farm for labour days worked	7000[a]
Sales on free market	14800[b]
Earned outside collective farm	6700[c]
Other	5000[d]
Total	33500[e]

[a] 376 rubles per household (*Kolkhozy* (1939), 110) for 18.5 million households (*ibid.* 1).
[b] Total sales 17800 (*Itogi* (1939), 107); sales by collective farmers and individual peasants in *1938* given as 83.3 per cent of total (1937 figure has not been traced) (*Problemy ekonomiki*, 3, 1940, 95). But according to another source sales by collective farms on urban markets alone amounted to as much as 4120 million rubles (Bergson (1953), 104), leaving less than 13700 millions for sales by farmers.
[c] According to *Planovoe khozyaistvo*, 9, 1938, 100 (M. Nesmii), collective farmers earned 19–20 per cent of their money income outside their collective farms in 1935–7. These data are for a limited number of regions.
[d] Residual.
[e] Money income per household 23.6 per cent greater than 1936, i.e. 1807 rubles (*Planovoe khozyaistvo*, 9, 1938, 100), for 18.5 million households. These data are for a limited number of regions.

It should be noted, however, that money income represented only a small part of the total real income of collective farmers. When grain and other products received by collective farmers for work on the collective farm, together with the products consumed from their household plots, are valued at free-market prices, the total real income of collective farmers amounted to some 108000 million rubles in 1937. Money income thus accounted for only 31 per cent of the total.[46] The peasant economy of the 1930s was still largely an economy in kind.

Agriculture in the 1930s – and this remained true fifty years later – was thus a paradoxical combination of an advanced degree of mechanisation with the extensive use of manual labour. The supply of machinery was inadequate for the comprehensive mechanisation of agriculture envisaged at the end of the 1920s. But most large-scale state and collective farms proved incapable of managing successful branches of farming requiring close individual attention – notably the cultivation of vegetables and fruit and the rearing of livestock. Abundant labour was still available on the collective farms in many areas, and the collective farmers still possessed the skills required for cultivating the individual plot. Thus in the social- ised sector of agriculture, as in the newly-established modern industries, advanced American machinery was used with far more labour than in the United States; and this technically more advanced sector existed in paral- lel with household plots cultivated manually by traditional peasant methods.

The parallel existence of the two sectors was legitimised by Stalin in a speech at a congress of collective-farm shock workers in February 1935:

There is artel farming, socialised, large, and of decisive importance, necessary to meet socialised needs, and there is side by side with it small personal farming necessary to satisfy the personal needs of collective farmers ...

The combination of the personal interests of the collective farmers with the socialised interests of the collective farms – here is the key to the strengthening of the collective farms.[47]

But Stalin regarded the household plot and the free market as transitional phenomena, permitted as long as the collective farm did not yet provide 'an abundance of products'. The Soviet authorities frequently attempted to restrict the operation of the private sector. In 1939 the household plots were rigorously cut back to the official norms, and discriminating measures were adopted against private livestock.[48] In consequence, while the number of socialised livestock increased in 1939, the steep decline in private livestock resulted in an immediate reduction of the total number of farm animals.[49] But, in spite of such actions by the authorities, the household plot remained a major source of food production.

(E) Labour productivity, 1928–1941

The socialisation of agriculture failed to produce any substantial increase in agricultural production in the 1930s or in the Stalin period generally. How far did it result in an increase in labour productivity, so that the same level of production was achieved with a smaller input of labour? We estimate that the number of adults engaged in farming declined from 61.6 millions in December 1926 to 48.2 millions in January 1939 (both figures exclude children under 16 and all persons above the formal retirement age, and should probably each be increased by about 10 million – see chapter 5). Thus *annual* output per adult engaged in farming increased by some 28 per cent. However, in terms of output *per day* worked the position is radically different, according to Nimitz. She estimates that the total number of days worked in farming was 10,459 million in 1937 as compared with 9,793 million in 1928. Her data for 1928 were based on a Gosplan labour balance which estimated that 8.5 million of the total adult population of 60.1 million were effectively unemployed in 1927/28; thus according to her estimates, in 1937 a smaller farming population was working on average for more days per year.[50] No attempt has been made to measure output *per hour* worked; anecdotal evidence suggests that on the collective lands the members worked for less hours per day than the individual peasant in 1928, and to this extent output per hour in the collective sector in 1937 was higher than in individual agriculture in 1928.

Some evidence is available about the division of time between the household plot and the collective sector in 1937. A sample survey of 28 regions and republics produced the following result (percentage of time of adults aged 16–59 devoted to each sector):

	Men	Women	Total
Collective farm	58.9	35.3	46.6
MTS	2.5	0.2	1.3
Working for hire, army, etc.	27.2	8.5	17.4
Household plot	5.7	24.1	15.3
Other	5.7	31.9	19.4
	100.0	100.0	100.0

Men devoted 153 hours a year to the household plot and women 620, an average of 398 hours.[51] Nimitz estimates from these data that output per day in the non-mechanised private sector was roughly 77 per cent of output in the partly mechanised collective sector.[52]

At the end of the 1930s, the labour productivity gap between agriculture and the rest of the economy was even wider than it had been in 1928.

According to all Western estimates, between 1928 and 1940 labour productivity rose substantially in the nonagricultural economy as a whole, and even faster in industry itself. According to Moorsteen and Powell, labour productivity in the non-agricultural sector was 95 per cent greater than in the agricultural sector in 1928; the percentage increased to 162 in 1939.[53] By 1940 the average person employed in industry produced four times as much as in agriculture (see chapter 12).

Further reading

N. Jasny, *The Socialized Agriculture of the USSR: Plan and Performance* (Stanford, 1949) remains the best survey of quantitative developments.

For the grain harvest, see S. G. Wheatcroft, 'The Reliability of Russian Pre-war Grain Output Statistics', *Soviet Studies*, xxvi (1974), 157–80. For grain marketings, see the controversy between J. Karcz and R. W. Davies in *Soviet Studies*, xviii (1966–7), 399–434 (Karcz), xxi (1969–70), 314–29 (Davies), xxii (1970–1), 262–96 (Karcz). For grain collections, see M. Lewin, *The Making of the Soviet System* (London, 1985), 142–77.

7   Industry

R. W. Davies

In the nineteenth Century the Russian Empire was the least industrially developed of the Great Powers. The humiliating Russian defeat in the Crimean War (1854–6) at the hands of Britain and France, with their more advanced armaments, convincingly demonstrated how the lag in Russian industry hampered and frustrated the military and political actions of the Tsars on the international stage.

Russia had long endeavoured to overcome industrial backwardness through state action. In the first quarter of the eighteenth Century Peter the Great used state power and serf labour to establish the iron industries of the Urals and to build St Petersburg as 'a window onto Europe'. In the 1890s, urged on by his Finance Minister Sergei Witte, Nicholas II used state finance and state power to accelerate the development of the capital goods industries. But the industries of the other Great Powers were also developing rapidly. In 1913 Russia still remained the least industrially developed of the Great Powers. Her industry was responsible for only 21 per cent of net national income. This included 15 per cent from large-scale industry, which employed a mere 4 per cent of the labour force.[1]

In October 1917 the Bolsheviks came to power with the objective of constructing a socialist society in the former Russian Empire. The economic foundation of the new society would be an industrial working class, expanded to include the majority of the population, and managing a technologically advanced industry.

But the Bolsheviks assumed that the socialist revolution would soon also triumph in the advanced countries, which would provide economic support for the developing Soviet economy. This project failed, and in the mid-1920s the Soviet Communist Party, headed by Stalin, embarked on its attempt to establish socialism in a single country. This involved the rapid industrialisation of the Soviet Union on its own resources, with the objective of 'catching up and overtaking the advanced countries in a technical and economic respect' (Stalin, November 1928).

Chapters 4 and 6 discussed some of the tragic consequences of this endeavour – mass repressions, and agricultural disaster culminating in the terrible famine of 1933. The present chapter, after briefly discussing developments up to 1928 (Sections A-C), deals with the industrial endeavour in pursuit of which so many sacrifices were demanded.

Between 1928 and 1940 capital goods industries advanced far more rapidly in the Soviet Union than in the capitalist world. By 1940 industry employed some thirteen million workers, as compared with over four million in 1928 and 1913; and industrial production was more than double the 1928 level. The armaments potential of Soviet industry, in contrast to the experience of the Russian Empire of 1914–7, and in spite of the disastrous defeats of 1941–2, proved powerful enough to furnish the weapons for the defeat of the invasion by Nazi Germany and her allies.

The rapid development of 1928–1940 achieved only a few strides along the road to industrialisation. In 1940 industry was responsible for 33 per cent of national income, as compared with 21 per cent in 1913. But its share of national income was still only slightly greater than that of agriculture (see Table 4). And industrial employment accounted for at most 18 per cent of the total labour force, while as many as 52 per cent were engaged in farming (see Table 11).

In international comparison, industrial output per head of population in 1940 was still substantially lower in the Soviet Union than in the other major European countries, and far lower than in the United States. The further Soviet effort, after the devastation of the German invasion, first to restore industry and then to overtake the industrial and military might of the United States, occupied 40 more years, from 1945 to 1985. The strain of this endeavour was a major factor in the collapse of the Soviet system.

(A) The eve of the First World War

By 1913, a modern factory industry was firmly established in the Russian Empire. Cotton-spinning and sugar-processing factories using foreign machinery already existed before the serf reform of 1861. After the reform, cotton-weaving factories were developed, and the 1890s saw the construction of large iron-and-steel making and railway engineering facilities. Between 1860 and 1913 the production of large-scale industry increased on average by nearly 5 per cent a year, more rapidly than in most other major European countries.[2] (For the definition used in pre-revolutionary and Soviet statistics of 'large-scale' ('census') industry, and 'small-scale' industry, see Glossary.)

With the advent of modern machinery, industrial labour productivity (output per person employed) more than doubled between 1860 and 1913. While the production of large-scale industry in 1913 reached some eleven times the 1860 level, the number employed in large-scale industry increased far more slowly:

	Index: 1860 = 100		Average annual increase (%)	
	1900	1913	1860–1900	1900–13
Production: Goldsmith's linked index[a]	714	1132	5.0	3.6
Number employed[b]	256	360	2.4	2.7
Output per person employed[c]	279	314	2.6	0.9

[a] Goldsmith (1955), 60–1.
[b] See Crisp (1978), 345, 349; *Ocherki* (1957), 192–3, 195 (Mints).
[c] Computed.

In this expansion of industry two related but separate major influences were involved. The first, in the terminology of Professor Crisp, was the 'autonomous stream', a response to the expansion of the market. The steady growth of the consumer industries, notably cotton textiles, and of food processing provide the classic examples. But throughout this half-century a second 'induced-growth stream', resulting from the positive actions of the state, supplemented the 'autonomous' stream and facilitated its further expansion. The growth of the iron industry, railway engineering and armaments depended on the state budget, state contracts, and state protective tariffs. Alexander Gerschenkron has argued that Russian industrialisation was primarily state-induced in the 1890s, but that by the eve of the First World War the 'induced' stream was declining in importance, so that industrialisation was primarily market-led in the 1909–13 boom. Available evidence indicates, however, that armaments were as important to industrial growth in the boom of 1909–13 as the railways were in the 1890s. Between 1909 and 1913, as in the 1890s, capital goods industries (Group A industries) continued to expand more rapidly than consumer goods industries (Group B industries).[3]

In spite of this half-century of industrial growth, Russian industrial production per head of population in 1913 was only 10 per cent of the French level and 7 per cent of the British and United States level.[4] Paul Bairoch has shown that, in spite of the rapid growth of 1860–1910, Russia's relative position, for a series of key indicators of industrial progress, failed to improve in relation to the other Great Powers.[5] Labour productivity, in spite of its substantial increase in the half-century before the First World War, remained far lower than in the more advanced industrial countries. In the major industries, labour productivity (output per worker per year) on the eve of the First World War was 50–60 per cent of the British level and a mere 20–25 per cent of the United States' level.[6]

Moreover, in spite of the vigorous efforts of the state to promote the development of modern heavy industry, in Russia the industrial structure remained relatively immature. Even by 1914 the textile and food industries in Russia were responsible for a far higher share of industrial production and of the industrial labour force than in Germany, and the mining and metal industries for a far smaller share.[7] Many capital goods industries were absent or in a rudimentary state of development in the Russian Empire. Non-ferrous metals such as tin, aluminium and nickel were not produced at all; and the basic chemical industry was extremely weak. The Russian engineering industries had undergone considerable development since the 1890s. With foreign technical assistance, Russia produced on a substantial scale her own locomotives and goods wagons, and her own sewing machines; and in the last decade before the war Russia began to produce pedal- and motor-bicycles, motor-cars, aircraft and even a handful of tractors. But Russia relied entirely on imports for iron-and-steel-making equipment, steel bearings and timepieces, for complex electrical and optical equipment, and for many types of machine tools and textile machinery. Half of all agricultural machinery was imported.

In spite of the rapid expansion of the advanced sectors of industry in Russia, small-scale industry remained extensive. The value of its output cannot be assessed with certainty. It accounted for between one-quarter and one-third of total industrial production, the proportion being considerably higher in the case of foodstuffs, woodworking and clothing. Two-thirds of small-scale output was produced by rural craftsmen (*kustari*), normally working on a seasonal part-time basis.

Industry in Russia was overwhelmingly concentrated into a few major regions (see Map 3). In 1912, European Russia (excluding Ukraine) contributed 64 per cent of large-scale industrial production, and within European Russia most production was located in the North West and Central Industrial Regions around St Petersburg and Moscow. Ukraine contributed 20 per cent. The Transcaucasus added a further 7 per cent with its oil production. All other regions of the country together contributed only about 9 per cent (see Table 30). Central Asia and Siberia, in spite of their vast reserves of raw material, remained industrially undeveloped.

The annual rate of growth of Russian industry was considerably slower in 1900–14 than in 1860–1900. This deceleration was primarily due to the effects of the depression at the beginning of the century, exacerbated by the Russo–Japanese war and the 1905 revolution. Production was lower in 1905 than in 1900, and even in 1908 it was only 17.6 per cent above the 1900 level. The depression was not peculiar to Russia; while it was particularly severe in Russia, it was one phase of the cycle of growth which affected nearly all the more advanced countries. The depression of 1900–5 and the boom of 1909–13 must both be seen not as unfortunate or lucky accidents but as part of this pattern of international industrial growth in the last period before the First World War.

(B) From Tsarism to NEP

In Russia, as in all the belligerent countries, the First World War changed both the composition and the organisation of industrial production. In chapter 11 the changes in world war and civil war are traced in more detail. The output of large-scale industry reached a peak during 1916, and is estimated to have been some 16–22 per cent higher than in 1913.[8] Defence production, and the production of machine tools and other equipment to serve the defence industries, expanded five-fold during these three years.[9] But the production of consumer goods, particularly in small-scale industry, substantially declined.

This expansion was followed by a rapid collapse of large-scale industry during 1918–20; by 1920 its production had fallen to a mere 13 per cent of the 1913 level. The production of certain capital goods industries almost ceased: the output of iron and steel, for example, declined to a mere 3.6 per cent of 1913. The decline in production of the large-scale consumer goods industries between 1913 and 1920 was even more precipitate than the decline in capital goods. Small-scale industry (including peasant crafts), however, declined much less rapidly, to some 44 per cent of the 1913 level (see Table 56.)

(C) During NEP, 1921–1928

According to Soviet estimates made in the 1920s, industry recovered from a mere 20 per cent of the 1913 level in 1920 to 4 per cent above that level in 1926/27.[10] The figure for 1926/27 is probably an overestimate, and in any case does not take account of the fact that capital goods and armaments production expanded substantially between 1913 and 1916, so that for these industries a better indicator of industrial recovery would be a return to the 1916 level. There is no doubt, however, that the rate of recovery was far more rapid than anyone had anticipated. At the end of 1923, when the recovery process had already been proceeding quite rapidly, a five-year plan presented to Gosplan assumed that the production of large-scale industry would amount to only about 50 per cent of the 1913 level in 1926/27;[11] and a plan for the iron and steel industry prepared in the same year assumed that pig-iron production would amount only to about one million tons in 1927, merely a quarter of the 1913 level.[12] It was widely (and wrongly) believed that even the 1913 level could not be achieved without substantial capital investment, owing to the destruction of industrial plant during world war and civil war.

The pattern of recovery over time also differed sharply from expectations. All plans and prognoses in the first years of NEP assumed that the annual rate of growth would diminish in each successive year as recovery moved towards the pre-war level.[13] The acceleration of the rate of growth in 1922/23 was not astonishing; the famine of 1921/22 had delayed recovery. But the further acceleration in 1924/25, variously put at 53 or 61 per cent for large-scale industry, was entirely unexpected: according to V. S. Groman, a prominent non-party official in Gosplan, 'there was not a single mind in the USSR which would have foreseen this'.[14] And the rate of growth in 1925/26, variously put at 34 and 39 per cent for all industry, also exceeded expectations. The attenuation of the rate of growth due to the absorption of most existing capacity did not occur until 1926/27.[15]

The recovery of different industries proceeded at markedly different rates. Within the capital goods industries, by 1926/27 the production of coal and oil was greater than in 1913, and the production of electricity, from modest beginnings, had more than doubled. The civilian engineering and chemical industries also exceeded the pre-war level. But the iron and steel industry, which had collapsed during the civil war, still lagged considerably; the reduced demands of the railways, and of ship-building and armaments, made it possible for the economy to cope with lower supplies of metal than in 1913.

Throughout the recovery period, the consumer goods industries suffered chronically from a shortage of raw materials, owing to the low level of agricultural marketings. As a result, in large-scale industry the production of food, drink and tobacco in 1926/27 was lower than in 1913, and it is unlikely to have increased in small-scale industry. Contrary to expectations, and to the assumptions of many historians, the consumer goods industries as a whole therefore lagged behind the capital goods industries. The large-scale consumer industries increased more rapidly than the large-scale capital goods industries only in the two years sometimes known as 'high NEP', 1924 and 1925, when agricultural production and the internal market were both expanding rapidly.

(D) Industry under central planning 1929–1941

(i) *The social transformation: goals and achievements*

Soviet industrialisation was the first attempt by a government to transform an entire economy – and a society – through conscious planning by the state. This was not a narrowly economic programme. The development of industry was seen as part of the strategy of constructing socialism in a single country, which was surrounded by a hostile capitalist world. Stalin argued that 'we have caught up and *overtaken* the advanced capitalist countries in a political respect' and now 'we must use the dictatorship of the proletariat ... in order to catch up and *overtake* the advanced capitalist countries *economically* as well'.[16] But he also insisted that 'we do not need *just any* growth of the labour productivity of the people, we need a growth which will ensure a systematic preponderance of the socialist sector of the economy over the capitalist sector.'[17]

Socialism was defined as the social ownership of the means of production; and state ownership was assumed to be the most advanced form of social ownership. In industry, unlike agriculture, the preponderance of the socialist sector as thus defined was easily achieved. In 1929 only 0.7 per cent of the total production of large-scale industry was attributed to the private sector; and most of the remaining private factories were closed in the course of the following year.[18]

Even in small-scale industry in 1929 less than one per cent of workers was employed by private entrepreneurs, and only 3.4 per cent of artisans were recorded as primarily selling their production to private traders. In this sense 'capitalist industry' had virtually been eliminated by 1929. But as many as 74 per cent of the 4 million persons engaged in small-scale industry were individual artisans working on their own account[19] – a grey area which was variously described as 'individual' or 'private' activity. During the course of 1929/30 many of these individual artisans were pushed or persuaded to join the industrial cooperatives. But it was estimated that even in 1932 as many as 45 per cent of the estimated 4.5 million artisans did not belong to cooperatives;[20] and the 1939 population census recorded that 25 per cent of the 2.5 million engaged in small-scale industry were individuals working on their own account plus members of their family (see Table 11, note j).[21] The individual sector in industry was slow to die out; like the household plot and the collective-farm market, it was accordingly incorporated into the 'socialist sector' by a redefinition of official doctrine.

(ii) Industrial plans and objectives

Within this framework of 'socialisation' or statisation, the protagonists of industrialisation in the Politburo, and in the party at large, were by 1928 in general agreement on their more specific industrial objectives. They may be summarised under five main heads.

First, the Soviet Union must overtake the advanced capitalist countries in industrial output per head of population as rapidly as possible. This proposition carried with it the corollary that Soviet industry must become self-sufficient as soon as possible, in the sense that it should not depend on the capitalist world for any major type of product. It would at first lean heavily on foreign equipment and know-how; but it must soon produce all the capital equipment and other major products which were lacking in pre-revolutionary industry.

Secondly, Soviet industry must overtake the West technically as well as economically. This required the construction of major new advanced enterprises; and these would be capital-intensive, even though there was an abundance of skilled labour in the Soviet Union. The case for this policy was that large technical changes would render present cost equations irrelevant. The introduction of modern technology in lumps would act as an example to pull up the rest of industry; and would enable training in the latest skills.

Thirdly, the output of capital goods would increase more rapidly than that of consumer goods, with the concentration of resources on 'means of production for producing means of production', i.e. on the industries producing machine tools and industrial equipment.

Fourthly, the consumer goods industries (together with agriculture) would nevertheless expand rapidly, so that the standard of living of the population would rise substantially.

Fifthly, location policy would be based on long-term needs rather than on short-term costs. A major part of industry would be located away from the old centres of industrial production. Iron and steel and the major engineering industries must be developed far from the frontier in the Urals and Siberia for defence reasons; modern industry must be established in Central Asia and other underdeveloped areas in order to pull up their economy.

These principles were embodied in long-term, annual and quarterly national-economic plans. Most prominent were the three five-year plans: 1928–1932, 1933–7 and 1938–42.[22] These set out elaborate investment and production goals for industry and the other major sectors of the economy.

The succeeding sub-sections of this chapter examine the main achievements and failures of Soviet industry in the 1930s, and then consider how far they have corresponded to these objectives.

(iii) *Rate of growth* (Table 24)

The rate of growth of Soviet industry in the 1930s has been the subject of a protracted debate among Western economists, and has been investigated in considerable detail. According to the official Soviet data, the volume of industrial production in 1940 was 642 per cent of 1928 (see Table 24), representing an annual increase of 17 per cent.[23] All students of Soviet statistics agree that this figure is greatly exaggerated. Two main factors are involved. The first results from the base year chosen in order to estimate index numbers – an *index-number effect*. The Soviet official series was

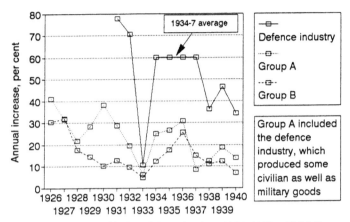

Figure 8   Growth of industrial production, 1926–1940: official figures.
Source: tables 29, 31.

measured in prices of the year 1926/27. As a result of the 'Gerschenkron effect' (see chapter 2) the rate of growth was far more rapid when measured in 1926/27 prices than in prices of the year 1937, or any later year. The more favourable 'initial-year' series preferred by Soviet statisticians and the less favourable 'end-year' series preferred by Western economists provide upper and lower limits to the rate of growth, each of which is methodologically legitimate.

The second important factor which pushed up the official Soviet index was *hidden inflation* in the prices used. Unlike the Gerschenkron effect, this is unambiguously a distortion which needs to be removed in order to obtain accurate figures for Soviet industrial growth. In preparing their index the Soviet statistical authorities often did not use 1926/27 prices, but prices of a later year. In the case of new products, the prices used were those of the year in which they were introduced. As the general level of prices was rising rapidly from 1929 to 1933, the production of later years tended to be overvalued, and this illegitimately pushed up the index.

The Soviet estimates also assumed that there was no change in quality during the 1930s in the case of items bearing the same name. In practice quality of production in almost every industry sharply deteriorated in the years 1929–33, followed by a steady improvement. Thus Soviet growth figures for at least the period 1929–33 should be discounted to allow for quality deterioration.

Faced with the unreliability of Soviet statistics of industrial production, during the first decade after the Second World War several Western economists undertook the laborious task of preparing independent estimates.

They had to proceed by combining together discrete series for the production of particular products in physical terms, using appropriate weights. The number of products involved was necessarily limited, ranging from a few key products in the case of the Seton index to over 100 in the case of the Nutter index. The alternative results are set out in Table 24.

The Western series certainly present a more reliable account of industrial growth than the Soviet official figures. With the exception of the Seton index, which was estimated on different principles, they may somewhat underestimate the rate of growth because they omit a large number of products; in particular, they usually exclude armaments, for which data were not available. On the other hand, they usually make no allowance for quality deterioration.

Recent Soviet commentaries concur with the Western criticisms of the official Soviet series. In their famous article 'Crafty Figure' Selyunin and Khanin claimed that the inflation of wholesale prices had not been allowed for adequately in Soviet statistics, and stressed even more emphatically than Western observers the unreliability of data in physical terms due to the change in quality.[24] But the Soviet critics have so far published only index numbers, both for national income as a whole and for industrial production, without data in value terms or any precise explanation of how they obtained their figures. Such estimates as they have produced broadly concur with the Western studies; and they also rely heavily on output data in physical terms.

One curiosity about the Soviet official statistics is worth mentioning. Most Western students have assumed that the Soviet index was particularly distorted in the case of machinery, not only because of the Gerschenkron effect, but also because machinery was particularly capable of being included in the Soviet index at artificially high prices. But Moorsteen's independent and very elaborate index for machinery production in 1927/28 prices, covering 210 types of machinery, in fact rises *more* rapidly than the Soviet index in 1926/27 prices for machinery and armaments combined.[25] It is the Soviet index for foodstuffs and consumer goods which seems to be greatly exaggerated.[26]

The Western estimates of the annual rate of industrial growth from 1928 to 1937 or 1940 range from 7.1 to 13.6 per cent, as compared with the official estimate of 16.8 per cent; a recent unofficial Soviet estimate is 9.0 per cent (see Table 24). Even the lowest rate of growth is substantial, as high as in the boom periods 1891–9 and 1909–13 in the pre-revolutionary Russian Empire.

But the differences between these rival estimates make it impossible to reach reliable conclusions about industrial efficiency. Employment in industry grew by about 9.5 per cent a year in 1928–40. If the lowest estimated growth rate is correct, 7.1 per cent a year in 1928–40, it follows that labour productivity (output per employed person per year) actually declined during this period. On the other hand, the highest Western estimate, 13.6 per cent, implies a quite rapid growth of labour productivity.

We are in even more difficulty when attempting to estimate a production function which would show capital productivity and total factor productivity (so-called 'technical progress'). This is because there is great uncertainty about the real value of capital investment and hence of capital stock. Alternative estimates are summarised in chapter 9. These results confirm the commonsense view that industrial efficiency is unlikely to have increased substantially, and may even have declined, in these years of social disorder and rapid technical change, years in which the industrial labour force was largely recruited from peasants with little or no previous experience of factory work.

(iv) Structure

The rate of growth of industrial production is less significant than the immense changes in the structure of industry. In 1928, on the eve of the first five-year plan, about 40 per cent of the industrial labour force worked in small-scale industry and it was responsible for 21 per cent of gross industrial production. By 1937, the proportions had fallen to 15 and 5.6 per cent.[27] During the early 1930s the number of persons working in small-scale industry declined absolutely. As a low-priority sector, artisan industry was deprived of raw material and other resources. Many artisans moved into state industry or other occupations; others were labelled 'petty capitalists', and expropriated and exiled. The number of persons working in small-scale industry increased again from 1933 onwards, but did not regain the level of the 1920s. Meanwhile large-scale industry expanded very rapidly, and small-scale industry was reduced from a major sector of industry to a quite minor one.

The decline of small-scale industry was most rapid in the case of consumer goods. The production of all kinds of textiles by small-scale industry declined to 38 per cent of 1927/28 by 1937; thus the pre-revolutionary trend to large-scale production continued, but at a faster rate.[28] All branches of the textile industry were affected, but the production of garments declined less rapidly than the other branches of the industry, and accounted for two-thirds of small-scale textile production in 1937. Certain branches of the small-scale food industry also declined, notably flour-milling: small-scale enterprises were responsible for 63 per cent of flour production in 1927/28, but only 26 per cent in 1937; this was a decline of over 40 per cent in absolute terms, which apparently occurred mainly during the second five-year plan.

Against the general background of decline, a few small-scale industries expanded. Bread-baking was transformed from a household activity to an industry in the 1930s. While small-scale bread production was responsible for only 26 per cent of all production in 1937, this was nearly treble the 1928/29 level in absolute terms. The associated small-scale biscuits and confectionery industry also expanded considerably. Some small-scale activities serving the new processes of industrialisation also expanded. According to the official figures, small-scale production by smiths amounted in 1937 to over six times the 1928/29 level. This figure, which includes repairs, may exaggerate the real increase, but a substantial increase certainly occurred; numbers employed (in full-time equivalents) increased from 101,000 to 321,000. In the 1920s smiths were mainly engaged on shoeing horses, repairing metal ploughs and other activities associated with individual peasant farming; by 1937 they were mainly responsible for repairing tractors and other agricultural machines. Small-scale quarrying and production of mineral building materials (apart from cement, which was entirely produced on a factory scale) also expanded considerably in the 1930s.

The general decline of small-scale industry was accompanied by the precipitate growth of giant factories in certain priority industries. By the beginning of the twentieth Century factory industry was already concentrated in much larger units than in any other country when measured by the number of people employed (it should be noted, however, that this measure tends to exaggerate the size of plant in Russian and Soviet industry, where output per worker was lower than in the more industrialised countries). By 1927, 61.7 per cent of the labour force in large-scale industry were located in enterprises employing more than 1,000 persons; and nearly a quarter of the total were in giant enterprises employing more than 5,000 persons (for data on the size of plant, see Table 26). In the iron and steel industry, as many as 54 per cent of the labour force were engaged in enterprises employing more than 5,000 persons. And, with the establishment of giant works at Magnitogorsk and Kuznetsk, and the expansion of the major Southern works, this percentage rose to 79 by 1936.[29] In machine-building and metal-working, where the total number employed expanded more rapidly than in other industries, growth was entirely dominated by large factories: thus tractor production was overwhelmingly concentrated in the Stalingrad, Khar'kov and Chelyabinsk plants. In a number of consumer goods industries, with the expansion of existing factories and the construction of large new factories, there was also a considerable increase in the size of plant.

Some other industries, however, followed the opposite trend: they were able to cope with their increased production plans only by establishing relatively small units. The coal industry, where the attempt to rely primarily on huge new mines was not successful, provides a striking example.

In most industries, taken separately, there was a marked tendency for the size of plant to increase. This occurred even in the consumer goods industries, with the expansion of existing factories and the establishment of new larger factories, such as the industrial bakeries and meat plants of the food industry. But surprisingly, the net effect of all these changes in scale on industry as a whole was that the average size of plant did not increase (see Table 26). This paradoxical result is due to the particularly rapid growth of the machine-building and metal-working industries, where the average size of plant was smaller than in iron and steel and cotton textiles, which dominated the industrial statistics of the 1920s.

(v) New industries

The most outstanding achievement of the industrialisation drive of the 1930s was the establishment of major new industries which did not exist before, or existed only in rudimentary form.

Among the largely new industries the *armaments industry* deserves pride of place (Tables 28 and 29). Powerful naval ship-building, artillery and small arms industries already existed before the First World War, and here the primary task of the Soviet authorities was to greatly expand and modernise long-established facilities. But in the mid-1920s the aircraft and tank industries were in their infancy throughout the world. In the 1930s the Soviet Union had not only to close the technological gap which had emerged between 1917 and 1926, but also to keep up with rapid Western technological advance.

In the mid-1920s, however, armaments production was almost certainly lower than in 1913, and the technical level of Soviet armaments lagged behind the major capitalist powers. Artillery was entirely based on pre-war designs and wartime modifications. The Soviet Union had only a rudimentary tank industry. At the end of 1928 the Red Army possessed only 300 lorries. The aircraft industry alone challenged the advanced countries. Already before 1917 Tsarist Russia possessed aircraft design and production facilities which were good for their time. In the 1920s Tupolev's metal aircraft designs were unsurpassed elsewhere; but Soviet batch production of aircraft consisted almost entirely of simple machines of foreign design, and most aero-engines were imported.[30]

The need to establish an economic base for a modern armaments industry reinforced the claims of industrialisation. The fear that the Soviet Union would sooner or later be attacked by one or more of the advanced countries encouraged the rapid development of an industrial capacity which would sustain a modern armaments industry. At the same time the immediate requirements of the armed forces competed with the long-term programme

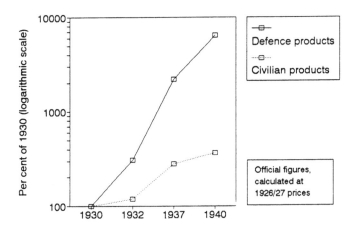

Figure 9   Civilian and defence industry, gross output, 1930–1940.
Source: table 29.

of industrial development. What proportion of capital investment should be allocated to aircraft and tank factories, what proportion to establishing basic metallurgical, chemical and civilian machine-building facilities which could in the future be used for armaments? And what proportion of current production should be devoted to armaments rather than civilian products?

During the war scare of the summer of 1927, which followed the abrogation of diplomatic relations with the Soviet Union by the British government, some resources were already diverted to the defence industry. But at first the Soviet leaders, believing that an immediate attack was unlikely, concentrated on the development of basic capital goods industries. And in 1929–31 the urgent need to provide tractors and other machinery to an agriculture in turmoil was afforded over-riding priority.

In developing the tractor industry, military needs were already given close attention. The large new tractor factories under construction at Stalingrad, Khar'kov and Chelyabinsk were designed for rapid conversion to tank production; the 'tractor and automobile industry' was known behind the scenes as the 'tank, tractor and automobile industry.'

During the early 1930s a series of external shocks impressed the political leaders with the urgent need to build a modern armaments industry immediately. In the summer of 1929 Chinese troops seized a railway in Manchuria which was jointly owned and managed by the Soviet and Chinese governments. In 1931 the Japanese invaded Manchuria, and threatened invasion of the Soviet Far East. And from 1933 onwards, with the assumption of power by Hitler and the Nazi Party in Germany, the threat of major war loomed over the European frontiers of the Soviet Union.

Against this background, the armaments industry gradually acquired greater priority. The increasing role of armaments is illustrated in Figures 8 and 9 and Tables 28 and 29. The share of armaments in total industrial production, a mere 2.6 per cent in 1930, increased to 5.7 per cent in 1932, the last year of the first five-year plan. This was a somewhat higher share than on the eve of the First World War, and a much larger absolute amount. By 1940 the proportion had increased to 22 per cent. By 1932 armaments production was already greater than that of the agricultural machinery, tractor and automobile industries combined, and amounted to over 11 per cent of total machine-building and metal-working production.[31] And on the eve of the German invasion of 1941, production of the armaments industry was planned to amount to as much as 62 per cent of all machine-building and metal-working production.[32]

The armaments industry made an even greater claim on capital investment. Its share of total capital investment in industry increased as follows (percent of total):[33]

1928/29	1932	1941(plan)
3.3	7.8	31.3

And in 1941 the armaments industry absorbed as much as 73 per cent of the investment allocated to the machine-building and metal-working sub-sector. By this time the urgent needs of defence dominated over all other needs. Even in 1938, three years before the outbreak of war, the industry was consuming one-third of all structural iron and steel and 42 per cent of high-quality steel.[34]

But the claims of the armaments industry are only palely reflected in these summary statistics. In many respects the establishment of a modern armaments industry required a more modern technology, and was more demanding in materials, workmanship and quality standards than anything previously produced in Russia. The industry demanded and swallowed up high-grade fuel for aircraft and tank engines, and high-quality steel, non-ferrous metals and sophisticated machine tools. None of these had previously been produced by Russian or Soviet industry.

Armaments became the top-priority sector of the whole economy. According to Julian Cooper:

It had first priority for the supply of fuel, materials and equipment; it received products of the best quality; and workers in the industry had better pay and conditions of work than those in civilian branches. The defence industry also absorbed considerable number of skilled engineering and design specialists ... This priority system must have had a deleterious effect on the rest of the economy and industry as a whole. Its use also means that the impact of defence production on the Soviet economy of the 'thirties cannot be measured simply by the volume of production of the defence industry.[35]

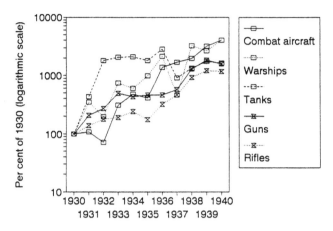

Figure 10   Products of defence industry in physical units, 1930–1940.
Source: table 28.

The armaments industry of the 1930s was the most outstanding success of the pre-war Soviet economy. Tank production started almost from scratch in 1930–1. At first the Soviet Union bought in British Carden-Lloyd and Vickers tanks, and the Christie tank from the United States; the Soviet designs of light, medium and heavy tanks were based on these foreign models. But within a few years Soviet original designs equalled those of their rivals. The T-34 medium tank and the KV heavy tank, first produced in 1939–40, and mass-produced during the war, outclassed the best German tanks in speed and firepower. Pioneering rocket and missile research, in spite of disruption during the 1937–8 repressions, resulted in the production of the famous 'Katyusha' rocket-gun. And the best Soviet military aircraft were comparable or superior to those of Germany, Britain and the United States.[36] These weapons, and the Soviet ability to produce them in large numbers, were a major factor in the Allied victory in the Second World War. Their rapid rate of growth is illustrated in Figure 10 and Table 28.

The armaments industry also had its failures and disasters. These were partly due to the inexperience of both engineers and politicians. The conversion of tractor factories to tank production proved much more costly and complicated than was originally envisaged. In 1932, when the partial conversion of the Stalingrad factory was under way, one of the officials involved, faced with an increase in the estimated cost of conversion from 11 to 90 million rubles, commented despairingly that it might have been better to build a tank factory and use it for producing tractors.[37] Later in the 1930s, the increasing weight and complexity of tanks made it necessary to build special production facilities at the tractor factories and elsewhere.

More serious were the gross miscalculations in relation to major lines of development of the arms industry. After considerable successes up to 1934, the industry failed to keep up with the rapid German technological advances after Hitler took power, and in 1937, during the Spanish Civil War, Soviet aircraft and other weapons were outclassed by the German. The feverish rush to catch up during the last three years before the war put a huge strain on the Soviet economy as a whole.[38] In 1939–41 the rising demands of defence outran the specialised capacity of defence plants and resulted in the conversion of civilian factories to defence production. Immense resources were diverted in the last years before the war to a surface ship-building programme which lacked strategic sense. Equally harmful was the poor location of the industry. In 1929–34 considerable efforts were made to develop a heavy industry and defence base in the Urals and beyond, safe from enemy invasion and enemy bombers. But during the armament drive of the last pre-war years, most armaments facilities were built in Ukraine and European Russia, in areas seized by the invaders in 1941–2. Construction in these more established industrial areas was cheaper; but the main reason for this mislocation was Stalin's compacent assumption that the invader would be immediately repulsed and would not succeed in capturing Soviet territory. Another political error with disastrous consequences for Soviet arms was the false assumption or hope that the German invasion would be delayed beyond 1941. The Soviet army was not on full alert and large numbers of aircraft, manufactured with so much effort, were destroyed on the ground in the first days of invasion.

Unquantifiable mischief was caused by the repressions. Periodic arrests of designers, engineers and managers gravely damaged the arms industry. Both in the early and in the late 1930s several major weapons and aircraft design teams worked as prisoners under armed guard. The execution of Tukhachevsky and most senior officers in 1937 during the 'Great Purge' removed the most talented military leaders, who provided designers and arms factories with a favourable atmosphere for innovation. They were mainly replaced at the top level by mediocrities with old-fashioned ideas of war. In the atmosphere of fear it was an act of bravery to challenge mistaken high-level decisions. The successes of the industry were achieved in spite of the repressions, owing to the high priority and huge resources devoted to defence, and the urgent pressure to produce modern armaments which was experienced by everyone from Stalin to factory worker.

The *agricultural machinery and motor-vehicle industries* were among the most important of the new civilian engineering industries which were established in the early 1930s. Enormous investments were devoted to the agricultural machinery industry. The original hope of rapidly establishing a highly-productive agricultural industry was abandoned with the collapse of agriculture in the early 1930s. But agricultural machinery was no less necessary in the desperate effort to introduce mechanical horse-power to replace the horses which died in the aftermath of collectivisation. The production of tractors increased from a mere 1300 in 1928 to a peak figure of 112900 in 1936; the first combine-harvesters were not produced until 1931, and output rose to a peak of 43900 in 1937.[39] The motor-vehicle industry also exemplified that aspect of Soviet industrialisation which was often referred to as 'sewing a coat onto a button' (rather than a button on to a coat): production of lorries increased from a mere 700 in 1928 to as many as 182,400 in 1938.[40] Tractors, combine-harvesters and motor vehicles were all produced in large new factories adapted from American designs, and the technological level of the basic production lines and their products was high.

The development of modern armaments, agricultural machinery and motor industries required the strengthening or establishment of a wide range of back-up industries supplying raw materials and components, and also supplying the capital equipment required by the new industries. Most prominent here was *the iron and steel industry*. For much of the 1930s iron and steel consumed more investment resources than any other single industry; its share of industrial investment rose from 9.8 per cent in 1927/28 to as much as 18.2 per cent in 1933, then slowly declined to the 1927/28 proportion by 1936.

This investment enabled the construction of vast modern facilities, based like the various machine-building factories on advanced United States models. In 1940 the production of pig-iron, and of crude and rolled steel, was four times as large as in 1928 (see Table 27). More than half the total production was concentrated in about ten giant works.[41] The new furnaces were highly productive as compared with the 1920s. The output of pig-iron per cubic metre of blast-furnace capacity increased by over 55 per cent between 1928 and the end of the 1930s; in the same period the output of crude steel per square metre of open-hearth furnace more than doubled.[42] As a result of the improved technology, output per worker also greatly increased: between 1928 and 1940, while output quadrupled in terms of the quantity of metal produced, the number of workers in the industry rose by only 73 per cent.[43]

The figures for the increase in the production of pig-iron and crude and rolled steel do not capture the immensity of the change in the industry. A careful Western estimate shows that in 1937 the value of the output of the whole iron and steel industry, when measured in dollar terms, was 472 per cent of the 1927/28 level, considerably higher than the crude physical indicators would suggest.[44] This was the result of the vast increase in the production of technologically complex and more costly special steels essential for the machinery and armaments industries. These were grouped under three heads in the Soviet statistics: (i) quality steels, (ii) ferro-alloys and (iii) pipes. All three categories were produced in very small quantities before the end of the 1920s; these were sub-industries almost entirely new to the USSR, and while they were being developed in the early 1930s it proved necessary to import substantial quantities of iron and steel in each category.

(i) *'Quality steel'*. This is a broad Soviet category referring to the new and better steels first developed in advanced industrial countries in the first decades of the twentieth Century for the machine-building and armaments industries: steel resistant to high pressure for use in turbines; dynamo and transformer steel; steels for internal combustion engines; light strong steels for aircraft frames; acid-resistant steel for the chemical industry; and the huge variety of steels required for the production of tanks and other weapons. Production of quality steel amounted to only 90,000 tons in 1927/28; it increased to 682,600 tons in 1932 and as much as 2,793,000 tons in 1940, rising from 2.7 per cent of rolled steel in 1927/28 to 21.3 per cent in 1940 (see Table 27).[45]

Quality steel was at first produced in existing factories, notably in a large group of long-established iron works in the Urals, which were converted to the production of quality steel in the early 1930s. But with the availability of hydro-electric power from the Dniepr plant, two major new quality steel works began production in Ukraine at Zaporozh'e (Zaporozh'stal' and Dneprospetstal'). The latter, like Elektrostal' near Moscow, which began production in the 1920s, manufactured steels of particularly high quality in electric furnaces; by 1940 over one-third of all quality steel was produced by this method. It has been estimated that as early as 1938 42 per cent of quality steel was directly consumed by the armaments industries, apart from quality steel consumed by intermediate products and industries.[46]

(ii) *Alloy steel*. The production of alloy steel requires the addition to ordinary rolled steel of ferro-alloys with a non-ferrous content ranging from ferro-manganese to ferro-molybdenum. In the 1930s lower-grade ferro-alloys were produced in blast-furnaces, higher-grade alloys in electric furnaces. Both types of production increased rapidly in the 1930s, from a very low level: blast-furnace production increased from 36000 tons in 1927/28 to 165000 tons in 1936, while production in electric furnaces increased from a mere 600 tons to 125000 tons. While most production in electric furnaces was located in Central and Southern USSR, a major facility was also established at Chelyabinsk in the Urals in the early 1930s.

(iii) *Iron and steel pipe*. Production of iron and steel pipe, which amounted to 78000 tons in 1913, was essential for oil extraction, machine-building, steam generation and housing. By 1927/28 it had already increased to 171000 tons, and by 1940 it reached 966000 tons. Thus the production of quality steels, ferro-alloys and iron and steel pipes became a major feature of the Soviet iron and steel industry, and was one of the major achievements of Soviet industrialisation.

Before the First World War and in the 1920s, Russian industry depended largely on imports for the *capital equipment and machine tools* which served its capital goods industries; and from the 1920s the Soviet government sought to become self-sufficient in 'the production of means of production for the production of means of production', and saw this as the indispensable nucleus of successful industrialisation. This task, already on the agenda in the 1920s, became much more complicated with the establishment of new armaments, agricultural machinery and vehicle industries, and of major new branches of established industries such as iron and steel.

The production of capital equipment for iron and steel mills provides a characteristic example of the establishment of a major new heavy engineering industry. Before the 1917 revolution, all major capital equipment for the iron and steel industry was imported, and the industry still relied on imports for its key equipment during the large-scale construction of new iron and steel capacity during the first five-year plan. In 1931 a modern blooming mill was constructed for the first time at the long-established engineering works at Izhora near Leningrad. But the most important new development during the first five-year plan was the construction of two new engineering works at Sverdlovsk in the Urals (Uralmashzavod) and Kramatorsk in the Ukraine (the Novokramatorsk works). From 1935 onwards these two works were both capable of producing most of the equipment for a 1.5 million ton iron and steel works in the course of a single year (in practice, however, much of their capacity was diverted to other heavy engineering products, and to armaments).[47]

Similar developments took place in other heavy engineering industries. During 1928–32 most of the equipment for the Dniepr hydro-electric project was imported, but the 1930s saw a huge expansion in the production of turbines, boilers and generating plant for all kinds of power stations.[48] Other major heavy engineering equipment produced for the first time in the Soviet Union in the 1930s included excavators, concrete-mixers and other machinery for the building industry.[49]

The machine-tool industry, which produced only 2000 metal-cutting machine tools in 1928, increased its production to 20000 in 1932 and 58000 in 1940 (see Table 27). During 1929–31 output expanded very rapidly as a result of the production in large batches of models designed during the First World War or in the early 1920s. From 1932 onwards, fundamentally new models were produced based on recent German and United States designs.

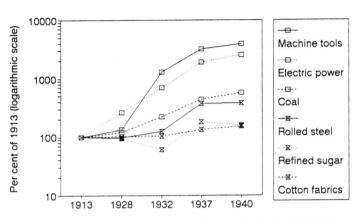

Figure 11   Products of civilian industry in physical units, 1913–1940.
Source: table 27.

The assimilation of high-precision technology proved extremely difficult; the technology was new to the USSR and the workforce was inadequately trained. As a result, production by the specialised machine-tool industry fell, and total machine-tool output increased between 1931 and 1935 only by expanding small-scale production at other engineering factories. But by 1934 automatic and semi-automatic lathes, centreless grinding machines and threadmilling machines were being manufactured in the USSR for the first time. By 1937 the Soviet Union was able to produce almost all types of machine tools, and the structure of output had been substantially modernised.[50] Figure 11 shows that machine-tool production increased more rapidly than the production of fuel and materials for industry, and far more rapidly than the production of food products or consumer goods.

(vi) Were the industrial objectives achieved?

Our account of industrial developments in the 1930s has shown that the first three of the five Soviet objectives outlined on pp. 137–8 above were at least partly achieved. Industrial production expanded rapidly; new industries were established at relatively high technological standards and were modernised; the production of capital goods received overwhelming priority. Moreover, this was in some respects a 'capital-intensive' industrialisation. Soviet industrialisation is often assumed to have relied on the massive increase in the labour force, which trebled between 1928 and 1940 (see chapter 5). But industrial expansion did not depend solely on the employment of additional industrial labour. Industrial capital – by Western as well as official Soviet measures – in fact expanded more rapidly than the labour force; the capital:labour ratio therefore rose. Moreover, a high proportion of the industrial labour force was employed in new factories or new industries. As early as 1 January 1935, according to official Soviet figures, as much as 73.5 per cent of total industrial capital stock was located in factories defined as 'new' in the sense that more than 50 per cent of their capital stock had been introduced since the 1917 revolution, and 37.6 per cent was in entirely new factories which started up in 1929–34.[51]

Substantial progress also took place in the achievement of the fifth objective – a shift in the location of industry from the older industrial areas. Industrial production shifted towards Urals and Siberia, and towards Central Asia and Kazakhstan (see Table 30).

The most obvious failure was in relation to the third objective: the consumer goods' programme (see Figures 8 and 11). While the factory production of consumer goods increased, this was largely the result of the transfer from domestic and small-scale to large-scale production. The most striking failure was in the production of foodstuffs. The decline in agricultural production resulted in a fall in food consumption per head in town as well as country; and even by 1940 food consumption per head had not returned to the 1928 level. Careful Western studies of Soviet real wages and incomes have concluded that while the industrial output of consumer goods per head of the whole population increased by 49 per cent between 1928 and 1937, real wages per person employed declined by between 17 and 43 per cent in the same period, depending on the prices used.[52]

But even in the capital goods industries the policies approved at the end of the 1920s were drastically modified in practice. The investment and production targets of the first five-year plan adopted in April 1929 were extremely optimistic; and they were drastically revised upwards in 1929–30. The most notorious plan proposed to produce 17 million tons of pig-iron in 1932/33 (some said in 1931/32), and this target was not achieved at all before the Second World War. Yet these plans influenced expectations about what could be achieved throughout the economy. It was estimated, for example, that the huge increase in the supply of iron and steel would enable the stock of tractors in the economy to rise from 391000 horse-power on 1 October 1929 to 9 or 10 million hp in 1932/33, while in practice the stock reached only 3.2 million hp by 1 January 1934.[53]

Vain hopes had harmful practical effects. The belief that large capital investment projects could be brought very rapidly to fruition led to many capital investment projects being started which could be completed only after long delays, and hence to a very large increase in unfinished construction in industry.[54] It resulted in the belief that tractors would replace horses throughout Soviet agriculture within a few years. In consequence, the leaders were insufficiently alarmed about the decline in the number of peasant horses in 1930 and 1931, and were thus encouraged to pursue rash policies towards the peasantry.

The most momentous of the unintended consequences of the unfeasible plans for the early 1930s – the deterioration of agriculture, and particularly of livestock farming – in turn had important repercussions on industrial policy. The need to replace dead horses by tractors was an urgent priority in the early 1930s.[55] As the plans for expansion of the iron and steel industry were not fulfilled, the large increases which took place in tractor and combine-harvester production, though much less than planned, were achieved only by a massive diversion of resources to the engineering industries serving agriculture. The big increases in production of quality steel of kinds never previously manufactured in the Soviet Union were at first mainly devoted to these industries: tractors alone consumed 252000 tons out of 502000 tons of quality steel in 1932.[56] This effort required the diversion of people and resources to quality steel production at existing plants which could have been used to complete the new iron and steel plants and put them into operation. Even the maintenance of the low levels of agricultural production of 1932–3 posed unexpected demands which haunted and mocked the industrializers. And the food shortages of 1932–3 forced the authorities to hold back the growth of the labour force in industry and reduce the number of workers in capital construction.[57]

By 1933 or 1934, relatively sober planning replaced the euphoria of the early 1930s. But planning in the later 1930s, and in more recent years, did not become a neutral and value-free process, for it continued to be influenced by powerful social and technological assumptions.

Economic decisions were constrained and spurred on by the deep-rooted Bolshevik enthusiasm for advanced technology, especially American technology. This enthusiasm over-rode resistance by many Russian specialists to foreign technology; and in industry the advantages of Bolshevik determination probably outweighed the disadvantages of their inadequate knowledge of the problems of applying advanced technology in Russian conditions. Certainly there were many blunders. In the machine-tool industry, for example, it was assumed for several years that the advanced path for machine-tool production was to follow the American pattern and produce specialized high-productivity machines; but it was not realised by the influential Workers' and Peasants' Inspectorate (Rabkrin) and its leading official M. Kaganovich (brother of the Politburo member L. Kaganovich) that this was incompatible with the mass production of a small variety of machines in large numbers. The difficulties of training a labour force with the special skills required for mass production were similarly greatly underestimated. But ignorance was overcome, and a technically advanced machine-tool industry, on the whole well-adapted to Soviet needs, was established by the end of the second five-year plan in 1937.[58]

Practical exigencies also led to the systematic modification of the ambitious policy of inculcating capital-intensive advanced technology throughout industry. As has been shown in an American study of the Soviet tractor industry, the pressures for more output and lower costs, together with the ready availability of unskilled labour, resulted in the employment of much more labour per unit of output, particularly in auxiliary processes, than in equivalent United States factories.[59]

The re-location of industry was also far less extensive than originally planned (see Table 30). Pressure for immediate output, coupled with complacency about the ability to halt the enemy at the frontiers, led to continued reliance on the established industrial areas in European Russia, and even to the construction of armaments factories in areas which were occupied by the invaders in 1941–2.

(vii) Production cycles under planning (Table 31)

We have seen that during NEP the expansion of industrial production did not follow a regular pattern. More surprising, perhaps, is the failure of Soviet industry to expand in a smooth and regular fashion in spite of the powerful central controls over every aspect of industrial activity. Soviet industrial production, unlike that of all the major capitalist countries in the 1930s, increased in every year between 1921 and 1940; and this remarkable success of Soviet industry has distracted attention from trends contained within this continuous boom.

Figures 8 and 12 and Table 31 show that during the 1930s two periods of very rapid industrial expansion (the three years 1928–30 and the three years 1934–6) were followed by years of much slower growth (1931–3 and 1937–40). These trends were first discussed by Naum Jasny, who named the four periods 'The Warming-Up Period' (1928–30), 'The All-Out Drive' (1930–3), 'The Three "Good" Years' (1934–6) and 'The Purge Era' (1937–40).[60]

The shape of the curve varies with the different series. In the 1931–3 depression, the Nutter series have the low point at 1931 or 1932, the official series at 1933. In the immediate pre-war depression, the Nutter series show a more or less continuous fall in the rate of growth from 1936; the official series shows a sharp improvement in 1939. These differences are largely because the Nutter series is incomplete: thus it excludes armaments, and does not incorporate either the relatively minor influence of the increase in armaments production in 1931–3, or the major influence of the increase in 1938–40. And the depression is much less marked in the official series,

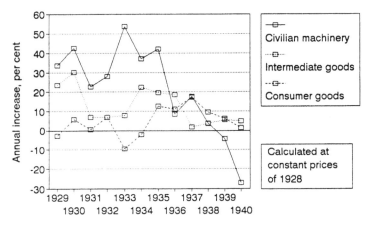

Figure 12   Growth of industrial production: Warren Nutter's estimate, 1929–1940. *Source:* table 31.

because of the distortions in the data for the Group B industries. But the broad trends appear in all the Western estimates.

How far were these alternative periods of boom and relative depression a result of inherent features in the Soviet economic system? Some economists have suggested that Soviet-type economies inevitably tend to over-invest, and that the consequent strain on the economy leads eventually to cut-backs in activity. The cycle is built in to the system.

The extraordinarily high level of investment in the early 1930s certainly played a major part in the boom and depression of 1928–30 and 1931–3. According to both Soviet and Western estimates, gross investment in fixed capital more than doubled between 1928 and 1931, increasing by 44 per cent in the single year 1930.[61] In this investment explosion, overwhelming priority was given to the capital goods industries. According to official figures, in 1931 investment in Group A state industries was 576 per cent of the 1928 level, and the increase in investment in this sector accounted for 54 per cent of the total increase in investment in 1928–31.

The rapid rate of growth of industry in 1928–30 was partly a result of the policy decision to expand investment. This in turn induced the expansion of industries serving investment, such as the fuel, iron and steel, metalworking and building materials industries. The possibility of this expansion was provided partly by the presence of spare capacity in certain industries. The metalworking industries, for example, had expanded rapidly during the First World War and had not yet reached their wartime level. The expansion was also achieved by the introduction of the 'continuous working week', and by some increase in the number of shifts worked per day.

But at the same time great expansion in investment automatically put a severe strain on the other sectors of the economy. Even according to the official figures consumption declined absolutely in 1931; and the rise in the non-agricultural population by some ten million persons in 1928–31 inexorably posed the acute problem of the redistribution of consumption between the agricultural and the non-agricultural population. Simultaneously, all kinds of resources were diverted to industrial investment. Thus the proportion of roofing iron used by industrial construction increased from 16 per cent in 1928 to 30 per cent in 1930, and the proportion of bricks from 20 to 30 per cent, and the amount used by agriculture dramatically declined.[62]

Much of this new investment did not provide an immediate return. Within the Group A industries a high proportion of investment was allocated to large-scale projects such as the Ural–Kuznetsk iron and steel combine, which took several years to complete. The proportion of incomplete construction increased throughout the period.[63]

The economy was therefore confronted from the summer of 1930 onwards with an 'over-investment crisis'. In the summer of 1930 industrial production and output per worker declined sharply. This was the first of a series of mini-slumps which worsened until an acute decline in production occurred in the first half of 1933.[64]

But the economic difficulties of 1931–3 cannot be attributed entirely to the high level of investment. The investment and production plans of 1930–2 were overambitious, and in spite of the severe strain were never achieved; this led to the misallocation of resources to infeasible objectives. The drive to collectivise agriculture, while partly motivated by the need to secure food and raw material supplies for the growing industrial sector, was brutal and inept; the upheaval in agriculture caused far greater damage to the urban standard of living than the political leaders had anticipated, and the unplanned death of millions of horses forced the diversion of industrial resources to investment and production in the agricultural engineering industries. Purges disrupted the industrial economy. The industrial reorganisation carried out in the early 1930s was confused and largely unsuccessful.[65] None of these factors, all of which exacerbated the economic situation, were automatic consequences of the industrialisation drive, and in major respects they hampered its success.

The 1931–3 crisis was resolved by modifying all the policies we have described. Total investment was reduced, and resources were concentrated on completing projects in progress; from the autumn of 1933 onwards the major projects of the first five-year plan supplied substantial increases in production. From 1933 onwards industrial and other plans were far more realistic. The pressures on agriculture were mitigated; and the supply of tractors and other agricultural machinery began to compensate for the loss in animal horse-power. The authorities sought a *modus vivendi* with industrial and other specialists; the purges did not cease altogether, but were far more restricted in their scope. In consequence, the years 1934–6 were perhaps the most successful in all Soviet industrial history.

The subsequent decline in the rate of industrial growth in 1937–41 was, like the 1931–3 crisis, partly due to the high level of investment. In 1936 total gross capital investment in the socialised sector increased by 32 per cent, more rapidly than in any of the previous four years.[66] In 1937 symptoms of over-investment again appeared.[67]

But other factors were almost certainly far more important. As we have seen, in 1937–41 a massive rearmament drive was launched, in response to the growing Nazi menace.

And the 'Great Purge' or Ezhovshchina of 1936–8 led to the arrest of officials, managers and engineers in industry and other sectors of the economy on an unprecedented scale. The mass arrest of key personnel was a major factor in the economic disruption. Economic crisis in the Soviet Union of the 1930s cannot be understood outside its political context.

Further reading

G. W. Nutter, *Growth of Industrial Production in the Soviet Union* (Princeton, N.J. 1962) is the foremost Western analysis of Soviet industrial statistics, and fully presents the raw data.

The various Western estimates are assessed by R. W. Davies, 'Soviet Industrial Production, 1928–1937: the Rival Estimates', unpublished Discussion Papers, SIPS No. 18 (CREES, University of Birmingham, 1978). Soviet official statistics of production and investment are presented in the *Occasional Paper* by Davies, Cooper and Ilič listed in the Bibliography of the present volume. Both these items may be obtained from The Secretary, Soviet Industrialisation Project, CREES, University of Birmingham, Birmingham B15 2TT.

The best sectoral studies are M. G. Clark, *The Economics of Soviet Steel* (Cambridge, Mass., 1956) and R. Moorsteen, *Prices and Production of Machinery in the Soviet Union, 1928–1958* (Cambridge, Mass., 1962).

8   Transport

J. N. Westwood

Russia is big, and the Russian Empire and its successor were even bigger. Political and economic cohesion depended on the means of transport. Water routes were traditionally important, whereas roads were few and nasty, but from the middle of the nineteenth century government-planned (and largely government-financed) railways were built, and these rapidly took the lion's share of the traffic originated by a fast-growing economy. In the twentieth century the railways were technically the most flexible mode of transport available and their relative importance increased in the first half of the century (see Table 32), in contrast to the United States where the railroads' share of freight traffic shrank from 75 per cent in 1929 to 62 per cent in 1939.

Stalin once went as far as an analogy between the function of Russia's railways and the British Empire's merchant navy, and it is clear what he meant. However, there was a fundamental difference in the economic situation of the railways in the late-tsarist industrialisation as compared with the Stalinist variant. Tsarist economic policy placed railway development in the forefront, as both end and means. In the Stalinist scheme of things, railways were simply means, an unwelcome necessity to be exploited for the benefit of production but benefitting as little as possible from that production. Under the five-year plans the USSR made a unique contribution to the history of railway transport, by carrying to extremes the policy of limiting investment while increasing traffic. The result of this under-investment may have been the faster development of industry, but certainly bequeathed to Stalin's successors a ramshackle transport system that remained a burden in the 1990s.

Surviving a test-to-destruction, although conferring some kind of historical distinction on Soviet railways, was only incidental to their role during industrialisation. That role was ostensibly a modest one. Far from being the leading edge of the great transformation, transport, and especially rail transport, was merely an auxiliary whose main care was to stay out of trouble. That is, to endure and adapt, providing the transport services needed for the assault. It was not helped by the policy of capital starvation and, additionally, the Soviet government's preconceptions about industrial location made its task more difficult. The government's urge to distribute industrial development more evenly, and in particular its emphasis on Eastern development, meant that industrialisation would produce not merely more tonnage to be carried but also greater distances over which to carry it. The transport burden imposed by this policy was multiplied by another feature of industrial policy, the preference for large-scale enterprises which, almost by definition, required very wide distribution areas for their products.

(A) The government and the railways

Transport policy was one of the most important cares of the Tsarist government. Although railway operations were entrusted to the Ministry of Ways and Communications (MPS), which had committees for technical decision-making and functional departments for administering the state railways, big decisions, like the approval of routes for new lines (both state and private), were reached by agreement inside the council of ministers, with the Finance, War, and Interior ministries, and sometimes others, wielding as much power as the MPS.

In the first two decades of Soviet rule the practice of appointing a professional railwayman as minister was abandoned. A party leader was entrusted with the transport commissariat (NKPS), with one or more deputy commissars appointed from the ranks of leading engineers. At crucial times strong and influential characters assumed the commissariat. Commissars who were also Politburo members were far more effective than those who were not. But when Kaganovich was eased out because of his alleged failures during the Second World War, he was replaced by a technical man, and the old tradition of a professional minister was re-established.

From time to time the party and government issued instructions in the form of declarations, decisions, orders and plans. Apart from the plans, which were necessarily parts of plans for the whole economy, these interventions were typically occasioned by the apparent inability of the NKPS to cope with a given situation. Quite lengthy debates, at both technical and political level, often preceded these instructions, and although such debates ceased once a decision was made it often happened that, in the end and despite the apparent finality of the decision, what actually took place was not at all what had been intended. The committees of Tsarist times, although cliquish and conservative, did at least foster continuity and long-term consistency, which cannot be said about their Soviet replacements.

In the second half of the 1920s there began a debate on the railways' future.[1] In the light of future economic growth, railway administrators pointed out that despite current successes the time was approaching when the railways would no longer be able to carry the increasing traffic. More investment was therefore needed, and the favoured aims were the introduction of more powerful locomotives, the consequent fitting of stronger couplings which would additionally be automatic, and the concentration of infrastructural work on 'super mainlines' over which the bulk of long-distance traffic would be funnelled.

While most participants agreed that more investment was needed, its extent and the source of the funds were controversial. The administrators initially hoped for substantial recapitalisation, to be largely financed from the state budget. Others, including Gosplan economists, felt that rationalisation of railway operations, aided by tariffs based on actual costs, could both reduce the traffic demand (especially if some degree of economic regionalisation could be achieved), and at the same time provide funds for investment. Super mainlines, they felt, just like discriminatory tariffs, would end by simply encouraging an unnecessary traffic growth. In 1929, with the execution of von Mekk, one of the advocates of thorough recapitalisation, it appeared that the rationalisers were winning the argument; implicitly and explicitly they placed their faith in planning. The derogatory term 'limiteer' would soon gain currency as a means of branding those who claimed that without investment there was a limit to traffic growth.

But the railway situation deteriorated, with a marked increase of accidents in 1930 accompanying a reversal of the previous trend toward ever-greater daily carloadings. In 1931 the party took determined action, the centrepiece of which was the plenum resolution of June 1931.[2] On the face of it, although this resolution mentioned the importance of more efficient management, its early reference to 'radical' recapitalisation and the shopping list that followed clearly suggested that this was the top priority. The list specified lines which were to undergo a heavy recapitalisation (at the end of which they would approximate to the super mainlines advocated by the late von Mekk and others), the size of new locomotives (not all that smaller than those envisaged by the earlier reconstructors), and among various other things the main lines to be electrified and secondary lines to be dieselised. Electrification, according to this resolution, was to be a basic part of the solution.

This policy, so emphatically pronounced, was not in fact carried out. For a time investment did increase, but nothing was on the scale envisaged. Table 36 shows that electrification proceeded at one tenth the speed specified in the resolution.

By 1933 things were again coming to a head. In 1935 the prominent Politburo member Kaganovich was at last sent to take charge, and the railway problem was, just, mastered. It was really a case of muddling through, of piecemeal investment at critical points. All in all, what was done was what any railway system would have done when faced with the same problems: investment in bottlenecks had first priority, investment in heavy-traffic lines had second priority, and a large number of overburdened lines were left to get through as best they could. At the same time, rationalisation was, after all, reinstated as a supreme goal and took its extreme form in the Stakhanovite drive for higher labour productivity.

(B) Railway traffic

Although different criteria may be advanced to evaluate a railway system, the essential question is whether the network carries the traffic that is offered. The short answer to this, both for the Tsarist and Soviet periods, is a qualified yes; the traffic was carried, but not all the traffic at all the time. In the Tsarist years, freight could sometimes accumulate at stations in peak periods. In the civil war years, train services in many areas disintegrated, although the economic effect of this was mitigated by the failure of the economy to generate a significant traffic demand. In the period of the five-year plans, the policy of demanding vastly increased traffic capacity without a corresponding investment in facilities sometimes led to transport crises, of which the 1933 edition was the most noticed.

Traffic was usually measured in 'conventional ton/kms' which, treating one passenger as one ton, combined freight and passengers into a single traffic measure. Table 33 shows how this key performance indicator evolved over the period. The traffic increases resulted from two factors: more tons and persons, and greater average distance of movement (see Table 34). This increasing length of haul was a continuing subject of complaint by Gosplan, which regarded it as a symptom of poor management. But it was largely a consequence of the wider geographical spread of economic activity.

In 1913 almost half the freight tonnage consisted of coal, grain, and timber, with hard coal alone amounting to as much as 22 per cent. A particular feature was the aggressive marketing of Donets coal, which was already necessitating new railway lines as its consumption area, aided by discriminatory freight tariffs, expanded towards Moscow and even the Urals. The First World War, by terminating supplies of British and Polish coal, carried this expansion further. As economic life settled down in the 1920s Donets coal traffic grew as the economy grew. Grain exports, which had been so important to the railways, especially to those lines that had been built specifically for them, had practically disappeared, although grain flows to the consuming areas remained, and were likely to increase with urbani-sation.

With industrialisation came even greater emphasis on bulk traffic, the kind of traffic for which railways are best suited. Here an important and little-noted change was the relative decline of small shipments, the less-than-carload (LCL) traffic that in 1913 accounted for 90 per cent of the shipments and 25 per cent of the tonnage and which by 1934, according to a sampling, had fallen to less than half of shipments and about 3 per cent of tonnage;[3] by 1939 LCL had fallen to about a third of shipments.[4]

Coal remained dominant throughout the period, both in tons and ton/kms, but by 1940 the commodity group known as mineral construction materials (sand, stone, etc.) had displaced grain from second place for tons but not ton/kms. The changing percentage of traffic ton/kms can be seen in the following table.[5]

	1913	1928	1932	1940	1945
Hard coal and coke	19	20	22	26	31
Grains and flour	15	16	10	8	7
Forestry products	8	12	13	11	7
Oil	5	7	9	9	8
Iron and steel	..	5	6	6	8
Mineral construction materials	..	..	7	7	3
Other	53	40	33	33	36

The main changes in the inter-war freight traffic flows stemmed from the increasing proportion of traffic to and from the Eastern party of the country. For example, eastbound traffic through Kropachevo on the East-West trunk route rose from 604000 tons in 1927/28 to 2,575,000 in 1932.[6] More generally, and over a longer timescale, the same shift can be seen in the figures for annual car-loadings: in 1934 total carloadings were almost four times greater than in 1923/24, whereas for the group of four Siberian railways (the Omsk, Tomsk, Trans-Baikal and Ussuri railways) there was a sixfold increase.[7] Dependence on Donets coal continued, and even intensified, although coal from other areas, notably the Kuznetsk Basin, began to replace Donets coal in, for example, the Urals. In the Urals, and in several regions (especially Leningrad and Moscow), industrial growth meant the appearance of new traffic flows and the intensification of existing ones. Increased oil production, surprisingly little of which moved by river tanker, became an additional burden. Much of it was carried by rail from Odessa, where it arrived in tankers from Batum.

Only in the late 1930s was it acknowledged that the policy of building huge industrial complexes in remote areas was placing an unbearable strain on the railways. The party congress of March 1939 was told this by both Molotov and Kaganovich, but no great change had time to emerge before the war changed the picture. The realisation had been delayed because it was not until the mid-1930s that the big new enterprises actually came into full production, but the 1928 decision to go ahead with the Ural-Kuznetsk metallurgical combine was taken in full knowledge of the high ratio of railway ton/kms to unit of output. It was not simply that the coal and ore had to be hauled over the 2000km separating the two halves of the combine, although that was bad enough. Added to this was the need to transport most of the output over even greater distances to the consumption areas. By instituting concessional railway tariffs that were well below actual costs it was possible to disguise the true transportation expense, at least from those who were not closely involved, but in physical terms (rolling stock especially) the decision to execute this scheme was debilitating for the railways. Similar, though less dramatic, transport problems were created by other massive developments in remote areas.

However, industrial relocation played a small part in the crises that afflicted the railways in the first two five-year plans. Traffic crises of one sort or another have been characteristic of the twentieth century Russian railways. Most have been small-scale, although that has not prevented large-scale martyrdom performances by interested parties. The peacetime crises occurred because of a lack of 'hidden reserves', that extra, rarely-used, capacity that railways need to provide flexibility to deal with peaks and with the unexpected. There was a reluctance to invest, especially in goods wagons (freightcars), so long as existing assets stood idle some of the time.

The railways did well in the first year of the First World War, but the supreme effort during the retreat from Poland in 1915 left a legacy of disorganisation and deferred maintenance that began a decline that brought the first railway crisis in late 1917. Only in summer 1918 was the situation stabilised and then only because freight requiring movement had shrunk to the capacity of the railways to carry it. Moreover, there was a pent-up demand for passenger service, as eye-witness accounts throughout this period poignantly testify. During the civil war the physical condition of the railways rapidly worsened, and they could not satisfy a demand that had been swollen by the demands of internal warfare. 1919 was probably the trough, when there was a crucial shortage of wood fuel (which by then accounted for 86 per cent of the railways' fuel requirement).[8] Early in that year, from 18 March to 10 April, all non-suburban passenger services had been withdrawn to free the few available locomotives for work with food trains. This willingness to sacrifice the passenger in favour of freight was repeated in subsequent crisis years. According to one source, freight in 1919 was down to 30,500,000 tons from 115,245,000 in 1917[9] and the quantity of unshipped freight amounted to 5351 wagonloads in December 1919 and 6651 in February 1920.[10]

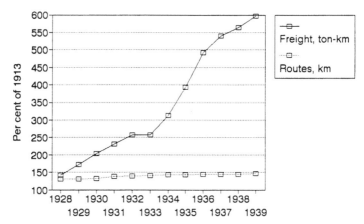

Figure 13   Railway routes and freight traffic, 1928–1939. *Source:* tables 33, 35.

In early 1921 another fuel shortage led to many train cancellations and an annual traffic figure slightly inferior to 1920. Henceforth freight traffic grew each year and by 1925 there were sporadic shortages of available locomotives and wagons. 1926 was the same but more so, and bottlenecks developed on some routes, due now not to rolling stock shortage but to insufficient line and station capacity. In general, constraints were tackled either by improved working methods or by selective investment. By the year 1927/28 freight traffic amounted to 150,600,000 tons, which implied a doubling over less than four years. In 1927 the railways were said to have 'completely satisfied the country's requirements for freight movement',[11] but almost certainly not all would-be passengers were carried; a doubling of passenger fares in 1926 brought demand closer to supply, and 1927 passenger traffic was less than in 1926. The slowing of industrial and agricultural growth in 1927/28 gave the railways a breathing space. They had already regained the 1913 level of freight ton/kms in the 1925/26 operating year, and in terms of tonnage in the following year. However, total passenger/kms did not reach the 1913 figure until 1928/29, although this was masked by the growth of commuter traffic, which brought the number of passenger-journeys to the 1913 level as early as 1924/25. From Table 33 it may be concluded that the railways reached their 1913 level in 1926, when passenger/kms and freight ton/kms together exceeded the 1913 total.

The rapid but irregular growth of freight traffic in 1929–39 is traced in Figure 13. As industry got moving under the first five-year plan the railways began to lag behind; although in 1929 railway freight tonnage rose by a hefty 19 per cent, this was not enough to keep ahead of all demands at all times.

This meant that transport crises, usually short-term and local, became a source of anxiety and friction.

It is difficult to judge how critical each alleged crisis really was. Industries and individual enterprises would have had a natural tendency to blame transport for their own failures, and the citation of particular industrial hold-ups caused by railway problems does not indicate the extent of a crisis. So far as 1929 is concerned, it was said that industrial enterprises were put into a difficult situation. In particular, from the autumn the oil industry had to limit its development because of non-delivery of pipes and cement, while rolling stock shortage meant that not all the oil could be shipped out of the Caucasus. This in turn embarrassed several metallurgical enterprises that were dependent on the oil. At the same period, some Donbas coalmines limited their production because of a goods wagon shortage and the accumulation of massive pithead reserves. The Krivoi Rog ore mines were in a similar situation. On the other hand, it appears that when the crisis was at its height the smelting enterprises had 18 days' stocks of ore (presumably on average) which was far below the normal 45 days but hardly represented a dire situation.[12]

The 1930 picture was similar, although worse, with the railways substantially increasing their traffic but being outpaced by industry. In the autumn and winter of 1930 failures to deliver fuel and other materials seem to have had some effect on certain enterprises, a delayed consequence of troubles experienced earlier in the year. What seems to have happened, according to an NKPS report,[13] is that the railways coped valiantly with rising traffic in the spring and early summer, but by June the goods wagon reserve was practically exhausted. On June 12 a record number of wagon-loadings, 54900, was achieved, and there could hardly have been an available empty goods wagon anywhere on the system on that day. The average daily loading for that month was 51039, but after this extraordinary effort loadings fell, despite a vigorous campaign to bring Sunday and festival loadings up to the average daily level. Interestingly, the record June monthly figure was only 94 per cent of the planned wagon-loadings, and when loadings relapsed to a more reasonable level in July and August they were seriously behind plan, with only 77 per cent fulfilment in August. August, moreover, was a peak traffic month because of the harvest, and the tautness was heightened by the long-distance passenger peak of that time. Storage space at stations was soon congested, as were many freightyards; this led to temporary embargoes on certain destinations, and they were less temporary than in previous periods. Also, to evade overworked yards and lines, a good deal of roundabout routing was necessary, which meant that goods wagons might produce more ton/kms but carry less tonnage per month. In August 1930 over 1100 passenger trains were entrusted to freight locomotives, evidence both of the swollen passenger traffic and the number of freight locomotives that were surplus despite the increased freight traffic on offer. With daily wagon-loadings averaging 46404 in the July–September quarter, the backlog was carried over into 1931. Towards the end of 1930 capital construction in the economy at large was held up by the accumulation of 142000 wagonloads of unshipped timber, and when winter approached there were two million tons of unshipped grain lying exposed to the elements (and to the hungry) at various stations.[14]

Early 1931 witnessed the actual closure of significant enterprises, including steel furnaces, due to lack of supplies. Although there were signs that things might get better, the growth of ton/kms was only 13 per cent in 1931, compared to 21 per cent in 1929. But how much of this deceleration was due to the railways' own problems and how much to the actual decline in output on the part of certain main clients like the oil and metallurgical industries cannot be gauged from the traffic statistics. All the same, the railways in 1930 and 1931 failed to carry 20 million tons of freight, equivalent to 50 days' railway work, according to the railway press.[15]

Reference to Table 33 will reveal an astonishing growth of passenger traffic during the first five-year plan, a reminder that the economic turmoil of those years was reflected nationwide in a disturbed human anthill. Passenger/kms doubled from 1928 to 1930 and more than trebled from 1928 to 1932, and passengers accounted for a third of total traffic. Why so many people were travelling, how many of them were involuntary travellers, how many resulted from the conversion of peasants into urban workers, are interesting questions which really imply another: whose journey was really necessary? In the following five-year plan (1933–7) passenger traffic actually fell; such a fall, making more room for freight traffic, was easily managed because, in a situation where railway berths were short, priority systems easily guaranteed places for those whose journeys were considered to be in the public interest.

The last half of 1932 saw less freight traffic than the last half of 1931, although freight ton/kms for all of 1932 were 11 per cent higher than in 1931. The five-year plan targets had been well surpassed, but that was far from enough in the circumstances of the time. Goods wagon shortage was still the defining constraint, although here and there shortages of line capacity persisted. To cope with the 11 per cent traffic increase, the railways' working stock of goods wagons grew by only half a per cent. By this time it was evident, too, that the composition of the goods wagon fleet was not suited to traffic demands, with far too few wagons suitable for mineral traffic. By 1932 the physical state of the goods wagon fleet was threateningly inadequate; with virtually no reserve stock, wagons had not been sent for their normal repair and refurbishment.

In late January 1933 the extent of what was to be the worst of the railway crises was measured: it amounted to one month of railway work, or about 20 million tons. (Such an amount, two years' previously, had been regarded as equivalent to 50 days work.) As much as 60 per cent of the backlog consisted of timber shipments and 24 per cent of consumer goods; this suggests that in some way or other priorities had been set, with those sectors receiving low priority. In these years coal, metallurgy and machine-building received top priority generally. The timber-carrying railways had for years received only a negligible share of the meagre railway investment. The fact that the timber industry was traditionally slow in loading and returning goods wagons, and that the consumer goods industries tended to forward LCL freight, may have made things worse for these industries.

Freight traffic did not increase in 1933 (see Figure 13). The railways were now emphatically regarded as a crucial bottleneck in the economy. Certainly there were some key commodities like oil and iron ore whose production increased considerably faster than their railway shipments. In 1934 traffic growth resumed, aided perhaps by a more active stick-and-carrot approach to railway workers. But still the growth (21 per cent) was not really enough. In 1935 the party, in the form of Kaganovich, imposed radical changes in railway operation, work practices and management, while at the same time relaxing the long-practised and partly self-defeating limitations on railway investment.[16] Among other things, the new investment under Kaganovich sustained the special effort, mentioned in the next section, to overcome the goods wagon shortage. Both in 1935 and 1936 25 per cent increases in ton/kms were achieved.

This growth declined to 10 per cent in 1937 and to around five per cent in the three following years. There were some anxious months during the coal famine of 1937–8 (the situation was so bad in the Urals that in the following winter the railways were allowed to hijack coal shipments for their own use).[17] In 1939 lack of line capacity in the Urals hampered some industries. But until 1940 there was nothing suggestive of a return to the bad days of 1933, and in general the slower rate of growth was matched by a slower rate of growth in the economy as a whole.

In 1940 the pattern of earlier crises was repeated. By reducing, in the guise of over-capacity, the reserves that gave railway transport the ability to face the unexpected, the government had gone some way towards cooking its own goose when the war with Finland broke out in late 1939. From September 1939 and spring 1940 the railways also had to assimilate the multi-gauge railways acquired by territorial expansion. The Baltic states, in particular, had a high mileage of narrow-gauge lines. But this was a mere inconvenience. What was much more serious was the problem of the main lines that had been converted in the inter-war years from the Russian broad gauge to the European standard gauge in both eastern Poland and the Baltic states. Operating economics, and above all strategic prudence, required such lines to be converted back to the Russian gauge. However, as a result (once more!) of the Soviet goods wagon shortage the NKPS preferred that the standard-gauge lines should remain standard-gauge as long as possible, thereby enabling their existing stock of some 120,000 standard-gauge goods wagons to remain in service. Only at the thirteenth hour, in spring 1941, did re-gauging work seriously get going.[18]

Meanwhile the railways were overwhelmed by the demands of the Russo–Finnish War. The war was fought in a relatively small region, where railways were sparse. Huge new traffic flows were concentrated on a few lines, especially those from the centre to the north-west. Unloading and wagon-return were slow, so goods wagons tended to accumulate in sidings. At least in Moscow and Leningrad, the consequences of the resultant crisis were probably as marked as in 1933. In February 1940 the Leningrad party organisation reported that many enterprises had stopped production because of fuel shortage. In Moscow, many factories were choked with loaded goods wagons that the railways had not managed to despatch. Not for the first time, passenger traffic was cut to make room for freight; in January 1940 the government ordered the railways commissariat to reduce long-distance passenger services by 25 per cent, and steam suburban services by 20 per cent. But after the end of the Finnish war in March 1940 recovery was swift, so the 1940 traffic figures showed a small growth over 1939. This achievement was at the expense of the passenger, however. In summer 1940, only 98 long-distance trains were originated each day, compared to 160 in 1939, and local and suburban services were also reduced. Yet the number of passengers rose, a conjunction that forced even more passengers than usual to travel on the train roof.[19]

In the Second World War there was a state of continual crisis. Military traffic was not enough to compensate for the loss of civilian tonnage. On the other hand, the average length of haul rose, partly because of the shift of industry to the East and partly because war conditions often necessitated roundabout routing. But for the most part the railways met the demands placed upon them.

(C) Railway investment

Sometime during the First World War, railway investment began to fall behind requirements and never caught up. This is the key to the Soviet railway situation, the successive difficulties and solutions being only variations on the theme of fitting a quart into a pint pot.

(i) Infrastructure

New railway construction was kept to a minimum, and there was a preference for concentrating it on access lines, rather than transit lines (access
lines, by obtaining new traffic, added to the railways' problems whereas
transit lines, producing little if any new traffic, relieved overburdened
routes). One source suggests that in 1901–13 only 25 per cent of new lines
were for access, compared to 60 per cent in the Soviet period.[20]

Figure 13 and Table 35 show how the route mileage grew and how more
intensive use enabled mileage to grow much more slowly than traffic.
Figures like these relate only to railways in the common-carrier network
controlled by NKPS. A substantial mileage was also owned, and usually
operated, by various industries, especially the coal, metal and timber commissariats. This mileage increased quite fast. Such increases were the
equivalent, for the NKPS network, of additional access lines, since almost
all traffic originated or received by the industrial lines passed over this main
network.[21]

Most of the lines planned in the last Tsarist years were eventually built,
or completed, by the Soviet government, the Turkestan–Siberian Railway
(Turksib) being the most celebrated of these projects. Both world wars
witnessed a flurry of new construction, most of which was of use in peacetime. What Table 35 does not show is that both during the civil war and the
Second World War lengths of main or second track were closed in order to
obtain scarce rails (1300km in 1943 alone).[22] In 1913 rail stocks had been
buoyant, but that came to an end in late 1918.

Table 35 is not precise, as measuring and dating new lines is not as simple
as it seems. During the Second World War the picture is obscured by the
lifting of lines, and the construction of new railways by the army, the
GULag organisation or individual industries (railways which might, or
might not, be handed over to the NKPS). Nor is it always clear whether
lines built but then closed are included. Such lines, evidence of large-scale
muddle, were comparatively rare, although they did include the quite
lengthy Novgorod–Smolensk line, begun in 1930, mothballed in 1934,
restarted in 1939 and again mothballed. By early 1938 5000km of line had
been begun and then 'conserved'.[23]

The shortfall in new lines (a shortfall both of intention and achievement)
was partially redeemed by the programme of double-tracking single lines.
Double-tracking cost between half and three-quarters as much as a new
single-track line, and could increase line capacity by two or three times. In
the first five-year plan, 3397km were doubled, as against the target of
2200km; and in 1928–41 as a whole about 9100km of second track were
laid.[24]

Track maintenance standards fell to the lowest possible level during the civil war and never returned to the 1913 quality. Economies here had a dire effect on railway operations and were still felt by the railways of the 1990s. Rails throughout this period were of a cross-section plainly inadequate for current needs. With the heavier traffic density, 50kg/m rails were the minimum that would assure a reasonable life and permit reasonable axleweights (that is, heavier locomotives than the 1913 standards). In 1940, however, four-fifths of the mileage was laid with rail of 38kg/m or less. On top of this, because of low-quality manufacture, rails were not capable of performing anywhere near their theoretical capacity. As late as 1938 46 per cent of the rails produced, it was said, were either too soft or too brittle. The rail factories themselves rejected from 7 to 22 per cent of their output (depending on which factory and, one surmises, on which inspector). After this weed-out the NKPS inspectors rejected a further 9–12 per cent.[25] And even then a high proportion of defective rails reached the railways, to be laid on main lines and eventually failing, sometimes catastrophically.

The annual rate of rail replacement on main lines was 5 per cent in 1935–40 – an average rail life in mainline service of twenty years – and as little as 2 per cent in 1931–4.[26] This represented a crippling deterioration of the infrastructure. According to a somewhat theoretical exercise presented by the NKPS in 1935 to the Council of Peoples' Commissars, the mileage requiring rail replacement was 472km in 1920/21, 2534km in 1926/27, and then took off to reach no less than 25104km in 1934.[27] The position with sleepers (ties) was just as bad, and in 1940 an average of 14.5 per cent of the sleepers in main tracks were unserviceable. This was a deterioration as compared with 1936, and said to be due to a timber shortage in 1937–39.[28]

(ii) Rolling Stock

Despite the threadbare track, the most limiting factor was the goods wagon (freightcar) shortage, because the culmination of railway crises was almost always the inability of the railways to provide industry with empty wagons for loading. A bigger reserve of goods wagons would therefore have moderated, at least, the successive critical situations. Neither Gosplan nor the government, it seemed, could ungrudgingly accept that goods wagon capacity needed to exceed traffic volume. Thus by 1940 the Soviet goods wagon stock per unit of traffic was only a third of that of US railroads. US utilisation rates were undoubtedly low, but the service provided to US clients was incomparable better.

Goods wagon production was as high as 30000 units in 1914,[29] but for the next two decades it remained much below that figure. Only at one period was a real effort made to bring wagon supply close to needs. This was in

1935 when a crash programme initiated in 1934 trebled goods-wagon output by halving coach (passenger-car) production, and building goods wagons in repair workshops and in other engineering works. So whereas output was 12000 wagons in 1933 and 19000 in 1934, it rose to 69000 in 1935, although by 1940 it had fallen back to 30000. By 1940, however, the rising proportion of four-axle wagons meant that production was equivalent to 53000 of the 1914-style vehicles.[30] In 1934 the number of wagons out of service after accidents would have cancelled out the accession of new wagons.[31] This casualty-rate was superimposed on the crisis resulting from the first five-year plan, when traffic grew four times faster than the wagon stock.

By 1941 two-fifths of the wagon stock consisted of 4-axle wagons (that is, they were supported at each end by four rather than two wheels and carried about double the load of 2-axle wagons). Half the wagons had automatic couplings; these were much stronger than the link couplings used by the Tsarist railways and therefore minimised the train-breaks that could result from heavy trains or poor-quality driving. Two-thirds of the goods wagons had the automatic brake, enabling heavier and faster trains to be operated without risking runaways. Although Soviet railways were advanced in the use of small containers that could be interchanged between road and rail vehicles, and the proportion of specialised vehicles was greater than in Tsarist times, the latter were still far too few. In 1913 only three per cent of the wagon stock had been in the form of open wagons, even though coal made up a fifth of the freight traffic. Carrying bulk freight like coal in boxcars (vans) or on flatcars was normal, and remained normal. As late as 1939 it was authoritatively stated that 10 per cent of freight required flatcars, another 10 per cent needed specialised wagons, 15–20 per cent needed vans (presumably to stay dry), whereas 60–65 per cent could move either by flats or vans.[32] Outside the USSR, this would have seemed an astonishing declaration, given that three bulk commodities alone (coal, ores, building materials) accounted for more than half of the traffic and could only be loaded and unloaded to and from vans with much time and effort.

Nevertheless, by late 1937 open wagons of various categories accounted for 7 per cent and vans for 53 per cent of the stock. Two-axle flats accounted for as much as 29 per cent: this did not, however, avert a critical shortage of flatcars in the Finnish campaign.[33]

The goods wagon stock was 485600 units in 1913.[34] At the beginning of 1941, excluding units acquired by recent territorial acquisitions, there were 650800,[35] and they were bigger; two-fifths of them were 4-axle, of more than double the capacity of the 1913 designs, and the recent 2-axle types were bigger, by 2–6 tonnes, than their Tsarist predecessors. So the 1941 figure was equivalent to about 920000 of the 1913-type cars, a doubling of capacity in the face of a six-fold traffic growth. Improvements of the utilisation indices bridged this substantial gap, together with the acceptance of a very taut situation that engendered local crises, inconvenience for clients, and occasional countrywide crises.

Passenger vehicles were even less favoured than freight vehicles. Moreover, there was no technical advance. It was only in 1939 that an experimental all-metal long-distance passenger train appeared; batch production up to the late 1940s was of wooden-bodied Tsarist designs. True, these were the latest Tsarist designs, 8-wheelers and six-wheelers which steadily relegated to minor services the older four-wheel, candle-lit bone-shakers. But the poor fulfilment of the already small five-year plan targets (53, 42 and 48 per cent fulfilment in 1938, 1939 and 1940) meant that in 1941 about 60 per cent of passenger vehicles had been manufactured before the First World War. These figures exclude the new electric multiple-unit trains for suburban service, whose production more or less kept up with demand.[36]

(iii) Locomotives

There was probably no general locomotive shortage at any time, although there may have been problems with locomotives *available for traffic*. The main issue concerned the size rather than the number of locomotives. As the following table shows, locomotive production was substantial, with the new Soviet designs being bigger than their Tsarist predecessors.[37]

Locomotive deliveries to the railway system (units)

	Tsarist designs			Soviet designs		
	Total	Passenger	Freight	Total	Passenger	Freight
1906–13 (annual average)	785	..	..	–	–	–
1928/29	521	84	437	54	54	0
1932	827	147	680	2	1	1
1937	179	179	0	999	105	894

Bigger locomotives, and hence heavier and faster trains, eased the problems of line capacity and goods wagon shortage. But bigger locomotives implied stronger track and bridges, and the meagre supply of heavier rails placed a limit on both the size and the route-availability of heavier locomotive designs.

In the 1920s those who favoured railway reconstruction envisaged the use of American-size locomotives with 30-ton axleloads. But after ordering ten

US prototypes it was the smaller FD, designed in the USSR but US-style, which was approved by the party in its June 1931 resolution. (The FD was named after the late head of the political police, Feliks Dzerzhinskii.)

The FD was put into batch production and did enable the running of heavier trains on those few lines that were strong enough to take it. It was a step forward, but had undoubted design and construction faults. It tended to break even the heavier rails, and had a very limited route availability. So in due course it was joined by the SO, a new design representing a combination of two pre-revolutionary designs, which was a further step forward. But efforts to design radically new locomotives especially suited to cope with Soviet conditions were concentrated on no-hope innovations, to the detriment of less revolutionary initiatives that would have had a better chance of success. Kaganovich, with his preference for exciting rather than sound innovation, seemed fated to back the wrong horse on all possible occasions or, more accurately, to listen to the wrong voices.[38] The mass production of condenser locomotives is a good example of his skill in solving one problem (water supply) by introducing another (unreliable locomotives) and then another (arrests of locomotive maintenance engineers).

There were positive achievements as well. The locomotive industry benefitted from the reconstruction of the Lugansk (Voroshilovgrad) works and could divert some of its capacity to other, non-railway, work. The USSR in the 1920s took a leading role in the development of main-line diesel traction. But here again indecision posing as decisiveness turned victory into defeat. In 1937, just as batch production of a successful diesel locomotive was getting under way, it was decided (or, rather, Kaganovich decided) that the diesel programme should be scrapped.

Electrification which, in the June 1931 decision, was to be the leading feature of the new railway age, suffered heavily from the economy's inability to supply what was needed (see Table 36). Some newly-electrified main lines were steam-operated because they lacked electric locomotives or, quite often, electric power.[39]

(D) Labour

By 1928 labour productivity, expressed in conventional ton/kms per operating worker per year, had recovered to approximately the 1913 level (see Table 37). In the 1920s productivity had its ups and downs partly because, as in Tsarist times, short-term changes in the size of the workforce did not match short-term changes in the volume of traffic. Although the long-term trend was undoubtedly upward, the allegation that for the most part the railways were over-staffed in this period is probably true. It should be

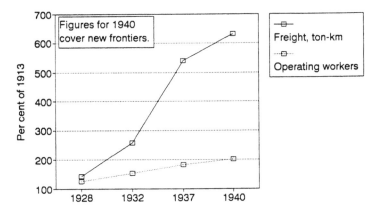

Figure 14   Railway output and workforce, 1928–1940. *Source:* tables
33, 37.

remembered, however, that their poor physical state meant that a larger
number of workers was required for maintenance.

Although in the 1930s, as Figure 14 shows, productivity moved unstea-
dily upwards, it was usually described as unsatisfactory. Certainly, in
relation to what railway transport was capable of, the output per worker was
not high. Soviet railway productivity increased from its low figure faster
than that of US railroads over the same period, but it never caught up the
US level of productivity. The Class 1 US railroads, even while labouring
under the notorious full-crew legislation, produced 473000 conventional
ton/kms per worker in 1929, 589000 in 1939, and 961000 in 1944,[40] whereas
the Soviet railway worker was only producing 368000 tons in 1940. It seems
most likely that the main factor in improving Soviet railway productivity
was the more rapid increase of the kinds of traffic which produce high
ton-mileage while demanding minimal labour input; that is, most bulk
freight (see p. 161 above). Substantial capital investment also played its part.

The various governmental or managerial measures probably contributed
less to enhanced productivity than was claimed. Measures taken in early
1931 may, in fact, have contributed to improved locomotive maintenance at
the expense of a deterioration of the productivity indices. The previous
practice of giving a locomotive to the first available crew should have
improved both labour and locomotive productivity but in fact resulted in
the neglect of locomotives. In 1931 it was replaced by a system of having two
crews allocated to a given locomotive. At the same time, main-line locomotives, apart from oil-burners, were to be served by three-men rather than
two-men crews.

Measures in July 1933 included a strengthening of discipline, both of workers and management. Absenteeism and failure to look after equipment were two of the targets. The multitude of job-rates was also attacked, as was the large proportion of skilled staff working in offices rather than out on the line.

From the mid-1930s the railways were dominated by the Stakhanovite movement (see Glossary), said to have been the motive force behind the improved productivity of those years. How far the movement was cause, clothing, or reflection of a widespread revision of working practices which undoubtedly took place is easier to ask than to answer.

The first railway Stakhanovite was Krivonos, a Donbass freight locomotive driver, who broke many of the written and unwritten rules governing locomotive handling and thereby succeeded in hauling trains heavier and faster than was customary. The importance of this achievement lay in its apparent proof of the party's assertion that the railways had spare capacity; to handle their increased traffic they did not need as much investment as their managements claimed.

Although Krivonos was soon followed by Stakhanovites in other railway trades, whose new working methods in most cases were less blatantly opposed to previous working rules, it can hardly be doubted that railway managers' attitudes to Stakhanovism were flavoured by the Krivonos example. This example was a bad example, because in flouting time-honoured caution Krivonosites simply wasted fuel, imposed high maintenance costs, and in the long run shortened the lives of locomotives and track. Moreover, the higher speeds at which they ran were often unsuited to track and trains and may be presumed to have contributed to the higher accident rates.

It can hardly be doubted that railway managers were aware of these negative results of Stakhanovite locomotive driving, so the allegation that many of them shunned Stakhanovism rings true. How far this reluctance led to the poor performance of the 1937–38 winter is uncertain. It was probably far less important than was claimed at the time, as that winter witnessed the promotion of hundreds of inexperienced officials, replacing predecessors picked up by the railway purge of summer 1937.[41] But undoubtedly managers did not expect great things from the movement. On the October Railway it was decided to increase the labour force by 18 per cent in 1938, even though this meant that labour productivity would fall.[42] At Yasinovataya, origin of Kozhukhar''s quite successful train-despatch technique, they had returned to the old pre-Kozhukhar' methods in 1937.[43]

The 1938 re-entry of Kaganovich into the fray changed all this. A new wave of Stakhanovism hit the railways. The purge, which had peaked in 1937 but still maintained some momentum, no doubt encouraged railway managers to show some enthusiasm for the movement. How far the purge was a necessary component of Stakhanovism is another of those interesting questions which do not belong to this chapter, but it may be remarked that Stakhanovism on the railways, as elsewhere in the economy, seems to fall into two phases, with the 1937–38 stagnation dividing them. By 1941 it could no longer fairly be termed an élite movement, for 45 per cent of the operating workers were entitled to call themselves Stakhanovites (and another 18 per cent could call themselves shock-workers); the total of railway Stakhanovites, which had been 69000 in 1935, was 701558 in early 1941.[44] This meant that there must have been very few railway operations that had not been touched by Stakhanovism, for better or for worse.

There is much about Stakhanovism that remains to be explained. That it accompanied a rise in productivity is true; that is was a prerequisite for such a rise is less certain. After all, the monthly mileages run by locomotive drivers rose faster in 1932–35 than they did in the five intensely-Stakhano-vite years of 1936–40.[45]

(E) Rivers

It is difficult to decide whether, in the family of transport modes, Soviet river transport was an ugly sister masquerading as Cinderella, or vice versa. On the one hand the waterways, with their apparent low costs, were extolled by transport economists and party specialists as the most attractive medium of transport. On the other hand, in practice capital allocations were niggardly, and even so were rarely spent because river transport was at the wrong end of the queue for metal supplies. Above all, shippers who used the waterways for the first time were reluctant to do so again if they could avoid it, and this hydrophobia has proved very long-lasting.

Enthusiasm for waterway transport varied directly with the distance from the scene of operations. Party and Gosplan transport specialists, noting the 'free' route mileage and the low ton/km costs, and blissfully unaware that the lowest ton/km costs do not ncesssarily guarantee the cheapest transport, repeatedly urged the transfer of freight from rail to water. But there were many reasons why shippers thought differently. The winter freeze-up meant that clients had to rearrange their transport procedures twice every year; this was a bureaucratic as well as economic deterrent. Moreover, the precise start and end of the navigation season depended on the weather and could vary by a month at each end. In the summer, when traffic peaked, rivers tended to run low, so craft could take only a reduced cargo. River transport was slow, even disregarding port delays, and it was less punctual than the railways. Trouble-free navigation depended on standards of skill and sobriety that were not always forthcoming. Industrial managements valued punctuality and speed of transport (which, for example, might compensate for delays in production). That the rivers might have lower tariffs was of small importance, especially as it was usually the shipper who chose the means of transport and the receiver who bore the cost. On top of all this, investment in waterways was hardly noticeable, which meant that everything, boats, wharves, crews, was unpreposessing and inefficient.

Even if investment had been more generous it is doubtful whether the waterways could have taken as great a proportion of total traffic as they did in Tsarist times. One way to mitigate the problem of the irregular navigating season was the stockpiling of shipments at the river ports during the winter, so that movement could begin as soon as the thaw came. In the hand-to-mouth conditions of Soviet industrialisation, there was no room for the luxury of stock accumulation, and little room for a transport mode that could promise neither fast delivery nor flexible schedules.

In 1913 the common-carrier river shipping lines carried 35 million tons of freight and achieved almost 29 billion ton/kms. In addition, 14 million tons were floated down the rivers, accounting for another 8 billion ton/kms. Half the tonnage and 70 per cent of the ton/kms were accounted for by the Volga/Kama system. A third of the total tonnage represented timber, and one-sixth was oil (which was as much as one-third in terms of ton/kms). Grain amounted to 17 per cent of the total, both in tonnage and in ton/kms.[46]

The corresponding 1940 figures show an unusually low growth, compared to other transport modes. The tonnage shipped by common-carrier shipping lines was 73 million tons, and the ton/kms 36 billion (self-floating traffic excluded).[47] The traffic carried by ships owned by other organisations is not known, but it was almost entirely short-distance. Timber and firewood accounted for 55 per cent of the tonnage, followed by oils (13 per cent), mineral construction materials (10), grain (7) and coal (3 per cent).[48]

The relative decline in water transport is a feature of the whole Soviet period. Although in 1928 passenger traffic was higher than in 1913, freight ton/kms were little more than half those of 1913 (see Table 38). A large factor in this depressing performance was the havoc imposed by the civil war, with so many vessels sent to the bottom in shallow water. Resurrecting these craft was a slow process for which there seemed to be little incentive, because only in a few areas, usually remote, was river transport indispensible. Despite this situation, some work seems to have been done on rehabilitating the routes themselves; the length of buoyed riverways was slightly greater in 1928 than in 1913. Coastal sea transport faced a somewhat similar situation in 1928.

In 1925 the state river shipping lines accounted for 53 per cent of the tonnage, other state organisations and cooperatives for 42 per cent, and private owners for 5 per cent. The state companies' share was considerably greater in terms of ton/kms, because they handled almost all the long-distance traffic.[49]

In an attempt to make waterway transport more attractive, freight tariffs were reduced for the 1925 season. In later years tariff-juggling was a frequent resort, and must have had some effect in retaining clients even if it did not do very much to attract new traffic.

New traffic was carried by old ships restored to service, since new construction fell far behind the attrition rate. In 1921–24, for example, only three new self-propelled vessels were added to stock. In the following years, although money for shipbuilding was made available, metal shortage and yard shortage kept new construction to a minimum.

Fresh demands were laid on water transport by the first five-year plan. But, far from relieving the railways of part of the freight burden, the waterways actually lost some of their traditional freight to the railways, oil being the most obvious example. To carry the traffic, the shipping lines were forced to resurrect some of their very oldest reserve ships. New ship construction remained low. Although in 1929–32 the plans specified new self-propelled ships to the extent of 138000 h.p., only 51300 h.p. was actually delivered. Barges were delivered more satisfactorily, but only because wooden craft, with their short life and high maintenance cost, remained in production. Self-propelled vessels were built to old designs, and a quarter of them used imported engines, as domestic industry could not supply these in sufficient numbers.[50] Shortage of materials also meant that capital repairs fell behind requirements. On the whole, the obsolescence and availability of the fleet were worse in 1932 than they had been in 1928. On the other hand, some useful work was accomplished in creating or modernising river ports, and steady if slow progress was made with extending navigable rivers. The operated length of waterways, which had been 59400km in 1913 (inter-war frontiers) had risen to 71600km in 1928 and then to 84000 in 1932, with the length of river suitable for night navigation falling from 33000km in 1913 to 29300km in 1928 and then rising to 47300km in 1932. By 1940 the corresponding figures were 107300 and 69600km.[51] Two big boat repair works were built on the Northern Dvina and Lower Volga.

Common-carrier waterway shipping produced 15.9 billion ton/kms in 1928, and 25 billion in 1932. This was below requirements. At times the disappointing performance seriously affected the economy. In summer 1931, for example, harvest delays were caused by non-delivery of fuel and lubricants. In the autumn of the same year, construction slowed down at Magnitogorsk and Kuznetsk because empty boats had not been made available for cement. Traffic in 1932 was actually less than 1931 (by one per cent for tonnage, 7 per cent for ton/kms). River transport continued to be badly organised, chaotic and unpredictable in its operations; much of the fleet was sent for unplanned repair at the height of the season. Workers tended to quit in mid-season and those that did not dispersed when the ice came.

In the later pre-war years there was an improvement in the supply of new craft, which tended to be larger than their predecessors; the USSR's 12000-ton barges were the world's biggest. But diesel dry-freight carriers, which had long been popular in Europe, only began to be built in batches in 1940. Moreover, new arrivals were insufficient to cover the number of vessels that reached the end of their depreciation life. The intention during the second five-year plan to increase barge capacity by 43 per cent was realised only to the extent of 11 per cent. Shortage of vessels was exacerbated by lengthening port delays. After 1937 ship deliveries fell off because of the move towards naval work. In the late 1930s the proportion of barges that were of metal construction was about the same as it had been in 1913, around one-tenth. Total barge construction was just about enough to cover attrition. The average age of barges was eight years in 1940, compared to 5.4 years in 1932.[52] For a wooden barge, ten years was an over-ripe old age. During this period canal rehabilitation, in many cases amounting to new construction, continued at an intensified pace. Although this activity did not demand much metal, it was not perhaps the most rewarding of investments for the labour, organisation, cement and enthusiasm that were put into it; the shipping lines were simply not in a position to take full advantage of it. The concept of a unified waterway network, adopted as a policy by the seventeenth party conference in January 1932 was a good one in principle, but premature in the 1930s. It was not realised in practice until well after the Second World War.

(F) Roads

Highway traffic was essentially short-distance traffic. Table 39 illustrates this. It also suggests that those tables so often used in Soviet textbooks, showing the percentage distribution of traffic between transport modes in terms of ton/kms, are misleading in their portrayal of highway traffic as a very minor component of the total. In terms of tonnage road traffic is the biggest. In 1940 total highway traffic in ton/kms amounted only to 8.9 billion ton/kms, compared to the railways' 415 billion. But in terms of tonnage the relationship was reversed, with road carrying 858.6 million tons and rail 592.6 million.

Both roads and vehicles fell far short of requirements. Most roads were unpaved, pitted, and corrugated, and imposed high maintenance costs and slow speeds on the vehicles using them. The mileage of hard-surface roads greatly increased during the 1930s (see Table 40). But they usually presented only a thin skin of tar and gravel. Few roads could be used in the thaw or in rainy periods.

Of the 143200km of hard road in 1940, 43800km were central state roads, 28000 republican, and the remainder regional or local.[53] During the 1930s a start was also made on inter-city (Moscow-Minsk and Moscow-Kiev) improved-surface roads.

In 1913 there were less than 9000 motor vehicles (lorries, cars, buses), but the import of about 25000 vehicles during the war meant that in mid-1919 the total of serviceable vehicles was as high as 13500. Imports recommenced in 1921, and in 1921–27 5275 vehicles were added, of which 4500 were imports,[54] but this influx was approximately balanced by write-offs. Total motor vehicles in 1928 were 16663.[55] With the establishment of a domestic motor industry this situation soon changed. At the beginning of 1933 there were 71029 vehicles, and this rose to 554500 at the beginning of 1938.[56]

Public-service freight vehicle stock rose by an annual average of 8.7 per cent 1933–38,[57] while traffic increased by a rather smaller percentage. Obviously, vehicle utilisation must have been falling, and this is confirmed by some scrappy archival figures quoted by Orlov.[58] The average daily percentage of total vehicles actually put to work, 55 in 1932, rose to 57.6 in 1934, but then fell to 47.6 in 1937. With average annual vehicle mileage the peak was in 1936 at 25,700 km, but then dropped drastically to 21,000 in 1937, which was less than the 22,000 logged in 1932. Moreover, these figures relate only to the bigger common-carrier enterprises; the general picture must have been even worse. Lack of spare parts and tyres seems to have been the major cause of this poor performance. In 1934 seven outer-cover tyres were produced per vehicle (which is about what would have been needed) but, perhaps as a result of defence requirements, this fell to 2.5 in 1937. The 24 workshops planned in the second five-year plan for major automotive repairs did not materialise. Other negative factors were the long times spent loading and unloading, which often amounted to 40 per cent of working time. Orlov calculates that in 1940 about three-fifths of highway traffic was still dependent on animal traction.[59]

Like air transport, highway transport emerged stronger from the Second World War. The sheer impossibility of the roads impelled the Red Army to take a hand, and its specialist road-building units ensured that during the war hard-surfaced roads actually grew by eight per cent (and improved roads by 40 per cent). The war also left a useful legacy of second-hand vehicles. All the same, in 1945 Soviet road transport lagged far behind that of other developed countries. The cost of this neglect could not easily be measured, but its consequences included the misuse of rail transport in the carriage of short distance freight, the spilling of agricultural traffic and other traffic entrusted to roller-coaster roads, and the economic sterilisation of countless enterprises during heavy rain and thaw.

(G) In retrospect

On the whole the transport system that emerged from industrialisation was powerful, but badly tuned. One plank of industrial policy, the wider geographic distribution of large-scale industries, had, in due course, been acknowledged as an unbearable strain on the under-capitalised railways. In this sense, and perhaps only in this sense, a tenuous argument could be made that transport policy failed. Another plank that turned out to be rotten, the hoped-for transfer of substantial freight from the railways to the waterways, was a blessing in a see-through disguise.

The history of Russian transport from the start of the First World War to the end of the second is a history of things not quite going to plan. It is therefore a history of achievement, because at the end of the period the basic transportation needs of the economy were nevertheless being met. A factor in this success was, above all, the resilience of railway transport and of the human spirit.

The government and its planners, in the end, also triumped, but it was a triumph with reservations. Having a rail and water transport system already in place, the government decided that the burden imposed by industrialisation could be handled with a disproportionately small allocation of capital resources, and this policy was an overall success despite a succession of misjudgments. Such misjudgments included, notably, the delay in acting to head off transport crises that were clearly threatening. Too little and too late is not an excessively harsh comment; having seen that squeezing worked, the government found it difficult to know when to stop.

There was a cost attached to this, paid by those branches of the economy that were held back by a transport service that was less prompt, reliable and generally helpful than it might have been.

Further reading

The classic study is H. Hunter, *Soviet Transportation Policy* (Cambridge, 1957). On the railways, see J. N. Westwood, *Soviet Locomotive Technology during Industrialisation* (London, 1982).

9 Technology and the transformation of the Soviet economy

Robert Lewis

Post-war discussions and studies of technological transfer and economic development have demonstrated that the advantages of being backward can be elusive. With a technical lag, new technology can apparently be borrowed 'off-the-peg'. But the new technology cannot automatically be easily assimilated into the lagging economy. Institutional structures, organisational styles, and the varying characteristics of inputs can all entail adaptations and modifications to ensure successful borrowing. Making these changes can often depend on the existence of domestic scientific and technical expertise. In this respect, the Soviet Union was in a relatively favourable position. It had inherited the beginnings of an industrial base from Tsarism. It also had a small but lively scientific and technological community to provide the foundations of a substantial R&D network. It therefore had the capacity to make the necessary modifications to imported technology.

The key area of technological failure was that, in spite of these advantages, the Soviet Union was not able to use large-scale technical borrowing to build the foundation of further widespread and domestically initiated technological change. Institutional factors, such as the organisational structures for research, development and innovation, are important in explaining this failure, but the political and social conditions of the late 1930s were such that it was not a propitious time to be attempting such a transformation.

(A) Under Tsarism

The technological level of the pre-revolutionary economy of the Russian Empire was far below that of the industrialised nations. Agricultural techniques were backward over most of the Empire, and much of industry, including oil, coal and many branches of engineering, was at a low technological level.[1] There were exceptions to this picture. Industrial growth had been closely linked with the involvement of foreign capital; foreign entrepreneurship and in some areas foreign firms had helped Russian industry to reach technical levels more comparable with those of the more industrial economies. For example, on the eve of the First World War, Ukrainian blast-furnaces had an average yearly output which matched that achieved in Western Europe, (although by this time, however, Western Europe lagged behind the United States in this respect).[2] In isolated fields the small Russian scientific and technical community had put the Empire near the cutting-edge of technological change. There was considerable domestic design activity in the field of railway locomotives.[3] While indigenous military technology was generally at a low level, Russian work on naval mines had put it ahead of the other Great Powers.[4] Russian aviation pioneers also made notable advances, despite problems with the supply of materials and components of the necessary quality.[5] But in many instances Russian inventors found it difficult to attract support for their activities.[6]

In the engineering industries as a whole, according to Gatrell, 'Russia resembled Germany or Britain in the preceding generation'. Modern factories in some fields 'coexisted with plant where manual skill and power continued to dominate'.[7] In aggregate terms, Tsarist economic growth stemmed largely from increases in the capital stock and an elastic supply of labour which resulted from rapid population growth. The transformation of the economy through the use of new technology played a relatively minor role.[8]

(B) Technological change, 1917–1928

The October Revolution of 1917 brought to power a government which saw modern science and technology as an important factor in economic progress and the building of a new, socialist, society.[9] Its leaders, and Lenin in particular, showed themselves to be receptive to proposals by the scientific community to establish their research activities on a firmer basis; the immediate post-revolutionary period saw the formation of the first research institutes in what was later to become a comprehensive system of Research and Development (R&D) organisations covering all branches of industry and the other areas of the economy.[10] Also, in spite of the background of civil war and economic turmoil, Russian technical specialists forged ahead with schemes for the technological transformation of the economy. The GOELRO plan for electrification is the most notable example.[11] With the initial backing of Lenin, Soviet Russia was also to embark on a pioneering programme in the development of diesel railway locomotives.[12]

However, technical development largely came to a halt between the revolution and the mid-1920s. The main task during the civil war was to keep plants operating in the face of overwhelming shortages. With the introduction of NEP, the immediate need was to bring back into operation factories which had stopped working during the previous period of hardship. There was correspondingly little industrial investment. The fixed capital of factories newly constructed or fundamentally reorganised between 1917 and 1926 amounted to less than 10 per cent of all fixed industrial capital.[13] The rising average age of the capital stock meant an increasing lag between the technical level of Soviet plants and those abroad, particularly those in the United States, where the post-war years brought a wave of new investment.

In those areas of the engineering industry which can be looked on as the equivalent of today's 'high-technology' branches, and consequently as one of the keys to industrial modernisation, recovery was further held up by the loss of imported engineering skills. A recent comparison of these branches in the pre-revolutionary period and the mid-1920s points to a performance which was not in general very impressive; the Soviet Union fell even further behind in the vast majority of the advanced technology sectors of engineering.[14] An exception was aeroplane construction where, as we have seen, alongside foreign involvement there was an indigenous pioneering base. However, even in this field the success in designing airframes contrasts with the failure of Soviet industry to provide an adequate supply of engines.[15]

In agriculture, post-revolutionary land redistribution, which saw the break-up of most of the large estates, increased the number of small subsistence holdings (see chapter 6). Thus the areas of technological backwardness in agriculture grew after the revolution. It is estimated that nearly one-half of all the ploughs in use in 1924 were still the primitive sokha (wooden scratch-plough).[16] In the middle of the 1920s, the yields on Soviet peasant farms were little better than those on estates in medieval England.[17]

The overall technological backwardness of the Soviet economy was reflected in estimates for the comparative consumption of energy which were published in the Gosplan control figures for the economy in 1927/28. Per capita mechanical energy consumption in the USSR was 15 per cent of the German, 9 per cent of the British and under 5 per cent of the United States level. Nearly 70 per cent of Soviet energy consumption was the result of the application of human and animal muscle power. In Germany, the UK and the United States, the shares were 14, 5 and 10 per cent respectively.[18]

(C) Technology and the industrialisation debate

The level of backwardness of the Soviet economy and post-revolutionary technological stagnation provided an important part of the background to the discussion of industrialisation and the future shape of the economy which took place from the mid-1920s. On virtually every important occasion when the industrialisation programme was discussed, reference was made to the need to modernise the economy and to adopt up-to-date technology. Such remarks became a cliché in all pronouncements on industrialisation.[19]

Discussions of technical modernisation were not limited to industry alone. Agricultural policy, too, became closely linked with increasing the stock of machinery and equipment available to the Soviet peasant. There was talk of the 'industrialisation' of agriculture.[20] 'Tractorisation' was seen as the key to raising the level of agricultural technology.[21] A Soviet government resolution claimed that an advantage of collective agriculture was that it enabled the 'application in the countryside of complex machines, which create the technical basis for large-scale agricultural production'.[22]

The Soviet discussions on future industrialisation were, of course, marked by heated debate about the pattern of future growth and the means by which it could be funded. Similarly, while there was agreement that the growing programme of capital investment would bring the opportunity to introduce new technological processes and new products, the more detailed technical questions were the subject of vigorous discussion. This discussion was also coloured by the growing problem of urban unemployment. The possibility of absorbing this seemingly excess labour into the newly developing industrial economy was also to be an issue.

In broad terms, Soviet experts and decision-makers saw the country as having a choice between American and European technology and production organisation. Underlying this view was the perception that, as a consequence of fundamental differences in the relative availability and, hence, price of the factors of production, the second half of the XIX century brought a diverging path of technological change in the United States and Britain (and by implication Europe).[23] In the United States, as a result of relative labour scarcity, labour costs were high in relation to the cost of capital, and entrepreneurs were encouraged to use machines rather than workers. Consequently a more capital-intensive technology was seen to have emerged, with the United States using more capital and less labour to produce a unit of output. The distinctive feature of United States industry which reflected this different combination of capital and labour was the use of mass-production techniques in the manufacture of long runs of standardised items. These were based on the widespread use of jigs and fixtures with a correspondingly low application of manual craftsmanship skills in the basic manufacturing processes. The European model, in contrast, made use of more general purpose machinery with a greater degree of craft skill. European production was seen as geared towards the manufacture of less specialised products in shorter runs. In general terms, it was this European model which the Soviet government had inherited from Tsarist Russia. It reflected the heavy involvement of European firms in pre-revolutionary manufacturing industry and the close links between Russian scientific and technical specialists and their western European, particularly German counterparts.[24]

One branch of industry where the debate about technology took place in very clear terms was textiles. In the review of the future development of the textile industry, it was felt that the Soviet Union had a clear choice between capital-intensive and labour-intensive technology. The Scientific and Technical Council for the industry came out strongly against the adoption of the approach and methods of the American textile industry. Its chairman Professor A. A. Fedotov, who was also head of the main textile research institute, pointed out that 'much that is wholly applicable, justified and profitable in America can turn out wholly inappropriate for the USSR'. He went on to say that for the Soviet Union capital was 'at a premium, it is very expensive and at the same time we have sufficiently large reserves of labour. But in America capital is cheap and labour expensive'. He considered that the Americans used capital wastefully by building cheap factories. For Fedotov the Americans built these cheap factories 'because they are rich and it matters little to them to throw away machines after a few years and to build the factory anew'. He pointed out that the Soviet Union could not afford to discard its equipment so quickly.[25]

However, this kind of choice was not always available. Given that the Soviet Union wanted to develop a large tractor industry to modernise its agriculture, it could rationally model itself only on American experience. In Europe, the production and utilisation of tractors lagged throughout the inter-war years. The European industry at this time was still in the era of small-scale, virtually handicraft production.[26] Modern tractor production was achieved in Europe only with the large-scale involvement of United States' firms. The high level of demand for tractors in the United States had led to a much more rapid expansion of the industry, bringing radical changes in production technology. American tractor manufacturers used their resources so much more productively that they required not only less labour but also less capital to produce a tractor than European firms.[27] Thus, notwithstanding its different capital/labour price ratio, the Soviet Union would be able to save both labour and capital by adopting American rather than European technology.

The arguments for or against a particular technological model were backed by data on such variables as investment per unit of output, manning levels and speed of machine operation. However, in the environment of the Soviet Union in the late 1920s, the final decision was often based on political rather than economic arguments. The Stalinist leadership and the specialists associated with it saw the United States as the growing economic world power and both came to identify American technology as really the only modern technology. 'Americanisation' became the watchword for future growth and modernisation.[28] The European model was seen as 'conservative'; on this view, Russia had greatly suffered from following the latter road.[29]

In the Western literature on economic development, there has been much discussion of the need for developing countries to adopt technology which is more appropriate for their particular pattern of the factors of production. The implication of the preceding discussion is that there were some Soviet industries in which a decision to adopt American technology was not economically justifiable. But the Western literature has also demonstrated the complexity of the choice.[30] In the Soviet case there are several arguments which point to the selection of American technology as economically justifiable.

First, once a decision had been taken to maximise industrial growth then the adoption of capital-intensive technology would result in a slower growth of wage payments and consumption and correspondingly release greater resources for reinvestment.[31]

Secondly, our discussion has so far been in terms of aggregates. But the distorting effects of treating capital and labour as homogeneous aggregates have been at the centre of much of the debate about technology. Above all, American technology enabled the use of a greater proportion of unskilled labour which was a definite advantage in Soviet conditions. For example, it was noted that German blast furnaces required skilled operating teams, while in the United States expensive skilled labour was, wherever feasible, replaced by equipment with an accompanying deskilling of the labour force.[32] With regard to capital, Field has argued that American technology, while relatively costly in terms of machinery, reduced stocks (working capital) by standardisation and specialisation.[33] Furthermore, fewer stocks require less factory space, so that there are economies in fixed structural capital as well.[34] It should also be noted that a reduction in the number of high-productivity machines which are needed for a given level of output will again mean savings in floor space.[35] Moreover, the flimsy wooden factories which Fedotov considered to be a sign of wealth may, in fact, be a way of saving capital in the longer run.[36]

Thus, it can be argued that, since American technology was much less capital-intensive than it appeared at first sight and since it economised on skilled labour, the decision to adopt American technology may not have been generally economically inefficient. But our current knowledge of the variables underlying technical choices made in the Soviet Union in the middle and late 1920s is not sufficient for firm conclusions to be drawn; in particular, it is difficult to assess the extent to which the long runs of output characteristic of American technology were feasible in Soviet conditions.

(D) Technological change, 1928–1940

Empirical studies by economists and economic historians point to a close correlation between the rate of growth of capital stock and the rapidity of technical change.[37] This relationship was indeed a feature of the Soviet Union in the years after 1928. Rapid increase in investment produced a radical restructuring of the economy which was accompanied by both product and process innovation.

The 1930s brought the production for the first time in the Soviet Union of a wide range of new products. Among these were motor cycles, wrist watches and cameras, and the new types of machine tools which were needed to produce these and other goods. In chemicals, there was the development of a plastics industry. In metallurgy, new types of high-quality and alloy steels and various non-ferrous metals were manufactured for the first time (see chapter 7).

The scale and efficiency with which existing products were made also greatly increased. In the iron and steel industry, by the end of the 1930s, the average size of a new blast-furnace was 40 per cent larger than those blown in at the end of the 1920s.[38] Open-hearth furnaces had also increased in size and their productivity as measured in the output of steel per square metre grew at an average annual rate of 3.3 per cent between 1928 and 1940.[39] Coal-mining saw the diffusion of explosives, pneumatic picks and cutters in the winning of coal.[40]

Some innovations were based on indigenous technical developments. In the aircraft industry Soviet engineers produced airframes which were in many cases comparable with foreign designs. Unrivalled tanks were developed in the later 1930s. The Soviet Union was also the first country to produce polybutadiene synthetic rubber. However, in most Soviet industries, technical change was closely linked with the introduction of foreign and particularly of American technology and production organisation. Leading United States' firms were closely involved in this process of technology transfer. Prominent examples included the new Nizhnii Novgorod (Gor'kii) car plant, which was based on Ford's River Rouge works, and the giant Magnitogorsk iron and steel combine (based on the United States Steel works at Gary, Indiana). These giant projects were the most notable examples of a widespread American and, to a lesser extent, European involvement.[41]

Notwithstanding these close and influential links, foreign technology was not adopted unchanged. Both the Soviet institutional structure and the different relative availability of the factors of production within the Soviet economy resulted in Soviet plants being far from mirror images of their American models. In his study of Soviet metal-working, Granick demonstrated that there was a consistent and widespread substitution of labour for capital.[42] On the surface, given the prices charged for the factors of production, this would appear illogical. No interest charges were levied on capital in the Soviet Union, while workers had to be paid wages, so economic logic pointed to a pressure to substitute capital for labour. However, capital was physically rationed and limited, while labour was generally available and the wage-bill a soft constraint. Plant managers therefore had an incentive to substitute labour for capital and to use their labour to produce items of capital 'in-house'.[43] Materials handling provides a striking example of the consequences of the relative shortage of capital and abundance of labour in the Soviet Union. In the American factories from the 1920s materials handling underwent a process of mechanisation, in Soviet plants in the 1930s it was largely undertaken by manual labour.[44] Similarly, while coal-winning was being mechanised, the driving of road-ways and underground transport continued to be the province of human and animal power.[45]

In cases where American technology was superior to European technology for all relative factor prices, the substitution of labour for capital could enable considerable gains in efficiency to be made. However, as Granick notes, institutional factors still resulted in a 'lavish' use of capital, despite its relative shortage and the associated tendencies noted above; in consequence, the capital-intensity of the metalworking industry was not optimal.[46] In the situation where there are two distinct choices available and the capital-intensive technology is chosen despite the prevailing capital/labour price ratio, there are still gains from substituting labour for capital, but they are much more limited.

The implication of this analysis is that the particular institutional structure and the (largely implicit) price relationships of the Soviet economy resulted in important differences in the Soviet version of an imported technology, in terms of both production organisation and factor inputs. At the same time there are other, more technical, reasons for making adaptations to foreign technology to fit Soviet circumstances. The inputs and outputs of the iron and steel industry can be considered relatively homogeneous compared with many other branches of industry, yet even here the differences in basic inputs can make it necessary to undertake research into their specific characteristics and to adapt imported plant and equipment. Soviet coals varied greatly in their coking characteristics from each other and from their American equivalents. Iron ore was similarly very diverse and in many cases quality was such that successful blast-furnace operation could only be achieved with the prior use of such processes as concentration and sintering.[47]

(E) Closing the technological gap?

The implication of much writing on Soviet economic development, both Western and Soviet, is that the vast programme of investment which was undertaken during the 1930s enabled the Soviet Union to close the technological gap which had existed between Tsarist Russia and the advanced industrial powers. While it is certainly true that between 1928 and 1940 technical development in the Soviet economy accelerated, such developments had first to offset the widening of the technological gap between the Soviet Union and Western countries due to the limited amount of Soviet technical change between 1917 and 1928. International comparisons are also made more difficult by differences in the economic experience and pace of change in the industrial economies over these years. There were perhaps twice as many tractors in the Soviet Union in 1940 as in the whole of Europe; but its tractor stock was only approximately one-third that of the United States.[48] Similarly, in 1940 there were only three continuous strip mills in the whole of Western Europe, while at this time five were apparently operating in the Soviet Union; but in the United States there were as many as 28. The European industry was lagging some 15 to 20 years behind its American competitor.[49]

One of the most successful areas of Soviet technological development was the aircraft industry. Although the supply of aero-engines remained a problem throughout the period after 1917, much Soviet airframe design was on a par with the world's best. Consequently, one study of the Soviet aircraft industry has concluded that 'between 1918 and the Second World War, the Soviet Union was closing the gap between its aircraft and those of the leading western industrial nations'.[50] In other areas of the armament industries, Soviet technology had also closed the gap or even become a leader. Tank production is one of the clearest examples. The T-34, introduced at the very end of the 1930s, was widely considered to be the world's best tank of its type.[51]

It seems clear that some closing of the technical gap was also taking place in other sectors of the economy. The two key sectors of the 'second industrial revolution' at the end of the nineteenth century were the electrical industry and science-based chemicals. In the former, where some momentum was maintained in the 1920s as a consequence of GOELRO, the 1930s brought a rapid expansion in the production of modern equipment.[52] Power-distribution technology also advanced. By 1940, the Soviet Union had caught up with Western Europe in high-voltage electricity transmission, although both lagged behind the United States.[53] In chemicals, too, the Soviet Union had some success in making inroads into the lag which had emerged before the First World War and which widened again between 1917 and 1928. There were some indigenous technical developments in the chemical industry, but in the main the Soviet Union imported foreign technology to boost the production of basic chemicals and to try to keep pace with fast-moving developments in fields such as plastics and artificial fibres. While the Soviet Union largely kept up with new developments in plastics, the technical modernisation and development of artificial fibres may have been less successful.[54]

Up-to-date machine tools were vital for the modernisation of many areas of industry and a key to the manufacture of high-quality armaments. In machine tools rapid strides were made after 1928; many new types were manufactured in the Soviet Union for the first time. By the end of the 1930s this industry was capable of producing any type of machine tool, and Soviet technologists were undertaking further development of previously imported technology and machines.[55]

The technological level of the transport system was far lower. In the long-established field of railway locomotive engineering the technological gap may even have widened in the inter-war years. The innovative programme in main-line dieselisation was stopped in the mid-1930s at a time when the role of the diesel was greatly increasing in the United States. As we have seen, there was little development in railway electrification. Furthermore, steam locomotive design also showed shortcomings, with new engines introduced in the 1930s having serious defects and 'built-in mediocrities'.[56] The urban transport systems of Soviet towns and cities generally appear to have been no more advanced in relative terms than those in pre-revolutionary times.[57]

Such examples may not be fully representative, but they do suggest that as a result of the industrialisation drive, the Soviet Union by 1941 had more than made good the lag which developed between the Revolution and the start of the first five- year plan in overall terms. Moreover, while Soviet *best-practice* technology was catching-up with the best practice abroad, the *average* technical level was no doubt closing the gap even more quickly. The rapid expansion of capital stock meant that the average Soviet machine or piece of equipment was younger than its equivalent abroad. In 1940 71 per cent of the Soviet machine-tool stock was less than 10 years old, compared with 28 per cent in the United States and 34 per cent in Germany.[58]

But the technological momentum achieved at the start of the 1930s was not maintained later in the decade.This was true even in some of the high-priority industries. A study of technology transfer in the automotive industry points out that the GAZ-AA truck, introduced at the new Gor'kii plant, had fallen behind comparable western models by 1936. While there were model changes, these were generally of a minor nature. The Gor'kii plant made no attempt to incorporate major innovations such as the V–8 engine which Ford had introduced in the United States in 1932, even though the Soviet Union had an option to acquire the engine technology from Ford.[59] In the mid-1930s a Soviet author claimed in the industrial newspaper that a widening gap was reemerging in various parts of electrical engineering and elsewhere.[60] He blamed this situation on the poor performance of the Soviet R&D network.

The ability to make the transition from imported to domestically improved and then independently-developed technology is a key to the achievement of technological dynamism. By the late 1930s the Soviet R&D system was extensive.[61] But its organisational structure, the pattern of provision of resources and facilities and the economic planning system all set up barriers to the widespread development of indigenous technology and its speedy innovation. During the first stage of the industrialisation drive, technical progress was imposed on the factories from the centre and it proved difficult to persuade it to bubble up from below.[62] Political factors were also involved. The purges of the late 1930s had a devastating effect on many parts of the Soviet scientific and technical community. The political climate also resulted in a drastic reduction in the international links vital for progress in science and technology. It also encouraged people to be cautious rather than innovative.[63] Various areas of Soviet scientific and technical life were to fall under the control of party-supported pseudo-scientists such as the plant biologist T. D. Lysenko.

Thus technological performance may be summarised as follows. After 1928 Soviet technology underwent a virtual revolution in many areas. But by the end of the 1930s the Soviet Union had started to slide into a situation where, across much of the economy, substantial further technical modernisation only occurred piecemeal and intermittently in response to central drives to modernise particular areas.

(F) Technology and Soviet economic growth

Technological change played a very minor part in the recovery of the economy during the 1920s. The rapid growth of output from the trough of the civil war was largely based on the restoration and return to full production of already existing capital. In assessing the role of technological change as a factor in Soviet economic development in the inter-war years we will therefore concentrate on the years of rapid technical transformation after 1928.

Production function

A production function shows the presumed relationship between inputs and outputs. The *Cobb-Douglas* production function is a form commonly used for applied purposes, mainly because it is easily handled mathemetically. The most important assumptions are that products are homogeneous; inputs are also homogeneous and can be substituted for each other within certain limits. There are diminishing returns to each input taken separately, and no economies of scale.

An important aspect of the production function approach is the concept of *total factor inputs*. This total is the weighted sum of the capital, labour, and land used up in production (the weights are sometimes estimated, but are frequently just guessed or assumed). Total output, divided by total factor inputs, is called *total factor productivity* (TFP). And the growth of TFP – the 'residual' left after subtracting the growth of total factor inputs from the growth of total output – is usually viewed as *that part of economic growth attributable to increased efficiency of technology and resource allocation.*

Aggregate studies of the effect of technical change with the aid of production functions (see Box) are based on isolating that part of overall growth which is not explained by increases in the use of the factors of production – land, labour and capital. However, the residual which is calculated in this way may include various non-technological factors. For example, the quality of the inputs may change. Rising educational levels improve the quality of labour and lead to increased labour productivity. Labour quality can also improve as a result of growing experience. By 1940 the average Soviet shop-floor worker, who had been a peasant in the 1920s, was a better worker than he or she had been ten years before. Similarly, organisational changes unrelated to technological innovation may result in improved productivity.

Furthermore, the measurement of total factor productivity growth in the Soviet context brings its own problems. To produce an index for the growth of inputs into the economy, we need to know the shares of the individual factors of production in national income. The lack of a market-based measure of the marginal product of capital has meant that economists have had to make a series of assumptions. The Cobb-Douglas production function (see Box) is often taken as applicable to the Soviet case in these studies. Estimates of total factor productivity have relied heavily on the work of Bergson and make use of two of his key assumptions.[64] First, it is usually

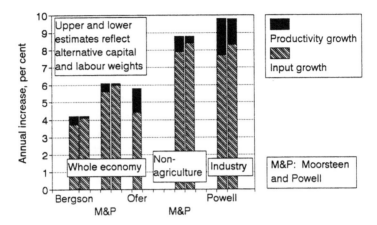

Figure 15 Accounting for GNP growth, 1928–1940. *Source:* table 41.

assumed that rent on agricultural land can be set at 40 per cent of Soviet farm labour income.[65] Secondly, Bergson suggested upper and lower boundaries for the rate of return on fixed capital, namely 8 per cent and 20 per cent, based on United States' experience. These assumptions produce alternative estimates of 80.5 per cent and 70.4 per cent for the share of labour in national product in 1937, capital (including land) comprising the remaining 19.5 per cent and 29.6 per cent respectively.[66] More recent writing points to the higher figure as being more appropriate.[67]

Figure 15 and Table 41 present some of the existing estimates for the years 1928–1940 using 1937 prices for valuing both GNP and the capital stock. They suggest that the major influence on growth was an increasing mobilisation of capital and labour. The contribution of technological progress and the other factors which are incorporated in the residual appears to have been small. Even in the estimate of Ofer, it only explains 24 per cent of growth, and the estimates of Bergson and Moorsteen and Powell are much lower. The application of the lower 8 per cent interest rate lessens the importance of capital as an input; correspondingly, there is a relative leap in the figure for total factor productivity, but its absolute level still remains low. Recent recalculations of Soviet growth rates by Khanin also point to a minimal role for technical progress in growth. He considers that both the productivity of fixed capital and output per unit of raw material input fell between 1929 and 1941. Depending on the weights used to produce an index of total inputs, the growth of labour productivity may not have been large enough to offset this decline and total factor productivity may have also fallen.[68]

When compared with Gregory's estimate for the Tsarist period, these figures suggest that simple increases in labour and capital were more important for Soviet growth between 1928 and 1940 than they had been for Tsarist growth between 1885 and 1913.[69] With the exception of Ofer, these estimates are also significantly lower than those for the major industrialised countries during the period 1913–1950, and for Germany, the United Kingdom and the United States during the main phase of their industrialisation.[70]

However, estimates of total factor productivity for the economy as a whole may conceal a wide variation in the role of technology in the different areas of the economy. The methods of calculating output in such areas as services and housing tend effectively to exclude the possibility of productivity growth.[71] Further, radical technical modernisation did not reach all parts of the Soviet economy to the same extent. As can be seen from part B of Table 41, Moorsteen and Powell measured total factor productivity for broad sectors of the economy. Their figures suggest, somewhat surprisingly, that total factor productivity growth in the non-agricultural and non-residential area of the economy was lower than for the economy as a whole. But, in a calculation based on industry alone, Powell produced the higher but still not impressive result that total factor productivity contributed 15–21 per cent to output growth. In an earlier study using a different approach Seton estimated that in large-scale industry the share of total factor productivity was 10–12 per cent over the same period.[72]

In any study of productivity movements, the choice of period can have an important effect. Economic historians analysing Western economies are careful to try to choose years which lie at a comparable level on the business cycle as the beginning and end of a period, so that there is no difference in the extent to which the capital stock is being used. The Soviet administrative planning system also brought with it a cyclical pattern.[73] In particular, the last years of the 1930s saw a virtual stagnation in many basic industries, and a slowing in the rate of economic growth. This has been attributed by economic historians both to the purges and to the effects on the industrial structure of a massive reorganisation onto a war footing. The implication that this was also a time during which the Soviet economy operated less efficiently is borne out at the aggregate level by the quantitative evidence. As can be seen from Table 42, for the period 1928–1937 the contribution of total factor productivity to economic growth looks much more important, representing 19–29 per cent of GNP growth. However, Powell's estimate of the movement in productivity in the industrial sector shows very little change between the two periods: this suggests that the causes of productivity slowdown were to be found elsewhere in the economy. Katz attempted a quantitative analysis of the effects of the purges and war preparations on industrial performance; as a by-product of her analysis she suggested that, in the late 1930s, the marginal productivity of labour may have risen, while the marginal productivity of capital declined.[74] Within industry it would appear likely that gains in efficiency in the expanding armaments sector offset any decline in the basic industrial branches.

In assessing the role of technology in the Soviet economy, we should look not only at rates of productivity growth, but also at the absolute level of productivity. Unfortunately, there are no available comparative estimates for the level of total factor productivity in the Soviet Union and the industrialised economies. Work by Bergson on the comparative perform-ance of the Soviet Union after the Second World War has suggested that there is a close correlation between the level of total factor productivity and national income per employed worker; this correlation is a reflection of the large weight usually attached to labour in the underlying production func-tion.[75] Thus, it is likely that the relative levels of GDP per head reported in chapter 3 provide a guide to relative total factor productivity in the Soviet Union.

While there is a considerable margin of error surrounding all these estimates, it seems reasonable to conclude that the role of technology in Soviet economic growth during the years after 1928 was not as great as might be assumed from a listing of the technical developments of the period. In the context of the modernisation which undoubtedly took place in the Soviet industrial structure, the suggestion that technology may not have played the crucial role in Soviet economic growth may seem surprising. There are five features of economic and technical change in the period which support the view that the role of technical progress was not decisive.

First, the most modern technology was concentrated in certain sectors. In fields which had low priority the pace of technical change was not so fast. For example, the building materials industry produced bricks and timber rather than reinforced concrete.[76] On the railways, as we have seen, the innovative diesel developments were shelved and the total length of elec-trified line in 1941 was only 1870km.[77] The Soviet Union retained funda-mentally a steam railway system. The large agricultural sector remained backward (see chapter 6).

Secondly, the permeation of modern technology was limited in extent, even in those branches which had been given priority in the modernisation process. As we have noted, many of the auxiliary processes in metalworking did not experience the technical revolution which occurred in the basic production processes. The gains from introducing new technology were offset by the overwhelming pressure for vertical integration, which stemmed from the institutional structure of the economy. While the basic production process of Soviet engineering plants approached American levels of productivity, at the same time they were producing a much larger proportion of their semi-fabricates and components than their role models. At the end of the 1930s about one-fifth of Soviet steel was produced in engineering plants.[78] Rolled steel produced 'in house' met as much as one-third of the needs of these plants.[79] Plants also undertook small-scale production of components and spare parts. In the Soviet automotive industry in 1937 roughly one-half of the workers were employed in auxiliary shops.[80] Much of this production was conducted at a relatively low technical level.[81]

Thirdly, productivity gains were adversely affected by overmanning in areas of Soviet industry.[82]

Fourthly, if the surge in productivity growth which flowed from the introduction of new plant and equipment was to be maintained, the Soviet Union would have needed to use imported technology as a base for further development. In some fields, such as the key area of machine tools,[83] a transfer to Soviet technical resources was partially achieved. But even here, as in other areas, the Soviet Union was showing signs of a new retardation, as further development took place abroad. The target for 'catching-up and surpassing' was moving ahead; as Cooper notes, '"keeping" up became a real problem'.[84]

Finally, in some branches there may have been diseconomies stemming from the scale adopted for the newly introduced technology. While the very large scale of some of the new plant and factories produced 'technical' economies of scale, such gains may have been outweighed by 'organisational' diseconomies; these plants were beyond the size at which Soviet managers could run them efficiently.[85] 'Gigantomania' was eventually seen as a serious problem.[86] Katz' research has provided some econometric support for this view, as her results suggest that Soviet industry suffered from decreasing returns to scale.[87]

Further reading

On science policy and results in Soviet economic development see R. A. Lewis, *Science and Industrialisation in the USSR* (London and Basingstoke, 1979). A standard work on industrial technology, sharing a strong historical perspective, is R. Amann, J. M. Cooper and R. W. Davies (eds.), *The Technological Level of Soviet Industry* (New Haven and London, 1977). The role of foreign technology is strongly stressed in two volumes by A. C. Sutton, *Western Technology and Soviet Economic Development, 1917–1930* (Stanford, 1968), and *Western Technology and Soviet Economic Development, 1930–1945* (Stanford, 1971); see also G. D. Holliday, *Technology Transfer to the USSR, 1928–1937 and 1966–1975* (Boulder, Colorado, 1979). The evaluation of Soviet factor productivity is pursued by A. Bergson, *Planning and Productivity under Soviet Socialism* (New York, 1968), and more recently by G. Ofer, 'Soviet Economic Growth: 1928–1985', *Journal of Economic Literature*, xxv (1987).

10 Foreign economic relations

Robert Lewis

The foreign economic relations of the Soviet Union took a very different course from those of the Russian Empire in the decades before the revolution. While world trade as a whole was depressed in the inter-war years, the trade of the new Soviet state was at an even lower level. On the eve of the Second World War, the volume of Soviet foreign trade amounted to only about one half of its level in 1913. The volume of exports reached the 1913 level of imports only in the single year 1931. During this period trade and other foreign economic relations were also marked by their instability. An important reason for this was the fluctuations in Soviet international political relations. It is also clear, however, that the response of the state to the effects of political changes on the prospects for economic relations with the capitalist world was tempered by a 'love-hate' relationship. The need for trade to acquire modern technology was recognised, but there were worries that international links could be manipulated by foreign business to the detriment of the Soviet Union. The import of foreign technology, and the effort to obtain adequate exports to finance this import, was a crucial if intermittent feature of Soviet economic development in the inter-war years.

(A) Under Tsarism

The foreign sector played an important role in the development of Tsarist Russia during its modernisation push in the years before the First World War. The patterns of trade and international payments were determined by the economic structure and by state tariff and foreign exchange policy.

As might be expected from the large role of agriculture in the Russian economy in the second half of the nineteenth century, the comparative advantage of the Tsarist Empire lay in primary products. Exports came overwhelmingly from this sector, mainly foodstuffs and forest products. This is reflected in Figure 16 and Table 46.

In contrast to exports, the pattern of imports was more varied and reflected the status of Tsarist Russia as a newly industrialising economy (see Figure 17 and Table 46). Modern machinery was bought abroad for investment in

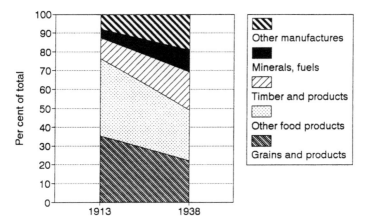

Figure 16   The structure of exports, 1913 and 1938. *Source:* tables 46, 47.

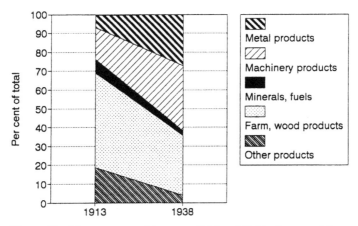

Figure 17   The structure of imports, 1913 and 1938. *Source:* tables 46, 47.

the developing branches of industry, and a substantial volume of industrial raw materials was imported, particularly cotton, wool and silk for the expanding textile industry. Manufactured consumer goods were also imported for the growing domestic market.

The major trading partner was Germany which purchased nearly 30 per cent of Russian exports and was the source of a massive 47.5 per cent of imports. Britain, which was the second most important market, lagged well behind; unlike Germany, it ran a trade deficit with Russia, buying about 18 per cent of Russian exports, but providing less than 13 per cent of imports.[1]

The government pursued an active trade policy within the framework of a market mechanism. High tariff barriers on many industrial products encouraged Russian production at costs higher than the price of imports in key sectors such as iron and steel – import substitution industrialisation. The tariff policy also encouraged direct foreign investment into developing industry. Foreign funds and expertise made a vital contribution to the establishment of a modern industrial core.[2] Currency stability was an important prerequisite for foreign businesses, and was enshrined in the adoption of the Gold Standard and a fixed exchange rate in 1897. The stable currency also facilitated the borrowing of funds abroad by the government itself to support expenditure in areas such as railway construction.

In the years before the First World War, the servicing of foreign-owned state debt and the remittance of profits by foreign investors in the Russian economy consequently became important items in foreign economic relations. This net outflow of invisibles had to be funded through the maintenance of an export surplus, and the balance of commodity trade was generally very favourable. Between 1900 and 1913 the value of imports was on average only about 75 per cent of export earnings.[3] However, as can be seen from Table 43, in the years after 1900 a sum equivalent to the whole of this trade surplus was being remitted abroad every year in payment for previous capital borrowing and as returns on foreign direct investment. Consequently, when other items, such as the difference between expenditures by Russian tourists abroad and receipts from visitors to Russia, are taken into account, there was a sizeable deficit in the balance of payments. This gap had to be funded through further borrowing. It has been suggested that, from the start of the 1890s, Russia was in the same position as many Third World countries in more recent times: the cost of servicing its past debt, together with the outflows of profits, exceeded imports of new capital (see Table 43).

(B) War, revolution and civil war

With the outbreak of war in 1914, the Russian balance of trade went sharply into deficit. At a time when imports were vital for the viability of the war economy, exports collapsed. Russia was at war with its major trading partner. In 1913, as we have seen, Germany had taken approximately 30 per cent of her exports. The Allies supplied imports for the war effort, and consequently the Russian foreign debt rose sharply. This was a factor behind a considerable tightening by the state of its controls over foreign trade and the foreign exchange market. The Provisional Government during its brief existence attempted to increase controls still further.[4]

The October Revolution set in train events which disrupted foreign trade

---

Problems of Soviet foreign trade statistics

Comparisons of Russian and Soviet trade values and volumes are made difficult by the boundary changes which took place after the Revolution. Dohan, who has done the most detailed work by a western scholar on foreign trade in the period spanning the Revolution, considers that 'it is not clear that the overall volume of pre-1913 trade of the territory destined to become the USSR was significantly different than that of Tsarist Russia' (Dohan (1976), 234). In presenting the quantitative picture of Soviet trade, the situation is complicated by the fact that one of the major statistical sources for the inter-war years (*Vneshnyaya torgovlya* (1960)) excludes trade with Estonia, Latvia and Lithuania – in 1928 these countries took 8.5 per cent of Soviet exports and provided 0.9 per cent of imports, in 1937 trade with them was 1.7 per cent of both exports and imports (*Vneshnyaya torgovlya* (1939), 11, 27, 31).

It should also be noted the published Soviet foreign trade figures are given in rubles based on the gold value of the ruble ('foreign trade rubles'); this was changed in 1936 and 1937, and conversion ratios are used to produce a consistent series for the whole of the period (see *Vneshnyaya torgovlya* (1960), 9; a fuller discussion of foreign trade rubles can be found in Dohan (1969), 701–708). As a consequence of the inconvertibility of the ruble and the government's monopoly over foreign exchange transactions there was no direct link between foreign trade rubles and the domestic currency.

---

and foreign economic relations more than virtually any other part of the economy. With the blockade of the new Soviet republic, the allied intervention and the civil war, foreign trade almost totally disappeared. In 1918, 1919 and 1920 trade turnover was less than 1 per cent of its 1913 level.[5] At the same time the national and international structures which had organised and supported trade were destroyed. Shortly after the revolution a system of export and import licences was introduced; this greatly increased the state control over trade which had been inherited from the previous regime.[6] In January 1918 the debts of the Tsarist government were repudiated for economic as well as ideological reasons. Then on 22 April 1918 foreign trade was nationalised.[7] This policy was adopted at that time partly in order to evade the economic conditions of the Treaty of Brest-Litovsk, which obliged the new Soviet republic neither to raise tariffs against German goods, nor to impose prohibitions or export duties on the export of forest products or ores.[8] After nationalisation foreign trade was controlled by a separate state agency, which was sometimes part of a People's Commissariat concerned with both internal and external trade, but for most of the Soviet period was a separate commissariat. Foreign-owned property and firms were expropriated and nationalised as part of the general process of establishing state control over the economy which took place during this period.

(C) The NEP years

The inauguration of NEP as a policy for the rebuilding of a shattered economy and the partial return to a market economy had important consequences for foreign trade. The possibility of restoring foreign trade emerged initially in 1920 with the removal of the blockade; this was followed by the dispatch of some trade delegations abroad. However, it was the signing of a trade agreement with the United Kingdom in 1921 which marked the start of a return to more normal international economic relations. Within the Soviet government there was a heated debate on whether a foreign trade monopoly was the right policy for the new times. Much was made of the ineffectiveness of the Commissariat for Foreign Trade. It was argued, for example, that those bodies which were directly responsible for industrial production were much better qualified to buy and sell abroad than the staff of the foreign trade commissariat. Lenin's support for the monopoly ensured its survival. However, while trade remained fully under state control, the power to engage in foreign trade was delegated to a number of other state and cooperative bodies and some joint ventures were established for this purpose.[9] These moves severely dented the authority of the Commissariat of Foreign Trade. Nevertheless, the difference from the Tsarist economy remained fundamental: control over trade was exerted not by the use of tariffs within a basically market system, but through direct controls over the flow of trade and currency exchange. Plans were drawn up for exports and imports.[10] The Soviet government also sought to attract foreign industry back into the economy and recognised that economic recovery needed technological help from abroad.[11] As early as November 1920, before the launching of NEP, a decree was passed on 'concessions'; these resembled the joint ventures which have been encouraged in the Soviet Union since the mid-1980s. The decree promised long-term agreements under which foreign participants would be allowed to invest in the country and gain a full return on their investments, with the ability to repatriate part of the profits. There was a guarantee that no unilateral changes would be made in agreements.[12]

Under NEP foreign trade, like other sectors of the economy, recovered from the nadir of the years of War Communism. However, in foreign trade it proved particularly difficult to rebuild or replace structures and economic mechanisms which had been destroyed, and to reestablish confidence. The balance of trade was helped by the ability of the state to limit the import of consumer goods; in any case, the demand for such imports declined as a consequence of the large-scale emigration after the revolution of the better-off stratum in society which had the highest propensity to consume imports, and the dramatic decline in wealth of those who remained. These were also the people who had been spending money on the foreign holidays which appeared as a substantial negative item in the pre-war balance of payments (see Table 43). With the removal of this large net outflow, the repudiation of the Tsarist foreign debt and the nationalisation of foreign property, there was clearly less need to run a large balance of trade surplus than in 1913.

Since the government sought to avoid a trade deficit, the recovery of trade was regulated by the ability of the economy to generate export products. As can be seen from Figure 16, this meant not only grain, the largest single export item before the war, but also the wide variety of other agricultural products which had played an important role in the trade of the Russian Empire. The overwhelming proportion of these products came from the livestock sector. Thus the performance of the foreign trade sector was closely tied to government policy towards the peasantry and agriculture. Restoration of trade to anything near pre-1914 levels was dependent on the ability, first, to restore the level of agricultural output, secondly, to raise the level of grain marketings to pre-war levels, and thirdly to reestablish fully the export of livestock and livestock products. However, agricultural policy was not able to bring about this recovery. As can be seen from Figure 18 and Tables 48–9, there was a sudden surge in grain exports in 1923/24 and a trade surplus was achieved. However, the optimism which this engendered was shortlived. In the following year 1924/25, the poor harvest resulted in a sharp curtailing of grain exports and the total volume of exports correspondingly fell. Precious foreign exchange was also spent on grain imports in the economic year to stem rising prices.[13] Other agricultural exports were not as volatile, but also remained considerably below pre-war levels. An important factor in the lack of agricultural exports was the increase in subsistence farming across the whole of the agricultural sector, a consequence of the redistribution of land after the revolution (see chapter 6).

The balance of payments problems which resulted from the need to import grain after the 1924 harvest had important consequences for the currency: the ruble, which was to some extent convertible after the currency reform early in 1924, became non-convertible. In March 1926 the financial authorities ceased to exchange the ruble for gold or foreign currency and in July of the same year a decree was passed which prohibited the export of Soviet currency. Thus the Soviet Union finally uncoupled itself from

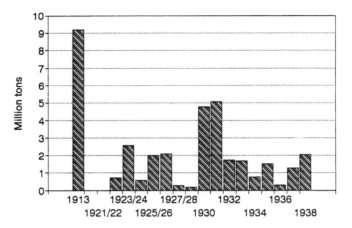

Figure 18   Soviet grain exports, 1913–1938. *Source:* table 48.

international financial markets.[14]

Against this background it was not surprising that foreign trade recovered more slowly than the other sectors of the economy. By 1927/28 exports were only about 40 per cent of the 1913 level (see Table 51). In that year a poor harvest and growing grain collection difficulties led the state to increase the exports of other primary products, despite some resulting problems for the domestic economy.[15] The continuing struggle to increase exports in a situation where home demand tended to absorb production meant that the central authorities played a key role in the allocation of the resulting limited import capacity. There is some evidence to suggest that the problems which were experienced with trade in 1927 and 1928 led to serious consideration of the possibility of relaxing the foreign trade monopoly at a time when international relations appeared to be improving.[16]

Over the whole of the period of NEP the Soviet balance of payments was under pressure. As can be seen from Table 49, in surplus years the positive balances of trade were small; they were considerably outweighed by the size of the intervening deficits. This gap was bridged by exports of precious metals and by borrowing in the form of short and medium-term trade credits. Between 1924/25 and 1926/27 nearly 60 per cent of the deficit was funded by borrowing. However, there were clearly problems in continually increasing short-term borrowing in an uncertain political situation. When the balance of payments slumped from a virtually neutral position in 1926/27 to a large deficit in 1927/28 as a result of the trade difficulties of that year, the government responded by dramatically increasing gold exports to 145 million rubles; total exports of precious metals were worth 155 million rubles (see Table 45). But, with the deficit estimated at 247 million rubles, borrowing also increased sharply. The total foreign reserves of the Soviet Union may have fallen by 30 per cent in the single year 1928. Clearly such a haemorrhage could not often be repeated. If exports fell below desired levels, or the terms of trade moved against the Soviet Union, such problems and a serious dislocation in foreign trade could recur. This provided a strong argument for the adoption of a policy of industrialisation through import substitution.[17]

The policy of encouraging concessions was even less successful than the attempt to encourage the recovery of foreign trade. Under one of the best known of these agreements, the Swedish SKF firm took back the important Moscow bearing factory in 1921. But in most cases western industrialists were too wary to make long-term investments in Soviet industry, and the Soviet authorities themselves were not wholeheartedly behind the policy. The number of concession agreements remained relatively small;[18] the majority were in trade, and in the extraction and export of raw materials such as timber and mineral ores, activities which guaranteed some short-term return.[19] The output of concessions was reported as less than 1 per cent of total industrial production in 1926/27; but they were responsible for 40 per cent of the output of manganese ore (primarily from the Harriman concession in the Caucasus), and one-third of the output of silver and lead ores.[20] Further, these data did not apparently include the gold-mining industry, in which the British-owned concession, Lena Goldfields, played an important role. In 1925, under a 30-year agreement, it took over the area of eastern Siberia which it had mined before the Revolution. In the next few years it provided about one-third of Soviet output of this crucial metal.[21] By the summer of 1927, however, approximately one-third of the concessions which had been taken up had been discontinued or were in the process of closure.[22] At the XV Party Congress Mikoyan noted the failure of the concessions policy to live up to expectations.[23]

In terms of both the expansion of trade and the import of technical expertise, the years between 1921 and 1927 were disappointing. But it was still generally recognised that the foreign sector had a key role to play in economic development. The various views expressed in the industriali-sation debate of the mid-1920s differed greatly on many aspects of possible future development. As regards trade, widely differing considerations were advanced in support of the general belief in the importance of foreign trade. Those such as Shanin and Sokolnikov who supported the encouragement of agricultural investment saw agricultural exports as the way of providing the means to modernise industry through the import of machinery and equip-ment. Comparative advantage would mean that these capital goods would be obtained at less resource cost than if they were to be produced at home.[24] At the other end of the political spectrum, the Left-wing economist

Preobrazhenskii foresaw that a recovery in agricultural exports could be utilised through the foreign trade monopoly to increase the possibilities of primitive socialist accumulation from the peasant sector.[25] The resolution of the XV Party Congress on the five-year plan considered it 'necessary in the field of international relations to proceed on the basis of very wide inter-connections, since these inter-connections (the organisation of foreign trade, of foreign capital, of concessions, the attraction of foreign technical forces, etc.) increase the economic strength of the USSR'.[26] However, the goal was not to establish the old pattern of trade based on a comparative advantage in agricultural and other primary products, but instead to orient trade towards an industrialisation programme, and to reduce the imports of consumer goods and other manufactures. This approach also reflected the continuing difficulties in mobilising exports under NEP. But despite Mikoyan's remarks to the Congress about the failings of the concessions policy, the Soviet government was apparently not prepared wholly to accept that they had no real future. In the summer of 1928, when the Council of People's Commissars discussed the report of its Chief Concessions Committee, it looked to a future in which concessions would still have a role, and approved a 'sales drive' to attract foreign investors to a wide range of economic activity.[27]

(D) The plan era, 1929–1941

(i) *The first five-year plan, October 1928–December 1932*

The first five-year plan targets for foreign trade reflected the optimism of the XV Party Congress rather than the realities of the trade situation of 1927/28. According to the plan, exports were to grow steadily to reach two and one-half times their 1927/28 level during its last year. Grain exports should increase to 5–8 million tons. Imports would initially be cut in order to pay off the deficit from 1927/28, but would then rise. It was envisaged that there would be a trade surplus in each year of the plan. Reaching the goals of the optimum (higher) variant of the plan was seen as linked to 'the mobilisation of export resources, the activisation of the concessions' policy and to a policy of attracting foreign credits'.[28]

In the event, all these desires proved to varying degrees unrealisable. The key feature of the international economy in the years of world depression after 1929 was falling prices, rising controls and declining trade. The volume of world trade fell by one quarter between 1929 and 1932.[29] In particular, the problems which had been building up in the world grain market in the 1920s finally came to a head. Rising post-war production coupled with virtually static international demand resulted in excess supply.

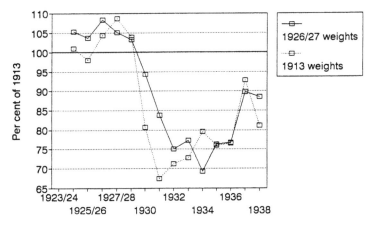

Figure 19   Soviet international terms of trade, 1924/25–1938. *Source:*
table 50.

By the middle of 1929 roughly the equivalent of a year's grain exports was in
store around the world.[30] With the onset of the depression grain prices
collapsed, falling much more quickly than those of industrial goods. This
picture was soon to be repeated for a wide variety of primary products. The
consequence for the Soviet Union, as for her neighbours in Eastern Europe,
was a sharp decline in the terms of trade. By 1932 they had fallen to about 70
per cent of their 1927/28 level (see Figure 19 and Table 50). Changes in the
terms of trade can reflect the rates of productivity growth within an
economy. Falling export prices may reflect increased efficiency in production in the export sector. In these circumstances, despite deteriorating
terms of trade, an economy does not have to commit more resources to
maintain its level of imports. This was certainly not the case in the Soviet
Union at this time. There is no doubt that world price changes imposed an
increased burden on the economy and limited Soviet ability to purchase
abroad the equipment and machinery which was needed for the industrialisation drive.

   A country can respond in three ways to such a deterioration of the terms
of trade; it can cut imports to maintain a balance at the new lower level of
export earnings; it can seek to raise exports; and it can borrow. Policy
adjustments, however, take time. In the short term the likelihood is that
the severe deterioration in the terms of trade will result in the accumulation of debt as the balance of trade goes into deficit. In the Soviet case
the state monopoly of trade potentially gave the government more control
over a worsening trade position. And in 1930, with the growing
centralisation of all economic management, control of foreign trade was

strengthened with the elimination of a multiplicity of foreign trade organisations.[31]

The initial response of the Soviet government was to seek to expand exports above the levels envisaged in the plan, so as to maintain large-scale imports for the industrialisation drive.[32] In particular, grain exports were increased (see Figure 18 and Table 48). But the price fall was extremely damaging. In 1930 the Soviet Union exported nearly two-and-one-third times as much grain as in 1926/27, but it received only about 6 per cent more proceeds from these sales.[33] The resolution of the sixteenth Party Congress in July 1930 on the progress of the five-year plan called for special attention to be paid to the development of the export branches of industry.[34] As a result of these efforts, the volume of Soviet trade continued to rise while world trade volume was falling; it reached its peak for the inter-war years in 1931 (see Table 51). However, it was impossible to squeeze out enough exports from the economy. The positive balance of trade which was envisaged in the five-year plan could not be achieved at the planned or even the existing import levels. Government and party statements began to refer to the need for import substitution;[35] and substantial cuts were made in imports. These fell most heavily on the consumer and the consumer goods sector. For example, imports of wool declined by 40 per cent between 1929 and 1932; in the latter year they were less than a quarter of the level envisaged in the five-year plan.[36] In the same period, imports of cotton cloth fell from over 10.5 million metres to a little over 800,000 metres. But these measures were not sufficient to shield heavy industry from the need to reduce imports. Imports of steel were slashed from the beginning of 1932, even though they were desperately needed to compensate for a shortfall in supply, resulting from the failure of the investment and expansion programme for the domestic iron and steel industry. There was an immediate impact on major industrial projects.[37] The government also cut payments in foreign currency to foreign specialists.[38]

In the short term trade flows could not be adjusted adequately. After a small surplus in 1929, the Soviet balance of trade was in deficit for the rest of the first five-year plan (see Table 49). This resulted in serious balance of payments problems. As we have seen above, the years since the mid-1920s had already seen an increase in foreign debt in spite of the export of precious metals. In the early 1930s gold exports were again increased, but further short-term borrowing was required to plug the gap in the balance of payments. The ability to import became closely linked with the ability to obtain credits. It had been envisaged that short-term debt would disappear; in the changed circumstances it increased sharply. Soviet foreign debt more than doubled between 1929 and 1931 (see Table 45). This debt was expensive, and the direct cost of borrowing was accompanied by the padding of the prices of goods bought on credit.[39] Some relief was provided by the devaluation of sterling after the United Kingdom withdrew from the Gold Standard in October 1931. By the end of the year the value of sterling had fallen by 30 per cent. This reduced the gold value of Soviet debt, much of which was payable in sterling.

Germany and the United States, the major suppliers of industrial equipment, increased their share of Soviet imports (see Table 52). This led to major problems in trade relations with these countries, especially with the United States. In 1929, 1930 and 1931 exports to the US ran at only 20 per cent of the value of imports from that source. Soviet efforts to increase exports to the US met with vocal campaigns against dumping; in response, the Soviet Union attempted to keep tight control over the level of imports from the United States. Credits were also more difficult to obtain from the United States.[40] As can be seen from Table 52 all these factors were reflected in a sharp drop in the United States' share of Soviet imports in 1932. The direction of Soviet trade was determined by the availability of credit rather than by competitive factors. In view of the radical change in the world economy, the failure of the first five-year plan for foreign trade was not surprising.

In 1929, as we have seen, the five-year plan favoured further concessions and foreign loans. But this did not reflect the policy changes which were already underway. In practice the place of concessions was soon taken by a policy of directly purchasing foreign technical assistance. Over the next few years the major concessions agreements were wound up or repudiated. The important Harriman manganese concession was ended in 1928, a result of a combination of high production costs, falling prices, and friction with the authorities. In 1930 SKF again lost control of its Moscow bearings plant for the second and final time. In that same year, the Lena Goldfields concession came to a disputed end, followed by lengthy British litigation against the Soviet government.[41]

The large investment projects that provided the foundation for Soviet industrial expansion were built on Soviet internal financial resources. For example, in 1926 direct foreign participation in the giant Dneproges hydroelectric scheme was seriously considered, but the final decision was to build it from Soviet internal resources. At the same time the Cooper Company, which had built the Muscle Shoals dam in the Tennessee valley, was employed to provide technical expertise and advice.[42] Such agreements expanded rapidly. Seventeen were in existence in 1927/28.[43] In 1931, at the height of the construction activity of the first five-year plan, there were 124 contracts with foreign firms and organisations, mainly from Germany and the United States, for the provision of technical assistance to Soviet industry. Their numbers began to fall sharply even before the end of the first five-year plan, as existing agreements were terminated. By 1933 only 46 were still in force.[44] The desperate need to save foreign currency as a result of the trade and payments crisis of 1932 must have encouraged the Soviet government to liquidate technical assistance contracts. But other factors also contributed to this change of policy: the view that industry was strong enough to develop further independently; the growing political isolationism, a feature of Stalinism; and the stormy disputes during the operation of some contracts.

As might be expected the technical assistance agreements largely concerned projects in the capital goods industries. They covered virtually all the major new plants of the capital investment programme. McKee Corporation were involved in the planning and design of the giant Magnitogorsk iron and steel works in the Urals, while Freyn Engineering provided similar assistance at Kuznetsk in Siberia, the matching major site in the development of the Urals-Kuzbass combine; this became the second main Soviet metallurgical base. An agreement with Ford provided assistance in the establishment of a major car plant at Nizhnii-Novgorod (Gor'kii) on the Volga east of Moscow. Several other American firms were involved in this project. Similarly American companies and engineers were involved in the giant tractor factories at Stalingrad and Khar'kov.[45] The total value of the contracts in operation in 1931 is reported at 83 million rubles.[46] In that year the payments on these agreements and to directly employed foreign specialists and workers may have amounted to 25 per cent of the value of grain exports.[47] But the expenditure on technical assistance was far outweighed by the purchases of technology in physical terms through the direct import of machinery. Although some Western writers, such as Sutton, have argued that this assistance played a crucial role in the industrialisation drive, it is very difficult to disentangle the respective contributions of the various channels for importing technology.

(ii) 1933–1941

In the foreign sector, as in the economy as a whole, the strains produced by the first five-year plan led to a period of adjustment. A major concern was now to pay off the accumulated debt (see Table 45) and to reach a more stable trading situation. This process was made more difficult because the British government ended most-favoured-nation status for the Soviet Union and the German trade policies were tightened up when the Nazi government, in power from January 1933, sought to strengthen earlier measures to manage Germany's own debt problems.

In spite of these difficulties, the debt was largely paid off by the end of the second five-year plan. Several factors were involved. Firstly, the Soviet

Union ran a surplus in commodity trade (see Table 49); this continued the policy of import stringency introduced at the end of 1931. Soviet industry was called upon to manage without equipment imports and to use previously imported materials now available from domestic plants.[48] But it proved extremely difficult to increase export revenues. The world market for primary products continued to be poor. The low point in the Soviet terms of trade depends on the base year which is used, but there was little improvement between 1932 and 1936 (see Table 50). Simultaneously, the agricultural crisis following collectivisation meant that the high grain exports of 1930 and 1931 could not be maintained. Yet the squeeze on imports was so great that the fall in import volume more than matched the decline in exports (see Tables 48 and 51). In the years between 1932 and 1936, the cumulative trade surplus was 300 million rubles.

Secondly, precious metals continued to be exported. In 1933 and 1934 they remained at the level of 1931 and 1932; in total they amounted to 411 million rubles during 1932–1936 (see Table 45). The Soviet Union was able to maintain these exports at this level without exhausting gold stocks as a result of the a rapid increase in gold production. Output in 1933 is estimated to have increased threefold over its 1928 level.[49]

Thirdly, the devaluation of sterling was followed by devaluations in other creditor countries, most notably by the United States in 1933. As in the British case, this helped to ease debt repayments. However, it should be noted that the Reichsmark, like the ruble itself, was now being uncoupled from the international exchange rate system, while notionally maintaining its gold parity. Thus, there was to be no alleviation of foreign trade debt to Germany. The precise impact of the devaluations is very difficult to establish, but it has been suggested that the Soviet Union benefited by 300–350 million gold rubles.

Fourthly, unsold products in warehouses abroad had increased during the first five-year plan as a result of the slump in world markets as a result of the depression. These stocks were now reduced. There was a concomitant saving in expenditure on storage space. Staff numbers in trade organisations abroad were also cut.[50]

Fifthly, the Soviet government accumulated foreign currency and precious metals through Torgsin, its chain of foreign currency stores. These served tourists and foreign workers; and also Soviet citizens who possessed foreign currency or gold and silver. Between 1932 and 1935, the sales through these shops were worth 280 million gold rubles.[51] Their net contribution may have been 90–100 million gold rubles.[52]

Sixthly, the negative balance on invisibles was eased by the expansion of the Soviet shipping fleet. It was reported that during the period 1933–1935 a total of 30 million rubles were saved on the carriage of imports and exports.[53] In the balances of payments for 1935 and 1936 which were supplied by the government to the League of Nations, net shipping income is given at 47.5 and 71.6 million rubles.[54]

This discussion suggests that the contributions of these factors to the liquidation of the debt between 1932 and 1936 may have looked roughly as follows:

	million gold rubles
Trade surplus	300
Exports of precious metals	411
Favourable impact of creditors' devaluations	300–350
Elimination of stocks abroad and economies in foreign trade apparatus	unknown
'Net receipts' from Torgsin stores	90–100
Net shipping income	100 +
Total	1201–1261 +

The improvement in the balance of payments as the debt was paid off, and the sharp improvement in the terms of trade in 1936, did not lead to radical changes in the pattern of trade which had been established earlier in the decade. There was little change in either the value or the volume of imports between 1933 and the outbreak of war in Europe, while exports showed a continuing tendency to fall. In 1939 trade was virtually cut in half, but recovered sharply in 1940 as a result of a dramatic increase in trade with Germany after the signing of the Soviet–German Molotov-Ribbentrop Pact in August 1939 (see Tables 44 and 51). On the plausible assumption that the government wished to build up its gold reserves,[55] the failure to increase exports was the key to the lack of growth of imports and the continuing low level of foreign trade as a whole.

The crucial issue in assessing the size and pattern of foreign trade in the second half of the 1930s is whether the Soviet government had adopted a conscious policy of autarky. Did it intend to withdraw as much as possible from international trade, so as to avoid involvement in a potentially unequal economic relationship? If this was the case, then the boost in trade in 1929–31 was a temporary measure, to be discontinued at the earliest possible opportunity; and the failure of trade to recover after the problems of the early 1930s reflected the view of the Soviet leadership that the Soviet economy and Soviet industry were growing in strength.[56] However, the existing evidence for the early 1930s suggests that the government was then looking towards renewed trade expansion rather than towards continuing trade decline.[57] But a decline in the volume of trade was inevitable, given the problems which faced the Soviet Union as an exporter of primary products at the beginning of the 1930s. It can be argued that this decline would have taken place irrespective of any government drive to achieve autarky. At the same time, Soviet markets were increasingly surrounded by growing trade barriers.[58]

Dohan argues that this unfavourable situation forced the Soviet planners and government to reconsider whether it was rational to continue to use foreign trade to supply large amounts of equipment for industrial development. The structure of Soviet exports meant that any growth would have to be achieved by increasing the sale of food products. But international food prices were still low; and the failings of Soviet agriculture meant that domestic food supplies were struggling first to match the rise in population, and then to provide a modest increase in living standards following the end of rationing in 1934.

A further difficulty for Soviet foreign trade was the continuation of restrictions in major markets. The United Kingdom wished to keep its trade deficit with the Soviet Union under control. The two countries signed a trade agreement in 1934, under which the ratio of Soviet exports to Soviet imports was to be reduced from 1.7 to 1 in 1934 to 1.1 to 1 in 1938.[59] In Germany, the coming to power of the Nazis with their strongly anti-communist policies in 1933 meant that the Soviet Union could not envisage a strong recovery in trade with its major trading partner. The German government itself pursued an autarkic policy and maintained tight control over the size and direction of its foreign trade.

Taking all these factors together, there is reason to believe that Soviet trade stagnation in the 1930s was caused by the prevailing economic circumstances and the state of the world market, rather than the result of a deliberate policy involving the sacrifice of economic efficiency.

These years also saw the Soviet Union signing fewer and fewer contracts with Western corporations for the supply of technical assistance. This was a reflection of the growing strength of the economy, but it was also related to the changing political and ideological position at home and abroad. As we have noted, the Nazi government in Germany was strongly anti-communist. This factor and the purges in the Soviet Union itself, which contained a strong xenophobic element, both tended to militate against the further development of such agreements.

Thus the foreign economic relations of the Soviet Union at the end of the 1930s looked very different from those of the Russian Empire in 1913. Under the Soviet regime there were substantial differences both in institutional structures and in policy. First, the state took direct monopoly control over trade; it cut itself off from the international financial system, did not encourage foreign direct investment, and did not itself borrow funds for the development of industry and infrastructure. Secondly, the volume of foreign trade amounted by the end of the 1930s to approximately only half the pre-war level (Table 51), and it was an even smaller proportion of the expanded national income. Thirdly, the structure of imports had changed markedly (see Figure 17 and Table 47). In 1938 machinery and metal products amounted to nearly two-thirds of the total. Their increased share was largely at the expense of imports of consumer goods; the share of industrial raw materials in total imports had also fallen. On the other hand, while industrial exports had grown in importance, Soviet exports, like those of the Russian Empire, were dominated by agricultural and forest products (see Figure 16 and Table 47). Fourthly, the geographical distribution of foreign trade was more dispersed. As a consequence of the changing political climate, in 1938 Germany bought less than 7 per cent of Soviet exports and provided under 5 per cent of imports. Britain was now the largest purchaser of Soviet goods, taking 27.7 per cent of Soviet exports. The major supplier of imports was the United States whose share had grown from under 6 per cent to over 28 per cent.[60] Fifthly, although we do not possess for the end of the 1930s the equivalent of Gregory's careful analysis of invisibles, there is no doubt that there was a great difference in this sector. There were no substantial debt repayments; and net tourist expenditures did not feature as a drain on foreign currency. Payments deficits were met not so much by borrowing abroad, as by exporting precious metals.

While the institutional structures for controlling foreign trade, the pattern of trade, and the foreign economic policy underlying this pattern were substantially different, in both periods economic relations with other countries were closely interrelated both with trends and policies in the domestic economy and with the attitude of the state to industrial development.

(E) The foreign sector in Soviet development

In view of the small scale of foreign trade throughout the inter-war years, it would seem difficult to argue that the foreign sector was as important in the Soviet as in the Tsarist economy. It should be borne in mind, however, that the Soviet Union was not 'burdened' to the same extent by the import of consumer goods or by the leaking abroad of potential imports through the tourist expenditures of its citizens. Strict central control of trade enabled the government to concentrate on the import of products, particularly producer goods, which were considered important to the industrialisation drive. The large purchases of foreign machinery and equipment during the first five-year plan clearly enabled the Soviet economy narrow the technological gap which had opened up since 1914.

The relative weight of imports in the machinery and equipment installed in Soviet factories is difficult to assess. Data are absent or unreliable; imports were measured in 'foreign trade rubles', which were not clearly related to the domestic currency. As part of an attempt to assess the changing price of machinery in the Soviet Union, Moorsteen has estimated the weight of imports in total investment in new machinery for selected years. He notes a declining relative share in the late 1920s; on his estimate the proportion of machinery which was imported declined from 22–24 per cent in 1927/28 to 16 per cent in 1929/30; these shares correspond to those given in the Soviet publication which reviews the results of the first five-year plan. Further, he considers that in the period 1934–1940 machinery imports were of negligible importance.[61] In contrast, in a recent work Khanin uses a conversion ratio from foreign trade rubles to domestic rubles which produces an estimated share of imports in the supply of industrial equipment amounting to 25 per cent for the whole period 1928–1940 and reaching a mammoth 80 per cent during the first five-year plan. However, his ratio is based on an estimated growth rate of domestic machinery which economic historians would consider to be unrealistically low. He also assumes that all imported machinery and equipment was used in industry. But in the first five-year plan a quarter of machinery imports was intended for use in the agricultural and transport sectors.[62] On more qualitative grounds Sutton argues in his study of the contribution of foreign technology to Soviet development that producer goods imports and technical assistance contracts were crucial to any modernisation of the Soviet industrial structure. Indeed, the imported machinery was usually more advanced than that produced in the Soviet Union[63] There is evidence to suggest that Sutton overstates his case.[64] Nevertheless, there were signs in the latter part of the 1930s that the technological lag was again increasing in at least some sectors of industry (see Chapter 9). This implies that the low level of trade was hindering the further process of economic modernisation.

Further reading

On foreign trade and capital before the revolution, see P. R. Gregory, *Russian National Income, 1885–1913* (Cambridge, 1982); on the inter-war period, M. R. Dohan and E. Hewett, *Two Studies in the Soviet Terms of Trade, 1918–1970* (Bloomington, 1973), and M. R. Dohan, 'The Economic Origins of Soviet Autarky, 1927/28–1934', *Slavic Review*, xxxv (1976). On the import of Western technology, see further reading for chapter 9.

11 The First World War and War Communism, 1914–1920

Peter Gatrell

When the Bolshevik revolution took place, Russia had already experienced more than three years of uninterrupted war. The revolution held out the hope of a more just and democratic society, in which differentials of wealth and income would be sharply curtailed. It offered the prospect of harnessing the talents and energies of the people to the task of socialist economic development. This task was made difficult, not only by Russia's economic backwardness, but also by the legacy of a war that had taken a heavy toll on ordinary people, sapping their morale and depleting the resources on which they depended. To make matters worse, no sooner had the revolution taken place than Russia became embroiled in a bitter civil war. In the towns, the supply of food and fuel deteriorated still further. Unemployment soared. With renewed war came fresh privations and upheaval. As the war intensified, workers found themselves subject to ever tighter supervision and discipline. In the countryside, the seizure and redistribution of land offered the peasantry a moment of celebration. It was short-lived. Desperate to obtain food for hungry workers and soldiers, the Bolsheviks resorted to coercive measures, culminating in a policy of nationwide grain requisition. As a result of this protracted period of upheaval, the men and women who tasted the fruits of liberation in 1917 quickly found that they turned to ashes in the mouth.

This chapter focuses on productive activities, whose behaviour has received much less attention than wartime economic administration and regulation.[1]

(A) The work force

(i) Population and employment

Chapter 4 demonstrated the impact of war and other catastrophes upon the civilian population. Other socio-demographic consequences of the First World War are less easy to measure, but should not be dismissed lightly on that account. Many of the conscripts who escaped death had to adjust to the practical and emotional consequences of disablement. The scars associated with capture, with 'shell shock' or involuntary displacement also took time to heal. Subsequently, the revolution and civil war took a toll on the minds of participants, as well as their physical health, adding to the strain on an already overburdened health service.[2]

The wave of urban migration that characterised the First World War was succeeded by an equally dramatic contraction of urban population. The population of Russian towns and cities increased by 25 per cent between January 1914 and January 1918. Over the course of the next three years, the urban population fell by over 20 per cent. Of all Russian cities, Petrograd exhibited the most dramatic changes. At its wartime peak, the population of the Russian capital numbered two-and-a-half million, including refugees from the western provinces. But shortages of food, fuel, and jobs rapidly decimated the population. The census conducted in June 1918 recorded one and a half million. Two years later, Petrograd supported fewer than three quarters of a million people. Those who stayed behind waged a constant battle to survive. Class distinctions ceased to have any meaning, as all urban dwellers became 'assimilated into the mass of trading townspeople', who struggled to obtain food and other basic necessities.[3]

One issue of unprecedented magnitude that confronted both the Tsarist government and its successors concerned the provision to be made for the refugee population. By the end of April 1916 more than 3.2 million refugees had settled on Russian soil.[4] Local authorities (*zemstva* and municipalities) spent much of their time on relief efforts, but were hampered by interference from central government and the military. By 1 January 1918 the numbers of refugees had swollen to 7.5 million people, representing five per cent of the entire population. Around 3.5 million refugees subsequently left Soviet territory and re-established themselves in the new successor states, particularly Poland. But around 4.75 million men, women, and children remained on Soviet territory and required resettlement by the authorities.[5]

The involuntary migration of millions of vulnerable people contributed to the spread of infectious diseases. Refugees and prisoners, as well as combatants, were particularly at risk and acted as human vectors for typhus and other diseases. Demobilized soldiers spread typhus among the civilian population. The influx of people from the city to the countryside after 1917 contributed still further to the spread of disease. In 1918, an estimated 115800 people died from typhus, smallpox, dysentery, and other infectious diseases. In 1919, the figure jumped to 910200, and in the following year it peaked at 1,091,000, most of whom were victims of typhus. Ironically, the Red Army succumbed far more frequently to the diseases spread by the defeated White troops than it did to their bullets.[6]

During the First World War, the Russian army absorbed virtually two-fifths of all males aged 15–49.[7] The mobilization of men on this scale could not fail to have profound consequences for the civilian economy. Their place was taken by hitherto unwaged labour (women and juveniles), and by people who had settled involuntarily on Russian territory, that is refugees and prisoners of war. Little substitution of capital for labour took place in the basic sectors of the economy, except in a handful of industries closely tied to the war effort. The main burden of carrying on production, in industry as in agriculture, rested with manual workers.

The dynamics of employment in large-scale industry can be established with some degree of confidence, but trends in employment in other sectors of the economy are difficult to reconstruct. Employment in large-scale industry rose steadily until 1916. In 1917, despite widespread concern among factory workers about unemployment, the figure remained stable. In 1918, and especially 1919, employment fell. By the end of the civil war, employment had fallen by 47 per cent, compared to the pre-war figure, and by 55 per cent, compared to 1917. The growth during the First World War reflected the rapid increase of employment in coal, iron and steel, and in metalworking and machinebuilding, sectors most associated with the war effort. Employment in textiles registered no increase during the war.[8] By contrast, small-scale industry registered a decline of between 13 and 21 per cent between 1913 and 1917. All sources agree that employment fell between 1917 and 1920, perhaps by as much as 50 per cent.

The building trade suffered a haemorrhage of workers to the armed forces. Precise figures are not available, but the output of brick, timber, and cement fell by more than two-fifths between 1913 and 1917, and this may serve as a rough indicator of the magnitude of the loss. During the civil war, employment probably fell to an insignificant level. Building workers who escaped the draft simply had neither the wherewithal nor the incentive to carry on their trade.

The fact that Tsarist Russia had a large rural population led contemporaries to believe that this would confer superiority on Russia in wartime. The rural population would generate a virtually inexhaustible supply of recruits for the armed forces; those left behind would continue to produce food. These expectations were ultimately confounded. The mobilization of peasants immediately deprived large landowners of agricultural labourers. Employers began to substitute refugee and prisoner-of-war labour on a significant scale. Even so, the agricultural hired labour force probably fell by as much as two-thirds between 1913 and 1916. A very substantial decline also occurred in the numbers of peasants capable of working their plots of land. One in two able-bodied rural males was conscripted into the army. At the end of 1916, the government reported that the able-bodied male workforce in agriculture, forestry, and fishing had declined by 57 per cent since the outbreak of war.[9]

By the end of 1915, the captains of industry faced an acute bottleneck in the supply of labour. They petitioned for the introduction of exemption certificates for skilled labour. In due course, one million men received exemption certificates. The return of men who had already been conscripted posed a bigger problem. Army leaders complained that their return to civilian employment would sap the morale of the men still at the front. The Russian government never devised a coherent labour policy. Unlike Britain and Germany, where government leaders were quick to reach an accord with organized labour and employers alike, the Tsarist regime kept its distance from industrialists and offered no concessions to trade unions.[10]

The shortages of labour in the most arduous occupations, such as mining, railway construction, and agricultural labour, were to some extent offset by the use of prison labour. By autumn 1916, prisoners constituted 54 per cent of the labour force in Krivoi Rog iron mines, and 25 per cent of the labour force in the Donbass coal fields.[11] In manufacturing industry, female workers and juveniles took the place of adult men. Between 1913 and 1917, female employment in large-scale industry increased by 60 per cent, compared with just eight per cent for male employment. The female share of industrial employment (excluding state-owned establishments) rose from 31 per cent in 1913 to 42 per cent in 1916. In some branches of industry, such as textiles and chemicals, which traditionally employed large numbers of women, the war did not bring about profound changes. But in metal-working, women made up 18 per cent of the labour force in 1917, compared to five per cent before the war. Nor did the general decline in industrial production after 1917 altogether erode the advances made by women during the First World War. For instance, in 1920, women comprised nearly half the labour force in the food and drink trades, compared to one-fifth in 1913. In wood-working, one-third of the labour force was female in 1920, compared to a mere five per cent in 1913. The Bolshevik decree on child labour eliminated most children under 15 from the factory labour force.[12]

(ii) Productivity (Table 53)

Trends in labour productivity in large-scale industry are difficult to establish with any degree of certainty. According to Gukhman, output per person rose slightly during 1915. A catastrophic decline ensued in 1917 and continued in 1918 and 1919. By the end of the civil war, labour productivity fell to below one-quarter of its pre-war level (see Figure 20 and Table 53).[13]

Aggregate data conceal wide variations in the behaviour of individual branches of industry. Between 1913 and 1916, output per day worked in machinebuilding increased by 32 per cent and in chemicals by 27 per cent. Other sectors, such as metalworking and clothing, also recorded an increase. In each instance, labour had been reorganized and new plant installed, in order to cope with the volume of military demand. Mass production of a standard product was particularly marked in shell manufacture where productivity increased as a result of new shift work, improved machinery and 'the elimination of teething troubles connected with the introduction of new products and the acquisition by the workforce of the necessary habits and methods'.[14] The clothing industry, uniquely, managed to sustain the increase in labour productivity in 1917. Here the 'Union of Towns and *Zemstva*' reorganised production, supplying knitting frames to producer cooperatives.[15] By contrast, labour productivity declined in branches such as foodstuffs, leather, cotton textiles, woodworking, and mining. In most cases a reduction in the quality of equipment seems to have been to blame.

During the civil war, the need to stem the decline in labour productivity was never far from the centre of attention in the Bolshevik Party. In theory, the Bolsheviks had an advantage over their predecessors, in that the party could appeal to its working-class adherents to maintain productivity. In practice, matters were not so simple. The Bolsheviks enjoyed support among many sections of the industrial working class and they attempted to capitalize on this support by instituting campaigns for greater productivity. 'Shock work' and Communist '*subbotniki*' (voluntary work at weekends) were creations of the civil war years. The Bolsheviks also enlisted trade unions and factory committees in the campaign to boost labour productivity. In April 1918 the All-Russian Council of Trade Unions approved regulations which emphasized the need to increase productivity, for example by the use of piece-rate payments. On the other hand, Russian workers did not offer unconditional support to the Bolshevik government. Lenin's emphasis upon one-person management did not commend itself to most rank-and-file workers. Furthermore, workers felt that the leadership of factory committees – which now administered many enterprises – lost touch with conditions on the shop floor. As food shortages worsened and enterprises laid off employees, workers began to question the wisdom of their leaders and challenged the exclusive right of the Bolsheviks to govern the country. The summer of 1918 saw a series of protests from the very quarter which had brought the Bolsheviks to victory. Bolshevik candidates suffered defeats during fresh elections to the soviets. Strikes and even uprisings against the government threatened the survival of the regime, and had a direct impact upon the course of industrial production.[16]

The civil war brought workers and the Bolshevik government closer together, because organized opposition to the Bolsheviks raised the spectre of a White regime, hostile to the working class. When war against the

Whites began in earnest, the Bolsheviks took more determined steps to combat the decline in productivity. During 1919, the government instituted differential rewards for workers in military and non-military industry. In the middle of 1920, Vesenkha (the government department responsible for industry) allocated scarce foodstuffs and other materials to factories engaged on 'shock work'. Productivity probably improved, but it is unlikely that these incentives were responsible. In many industries, bottlenecks in supply caused interruptions to production; by eliminating some of these bottlenecks, Vesenkha contributed to improvements in output per worker.[17]

The use of material incentives to reward improvements in labour productivity foundered on their unpopularity with the rank and file and on food shortages. The sad truth was that overall labour productivity could not be improved in conditions of acute exhaustion, sickness, and absenteeism. Skilled workers left their place of work either to search for food, or because they were mobilized for the Red Army or for Party duties. Measures taken during 1919 and 1920 to combat absenteeism do not appear to have resolved the problem: in 1920, workers took around 71 days' unapproved leave (in 1913 the figure was a mere 13 days) and 59 days' holiday (in 1913, when Russia celebrated numerous religious festivals, the corresponding figure had been 89 days). In 1920 they worked only 228 days on average, 29 days fewer than in 1913.[18]

In other sectors of the economy, the main problem was that basic activities, such as mining, fuel procurement, and the construction or repair of buildings and roads were threatened by a shortage of labour. The problem intensified during the winter of 1919, causing Trotsky to advocate the 'militarisation' of labour. Red Army troops were put to work on the most arduous tasks. Initially, the notion that able-bodied civilians had a duty to work for the state was applied to peasants, who were required to gather and load fuel. Early in 1920, the scheme was extended to all Soviet citizens, a far cry from the tentative measures adopted by the Tsarist regime.[19]

(B) Investment

The First World War led to a substantial fall in net investment. Investment probably declined by more than national income, which was 25 per cent lower in 1916–17 than in 1913–14. The war also changed the pattern of investment. Defence industry and railways claimed the lion's share of investment, at the expense of investment in agriculture, trade and residential construction.

In 1913, industry accounted for just over one-third of total net investment, agriculture for one-quarter and urban house-building for around 17 per cent of the total. Net investment in transport and communications, and in the trade sector, each made up ten per cent. The remainder comprised capital outlays on government projects. Expressed differently, in 1913 net investment in structures represented the largest component of the total (45 per cent). Equipment and stocks (including livestock) accounted for 29 per cent and 21 per cent respectively.[20]

The main difference between the pre-war situation and the First World War is that investment in agriculture and in residential structures diminished sharply. Public investment increased, with the construction of new railway lines. Industrial investment probably accounted for close to 40 per cent of total net investment by 1916. Net investment in railways perhaps accounted for 45 per cent of the total, a huge increase in its percentage share. By contrast, agriculture all but dropped out of the picture.

(i) Industrial investment (Table 54)

Industrial investment during the war years presents a confused picture, complicated by the fact that we know virtually nothing about small-scale industry. Contemporary sources testified to an impressive increase in capital investment in defence industry during the First World War.[21] Domestic output of equipment in 1916 was already some 24 per cent higher than in 1913. In addition, supplies of equipment were boosted by imports from Russia's allies. The overall dynamic of industrial investment in wartime is indicated in Table 54. Gross investment in industrial equipment and structures amounted to around 1,050 million rubles between January 1914 and January 1918. Thereafter, with the cessation of imports – the result of the Allied blockade – and the decline in domestic machinebuilding, virtually no fresh investment took place. The destruction of assets during the civil war reduced the capital stock from the peak it attained at the beginning of 1918. In addition, the intensity with which equipment was used, and the failure subsequently to maintain and repair the capital stock in industry, led to negative net investment after 1918, which lasted well into the 1920s. On the eve of NEP, the stock of industrial assets, after allowing for depreciation, was 13 per cent below its peak, no higher than the level reached in January 1914.[22] (See Figure 20 and Table 54.)

During the First World War, the Tsarist state poured millions of rubles into the industrial economy, in order to expand munitions output. Private firms drew upon generous credit, to finance the acquisition of new machine tools. New enterprises were built by the government, and others were reconstructed. Not to be outdone, the war industry committees (non-government agencies, established in 1915 to promote the mobilisation of industry) also invested in new plant. At the height of the war effort, the government advanced more than 1000 million rubles to its contractors.[23]

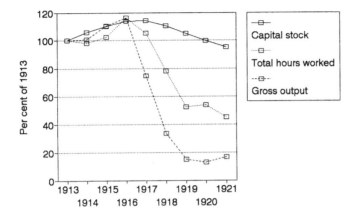

Figure 20   Large-scale industry, 1913–1921. *Source:* tables 53, 54.

Other sources of finance played a less significant role. Except in isolated instances, foreign investment, which financed as much as half of new corporate investment on the eve of the war, now ceased. Commercial banks, whose supply of credit had been growing in importance before 1914, guaranteed the enormous advances received by their clients. Corporate profits offered another source of finance. Generous depreciation allowances permitted companies to retain more of their pre-tax profits. A survey of 72 firms in 1917 indicated that, after tax, profits increased from 11.4 per cent of share capital in 1913 to 19.4 per cent in 1915 and 30.8 per cent in 1916.[24]

None of these mechanisms survived the Bolshevik revolution. Profits were squeezed by the rise in labour and raw materials costs during 1917. By the end of that year, the system of commercial credit had broken down, initially because the banks refused to finance enterprises that had been taken over by factory committees and, subsequently, because of the nationalisation of the joint-stock banks. The transfer of the Tsarist Special Council for State Defence to Soviet control was followed quickly by the liquidation of military orders and the collapse of state-financed investment. During the civil war, the Bolshevik authorities devoted little attention to investment. Capital assets were either destroyed, or deteriorated through constant use (in the case of munitions factories) or inescapable neglect.

(ii)   The agricultural sector

The First World War halted investment in agricultural equipment and machinery. Factory output of agricultural implements and machines declined by around 50 per cent between 1913 and 1916. Small-scale production could not possibly offset this decline. Imports, which had accounted for around 45 per cent of the market in 1913, fell sharply. As a result of these changes, total consumption of agricultural machinery by 1916 stood at little more than ten per cent of its pre-war level. During the civil war, the production of agricultural machinery continued to decline. In 1919, output barely exceeded four per cent of pre-war production, which was not regained until 1925/26.[25]

No less serious a problem for the agricultural sector was caused by the mobilization, and subsequently the destruction, of livestock. By spring 1916, the army had appropriated ten per cent of the horse population. Villagers were left with the oldest or youngest animals, that is those least suited for strenuous field work.[26] We know very little about the behaviour of the livestock component of investment. In 1915, livestock herds may have been slightly higher than before the war (1909–13). However, a decline set in some time between 1916 and 1920, when the stock of horses probably declined by ten per cent in relation to the pre-war average (less than the percentage decline in the sown area). By 1921, the stock stood 18 per cent below the 1909–13 average. The famine of 1921–22 devastated village livestock, reducing it to just two-thirds of the pre-war level. Thus, the grim reaper carried off what the contending armies had left behind.[27]

In money terms, the loss of draught animals and of farm implements during the civil war amounted to 2000 million rubles, in pre-war prices. The value of these elements of the agricultural capital stock in 1913 has been put at 8,050 million rubles (USSR territory), implying that wartime losses represented one-quarter of the pre-war stock. Total losses of capital in the agricultural sector (that is, including inventories and structures) amounted to 3,570 million rubles, or around 19 per cent of the pre-war total. It is against this background that the subsequent recovery of agriculture during NEP must be set.[28]

(iii) Transport and communications

The Tsarist government made the construction of new lines and the production of rolling stock one of its wartime priorities, making up for sluggish investment before the war. Between 1914 and 1917, the government laid down 11000km of track, some two-and-a-half times the amount achieved during the entire pre-war decade. By the end of 1916, the network was nearly 20 per cent longer than on the eve of the war. During 1917, construction slumped to 980km, although it picked up slightly during the following year. However, the average length of new track completed in 1919–21 was a mere 156km. The Soviet authorities concentrated upon repairing of track that had been destroyed, frequently more than once (more than one-third of the total railway track was destroyed at least twice during the civil war). As a result of these setbacks, on one pessimistic estimate the net value of track at the end of 1921 did not exceed 26 per cent of the 1913 level.[29]

The supply of rolling stock improved steadily during the First World War. Production of locomotives and wagons increased substantially during 1915, and supplies were supplemented subsequently by imports. But the war inevitably imposed an enormous strain on the rolling stock. Reports during 1917 spoke frequently of an increase in the number of locomotives in need of repair. The civil war exacerbated these difficulties: output slumped and imports ceased. By 1920, the proportion of wagons classified as 'sick' had increased to 30 per cent, five times the pre-war norm. As much as 56 per cent of locomotives were currently inactive, more than three times the peacetime norm. The civil war wrought additional havoc on the transport sector, by destroying bridges, railway stations and other fixed assets.[30]

(iv) Residential structures

Shortages of building materials and the mobilisation of construction workers disrupted the construction industry. Little house-building took place during the First World War. The civil war presented a more complicated picture. The battles that raged on Russian territory led to widespread destruction of homes in the countryside. Some attempts were made to maintain the stock of housing, by substituting cheaper accommodation for the substantial structures that were destroyed by bombardment or fire, a regular hazard in rural Russia. In addition, the increased numbers of peasant households – the result of land redistribution and other social changes associated with the revolution – necessitated at least some basic addition to the housing stock. According to Strumilin, the total stock of farm buildings increased by around 23 per cent between 1913/14 and 1924/25; but this must be regarded as a rough approximation, first, because we have no firm data on the number of peasant households and, secondly, because Strumilin assumed that the unit value of farm buildings did not change.[31]

During the revolution and civil war, more than 300000 urban buildings were destroyed. Wooden structures were quickly replaced, but shortages of brick and cement severely hampered attempts to repair or replace the more sophisticated urban structures. The stock of urban housing actually increased fractionally between 1913 and 1923, but this was entirely due to the increase in wooden structures. Total living space probably declined by around 15 per cent, reflecting the fact that it was more difficult to offset the loss of larger structures. In all likelihood, most municipal authorities, like those in Petrograd, devoted more attention to the redistribution of the inherited housing stock, rather than to its repair and replenishment. This strategy embodied Bolshevik ideology; but it was also dictated by the shortage of funds and building materials. In house-building, as in other spheres, a massive reconstruction programme would be required, if the new regime were to meet the needs of Russian citizens.[32]

(C) Agricultural production and food supply (Table 55)

No other country entered the war with better prospects of survival in a long drawn-out campaign than did Tsarist Russia (see chapter 6 for pre-war background). Russia's large agricultural sector appeared to guarantee that the country could never be starved into submission. However, symptoms of food shortage manifested themselves in Russia's cities as early as 1915. In the winter of 1916, the crisis in food supply toppled the old regime and threatened to create sufficient upheaval in towns, garrisons and trenches to jeopardise the war effort itself. Why did this crisis in food supply come about? Did it occur because of a failure in production, brought about by the notoriously erratic grain harvest, by a wartime shortage of labour and draught animals, or by some combination of these factors? Alternatively, did it take place because of a breakdown in the arrangements for obtaining grain from food producers, the result of peasants' reluctance to market grain?

After the Bolshevik revolution, the supply of food to the consumer deteriorated further. The revolutionary seizure and redistribution of land added to uncertainty in the agricultural sector. The Bolsheviks adopted various measures, beginning with the direct exchange of manufactured goods for foodstuffs, experimenting with so-called 'committees of the poor', and culminating in a grain levy (*prodrazverstka*). To what extent can the effect of these procurement policies on food supply be distinguished from other factors, such as adverse weather conditions or the physical exhaustion of food producers and draught animals?

(i) 1914–1917

In 1914, notwithstanding the disruption caused by mobilisation, the total sown area increased, but adverse weather conditions led to a sharp decline in yields. As a consequence, the overall grain harvest in 1914 was lower than the bumper harvest in the previous year. Nevertheless, the 1914 harvest corresponded almost precisely to the pre-war (1909–13) average. In 1915, the harvest was 10 per cent above the pre-war average. Sowings of grain declined slightly, but yields were five per cent higher than the pre-war average (Table 55).

The harvest in 1916 was a different matter. The area under crops probably declined slightly. To make matters worse, grain yields fell by around four per cent, compared with 1909–13. A regionally differentiated picture shows that production in the Northern Consumer Region (NCR) fell to 91 per cent of the pre-war level (see chapter 6). In the Southern Producer Region (SPR) grain output declined more sharply, to 86 per cent of the pre-war figure. A similar decline was registered in the Central Producer Region (CPR). In the Eastern Producer Region (EPR) the grain harvest also fell, although it remained above the pre-war average. Production here did not compensate for the losses in potential grain surpluses from the SPR and the CPR.

The war had a profound impact on the supply of labour, farm equipment and draught animals (see pp. 223–4 above). But its impact upon grain *production* should not obscure more profound wartime changes in grain *utilisation*. The most obvious change came about with the imposition of a blockade on foreign trade; as a result, the export of grain through the Black Sea came to a standstill. Russia thus had around 11 million additional tons of grain at its disposal (the average annual amount exported in 1909–13). But other changes worked in the opposite direction. As chapter 4 indicated, the war induced enormous spatial movements of people. The large Russian army required food and fodder. In addition, refugees imposed an additional burden on towns and cities. A more significant change in utilisation resulted from the unexpectedly large amounts of grain that Russian peasants retained in 1914/15 and 1915/16. Shorn of its export imperative, the rural economy took on a new dimension, as peasants consumed more grain themselves, fattened their livestock and distilled the residue into vodka.[33]

The impact of changes in population migration can best be gauged by considering the regional element in grain utilisation. In 1914/15, largely as a result of the increase in troop concentrations, the Northern Consumer Region (NCR) required additional grain, less than two-thirds of which could be supplied from within the regional economy. Fortunately, both the Southern Producer Region (SPR) and the Eastern Producer Region (EPR) had significant surpluses available, the first because of the cessation of exports, the second because of a sizeable increase in the grain harvest. In the Central Producer Region (CPR) the harvest was poor (see above), but the situation was not critical, because grain could be imported from areas of surplus and peasants could draw upon stocks accumulated from the 1913 harvest. Overall, there was a modest surplus of grain.

In 1915/16 the demands made upon food supplies by the NCR increased, as a result of the growth in the transient population. The grain harvest here increased by 20 per cent over the previous year's figure. The dependence of the region upon imports of grain from the major producing regions did not intensify and the situation in the first half of 1916 did not become critical. In the SPR, the decline in production in 1915 had few serious consequences. The bumper harvest in 1915/16 in the CPR allowed the region to build up stocks and satisfy the demands placed upon it by the NCR. In these circumstances, the decline in the harvest from the EPR was by no means alarming. The notional surplus of production over utilisation in 1915/16 more than doubled in comparison with the preceding year.[34]

The main problem in 1916/17 was that the demands from the NCR continued to grow, whilst the SPR had no surplus at its disposal to release to the towns and garrisons in the north. The sharp fall in the grain harvest in the CPR implied a pronounced reduction in the availability of grain for consumption, which could only be offset by the import of grain from other regions. Unfortunately, such was the decline in production elsewhere that neither the SPR nor the EPR could satisfy the claims of the NCR and the CPR. The aggregate decline in grain available for consumption in 1916/17 amounted to 10 million tons.

In the following year the situation deteriorated further. This probably reflected the continued decline in grain production in the NCR, rather than an increase in the regional grain requirement. In the SPR, production failed to recover in 1917 and this region persisted in its inability to generate a potential surplus. More serious still was the behaviour of the CPR where the harvest fell yet again, creating a deficit that amounted to nearly one-third of estimated regional consumption. The modest increase in output in the EPR simply could not compensate for the shortages experienced in the NCR and the CPR. In that year the notional grain deficit for the country as a whole amounted to more than 13 million tons.[35]

The delicate inter-regional balance of grain production and utilisation already came under pressure in 1914/15 and 1915/16, and broke down completely in 1916/17 and 1917/18. This is evident in the failure of the traditional grain-producing regions – the Volga provinces and Ukraine – to meet the demands of local consumption, let alone those of the northern consuming areas. Hence, it is misleading to identify a nationwide grain surplus in 1916/17.[36] The crisis in grain supply reflected the breakdown in inter-regional shipments, caused largely by the impact of the war on regional grain production and regional consumption patterns, and exacerbated by the disruption in interregional transportation.

To what extent were these potential shortages translated into actual shortages, as a result of transport problems or the choice of inappropriate policies by government? We should recall that peasants began the war by experiencing an increase in household consumption of grain. As the war progressed, demands from the military and the Russian government became ever more insistent. The main mechanism for grain procurement was a system of fixed prices for government purchases. Other transactions took place at unregulated prices, but the rise in prices did not call forth sufficient supplies to meet urban demand. Eventually, in November 1916 the government instituted a grain levy, anticipating the Bolshevik *prodrazverstka*. But this attempt to levy grain at fixed prices coincided with inflation in the price of manufactured goods. No subsidies were offered to food producers (as happened in Britain), and peasants lacked an incentive to market grain. They circumvented the levy and withheld grain, hoping to sell on the open market, or to secure an increase in the fixed price or in anticipation of a much-enhanced supply of consumer goods in due course. Neither the Tsarist regime nor the Provisional Government of 1917 (which imposed a grain monopoly in March) proved able to devise a policy of food procurement that could satisfy the wishes of producers and the needs of consumers. The catastrophic decline in urban and military food supply helped to overthrow the old regime and within a few months to de-stabilise the Provisional Government.[37]

(ii) 1917–1920

The revolution and subsequent redistribution of land from noble landowners to peasant smallholders entailed profound consequences for agricultural production and food supply. As a result of redistribution, many landless households received a small plot of land. In addition, peasants engaged in a hectic process of land redivision, in order to accommodate the needs of those who returned to the village from the front. Demobilised soldiers demanded a share of the enlarged pool of land, and established their own households as a means of registering their status within the village community. From the point of view of the peasantry as a social group, the revolution brought clear benefits. The poorest stratum gained a foothold in the community. The wealthiest households tended to disappear from the population, as they fragmented into smaller units under the pressure of land redistribution.[38]

From the point of view of food production and food supply, the benefits were less clear-cut. Although the new households had more land at their disposal, corresponding increases in the associated means of production were difficult to obtain. Fewer livestock meant a reduction in manure fertiliser and a shortage of draught power. Farm equipment was worn out and more peasants had to sow by hand. The new units were thus economic weaklings. As if this were not enough, the transformation of the rural economy had eliminated those sectors which had been responsible for a disproportionate share of total grain marketings, namely the landlords and the wealthier stratum of peasants. This structural change would have a significant impact on potential grain marketings.[39]

The civil war directly affected the conditions under which peasants farmed the land. Bitter military engagements took place in the grain-producing provinces of Samara and Simbirsk. Orel, a central black-earth province, was criss-crossed by railways whose strategic importance attracted the attention of the opposing forces. Elsewhere, the war did not disturb cultivation to the same degree, and output remained more stable.[40]

Changes in landholding and the impact of government procurement policy affected land use. Peasants planted crops for their own use, rather than for sale. The cultivation of flax in the Northern Consumer Region gave way to potatoes, millet and buckwheat for household consumption. In the grain-growing regions, peasants began to cultivate flax for their own use, at the expense of grain. In the Central Black Earth province, for instance, millet and buckwheat increased their share from 12 to nearly 30 per cent of total cereal production. The impact of government procurement policy was still more direct. *Prodrazverstka* did not apply to household plots (*usad'by*). Accordingly, peasants devoted more attention to these, rather than to their fields. The *usad'ba* became a source of cereal crops, as well as traditional products, such as fruit and vegetables. Before the First World War, arable fields yielded 59 per cent of the total output of crops in the main grain-consuming region (NCR); by 1921/22 the proportion had fallen to 39 per cent. Products from household plots increased their share from just one per cent to more than 10 per cent of the total. In the grain-producing regions, field crops declined from 63 to 39 per cent, whilst crops from the household plots increased from three per cent to around 13 per cent. The decision by peasants in the consuming region to devote rather more attention than hitherto to the cultivation of grain for their own household needs had the effect of improving average yields after 1919. By contrast, grain yields in the producing regions declined, whereas yields of potatoes in the SPR and CPR improved dramatically.[41]

As a result of these changes, the pre-revolutionary distinction between the Northern Consuming Region (which imported grain from the south, cultivated land more intensively and marketed technical crops, fruit and vegetables and dairy products), and two large producing regions (which concentrated on extensive cultivation of cereals) ceased to have any meaning. The NCR now produced more cereal crops than hitherto and less flax and hemp. In the CPR and SPR, the peasant switched to crops that could be consumed within the household. In the traditional producing regions, the peasantry sought to escape the requisition squads by curtailing production in the fields. In the consuming region, peasants cultivated more cereals, in order not to starve.

The size of the grain harvest in 1918 and 1919 is difficult to establish with any precision. Peasants concealed the sown area and harvest from the authorities. In 1920, the gross output of grain fell to 66 per cent of the pre-war average (see Table 55).[42] Faced with uncertainties about the size of the harvest, it is more useful to consider the government's own projection of the cereal surplus and the means whereby it could be extracted from the peasantry for non-rural consumption. Grain procurement must also be considered against the background of the shifting territory under Bolshevik control during the civil war.

In the winter of 1917–18, grain entered the urban economy in a haphazard and uncoordinated fashion. Attempts by the Provisional Government to organize the distribution of manufactured goods as a means of encouraging peasants to part with their grain at fixed prices were followed after October by local initiatives, in which factories and soviets entered into direct nego- tiations with peasants, exchanging stocks of commodities for grain and other foodstuffs. As a historian of War Communism has described it, the govern- ment 'chose to put commodity exchange under state control and to bend it to a central policy of food procurement'. In August 1918 the Bolsheviks decreed that peasants in key food-producing regions could acquire manu- factured goods, only in exchange for deliveries of grain.[43]

The attempt to procure grain during 1918 was severely hampered by the fact that most producing regions (Ukraine, Don and Kuban, North Cauca- sus and western Siberia) were in the hands of the White forces. Only the Volga region remained under Bolshevik control. It bore the brunt of the procurement campaign in 1918–19: more than two-fifths of the grain levy fell upon just four provinces, Samara, Saratov, Penza and Simbirsk. However, the size of the harvest was notional, and the estimated surplus was inflated by unrealistically low rural consumption norms. The authorities deliberately exaggerated the estimated surplus that could be extracted from the countryside, ignoring the increase in peasant consumption during the war and revolution and understating private sales by the peasantry. An official report observed that 'there can hardly be a more important explanation of the chronic failure of the procurement campaigns than the poor record of the actual production and consumption of cereals'. In the event, the government (or, rather, its numerous 'food brigades'), managed to obtain only two-fifths of the planned procurements, because of a break- down in local administration, shortages of capacity at state-controlled mills, transport bottlenecks and a shortage of manufactured goods to exchange for food.[44]

The harshness of the 1919–20 campaign reflects in part Bolshevik frust- ration with the limited success of the previous procurements effort. At the beginning of 1919 the government introduced the *prodrazverstka*, whereby provincial and district officials were assigned compulsory delivery quotas. In practice, the levies bore no systematic relation to the size of the harvest.

Rather than rely, as hitherto, on estimates of rural consumption norms, the government reverted to the experiment adopted in November 1916: it determined the total needs of the state and apportioned quotas among all regions. As a result of the government's scant regard for local reality, peasant households were deprived of food and seed needed to see them through the next twelve months. Once again, deliveries of manufactured goods that were supposed to sugar the pill never materialised.[45]

The harvest of 1920 was one of the worst on record, reflecting in part the seizure of seed grain in the previous year. The winter rye harvest did not exceed 50 per cent of the pre-war level; spring wheat fared even worse. Still the government was reluctant to moderate its demands. The government did cancel grain procurements in a number of regions during the winter of 1920; even so, procurements were more than two-thirds above the 1919/20 level. In eventual acknowledgement of the failure of administrative methods, the government resolved in March 1921 upon the substitution of a tax in kind, thereby hoping to regain the trust of the peasantry.[46]

Grain procurement campaigns enjoyed only limited success in supplying the Russian consumer. A large proportion of food consumed in the towns and cities came from various informal channels, rather than through the ration system. In 1919, for example, workers in the NCR received only 35 per cent of their cereals from the ration book. The remainder came from barter or from transactions on the free market. In the producing region, the story was the same; the central distribution of grain provided no more than half the requirements of the urban population.[47]

Bolshevik food policy was caught in a vicious circle. Peasants responded to attempts at coercion by curtailing sowings and concealing stocks. This prompted further administrative measures from the Bolsheviks, who believed that a rural bourgeoisie was intent on sabotaging the proletarian revolution. In the end, as one historian concludes, 'once the Whites had been defeated so that the requisitionings and punitive measures against deserters could no longer be easily justified, the peasantry put down its weapons of passive economic resistance and picked up those of armed struggle against the Bolshevik regime'.[48] Our survey began with the Tsarist Empire at war against imperial Germany; it ends with the Bolsheviks at war against the Russian peasantry.

(D) Industrial production (Figure 21 and Table 56)

The gross value of output in large-scale industry grew by about 17 per cent between 1913 and 1916, by which time defence requirements accounted for one-quarter of total production. But the aggregate increase disguised the very different fortunes of capital goods and consumer goods industries. In

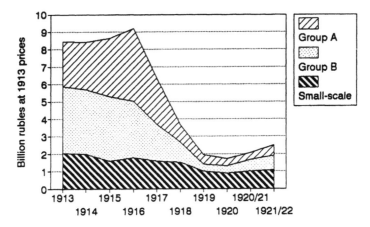

Figure 21   Gross output of industry in real terms, 1914–1921/22.
Source: table 56.

1916, output in Group A industries was already 62 per cent above the 1913 level; by contrast, output of Group B industries was 15 per cent lower. After this, both sectors collapsed. In 1917, the output of Group A industries fell sharply; in the following year a catastrophic decline occurred. In Group B industries the sharpest decline was reserved for 1918. In 1920, a modest recovery took place in Group B, a year in advance of the trend in output of Group A (Table 56).

The output of small-scale industry behaved in a less erratic fashion. Production declined at the outbreak of war, but then recovered between 1915 and 1916. Defence items accounted for around 12 per cent of output. Production declined during 1917 and 1918, but at a slower rate than in large-scale industry. Even at its nadir in 1920, the output of small-scale industry had reached 44 per cent of its pre-war level, compared to just 13 per cent in large-scale industry.[49]

(i) War production

Tsarist Russia entered the war in 1914 with supplies of munitions that broadly corresponded to expert assessments of the quantities required. But the predictions of a short conflict were soon confounded. So, too, were pre-war estimates of the rate of expenditure of artillery ammunition. Before the year was out, the Russian army found itself short of shell. The government responded by placing huge orders with the state works and with established private contractors. By spring 1915, the Tsarist regime faced a challenge on two fronts: an external challenge from Germany and Austria–

Hungary, and an internal challenge from liberal businessmen and professional people, who complained loudly about the bureaucratic incompetence that had brought nothing but defeat and privation to the Russian army. The government responded to the birth of the so-called voluntary organizations (the war industry committees and the Union of *Zemstva* and Towns) by embarking on an orgy of military production, designed simultaneously to defeat the 'enemy within' and the enemy without.

Considered in these terms, there is nothing very remarkable about the manufacture of shell in wartime. The government paid huge sums to state and private enterprises, which in turn purchased raw materials, acquired new machine tools, took on additional labour and passed the increased costs on to the state. However, this bald summary fails to do justice to three important aspects of the Tsarist war effort. First, an acute bottleneck in the supply of industrial equipment and, in particular, of machine tools placed industry at a huge disadvantage.[50] One means of resolving this shortage was by concentrating available stocks at a relatively small number of enterprises. This policy helped to promote still further the pre-war tendency towards industrial concentration. Secondly, the government intervened to smooth out disruptions in the supply of strategic raw materials to defence contractors. The third noteworthy development during wartime consisted in the reorganisation of factory work, for example by promoting the simplification and standardisation of the manufacturing process. This development was not unique to Russia. Where the mass manufacture of a standard product was relatively straightforward to accomplish, as in the production of shell, the gains in labour productivity were enormous. But so too was the military appetite. By contrast, Tsarist Russia was much less successful at producing heavy artillery, rifles and machine guns. For these items, the Chief Artillery Administration courted foreign suppliers, albeit with only limited success. Allied governments, juggling their priorities in a complex and changing situation, imposed strict limits to the export of munitions to Russia.[51]

The defeats suffered by the Russian army during the First World War owed something to the failure to achieve the right mix between different types and quantities of munitions. Nevertheless, Russia was not overwhelmed by the strength of its adversaries in terms of munitions, as Germany was in the Second World War. But military leadership was poor, compounded of a mistrust of infantry, a fatal attachment to fortresses and an overweening preoccupation with etiquette; and morale among the rank and file was low. The deciding factor in Russian defeat was the consequent inability of the Russian army to use similar types and quantities of munitions as effectively as its adversaries.[52]

The Bolshevik revolution and the call of the new leaders for peace provided a brief opportunity to begin the process of conversion from defence to civilian production. In the first few months of Bolshevik power, government attempts at planned demobilisation came to nothing, although individual factory committees organized the production of non-military goods, such as agricultural equipment. With the formation of the Red Army in February 1918 and the outbreak of civil war a few months later, it became necessary to make a careful inventory of the stocks of military hardware and to protect munitions from the encroaching German, Austrian and Romanian armies, not to mention deserters from the Russian army. These measures yielded disturbing news. In November 1918 the Red Army had at its disposal only one-tenth of the artillery and rifles, one-seventh of the cartridges and one-sixth of the shell held by the Russian army in September 1917. By the end of February 1919 the Red Army had only two-thirds of the rifles, one-third the number of machine-guns and two-fifths of the artillery pieces it required; Russian factories could supply no more than two-thirds of the required amounts of ammunition.[53]

The production of military goods during 1918 and 1919 was disrupted by the evacuation of Petrograd and hampered by the disorganized state of the enterprises that were relocated in the Central Industrial Region. Shortages of fuel and iron and steel compounded the problem. Machinery had been worn out by constant use. Skilled workers found themselves drafted into government, Party or army duties: in 1919, more than 55 per cent of workers in ordnance factories lacked skills. Serious shortages of food and other necessities led workers to absent themselves from work; in the autumn of 1918 this led to draconian laws on the militarisation of defence industry. The recapture of territory from White control brought with it the resumption of defence production in the Urals and elsewhere. Military success also enabled the Red Army to return skilled workers to factory work. However, the bulk of armaments 'production' during the civil war was attributable to repairs carried out on items inherited from the Imperial army. Repairs accounted for two-thirds of all rifles supplied during the civil war and for an even higher proportion of artillery pieces. The civil war was a massive exercise in recycling munitions.[54]

(ii) Civilian industry

The frantic attempt to boost armaments production curtailed the supply of finished goods to the civilian population. The Tsarist regime treated the claims of the non-combatant population as a residual, with disastrous consequences. The Provisional Government, by contrast, attempted to address the needs of the civilians, but without success. The Bolshevik government similarly struggled to meet the claims of both the civilian population and the military.

In 1915, the real value of manufactured output destined for final household demand was no lower than before the war, in part because of spare capacity. In 1916, the first cracks began to appear in the edifice. In 1917, with a substantial decline in total output, the value of output for household demand stood at no more than 64 per cent of the pre-war average.[55]

At the heart of the problem lay the diversion of resources to the war effort and the decline in labour productivity in consumer goods industry. Government regulation of raw materials, such as cotton, flax and leather, ensured that military contractors had priority in the supply of these products. Producers of finished goods for the civilian market went to the back of the queue. In July 1916 the government instituted fixed prices for all transactions in cotton yarn and fabrics, but this simply encouraged suppliers to hold out for higher prices.[56] Labour productivity in consumer goods branches declined throughout 1916, falling to 85 per cent of its pre-war level in cotton textiles and paper products, 82 per cent in food and drink and just 70 per cent in wood products.[57] Interruptions in supplies of fuel and raw materials, the mobilisation of skilled workers, and the high turnover of workers who sought more remunerative employment in the defence sector all wreaked havoc with attempts to maintain productivity.

During the civil war, labour productivity in group B industry continued to decline. Factories stood still for lack of fuel and raw materials. The labour force was ill-fed, ill-clothed and ill-housed, lacking the privileges accorded their counterparts in defence industry and in mining. The Bolshevik government established schedules of production and utilisation for a range of consumer commodities. By the beginning of 1919, plans had been drawn up for several foodstuffs (salt, sugar, fish) and other consumer necessities, such as clothing, leather, paper and rubber. The main aim was to allocate raw materials and semi-finished goods to government agencies and enterprises in accordance with detailed information about the size of the labour force and the stock of equipment. To this extent, the civil war promoted an experiment in rudimentary central planning. All the civil war experiments in state control, it should be remembered, took place in extremely difficult and uncertain conditions.[58]

Conclusion

In the twentieth century, economic factors played an increasingly important role in determining war potential. It is clear that the Russian contribution to Allied strength in the First World War was limited by the country's low level of economic development. In the civil war which followed, economic backwardness and disintegration contributed to the weakness of the opposing sides. A more detailed evaluation, drawn up in the light of Soviet economic performance in the Second World War, can be found at the end of the next chapter.

Further reading

For Russia's war preparations, see P. Gatrell's book (forthcoming). On Russian industry in wartime, see L. H. Siegelbaum, *The Politics of Industrial Mobilization in Russia, 1914–1917: a Study of the War Industries Committees* (1983); for a general international comparison, see G. Hardach, *The First World War, 1914–1918* (Harmondsworth, 1987). The economics of the civil war are surveyed by S. Malle, *The Economic Organization of War Communism, 1918–1921* (Cambridge, 1985). L. T. Lih, *Bread and Authority in Russia, 1914–1921* (Berkeley, 1990) is a study of food supply which spans both the world war and the civil war.

12   The Second World War

Mark Harrison

War broke out between Britain, France, and Germany, on 3 September 1939. At the end of August, the Soviet Union and Germany had entered into a pact of non-aggression. At this time, Stalin hoped to stand aside from the conflict in the west, and also to exploit it, expanding Soviet territory and military security at the expense of Polish and Baltic independence. But during the brief period of Soviet-German cooperation, Hitler's long-term perspective for German expansion remained fixed firmly on Soviet soil.

Already dominating half of continental Europe, German forces launched their surprise attack on Russia on 22 June 1941. The greatest land war of all time had begun. It would be fought with tens of millions of soldiers, and hundreds of thousands of aircraft, tanks and guns on each side, along a 2000 kilometre front.

By mid-autumn Kiev was taken, Leningrad besieged, and Moscow directly endangered. But neither Leningrad nor Moscow fell. The battle of Moscow in the autumn and winter of 1941–2 denied Hitler the lightning victory on which his hopes were pinned. Germany had lost the initiative, and now struggled to win it back. In the spring of 1942 the Wehrmacht advanced in a great arc across the south towards Stalingrad and the Caucasian oilfields. The Soviet encirclement and destruction of huge German forces at Stalingrad in the winter of 1942–3 marked the turning point. The Soviet drive to expel the German forces from Soviet territory was consolidated in another great battle at Kursk in the summer of 1943. After that, the story of the eastern front was one of almost continuous German retreat, matched by the advance of Soviet troops into Eastern Europe, and into Germany itself, the war culminating in the battle of Berlin (April–May 1945).

This was a devastating experience for the USSR. Its territory was deeply invaded. One in eight of its prewar population – some 26 million people – suffered premature death (see chapter 4); a third of its wealth was destroyed. Despite final victory, the Soviet economy, political development, and social and demographic processes were damaged and distorted for decades afterwards; the national pride of Soviet society, and great power aspirations of the Soviet state, also received a stimulus which was still evident in the events of 1991.

The outcome of the world war was largely decided on the eastern front. That the war in eastern Europe ended in Soviet victory raises many questions about Soviet economic development. How did the USSR mobilise its resources for victory, in spite of being the poorest of the Great Powers? How did the Soviet economy overcome its deep penetration by the German invader in the opening stage of the war? What was the relative importance of economic mobilisation, as distinct from the purely military role of the Red Army?

The statistical basis for answering these questions is richer in quantity than in quality. Published official data show realistically enough what happened on the changing territory under Soviet jurisdiction – the initial collapse of capital assets, of the workforce, and of production generally under the crushing weight of the German invasion; the difficulty with which industrial production was maintained but, at the same time, the rising graph of war production; the disaster which struck agriculture and consumer trade, and the long delay in recovery of these sectors.[1]

The official picture, however, suffers from all the defects which have driven western and Russian unofficial observers to attempt their own independent evaluations. Output is measured using material product concepts, not the GNP system. Real output is valued using 'fixed' prices of the distant past which not only give rise to large Gerschenkron effects, but also incorporate significant hidden price changes.

At a more detailed level a large volume of data is available to help us out. We have quite a lot of information about the underlying behaviour of physical output of different products, military and civilian. Wartime price trends may be estimated, although in a fairly freehand way. But published statistics on the workforce after 1940 are too aggregated, employment in munitions work is still officially concealed, and numbers employed in small-scale industry and agriculture have been generally neglected.

Reliable series for the Soviet national product, employment, and productivity must therefore be estimated indirectly, together with the real burden of defence, and the extent to which this burden was alleviated by Allied aid.[2] New information is continuing to throw further light on these trends.[3] Our estimates represent work in progress, which are subject to revision as more information becomes available.

(A) Production

(i) Military services and war production

In the Wehrmacht, Germany fielded by far the best fighting force of the Second World War. Wherever Germans met an opponent on numerically equal terms, man for man and gun for gun, Germany won. Neither side succeeded in developing a miracle weapon capable of winning the war quickly on its own until the atomic bombing of Japanese cities, which took place in August 1945 after Germany had already surrendered. Therefore, the main strategy available to the forces opposing Germany was to seek massive superiority in numbers of soldiers and quantities of equipment.

One of the most important factors affecting the demand for both soldiers and equipment in wartime was their rate of loss, both in combat and behind the front line in training and other use. The Second World War required such expenditures at unprecedented rates. In a typical month of the war, the Soviet armed forces would lose nearly 200000 men killed or died of wounds, and with them 300000 small arms, more than 6000 field guns and mortars, 2000 tanks, and nearly 2000 aircraft.[4]

There were several reasons for this. For one thing, the eastern front was contested with special bitterness. Much more than the British and the Americans, the Russians were faced with a war of national extermination. They carried on fighting under conditions in which Allied soldiers might have given ground, and their losses were correspondingly heavy. Moreover, the planning of Soviet military operations tended to ignore the likely human casualties and equipment losses. This habit, formed in the desperate days of 1941, persisted even when there was no compelling need to spend resources so carelessly, reinforced by the low valuation which the Stalinist system placed on the human 'cogs' which made up the military and economic machine. This was different from the German Nazi ideology and practice, which valued the lives of ethnic Germans but not those of others.

A particular factor affecting both combat and noncombat losses was the profound disadvantage of the Soviet soldier when it came to handling the equipment of modern war. Soviet weapon crews lacked the training, experience and battle hardening of the Wehrmacht, especially in the early stages. The typical Red Army man of 1942 was very young and green, as likely to write off his brand new aircraft or tank in training as under enemy fire. Official figures imply that combat accounted for less than half of Soviet wartime aircraft losses.[5]

Therefore, the first wartime task faced by the Soviet economy was to make good the huge losses of soldiers and equipment inflicted by the enemy under enormously adverse conditions of a deep invasion and terrifying defeats. Once this was accomplished, a second task was to supply yet more resources for the huge expansion of the armed forces which the war additionally required.

Soviet munitions output had accelerated in the years prior to the outbreak of war. In 1937 the Soviet Union was already producing a full range of modern weapons on a scale exceeded only by Germany. By 1940, Soviet munitions output had grown to nearly two-and-a-half times the 1937 level.

By the author's estimate (Table 57), between 1940 and the peak of the war effort during 1944, Soviet munitions output quadrupled again. At this time, monthly output stood at 3400 aircraft and nearly 1800 tanks, 10000 guns, 15,000,000 artillery and mortar shells and bombs, 500,000 small arms, and half a billion cartridges.

Contrary to all our findings about peacetime official production statistics in agriculture and industry, the official index of munitions output did not *overstate*, but greatly *understated* the real increase, as follows (1940 = 100):

	1941	1942	1943	1944
TsSU	140	186	224	251
Harrison	171	339	422	466

The underlying reason, however, was the same as in the case of peacetime statistical exaggeration – the failure of the official methodology to take into account changes in prices, which in the case of weapons *fell* by roughly 40 per cent, 1940–4. As the war proceeded, the improved, cheaper weapons which took the place of obsolete, expensive ones in the index were not given their due weight, leading to understatement of the increase in real output.[6]

The growth of munitions output was at first erratic and unstable. There was a first jump in the rate of production in the third quarter of 1941, followed immediately by a setback in the fourth quarter, which particularly affected aircraft, heavy and medium tanks, tank and anti-aircraft guns, shells, small arms, and cartridges. This setback, which reflected the impossibility of shielding the defence industry from the growing disruption and virtual collapse of the civilian economy, came when the outcome of the whole war hung by a thread, with Leningrad besieged, and Moscow threatened with capture.

The Red Army having survived this moment on the battlefield, the first quarter of 1942 saw resumed expansion of military goods. The expansion was now continuous, although the truth is that throughout 1942 it was continuously threatened by the danger of overall economic collapse, and a desperate shell shortage persisted. The foundations of the war economy could not be considered secure until 1943 brought stabilisation of the Soviet civilian economy. Now defence output rose towards its 1944 peak. Some military needs – e.g. for guns and mortars – were filled, and some lines of output could be cut back, though others continued to grow.

The Soviet contribution to overall Allied superiority over Germany was very substantial – more than 11,000,000 soldiers at the peak, together with huge quantities of munitions. During the war, Soviet industry produced 100000 tanks, 130000 aircraft, 800000 guns and mortars, one billion artillery and mortar shells and bombs, 30 million small arms of various kinds (including 12 million rifles), and 40 billion cartridges.[7] (However, the Soviet Union produced hardly any warships, jeeps or military trucks.)

How did the scale of the Soviet military effort compare with that of other countries? Numbers of military personnel are easily comparable, although they do not reflect the quality of combat organisation. Quantities of munitions produced are compared with greater difficulty, because of the different military specialisations of the Great Powers. (The United States and United Kingdom emphasised naval and strategic air power, the USSR built up huge ground and tactical air forces, while Germany was eventually forced to compete not only in ground and air forces but also in submarine warfare and air defence.)

For all these countries the most expensive weapon produced in large quantities remained the aircraft. The author has calculated the total (ground, air, and naval) munitions output of each country in standard units of single engined aircraft equivalents, with each country's ground and naval munitions being converted to single engined aircraft equivalents at national prices or costs, then valued in US dollar costs of 1945.[8] Numbers of military personnel at the peak of the war in 1944, and rough totals of war production cumulated over 1941 to 1944, can then be compared as follows (the figures cover the named Great Powers only, excluding their other allies, satellites, and colonies):

	Armed forces in 1944 (million)	Munitions output, 1941–4 ($1945 billion)
USA	11.4	140.6
UK	5.0	32.4
USSR	11.2	46.5
Germany	12.4	28.4

Thus the USSR provided two-fifths of Allied military personnel at the peak (the proportion of numbers in the European theatre would be larger), but perhaps little more than one fifth of overall Allied military equipment. Even so, if we assume that Germany disposed of two-thirds of her military assets on the eastern front, then the Soviet advantage of weaponry over Germany is given by a ratio of at least 2:1. If Italian and Japanese war production together amounted to as much as half the German total, the Anglo-American advantage over the Axis on the western front and in the Pacific was as high as 7:1.

(ii) Civilian industry and transport

What happened to the Soviet civilian economy during the war is, in outline, simple. In 1941 it suffered a catastrophic reverse. By 1942, real output of civilian industry (measured at 1937 prices by Edwin Bacon from serial data for 150 industrial products in physical units) had fallen to one third of the prewar benchmark; only the sternest measures held it back from outright collapse (Table 57). After 1942 civilian output began to recover, and to make new resources available once more. But by 1945 it still fell far short of pre-war levels.

Official measures of industrial production greatly overstated the performance of civilian branches, as compared with evaluation using serial data expressed in physical units and at 1937 prices. The official index numbers probably included some intermediate supplies to the defence industry, and may also have been exaggerated by an element of hidden inflation. Some significant discrepancies are shown below, expressing 1944 gross output as a percentage of 1940:[9]

	TsSU	Bacon and Harrison
Iron and steel	88	65
Chemicals, rubber	133	79
Timber, paper	55	21
Construction materials	35	26
Light industry	64	40
Food industry	47	39

The magnitude of the decline had the most serious implications. Without a minimum level of civilian output, there could be no war effort. As well as munitions, the army needed huge quantities of food rations, petrol and aircraft fuel, transport services, building materials and so forth – the means without which military construction and operations could not take place. The country's defence plant also needed metals, fuels, machinery and electric power; they needed workers, who themselves could not live without food, clothing and shelter. The munitions factories and their workforce also required transport services, training, and scientific, information and financial services. Thus the civilian economy was the foundation upon which the superstructure of defence output and combat organisation rested.

At first, the most threatening problems were found in heavy industry. In the autumn of 1941 many key branches were at a standstill, including all the factories making non-ferrous rolled metals, cable products, and ballbearings.[10] By the first half of 1942 the supplies of electricity, steel, and coal were respectively no more than one-half, two-fifths, and one-third of the levels achieved a year previously. Daily shipments of railway freight had fallen to one-third of the prewar level. The main factor was loss of territory and the decommissioning of evacuated plant, but there was also a downward spiral at work as coordination was lost. Coal shortages meant a lower level of railway utilisation. Moreover, coal accounted for a quarter of all pre-war ton-kilometres shipped by rail, so slower trains and more circuitous routes left power stations and blast furnaces without fuel, resulting in power cuts, and further loss of steel output.[11] The need to extend railway track and replace rolling stock to avoid further degradation of the railway system meant another downward twist of the spiral.

During 1942 things tended to get worse, not better. In the south the Germans renewed their offensive, and marched towards Stalingrad; more territory was lost. The Caucasian oilfields, until now protected by their remoteness, were directly threatened. Oil supplies had already begun to fall, because of equipment shortages and the difficulty of storing and transporting extracted oil; soon, production would be down by one-half. Although Soviet resistance before Leningrad and Moscow had averted complete defeat, everything remained desperate. The economy was regulated by emergency decrees, crash programmes, and panic measures to try to break out of the vicious spiral dragging industry down.[12] As each crisis was temporarily eased, new shortages would be felt; the strategic environment itself often changed more rapidly than plans and policies. Coal, steel, electric power, the railways and other forms of transportation were each in turn the object of attention; managerial shortcomings and wrong priorities criticised, new resources and cadres pumped in, along with exercises in boosting morale and tightening discipline.

The tide turned with the coming of 1943, for several reasons – victory at Stalingrad, large-scale American aid, and improved economic coordination. In all industries except nonferrous metallurgy, which was closely tied to defence output, output remained far below pre-war levels. After the winter of 1942–3, however, there was a partial recovery in most branches of civilian industry, and in transport. The war effort was no longer threatened by industrial collapse. But agriculture had not been restored, and in the food industry output continued to fall. During 1943–4, hunger continued to stalk the country.

(iii) *Agriculture and food industry*

In agriculture, 1941 was already very bad, and 1942 and 1943 were awesomely disastrous. In the autumn of 1941, as the Germans swept into the south and west, two-fifths of the whole Soviet grain harvest and two-thirds of the potato crop had been lost. The supply of livestock products had been held near to the 1940 level, but this was mainly because of heavy slaughtering of herds in face of the invading armies. In 1942 things got far, far worse. In that year total agricultural output fell to a mere two-fifths of the prewar level. In the meantime, the population under Soviet control had only fallen by one-third, from 196.7 million in June 1941 to 130 million in November 1942.[13]

The fall in output was partly a consequence of the temporary loss of the Ukrainian and Volga black-earth regions; this forced cultivation of field crops onto the inferior soils of the Northern and Eastern regions. But the agriculture of the interior regions was also forced into a sharp decline, as the following figures, dealing only with the territory untouched by enemy occupation, reveal:[14]

	1940	1942	1943	1944
Area under crops (million hectares)	72.7	77.7	66.4	59.0
Gross cereals harvest, barn yield (million tons)	57.7	60.4	51.0	45.1
Potatoes (million tons)	3.4	4.2	4.6	4.6
Meat, dead weight (million tons)	2.0	1.5	1.5	1.4
Raw cotton (million tons)	1.6	1.6	1.2	1.1

Having collapsed, output failed to recover in line with population. The 1943 growing season was relatively unfavourable; in central Russia there was too much rain, and it was too hot and dry in the south and east.[15] In spite of an increase in the area sown, yields declined further, and the 1943 harvest was barely maintained at the 1942 level. There was perhaps a small improvement in total agricultural production, but the increase was very small and all of it went to restoring livestock herds, so that the supply of food for human consumption did not increase at all. At the same time, the demand for food was rising because in 1943 significant territory was being recovered, and on it lived hungry people who had themselves lost the means of cultivating the soil. Only in 1944 was significant recovery achieved, and pre-war output still represented an unreachable goal.

The food processing industry was closely tied to agricultural performance. This branch supplied bread and bakery products, preserved fruit and vegetables, canned and cooked meat, dairy products, sugar and confectionary, tobacco, and alcoholic beverages. Food industry output fell with that of agriculture, and recovered more slowly. An increased share of processed foodstuffs was probably taken for Red Army rations – dried and tinned food for mobility, cigarettes for morale, and vodka for indifference to danger. As the war continued, town dwellers consumed less food, and in less processed forms. Starvation was widespread. In besieged Leningrad alone, a million people died of hunger and hunger-related conditions.[16]

(iv) National income and the defence burden

Soviet resources for war had to be found from within a rapidly diminishing total. This put the Soviet Union at a grave disadvantage. The war mobilisation of the other Great Powers was assisted by a significant increase in

Measuring Soviet wartime GDP

The author's calculation combines our present knowledge of the behaviour of the various branches of Soviet material production (including war production from 1937), and of employment in civilian and military services, with Moorsteen and Powell's estimates of the Soviet national product for 1937–40, by sector of origin, at 1937 factor cost. The result can be compared with other estimates for 1944 (1940 = 100):

		Excluding Lend-lease	Including Lend-lease
TsSU (1959)	NMP produced at 1926/27 prices	88	..
TsSU (1959)	NMP utilised, at 1940 prices	..	79
Bergson (1961)	GNP by end-use, at 1937 factor costs	89	100
Powell (1968)	NNP by sector of origin, at 1937 factor costs	80	..
Harrison (1993a)	GDP by sector of origin, at 1937 factor costs	78	92

Sources: TsSU figures: NMP produced, at 1926/27 prices, from *Nar. kh. 1941–5* (1959), 9; NMP used, at 1940 prices, calculated from index numbers and percentage shares for material consumption, accumulation, and defence outlays, in *Nar. kh. 1941–5* (1959), 55. Other figures from Bergson (1961), 210; Powell (1968), 7. For the author's GDP series, see table 57; GDP including Lend-lease is obtained from Table 58.

The present estimate is shown to be the most pessimistic of the Western studies; it is comparable with Powell's but the coincidence is accidental. (Powell's methodology understated the wartime increase in industrial production, and overstated the resilience of other branches; this point is discussed in Harrison (1991), 5–6.) It is also more pessimistic than the most widely cited official index (NMP produced in 1926/27 prices), but is surprisingly undercut by an alternative measure calculated from official TsSU data for NMP used (including Lend-lease revenues) in 1940 prices.

The burden of the war effort on supply

One official measure of the war-time defence burden was compiled within Gosplan on the basis of material balances for domestic products and their utilisation by the armed forces and defence industry, at state prices (which were at least relatively stable in wartime). The result, which is given separately for each production branch, shows the defence burden as a percentage of the gross value of output of the branch, as follows:

	1940	1942	1943 prelim
Industry	26	68	66
Agriculture	9	24	24
Construction	13	26	18
Transport	16	61	66
Trade	6	31	32

Source: GARF, 3922–4372/4/115, 19–22. Figures are given in more detail and reviewed in Harrison (1992b).

Such figures certainly understate the degree of economic mobilisation, for several reasons. One is that they ignore the contribution of service trades, both military and civilian (doctors, scientists, technicians). Another is that they rely on the material balance calculations of Gosplan, which were highly incomplete. For example, they show the gross value of output of the defence industry, and of the materials and transport services which the defence industry utilised, but not of the associated inputs into the fuel and transport sectors. Last, by the peak of the war effort munitions production was spread far beyond the specialised defence industry complex, and was also carried on under many civilian commissariats, whose claim on intermediate goods may not have been counted. For example, of the 646000 workers employed in the ammunition industry in 1943, more than half were outside the ammunition commissariat, and two-fifths were outside the defence industry complex altogether (GARF, 3922–4372/4/313, 165–9).

Still, the Gosplan figures show clearly the uneven incidence of war burdens, which pressed most heavily upon industry and transport (they also suggest the expected lessening of the pressure on industry and construction in 1943, as the inflow of foreign resources increased). If we weight them by value added in the various production branches, and include the value of military services (Table 57) they suggest that by 1942 the share of defence supply had reached just under 50 per cent of Soviet GDP.

The real burden of defence outlays

One official estimate of the war burden, based on material product accounts, compares defence-related expenditure on material supplies (including the material consumption and maintenance of military personnel) with the overall net material product (NMP) at 1940 prices. For 1940 this ratio is reported as 11 per cent, rising to 40 per cent in 1942 and a peak of 44 per cent in 1943 (*Nar. kh. 1941–5* (1959), 55). Some major items are left out of account however. Outlays other than on munitions, and pay and subsistence of personnel, may have been omitted in part or whole. Certainly, defence-related consumption of services, and the role of foreign supply in easing the burden of war spending on the domestic economy after 1942, are not reported; the increase in net imports was substantial enough to make 1943 significantly easier than 1942, even if we take the cited percentages at face value.

A more complete measure of economic mobilisation would be the ratio of total budget defence outlays to national income. But this is hard to compute and hard to interpret. Published budget statistics give wartime defence outlays only in current rubles, the reliability of which there is no reason to doubt. But national income, whether measured officially or by an independent western methodology, is only available at constant prewar prices. Naturally, for measuring the defence burden, both national income and defence spending should be measured in comparable prices. But which prices – current or constant? This is a very important choice, as Soviet officials discovered already in war-time when they estimated overall defence outlays as follows, per cent of NMP:

	1940	1941	1942	1943
At current prices	19	28	38	35
At prices of 1940	19	29	57	58

Source: GARF, 3922–4372/4/115, 50–3; figures are reviewed in Harrison (1992b).

The cause of this discrepancy was simple – between 1940 and 1943 munitions prices fell sharply, while prices of foodstuffs and consumer goods soared; the overall change in relative prices was roughly by a factor of 10 (Harrison (1991), table G–2). The war involved a huge change in the structure of output, away from civilian towards military goods and services; this is what we observe in the defence burden at fixed pre-war prices. However, rubles were expended on defence in war-time at the prices of war-time, not at pre-war prices. The war-time processes which made military goods cheaper, and civilian goods much more expensive, limited the share of national income which could be claimed by defence at current prices; the extraordinary scarcity and high cost of consumer goods and especially food set an effective upper limit on the degree of mobilisation.

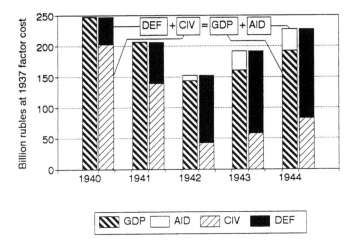

Figure 22   GDP and defence outlays, 1940–1944. *Source:* table 58.

their real national product, which greatly eased the problem of diverting resources to the war effort. Very different, and far worse, was the Soviet position.

The defence utilisation of GDP is shown in Table 58. One difference between GDP by end-use and a sector-of-origin approach to GDP is shown by the series for outlays on munitions (Table 58), which exceeded the net output (value added) of the defence industry itself (Table 57) by the value of intermediate goods acquired by the defence industry from other sectors. As Figure 22 shows, the share of defence spending in GDP at prewar prices, rising from 18 per cent in 1940, peaked at an astronomical 83 per cent in 1943. However, when the inflow from abroad is taken into account, the peak of domestic mobilisation is shown as having come in 1942, when the defence share of GDP reached a smaller (but still fantastic) figure of 70 per cent; in 1943, it was allowed to fall back somewhat, while foreign supply of the Soviet war effort reached nearly one-fifth of Soviet GDP.

What happened to the non-defence uses of national income in wartime is also clear from Table 58. In real terms, they fell from over 200 billion pre-war rubles in 1940 to well under 50 billion rubles in 1942, by which time the life was being squeezed out of the civilian economy. Not surprisingly, therefore, more than four-fifths of the 50 billion ruble improvement in real GDP in 1944, compared with 1942, was allocated to civilian uses.

The economic crisis of 1942 can be termed *a crisis of excessive mobilisation.* The mobilisation was excessive in the sense that the economy was faced with impossible demands, however justified they were by military necessity; the supply side could not long sustain the military burden at that level without collapsing within months. For mobilisation to have been 'excessive' in this sense, it is not necessary for there to have been avoidable mistakes, but with hindsight we can see how decisions and delays in 1941 deepened the difficulties in 1942.

Prominent among the factors deepening the crisis in 1942 was the continuing loss of territory and assets, over and above what had been lost in 1941. Other factors were a direct result of the pattern of mobilisation begun in 1941. First was the uncontrolled expansion of the Red Army and the munitions industries. Unrestricted recruitment into the army and home defence militia stripped the urban and industrial economy (including war factories) of key workers. The massive, uncoordinated conversion of civilian industry to war production also diverted huge stocks of labour, capital and material inputs away from the civilian economy. The army and defence industry commanded a larger and larger share of the civilian economy's outputs of refined fuels, machinery and transport and building services. The very success of the evacuation of defence industry from threatened areas added to the imbalance: to restart war production in the undeveloped regions of the remote interior usually required a fresh workforce and immediate provision of a new transport, service and residential infrastructure for the evacuated factory. The civilian economy, not being infinitely elastic, came close to snapping.

(B) Foreign economic relations

International transfers were generally very important in the economics of global war. All the Great Powers which engaged in the Second World War, except one, relied heavily on foreign supply to augment their national resources. Only America was rich enough to supply resources freely to other nations. The others – Great Britain, the Soviet Union and Germany – all imported heavily, and used their net imports to pay for the war in various ways. Germany did this by looting and taxing her new colonies in France, Scandinavia and eastern Europe, and also by transferring millions of slaves to the Reich to work on Germany's account. Britain and the Soviet Union also had access to large net imports, made available primarily by the United States under the Lend-Lease Act of March 1941.

For the Soviet Union, Allied aid did not matter very much until after Stalingrad. Eventually, however, it acquired a massive scale. Aid to the USSR (the great bulk of it from the United States) amounted to roughly $10 billions; nearly three-fifths of it arrived in the 18 months from mid–1943 to the end of 1944. There was also a comparatively slight British contribution, the bulk of which arrived in 1942–3.[17]

How important was this aid for the Soviet military? Through the war as a

---

The economic impact of Lend-lease

On the demand side, total expenditure consists of defence outlays (DEF) and civilian private and public consumption and gross investment (CIV). On the supply side are domestic resources (GDP) and foreign resources (AID). Thus, DEF + CIV = GDP + AID

If DEF was fixed by military requirements, and GDP was constrained by economic factors, it follows that any change in AID would be reflected in an equal change in CIV, the civilian use of resources. This would be the case, even if Lend-lease consisted solely of military goods.

However, to the extent that the Lend-lease program supplied goods which could not be produced domestically (or at least not quickly, or except at prohibitive cost), an increase in AID would be reflected in DEF, not CIV.

---

whole, up to the beginning of 1945, one in six combat aircraft supplied to the Soviet front, and one in eight armoured fighting vehicles, came from the West.[18], The Soviet Union supplied its own guns and ammunition, but its mobility and communications came to rely upon American trucks and jeeps, field telephones, tinned and concentrated foods. This confirms that the Soviet firepower which denied victory to Germany in 1941–2 was home produced. But the defeat of Germany in 1943–5 was significantly aided by foreign supply, and the Soviet capacity to chase the retreating armies thousands of kilometres from Stalingrad to Berlin depended on imported means of mobility.

Allied aid can also be evaluated in more general economic terms. According to the head of Gosplan, Voznesenskii, writing after the war, the industrial goods supplied in Lend-Lease summed to no more than 4 per cent of the value of output of Soviet public sector industry during the war as a whole.[19] Taking into account the low wartime ruble-dollar exchange rate, the wartime inflation of Soviet ruble prices, the double-counting inherent in the Soviet measurement of gross output value, and its inclusion of net indirect taxes, this figure is not entirely out of the question.[20]

Nonetheless Voznesenskii's 4 per cent clearly understated the importance of mutual aid for the Soviet economy in 1943–4. The flow of American machinery products and processed foods, cheap in dollar terms, weighed heavily in the Soviet resource balance when revalued in rubles. At Soviet factor costs of 1937, Lend-Lease may have amounted to one-fifth of the shrunken Soviet GDP in 1943–4 (See Figure 22 and Table 58). These figures suggest that without Lend-Lease the Soviet task in 1943 would have been far more difficult. To make up the shortfall and maintain the actual Soviet military effort of that year, a sum equivalent to one-fifth of GDP would have had to be withdrawn from civilian uses, tightening, not relaxing the pitch of overall mobilisation. (As the inset box demonstrates, this argument does not depend on the form of Allied aid – for example, combat gear for the army, or products such as industrial machinery for civilian use – so long as military and civilian goods were substitutes in production.)

To increase the degree of economic mobilisation in 1943 was almost certainly infeasible, and would have resulted in economic and military collapse – war factories without supplies, workers and soldiers without food or weapons. Therefore, without Allied aid, the authorities would have been compelled to withdraw major resources from fighting in 1943 in order to stabilise the economy; at best, victory in Europe would have been long postponed.

The Soviet achievement in 1941–2 is not affected by this judgment. The setbacks inflicted on Germany at Leningrad and Moscow in late 1941 were strategically decisive. Germany lost the initiative, temporarily at least, and the German strategy depended on holding it continuously. However, the initiative had not yet passed to the Soviet side, which was in no condition to hold it firmly until after Stalingrad. Moreover, the achievements of Moscow, Leningrad, and Stalingrad were based on an unsustainable degree of economic mobilisation. In order to pursue the war at all, the Soviet authorities had to relax their demands on the economy in 1943. They were enabled to combine this with a sustained military effort only by Allied aid.

(C) Capital

(i) Evacuation and conversion

One of the most important reasons why the Red Army was able to beat the Wehrmacht was that there were Soviet factories in the interior of the country in 1942–3, able to pour out aircraft, tanks, guns and shells at a faster rate than German factories. This depended partly on pre-war investment in the defence industry, but it also relied to a large extent upon wartime policies and decisions. This was for two reasons. First, the capacities created in peacetime were still hopelessly inadequate in face of the demands of a real war. Secondly, too much pre-war investment had been concentrated in the vulnerable western and southern regions close to Soviet borders; by 1942, they would be under enemy control. It had always been quicker and cheaper to add to plant which could produce immediately at a high rate, but in the wrong place from the point of view of an immediate war, than to incur the

---

The value of industrial assets evacuated in 1941

Lipatov (1966), 187, stated that the value of assets transferred exceeded three years' state investments under the first five-year plan (1928–32). According to official estimates, between 1929 and 1932 the fixed assets of Soviet industry grew by 3.8 billion rubles annually, or 11.4 billion rubles in three years. This can be compared with the value of all Soviet industrial assets, given as 92 billion rubles in 1941 in *Istoriya sotsialisticheskoi ekonomiki*, v (1978), 52–3, yielding a proportion of evacuated assets of one-eighth. But the evacuation zone accounted for one-third of prewar industrial production (see below), so the evacuation saved three-eighths (1/8 divided by 1/3) of assets in the evacuation zone. It also follows that the invasion resulted directly in a net loss of one-fifth (1/3 minus 1/8) of pre-war industrial production and capacity by 1942.

---

extra cost of building new plant in more remote industrial regions, which would add to immediate output only after a delay.[21]

On the territory occupied by Germany up to November 1941 had lived two-fifths of the Soviet 1940 population: 78 million people. This was one of the industrially most developed regions, producing one-third of pre-war industrial output (at 1926/27 prices), including half or more of pre-war aircraft, armament, and tank-building capacity, as well as of iron and steel (including rolled and armour steel), coal, aluminium, cement, soda ash and caustic soda, and raw alcohol. Devastating agricultural disruption also followed, since the occupied territories had accounted for nearly two-fifths of pre-war grain harvests and cattle stocks, 60 per cent of pre-war pig herds and virtually all the domestic sugar production.[22]

With the German invasion many of these capacities were simply lost. To try to save even a proportion required a tremendous effort of organisation and will. The evacuation began at the end of June 1941 and continued until the end of December. (In 1942, there was a second, much smaller wave of evacuation in the southern sector as the Germans advanced on Stalingrad.) Nearly half the evacuated factories went to the Urals, the rest to the Volga region, Western Siberia, Kazakhstan and Central Asia (a handful travelled still further to Eastern Siberia).[23] A permanent eastward shift in the Soviet defence industry's centre of gravity resulted.[24]

How much was actually evacuated? In a graphical metaphor, it is often written that the evacuated equipment filled a million ten-metre trucks; coupled end to end, they would have formed a solid line a quarter of the way round the world.[25] As shown in the Box, the whole process may have involved three-eighths of industrial capacity in the evacuation zone, or one-eighth of total Soviet industrial assets. This was an indispensable achievement since, without it, the Red Army would have had nothing to fight with in 1942.

It was claimed at the time that most evacuated plant had restarted production within 6–8 weeks of evacuation, but in retrospect this seems a minimum, not an average.[26] Of 94 iron and steel works evacuated in the second half of 1941, 40 were still not back in commission by mid–1942.[27] However, the usual reason for delay in recommissioning evacuated plant was not the efforts of construction agencies, which normally sufficed in the end, but the capacity of the new environment for supply of current inputs and labour to the relocated factory. The latter typically required not only ores, metals or components but also fuel and power, water, transport and communications, food and accommodation for the workforce, frequently a new workforce as well.[28] Of the 1523 big evacuated factories, 55 were still idle at the end of 1942 because a workforce could not be found to operate them.[29]

This reflected the negative side of the evacuation, which was a factor in the destabilisation of the civilian economy. While Moscow's attention was focussed exclusively on saving and relocating the key basic and military industrial plant, everything else was collapsing – transport, the fuel and power industry, iron and steel, food supplies. By 1942 it was not the shortage of munitions but the decline in these sectors which critically constrained and undermined the war effort.

The very success of the evacuation, which made possible military survival at the front, made these other matters worse. As huge defence and metallurgical factories were transported to the remote interior, sparsely settled rural communities were required to develop rail and road links, electric power lines and generating capacity, homes and services for workers, in a brief period of weeks and months. The established enterprises of the interior were also put under additional strain, since they now had not only to convert themselves to war production but also to service the new needs of relocated enterprises for materials, components and power supplies.[30] Only a completely inadequate proportion of these things could be accomplished in the time available, so the result was an economic crisis of awesome dimensions.

(ii) Conversion and construction

Regardless of the evacuation, productive capacity in the interior also had to be converted to wartime needs. While the evacuation was being carried out, the burdens of military supply had to be carried by the existing economy of the interior. Even after the evacuation, the specialised defence industries available for immediate military output still only represented a fraction of the total Soviet productive capacity. Therefore, side by side with evacuation, civilian capacities were converted to war production. Basic industries produced war materials and provided the army and defence industries with fuel, and power; engineering factories went over to making military equipment and components, while light industry produced uniforms and winter clothing, basic ration goods, and so on.

The conversion process began immediately, throughout industry and transport. But in many ways it lacked coordination. At first it did not go far enough, and eventually it went too far. Pre-war plans were drawn up on the basis of a short, offensive war. This meant that the likely losses of soldiers and equipment, and the huge increases in output required for years of total war, had been greatly underestimated. (It also fostered the shortage of ammunition relative to armament.) And the demands that war production would place upon the civilian economy, and the likely inroads upon civilian production, were not understood.[31]

Later, when the stark realities had become obvious to everyone, conversion of the civilian economy was carried far beyond anything envisaged in the pre-war period, and was eventually carried too far. While attention was fixed exclusively on saving and increasing the capacity to make military goods, the availability of steel, fuels, foodstuffs and transport services dwindled away. But without these the acceleration of defence output could not be sustained. Attention had henceforth to return to protecting and restoring the residual civilian economy.

In addition to converting existing factories to war production, the Soviet construction sector is also said to have built some 3500 big new establishments in the interior during the war years. These represented an annual rate of 780 commissioned plants, only a little less than the 860 per year under the third five-year plan (1938–41) or the 900 per year of the second (1933–7), and well above the 375 of the first (1929–32).[32] Probably, however, the new large-scale factory of the war years was smaller and more modest than the grandiose projects of peacetime, and locked up substantially fewer investible rubles.[33]

Moreover, the wartime rate of construction of new capital assets fell well short of the combined rates of depreciation and destruction. The official measure shows that by the end of 1942 the fixed capital stock, excluding livestock, had been reduced to two-thirds of the end–1940 level. Even at the end of 1945, when pre-war frontiers had been restored or even slightly enlarged, and the war had been over for several months, the value of fixed assets was still 9 per cent less than in 1940.[34] The overall loss directly attributable to the war can be set at roughly one third of the country's pre-war capital stock.[35]

In many branches of the economy, the capital stock decayed, and war losses were not replaced. This was especially true in agriculture, crippled by livestock and equipment losses. In peacetime, the shortage of draught power had been a principal constraint on the expansion of sown area and prompt performance of arable tasks.[36] When war broke out, horses were typically either handed over to Red Army units, or failed to survive civilian evacuation. (Cattle likewise died or were slaughtered.) The number of horses in the interior regions alone fell from 9.8 million in 1940 to 5.7 million in 1944. It is true that by 1940 half the draught power available to Soviet farmers was mechanised; but the production of tractors and combine harvesters had already fallen off because of the impact of pre-war rearmament on Soviet industry. With the outbreak of war the supply of machinery and parts to agriculture ceased altogether; again, in the interior regions alone, mechanical draught power in agriculture fell from 20.1 million horse-power in 1940 to 13.6 million in 1944.[37]

(D) Labour

(i) The pattern of employment

The war brought huge changes to the pattern of Soviet employment; the exact dimensions of change are obscured, however, by various uncertainties. Soviet employment in defence industry and defence-related sectors such as nonferrous metallurgy was traditionally classified information. Many other important figures (for example, the branch composition of industrial employment; numbers employed in transport, construction, and trade) were previously only published for 1940, leaving wartime changes to be guessed at. Figures for forced labour within NKVD establishments (mainly involved in construction, logging, and coal and gold mining) were also kept out of the official totals. Other areas were hidden by neglect – for example, employment in small-scale industry and collective farming.

Most of the missing data have now been uncovered, or can be reconstructed with some confidence. For example, the author has estimated wartime employment in munitions work from figures for defence industry output, combined with estimates of productivity change derived from price and cost data; these appear reliable from direct evidence in Soviet archives of both productivity change, and the change in employment, under the commissariats with special responsibility for defence industry.[38] Missing series for employment in small-scale industry have also been filled in from archival sources. We also have much more detailed information than before about the ration strength of the armed forces through the war years.

In considering the armed forces, I make a rough distinction between the defence forces (the army and navy), and the internal troops of the NKVD. The NKVD troops played only a limited combat role, and suffered few casualties.[39] Their main role was one of policing and domestic security, and I therefore exclude their maintenance and equipment from our estimates of the defence burden.

Official figures for public sector employment are assumed to include numbers of forced labourers leased by the NKVD to other agencies, but to exclude the population of GULAG camps, colonies, and labour settlements employed directly within NKVD establishments. The estimates given below make an allowance for the wartime scale of forced labour and its branch composition, based partly on estimates originally put forward 40 years ago by Jasny, whose work based on the captured annual plan for 1941 has been shown to be realistic, again, by new archival sources.[40]

Table 59 shows what happened to the Soviet working population and its branch composition, calculated on this basis. When war broke out, there were already five million soldiers in the Red Army, and five million more were mobilised from the civilian population in the first week of the war.[41] But this was just the first of several multi-million drafts; eventually, the defence commissariat had to find 11–12 million more men and women to replace early losses and lift force levels to the 11 million of 1942.[42]

In the economy, the production of military goods required substantial recruitment into the defence industry; its workforce grew eventually by more than a million, from 1.6 million in 1940 to 2.8 million in 1944. Since a majority of the existing defence industry workers in the occupied territories had been killed or left behind, or taken into the armed forces, total recruitment into the defence industry exceeded the net increase by a considerable margin; recruitment by the central agencies of the specialised defence industry complex amounted to over 800 thousand in 1942 alone (Table 60).

Even this was just the tip of the iceberg as far as war work generally is concerned. The number of other war workers supplying the means of munitions production, military construction, and military operations probably grew by a much larger number. Incomplete Gosplan figures showing the proportions of each branch's gross value of output claimed by the armed forces and defence industry were cited above (Box, p. 247). Those for 1940 and 1942 can be weighted by numbers employed in each branch (Table 59) to give numbers in war work.[43] A partial count is thus as follows (millions):

	1940	1942	Change, 1940–2
Army, navy	4.7	10.8	+ 6.1
War workers	9.0	14.1	+ 5.1
Working population	87.2	55.1	− 32.1

These figures suggest that within two years more than 11 million new workers were required for employment either in combat or in war work. At the same time, however, numbers in the working population collapsed. The result was an appalling labour shortage. Ultimately, civilian employment was devastated. Since the total supply of labour declined by 32 million between 1940 and 1942, and the number of soldiers and war workers grew by more than 11 million, numbers in nondefence employment (including agriculture) fell by at least 43 million.

Where did the millions of new war workers come from? Initially reserves were mobilised from the urban population. Thus in the second half of 1941 860000 women not at work, and school children between the ages of 12 and 15, volunteered for war work, together with thousands of students and veterans.[44] But conscripts graded unfit for combat duty were also directed into war work by the defence commissariat – 700000 in the same period.[45]

More detailed information is available for 1942 (Table 60). In that year, of 2.2 million workers recruited by the public sector agencies responsible for war work (defence industry, mining and metallurgy, transport, and construction), a further 655000 were found from the urban population (but now many were compulsorily mobilised), with another 480000 rejected conscripts. The growth of compulsory mobilisation was also reflected, although to a smaller extent, in the 240000 forced labourers contributed by the NKVD to commissariats engaged in war work.[46]

Most forced labourers, however, remained employed within NKVD establishments, engaged in construction, logging, and gold mining in the Far East. These probably totalled two million or more in 1940–1, falling to approximately 1.5 million in 1943–4.[47]

Increasingly the growth of war work made inroads on the numbers employed in inessential or administrative posts, or in training. Much of this encroachment did not require anyone to change their place of work or residence; it took place automatically, as a result of the conversion of civilian enterprises to war production. Steelworkers went on making steel, but their steel went to armour tanks rather than to plate road vehicles. Engineers continued to build machines, but the machines were for warlike, not peaceful use. However, there was still a need to find many new workers for such enterprises because established workers joined the armed forces or were promoted to administrative grades. For this reason, and because of the need to expand converted defence factories and create new ones, there was also significant recruitment into war work out of light industry and services through various channels – under the auspices of a wartime Labour Committee, 130000 in the second half of 1941 alone.[48] In subsequent years this channel would be greatly enlarged; in 1942–5 the Labour Committee directed nearly 12 million workers into war work or training, and half of them came from the urban economy.[49]

A major source of recruitment to the war was the rural population. Three-fifths of the wartime strength of the Red Army (11.7 million at its peak) were of rural origin. Of those mobilised in later years by the Labour Committee, a growing proportion was of rural origin; in 1943–4 three-fifths came from the countryside.

These recruits helped to fill the places of existing workers, mainly young men, taken into the armed forces. The result was a major change in the composition of the Soviet workforce. The share of women in public sector employment, 38 per cent in 1940, rose to 57 per cent in 1944, with figures for particular branches as follows (per cent of totals):[50]

	Jan. 1, 1940	Oct. 1, 1944
Industry	41	53
Construction	23	36
Transport	24	45
Trade	38	62
Government, administration	35	59

In beleaguered Leningrad, where virtually all male workers were enlisted in combat units, women's share in the factory workforce rose to 80 per cent or more.[51] Age was affected as much as gender. In the public sector as a whole, the combined employment share of the very young (under 19 years) and the relatively mature (over 50) rose from a sixth in 1939 to more than a quarter in 1942.[52]

The impact on rural employment was still more pronounced. The farm workforce on Soviet controlled territory was halved. In addition to the losses on territory under German occupation, the villages of the interior were stripped of working hands; there, the collective farm working population fell by more than one-third – in the Ural region and Siberia, by 45 per cent. Agriculture became the preserve of women, children, pensioners and evacuees. Young men disappeared from the countryside, recruited into war work in industry or the armed forces; the share of males aged between 18 and 49 years in the rural population, one-fifth in 1939, was reported at 6.4 per cent in January 1944. In the interior regions, able-bodied women outnumbered men by almost four to one.[53]

Most war work was skilled, and in the first months of the war huge skill deficits built up. As long as more unskilled workers were available, however, the skill deficit could always be overcome. Skilled labour had always been short in agrarian Russia and this was no new problem. Taking the war years as a whole, the shortage of skilled labour was acute but not decisive.

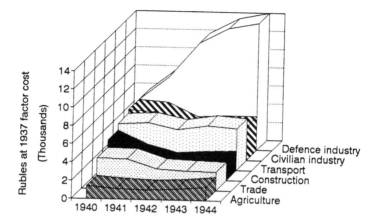

Figure 23   Net output per worker, 1940–1944. *Source:* table 61.

Ultimately, what constrained the Soviet productive effort was the shortage of working hands.

Excessive mobilisation characterised the Soviet labour market, just like supply and demand for output. By 1942 there were too many soldiers and too many war workers compared to the number left in the supporting civilian infrastructure; this placed the capacity of the Soviet Union for sustained military-economic resistance in doubt. Stricter controls on the mobilisation process, and the stabilisation of the civilian economy, came more or less together at the end of 1942. Only then could the country turn the corner of its economic crisis.

(ii) Productivity

In most branches of material production, the war saw a sharp decline in output per worker. According to the present author's estimate (see Figure 23 and Table 61), in civilian industry output per worker sagged by 30 per cent; since hours worked also rose by nearly 30 per cent, output per hour worked fell by even more.[54] In construction, output per worker probably fell by more than half. In agriculture, the largest branch in terms of peacetime employment, prewar productivity was already notably depressed, and output per worker fell by a quarter in 1940–2 before recovering in 1944. This means that, just when every spare worker was needed to fight or to make munitions, the labour requirement of each unit of other kinds of output rose sharply.

The reasons for the productivity setback were mixed. Official accounts stress the supply interruptions arising from the loss of economic coordination and reduced priority of civilian output.[55] In light industry, for example, there were continual supply interruptions in 1942; the number of day-length periods of idleness averaged over the manual workforce rose from less than 4 per worker in 1941 to more than 16 in 1942. But excessive working hours, and undernourishment, also played a part. For manual workers in industry as a whole, the working year rose from 270 7.6-hour days in 1940 to 292 9.3-hour days in 1943.[56] Western evidence suggests that at this level of intensity increased hours resulted merely in reduced output per hour worked, not increased output, as working time lengthened.[57] It remains to be established whether the moral impetus of war work in Soviet defence industry overcame this tendency. In light industry, the number of days lost through sick leave and other authorised or legitimate absence rose from 17 in 1940 to 37 in 1942.[58]

All the more important, therefore, was the capacity of the specialised defence industry to raise output far above the growth of employment. By 1944, output per worker in the defence industry was two-and-a-half times the 1940 level (see Figure 23 and Table 61). This was an international phenomenon, matched in German and American (and, to a lesser extent, in British) war factories.[59] What made it possible in each case was the mobilisation of reserve capacities, combined with the changeover from relatively slow, non-specialised, production of weapons in small batches to flow production and assembly of standardised parts on conveyor belts, allowing much greater specialisation and division of labour. The success of the Soviet war effort depended greatly on this achievement, and its importance was magnified by the disastrous productivity showing of other branches.

The degree of mobilisation of the workforce, although clearly excessive, was limited by low productivity in agriculture, and the setback to productivity in every branch except specialised munitions work. If productivity losses had been avoided, or if the productivity gap between industry and agriculture had been limited to Western European or North American proportions, millions of workers would have been freed for war work in industry or frontline duty. To the extent that the decline in agricultural productivity was a result of asset losses and efficiency losses stemming from the decision to collectivise agriculture at the end of the 1920s, then the Soviet economy continued to pay for this decision during the Second World War.

(E) Food

(i) Bread

The most important element in wartime consumption was food. Bread (600 grams, or 1300 calories) was the most important element in the daily ration for the Soviet industrial worker throughout most of 1942–3.

Between 1940 and 1942, the population under Soviet control fell by one-third. But the supply of consumer goods fell more. Per capita supply of basic goods – cotton and woollen cloth, grains and potatoes – was halved. Access to consumer services, ranging from catering and distribution to housing, health and education, suffered a similar squeeze. And in 1943, in proportion to the population, most supplies improved little, or got even worse. This was because the population under Soviet control increased more rapidly than civilian output. The territories now being liberated represented new demands for supplies which had to be diverted away from the consumers of the interior. There were 25 million homeless people to be fed and housed.

All the belligerent nations rationed food to civilians in the Second World War, and the Soviet Union was no exception. Food rationing was an inevitable result of wartime circumstances, especially the breakdown of market allocation of foodstuffs. The key factor was the development of overwhelming excess demand on the retail market. This in turn was a result of the fact that household incomes and purchasing power were maintained in face of the collapse in consumer supplies. The money wage of the public sector employee rose in wartime from 330 rubles per month in 1940 to 434 rubles per month in 1945.[60] This increase was not matched by any increase in real supplies for household consumption, which declined sharply. At the same time prices were significantly increased in state-controlled trade only for alcoholic drink. Even when the sixfold increase in the price of beers, wines and spirits is taken into account, official retail prices in state and cooperative trade in Moscow in 1942–3 stood at only 80–90 per cent above the July 1940 level.[61]

Only in 1944 was the reliance on rationing at fixed prices modified with the advent of 'commercial' trade – official shops where goods were sold off the ration at scarcity prices approaching free market levels. The 'commercial' price of a kilogram of white bread made from wheat flour in Moscow in 1944, for example, was a colossal 275 rubles (nearly three weeks' wages) compared to the ration price of 3.80 rubles.[62]

The rationing system emerged in stages between July and November 1941.[63] Rationing now covered the bulk of the nonfarm population, but this meant far from everybody. According to official figures, in 1942–3 no more than 48 per cent of the population on Soviet territory was supported by bread rationing.[64] The remainder had to rely on unofficial or 'local' resources (see below).

In deciding who was to get what, the rationing authorities were sometimes faced with unbelievably hard choices. There was not enough food to go round, and the food commissars were forced to exercise powers which amounted, in the extreme case, to powers of life and death. They had to take decisions (concerning whom to preserve and whom to abandon) of a kind familiar, perhaps, only to food relief workers in the midst of major famines in the world today.

As in 1930–4, a complicated system of differentiation between different categories of consumers evolved to reflect current economic priorities. In principle, there were the same four groups as in the early 1930s – manual workers, white-collar employees, dependents, and children under 13 years of age. But, as before, these categories soon acquired many fine internal gradations; the latter gave special status to defence industry workers, those working under particularly difficult or dangerous conditions, and a 'special list' of leading enterprises.

For those on rations, bread was all important. All categories of consumers received not less than four-fifths of their officially rationed calories and proteins from bread.[65] The energy content of food rations available in the interior of the country during the low point of the war, which lasted from the cut in the bread ration announced on 21 November 1943 until early 1945, is reported as follows (in calories):[66]

Children under 13 years	1067
Adult dependents	780
Non-manual workers	1074–1176
Most manual workers	1503–1913
Manual workers employed under particularly difficult or dangerous conditions in defence industry	3181–3460
Coalface workers	4114–4418

The extent of differentiation was such that the most privileged obtained five or six times as many calories and grams of protein as the least.

In fact, for almost all categories, official rations fell far below the minimum necessary to avoid serious malnutrition. The shortfall was roughly 50 per cent for the adult dependent and nonmanual worker shown above, and 20 per cent for the ordinary war worker. Only combat soldiers and manual workers in the most difficult and hazardous occupations were guaranteed sufficient nourishment to maintain health. Even so, the lowest ration in the interior of the country was considerably more generous than that available in Leningrad in the winter of 1941. In Leningrad, the low point was reached in the month from 20 November to 23 December, when workers' daily rations were cut to 250 grams (540 calories) of bread and all others' to a deadly 125 grams (270 calories). Even soldiers on the Leningrad front received no more than 500 grams (1080 calories).[67]

Under such circumstances, malnutrition was general and pervasive.

Deaths from starvation were not confined to Leningrad. Hunger did not just have individual consequences. 'Food crimes' were common, and were harshly punished.[68]

(ii) 'Local resources'

State rations alone were insufficient to sustain the lives of all but a minority of those entitled, and more than half the population – mainly farming families – did not receive state rations at all. Therefore, nearly everyone resorted to decentralised or unofficial sources of supply as well.[69] For some, they provided a supplement to official rations. For others – in fact, for the majority of the population – they were the only means of existence.

Local resources included sideline farming by large factories, the retained produce of collective farms and market gardens not claimed by government procurements, and the output of collective farmers cultivating allotments on their own account, marketed through the *kolkhoz* (collective farm) markets.

Even for the rationed population, the importance of nonrationed supplies can be seen from the following. It was shown above that in 1944 the adult public sector worker's daily ration provided not less than 1,000 calories and (in most cases) not more than 2,000 calories. But in 1944 the average daily intake of the urban adult was 2,810 calories. Of this, just over two-thirds (69 per cent) was met from central or local government stocks. The remainder came from 'local resources', in the following proportions (per cent of total calorie consumption):[70]

Sideline farming of enterprises and institutions	4.5
Private allotment gardening	12.4
Collective farm market purchases	14.5

By 1944 these sources made up the difference between starvation and survival. In 1942, in contrast, these decentralised supplies had made up a bare fifth of the urban adult's energy intake, which had only reached 2,550 calories per day.

No one was more dependent on 'local resources' than the peasant. How did collective farmers live under wartime conditions? It was not just that food supplies per head of the whole population had fallen disastrously. Food output per collective farmer had also fallen seriously, while the share of total grain and meat output taken by the government had risen.[71] The collective farmer was left with a reduced share in a smaller total than before the war.

Peasants depended substantially on potatoes. Potato consumption, per head of the peasant population, more than doubled, rising to 800–850 grams (600 calories) daily. Meanwhile, daily bread consumption fell to no more than 300 grams (650 calories) per head. Other proteins, fats and vitamins came from milk, grasses and acorns.[72]

Not all rural dwellers suffered equally. While food was fantastically scarce, those lucky enough to have disposable food surpluses could take them to market. (And this was part of the unofficial system which enabled the urban population to supplement official supplies and survive.) By 1943, when scarcity prices peaked, the seller could get 13 times the prewar return on food produce. On this basis, a few became ruble millionaires, on paper at least.[73] But the cash income from food sales on the free market did not contribute significantly to peasant living standards, since there was nothing to be bought in the village for cash.

(F) Two World Wars in economic comparison

Detailed comparison of the performance of the Soviet economy in the Second World War with that of the Imperial Russian economy in the First World War suggests a number of significant differences.[74]

A big difference lay in the scale of military mobilisation. Where Russia mobilised 10 per cent of its population for military service in the First World War, the USSR raised the proportion to 16 per cent. As for defence industry products for the army and air force, in the Second World War the USSR supplied at least 25 times the volume made available from the Russian economy during the first war, per year of fighting, without any allowance for the improved quality and assortment of weapons.

But the USSR also sustained far heavier losses – at least 8.7 million soldiers (compared with 1.8 million in 1914–17), 25–26 million citizens altogether, and a third of its pre-war wealth.

In the fate of the civilian economy in the two world wars we find both similarities and differences. In the Second World War loss of territory was combined with neglect of civilian requirements and diversion of resources into war production, leading to a sharp cutback in the availability of consumer goods. This, coupled with decline in food availability, led to steep deterioration in the real wage.

In the Second World War these things happened straight away, whereas in the First World War they had transpired only after two years' fighting. In both wars, despite productivity gains in war production, in many civilian sectors productivity fell back because of supply interruptions, excessive hours and workers' hardship. At the same time there were also major differences which operated to the advantage of the Soviet economy, most importantly in agriculture.

In the First World War, Russia suffered all the disadvantages of a low-productivity, semi-marketised agrarian sector. When war broke out, peasant responses to the wartime shortage of industrial goods forced the burden of adjustment onto the urban population. Peasant farmers preferred own consumption of their food surpluses to the sale of food in return for useless cash, given the prevailing shortage of industrial goods. Urban-rural trade broke down, and the countryside disintegrated into self-sufficient regions, withholding food surpluses from the food-deficit sectors of towns and industries. A weak transport and administrative infrastructure made it more difficult for government to intervene, impose rationing and controls, and direct food resources where they were needed.When the full extent of consumer shortages was revealed, the ensuing crisis toppled the old regime.

In the Second World War the decline in Soviet living standards and food availability was immediate, and was probably worse than in the First World War. However, this decline was shared to a greater extent amongst the population as a whole, especially (and forcibly) by the food producers themselves.The Soviet urban population was given a nominal floor to food entitlement through rationing, while the rural population was denied protection. The priorities of the Soviet food distribution system were maintained – despite the absolute insufficiency of food to keep everyone alive. Keys to this were the more highly developed transport and allocative system, and the *kolkhoz* and food procurement system, major elements of which had either not existed or not been effective in the First World War and the civil war. Despite shortages of industrial goods in exchange, the Soviet peasantry could not express a preference for own-consumption. This in turn contributes to an explanation of why Soviet urban society did not witness the mass resistance to officialdom and disillusionment with the war effort that were so characteristic of the popular response to the First World War. It also helps to explain how the Soviet economy was able to overcome the otherwise crippling disadvantage of what still remained in the 1940s the most technologically backward farming system in Europe.

Of course, part of Soviet military-economic success in the Second World War, in comparison with the miserable achievement of the First World War, can be ascribed to the intervening increase in available industrial, transport, and demographic assets, which gave to the USSR the advantages both of a larger GDP, and of a higher development level in terms of GDP per head (chapter 3).

At the same time, the record of the Second World War also suggests that the Soviet economy was mobilised with an intensity comparable to that of much more developed economies. This cannot be explained by the Soviet economy's size or development level. It can reasonably be attributed (in part, at least) to policy and system characteristics which were specific to the Soviet economy, and which made possible a very high ratio of defence spending to GDP.

However, it is worth remembering that the intensity of the Soviet mobilisation was more apparent in terms of GDP than employment commitment.
The ability to transfer workers to the war effort was limited by the pre-war
agrarian structure of the Soviet economy, especially the irreducible labour
requirements of a large low-productivity agricultural sector.

Further reading

J. D. Barber and M. Harrison, *The Soviet Home Front, 1941–1945: a Social and
Economic History of the USSR in World War II* (1991), provide an overview of
Soviet economic experience in the Second World War. A collection of very readable
essays by authorities on various special topics is S. J. Linz, ed., *The Impact of World
War II on the Soviet Union* (Totowa, NJ, 1985). M. Harrison, *Soviet Planning in
Peace and War, 1938–1945* (Cambridge, 1985) deals at greater length with the
wartime economic system and planning; Moskoff, W., *The Bread of Affliction: the
Food Supply in the USSR during World War II* (Cambridge, 1990) presents much
new material on economic and social aspects of the production and distribution of
food.

Finally, P. Gatrell and M. Harrison, 'The Russian and Soviet Economies in Two
World Wars', *Economic History Review*, xlvi (1993), offer a view of both wars in an
internationally comparative framework.

Tables

In all tables, 0 or 0.0 = nil or insignificant

               – = not applicable

               .. = not available

              ( ) = calculated as residual

Figures may not sum to totals shown because of rounding.

Metric tons (tonnes) and American billions (thousand millions) are used throughout this volume.

Data are given for Soviet frontiers before 17 September 1939 unless otherwise stated.

Table 1. *Russian and Soviet GNP and population, 1913–1940*

	GNP, billion rubles at 1937 factor cost	Population mid-year, millions	GNP per head, rubles
(A) Pre-1918 frontiers			
1913	134.1	166.0	810
(B) Pre-1939 frontiers			
1913	113.0	139.9	810
1928	123.7	153.2	810
1929	127.0	156.1	810
1930	134.5	158.6	850
1931	137.2	160.8	850
1932	135.7	162.4	840
1933	141.3	159.8	880
1934	155.2	157.5	990
1935	178.6	159.2	1120
1936	192.8	161.3	1200
1937	212.3	164.0	1290
1938	216.3	167.0	1300
1940	223.6	173.1	1290
(C) 1940 frontiers			
1940	250.5	194.0	1290

Sources:
GNP, 1913 and (within pre-1939 frontiers) 1940: GNP per head, multiplied by population; 1928–40, within contemporary frontiers, at 1937 ruble factor cost, from Moorsteen and Powell (1966), 622–3.

Population of the former Empire, 1913, less Finland and the Kingdom of Poland, and within pre-1939 frontiers (adjusted to mid-year): see chapter 4; of the USSR, 1928–40 – *Vestnik statistiki*, 7, 1990, 41 (ADK), adjusted to mid-year.

GNP per head, 1913 – 'permanent' income, assumed equal to 1928 (see chapter 3); 1928–40 – GNP within contemporary frontiers, divided by population.

Table 2. *GDP per head of the USSR in international comparison, 1913–1940 ($INT and 1980 prices)*

	1913	1928	1932	1937	1940
Japan	800	1150	1130	1330	1660
Russia (USSR)	900	900	930	1440	1440
Italy	1550	1780	1740	1960	2070
Germany	1960	2280	1880	2740	3190
France	2000	2550	2280	2590	2330
UK	2970	3110	2990	3610	3980
USA	3790	4690	3450	4570	4970

Note:

$INT are 'international' dollars in the meaning of Phase IV of the International Comparison Project.

Sources:

Russia (USSR) – GNP per head, in rubles at 1937 factor cost (table 1), converted to GDP and international dollars by setting Soviet GDP per head in 1937 at 40 per cent of the United Kingdom on the basis of Harrison (1992c), 10.

Other countries – per capita GDPs for 1980 from Maddison (1989), 112. Change in GDP, 1913–80, within present-day frontiers, from Maddison (1991), 212–19, adjusted to GDP within contemporary frontiers on the basis of notes to his tables. Mid-year population within contemporary frontiers from Maddison (1991), 232–9.

Table 3. *Gross investment and capital projects in progress, 1928–1940 (billion rubles and 1937 prices)*

	Gross investment	Increase in capital projects in progress			
		billion rubles		per cent of gross investment	
		(A)	(B)	(A)	(B)
1928	9.6	1.3	..	13	..
1929	12.2	1.7	..	14	..
1930	17.7	3.2	..	18	..
1931	19.9	3.7	..	19	..
1932	20.8	2.5	..	12	..
1933	18.5	0.0	0.0	0	0
1934	21.0	0.9	2.1	4	10
1935	26.3	-1.7	-1.3	-6	-5
1936	36.1	0.6	5.8	2	16
1937	32.5	1.8	4.8	6	15
1938	33.0	..	2.7	..	8
1939	33.0	..	0.6	..	2
1940	32.2	..	2.1	..	6

Source:
Gross investment from Moorsteen and Powell (1966), 387.

Value of capital projects in progress, at acquisition prices, 1 January 1928–40, from Davies (1982), 47 (series A), 48 (series B); the increase in capital projects in progress, 1940: gross investment at current prices, from Moorsteen, Powell (1966), 391, multiplied by 13.5 per cent, from the ratio of new capital in operation to investment in 1940, given by Sokolov (1946), 25, as 86.5 per cent. Acquisition prices are converted to constant 1937 prices using the procedure outlined by Moorsteen, Powell (1966), 448–9, which assumes that work in progress at the beginning of year t consists of work carried over from the previous two years, in the proportions of 60 per cent for year t-1 and 40 per cent for year t-2. Unfinished construction on 1 January 1928 and 1929, however, is derived using the deflator for 1928 only.

Table 4. *National income by sector of origin, 1913–1940 (per cent of net national product)*

	1913	1928	1932	1937	1940
Agriculture	50.7	48.3	32.1	31.0	29.5
Industry	21.4	20.4	28.8	32.2	32.8
Construction	5.1	3.2	5.1	5.2	4.5
Transport	5.8	3.9	7.5	8.3	8.2
Trade	8.1	7.9	6.2	5.1	4.7
Services	8.9	16.3	20.3	18.1	20.3
Total	100.0	100.0	100.0	100.0	100.0

Sources:
1913, at 1913 prices, from Gregory (1982), 73.
1928–40, at 1937 factor costs, calculated from Moorsteen and Powell (1966), 622–3.

Table 5. *National income by end use, 1913–1940 (per cent of net national product)*

	1913	1928	1937	1940
Consumption				
by households	80.5	81.6	54.9	52.2
by government				
defence	4.9	1.3	8.2	18.2
nondefence	6.0	6.9	14.3	14.9
Net investment				
domestic	11.4	10.2	22.6	14.7
foreign	−2.9	0.0	0.0	0.0
Total	100.0	100.0	100.0	100.0

Sources:
1913, at 1913 prices, from Gregory (1982), 57.
1928–40, at 1937 factor costs, calculated from Bergson (1961), 128 (gross product and investment are adjusted to net by subtracting depreciation, from Moorsteen and Powell (1966), 622–3).

Table 6. *Population recorded by censuses, 1926, 1937 and 1939 (millions)*

	17 December 1926		6 January 1937		17 January 1939		
	Official[1]	Adjusted[2]	Official[3]	Adjusted[2]	Official[2]	Adjusted A[2]	B[4]
Males	71.0	71.8	77.7	78.0	81.7	80.8	..
Females	76.0	76.8	84.3	84.7	88.9	88.0	..
Total	147.0	148.5	162.0	162.7	170.5	168.9	167.3

Sources:
[1] Lorimer (1946), 231.
[2] *Vestnik statistiki*, 7, 1990, 37.
[3] *Sots. issl.*, 6, 1990, 17–18.
[4] *Sots. issl.*, 8, 1990, 51.

Table 7. *Annual population increase, 1927–39: alternative estimates*

	Population on 1 January (millions)				Births during year (thousands)		Deaths during year (thousands)			Net increase in population (thousands)			
	From registration data	Lorimer initial	Lorimer adjusted	ADK	Lorimer	ADK	Lorimer initial	Lorimer adjusted	ADK	Registration data	Lorimer initial	Lorimer adjusted	ADK
	1	2	3	4	5	6	7	8	9	10	11	12	13
1927	147.1	147.1	147.1	148.7	6731	6950	3862	3862	3984	3339	2869	2869	2965
1928	150.4	150.0	150.0	151.6	6620	6944	3666	3850	3878	3768	2954	2770	3066
1929	154.2	153.0	152.8	154.7	6384	6876	3871	4239	4132	3248	2513	2145	2745
1930	157.4	155.5	154.9	157.4	6140	6694	3806	4358	4284	2986	2334	1782	2410
1931	160.4	157.8	156.7	159.8	5862	6510	3733	4469	4501	2650	2129	1393	2009
1932	163.1	159.9	158.1	161.9	5567	5837	3652	5493	4786	1893	1915	74	1051
1933	164.9	161.8	158.2	162.9	5272	5545	3547	4284	11450	–1315	1725	988	–5905
1934	163.7	163.6	159.2	156.8	4779	4780	3334	3886	3410	1111	1445	893	1369
1935	164.8	[165.0]	160.0	158.2	4829	5249	3238	3606	3282	2318	1591	1223	1967
1936	167.1	[166.6]	161.3	160.1	9447	5589	3147	3331	3223	2203	2300	2116	2366
1937	169.3	[168.9]	163.4	162.5	6542	6549	3071	3071	3557	..	3471	3471	2992
Discrepancy as compared with 1937 census	6.8–7.3	6.4–6.9	0.8–1.3	–					–				
1939	[175.8]		170.3	168.5	..	..		..	..	..	3456	3456	3033
Discrepancy as compared with 1939 census	5.3–8.5		0.2–3.0	–					–	–	–	–	–

Notes:

Discrepancy between his initial estimate and actual population in January 1939 was assumed by Lorimer to amount to 5,522,000 persons. As the population at the time of the 1939 census in fact differed from, and was less certain than, Lorimer's assumptions, the true discrepancy was between 5.3 and 8.5 million persons, and a discrepancy remained after Lorimer's adjustments (0.2 – 3.0 million persons). We have shown these figures, and the corresponding figures for 1937, in Columns 2 and 3. Population is assumed to have increased by 0.2 million between 1 January and the date of the census, 17 January 1939. A further adjustment would be needed to Lorimer's discrepancy of 5.5 million, if the population at the time of the December 1926 census was not 147.0 but 148.5 million.

Figures in square brackets are interpolated by the authors.

Sources:

Columns 1 and 10: from contemporary report of P. I. Popov (RGAE, 105/1/10, 20).

Columns 2, 5, 7 and 8: Lorimer (1946), 134.

Column 3: Lorimer (1946), 135.

Columns 4, 6, 9, 13: ADK (1990a), 41.

Column 8: derived from Lorimer's revised data for population cited in Column 3 and given in more detail in Lorimer (1946), 135.

Column 11: derived from Lorimer's initial data in Columns 6 and 9.

Column 12: derived from Lorimer's adjusted data for population (Lorimer (1946), 135).

Table 8. *Births and deaths in the period 1927–1936 (inclusive) (millions)*

	Raw registration data[1a]	Kurman: adjusted registration data[2]	ADK: Estimated population changes[1]
Births	47.5	(55.5)	61.0
Deaths	28.5	32.5[b]	46.9
Net apparent increase	19.0	23	14.1
Net actual increase	15.0	15	13.8
'Gap'	(4.0)	8[c]	0.2[d]

Notes:

[a] Covers only part of all Soviet territory; in 1934 it was estimated to include territory incorporating 90.7 per cent of the population, and 95.7 per cent of the population on that territory – i.e. 86.8 per cent of the whole population.

[b] According to ADK (1990a), 39, 34.3 million deaths were registered.

[c] For Kurman's explanation of this gap, see Box on p. 75.

[d] ADK attribute this small gap to emigration, which they give as 0.2 million 'as a minimum'.

Sources:

1 See ADK (1990a), 39.

2 *Sots. issl.* 6, 1990, 22–4 reprints the Kurman memorandum, dated 14 March 1937.

Table 9. *Birth rates and death rates, 1913–1950*

	Crude birth rate (per 1000 population)	Crude death rate (per 1000 population)	Net reproduction rate (per 1000 population)	Infant mortality (per 1000 population)
1913[1]	47.0	30.2	16.8	273
1926 (Official)[1]	44.0	20.3	23.7	174
1927 (registration data)[2]	43.7	21.0	22.7	..
1927 (Lorimer)[3]	45.0	26.0	19.0	..
1927 (ADK)[4]	46.3	26.5	19.7	182
1938 (Official)[1]	37.5	17.5	20.0	161
1938 (ADK)[4]	39.0	20.9	18.2	174
1950 (Official)[1]	26.7	9.7	17.0	81

Sources:

[1] *Nar. kh. 1963* (1965), 30.

[2] See text table, p. 66, note a.

[3] Lorimer (1946), 134.

[4] ADK (1990a), 41, 43.

Table 10. *Agricultural and non-agricultural occupations, 1926 and 1939 (millions of persons)*

| | 1926[1] | 1926[1] | 1939[2] |
	Raw data	Revised data	Raw data
Agricultural	71.7	61.6	48.2
Industry, building and transport	6.3	6.3	23.6
Other non-agricultural	5.3	5.3	15.3
Total	83.3	73.2	87.1
Pensioners, unemployed, etc.	2.9	2.9	5.0
Total gainfully occupied	86.2	76.1	92.1

Notes:
[1] Raw data for agriculture included family members engaged in agriculture: 11.8 million children aged 10–15 and 6.2 million men and women over nominal retirement age of 55 for women and 60 for men. The 1939 census includes only children over 15 and men and women under retirement age. For comparability with 1939, in col. 2 we have removed the 6.2 million men and women and (arbitrarily) one-third of the children aged 10—5 (we have assumed that a smaller proportion of children of that age was available for agricultural work in 1939 owing to increased school attendance). See also Wheatcroft, Davies and Cooper (1986), 273.

'Other non-agricultural' includes trade and credit; social and cultural and administration; free professions; casual labour, domestic servants, etc.; and armed services (see table 11).

Pensioners, unemployed, etc. includes unemployed; pensioners; students on grants; patients, children and invalids; prisoners, rentiers, beggars, etc; and not indicated or imprecise (see table 11).

[2] Figures obtained as follows (million):

Agriculture, etc.	40.20	employed in agriculture
	7.96	family members engaged in personal economy (families of manual and white-collar workers, collective farmers)
	48.16	Total
Industry, etc.:	14.94	employed in industry (including artisans)
	0.32	family members engaged in personal economy (families of cooperative and non-cooperative artisans)
	1.66	in timber industry (*lesnoe khozyaistvo*)
	3.23	building
	3.46	transport and communication
	23.61	Total

Other non-agricultural: includes trade and credit; social and cultural and administration; and 'not distributed by branch of economy' (see table 11).

Pensioners, unemployed, etc. includes 'stipends, pensioners and others' (see table 11, note o), and 'not stating means of existence' (see table 11, note p).

Armed forces are evidently included with 'other', and forced labour is apparently allocated to the sectors in which it worked. The 1939 census exaggerated the size of the total population, and this may mean that the size of the gainfully occupied population has also been exaggerated.

Sources:
1926: estimated from population census (*Vsesoyuznaya perepis'*, xxiv (1926), 120–42).
1939: estimated from population census (RGAE,1562/336/242, table 33, and 1562/336/242, table 25).

Table 11. *Gainfully occupied population, 1926 and 1939 (thousands)*

	1926[a]	1939[a]
Farming[b]		
Peasant households employing hired labour	738	0
Peasant households	21681[c]	1660[d]
Collective farmers		36499
Employed in private sector	882	0
Employed in socialised sector	320[e]	2038[f]
Family members working	38000[g]	7958[h]
Subtotal	61621	48155
Industry		
Large-scale: private employers	2	0
employed	2790	14393[i]
Small-scale: private employers	75	0
employed	301	0
householders, individuals and family	1490	2527[j]
Subtotal	4658	16920
Building		
Private employers	2	0
Employed	148	3232
Householders, individuals and family	215	0
Subtotal	365	3232
Transport and communications		
Private employers	4	0
Employed	1119	3463
Householders, individuals and family	170	0
Subtotal	1293[k]	3463
Trade and credit		
Private employers	23	0
Employed	679	3826
Individuals, householders and family	456	
Subtotal	1158	3826
Social and cultural; administration		
Education, science, etc.		3183
Health	1893	1628
Housing and municipal		913
State and public organisations		2425
Subtotal	1893	8149

Table 11. (*cont.*)

	1926[a]	1939[a]
Free professions	137	–
Casual labour, domestic servants etc.	1476	3339[n]
Armed services	631	
Unemployed	1014	0
Pensioners	501	
Students on grants	233	3922[o]
Patients, children and invalids in homes	378	
Prisoners	226	..[l]
Rentiers, etc.	231	0
Beggars, etc.	150	0
Not indicated, imprecise	146	1126[p]
Total	76106[m]	92134[q]

Notes:
[a] Respondents' main occupation.
[b] Includes timber cutting and hauling in 1926 but apparently not in 1939 (see note i). Includes peasants engaged in farming and resident in towns.
[c] Includes householders on their own and with family labour, including those who belong to collective farms.
[d] Individual peasant householders, not belonging to collective farms.
[e] Recorded as employed in agricultural enterprises.
[f] Residual (total engaged in agriculture – 40,197,000 – less 36,499,000 collective farmers and 1,660,000 individual peasants.
[g] Adjusted to correspond to coverage of 1939 census (see notes to table 10); original figure was 48,114,000.
[h] Collective farmers, and manual and white-collar workers, working in personal auxiliary farms (household plots).
[i] All employed in industry (14,945,000), less artisans (2,212,000), plus 'timber economy' (1,660,000). See also note j.
[j] Includes cooperative artisans (1,664,000) plus family members engaged in personal auxiliary economy (225000); individual artisans (548000), plus family members engaged in personal auxiliary economy (90000). We have assumed that all these artisans are engaged in industrial occupations, but this is an over-simplification.
[k] Excludes communications.
[l] Apparently all included with branch of economy in which they worked.
[m] Adds to 76,111,000; discrepancy is due to rounding.
[n] Listed as 'not distributed by branch of economy and not precisely indicating the branch'. Evidently includes approximately 2 million in armed services; rest unstated.
[o] Receiving stipends, pensions, and others on state and social maintenance.
[p] Persons not stating or not precisely stating sources of means of existence.
[q] Adds to 92,132,000; discrepancy is due to rounding.
Sources:
1926: estimated from population census of December 1926 (*Vsesoyuznaya perepis'*, xxxiv (1930)). Note that without the adjustments we have made so that the 1926 census corresponds to the 1939 census, the total in 1926 would be 86.2 million.
    1939: estimated from population census of January 1939 (RGAE, 1562/336/242, table 33, and 1562/336/242, table 25).

Table 12. *Non-agricultural employment by sector of the economy, 1928–1940ᵃ (thousands of persons)*

	1928	1932	1937	1940ᵇ
Industryᶜ	4339	9374	11641	13079
Buildingᵈ	818	2458	1877	1993
Transport and communications				
Rail	971	1297	1512	1767
Water	104	145	180	206
Other transportᵉ	227	704	1072	1552
Communications	95	224	375	484
Subtotal transport and communications	1397	2370	3139	4009
Tradeᶠ	606	2223	2551	3351
Science, education, culture and artᵍ	847	1512	2489	3213
Healthʰ	399	669	1127	1512
Credit and state insuranceⁱ	95	128	193	267
State and economic administration; voluntary organisationsʲ	1010	1650	1488	1837
Housing and municipal economyᵏ	158	711	1102	1516
Domestic help and day labourˡ	809	342	246	..
Other	40	83	99	166
Total	10518	21520	25952	30943

Notes:

ᵃ Annual averages. Includes members of industrial artels, amounting to (thousands): 700 (in 1928), 1600 (1932), 1800 (1937), and 2300 (1940) (from *Trud* (1968),22). Most of these persons are included with industry.

ᵇ Partly includes new territories incorporated in the USSR in 1939 and 1940; the increase probably amounts to some 700000 persons (*Pravda*, 19 February 1941, reports the number of employed persons in 1940 on the pre-1939 territory of the USSR at 30.4 million persons; and, apparently on the same definition, the number is given as 31.19 in *Nar. kh.* (1956), 190; these figures include persons employed in farming and forestry, but exclude members of industrial artels).

ᶜ 'Industrial production personnel' – includes managerial and administrative staff of enterprises, but excludes persons engaged in capital repair of buildings and installations, or working in housing and municipal, cultural and other non-industrial organisations, even if they form part of an industrial enterprise. These categories appear under the appropriate heading. (See *Nar. kh. 1959*, 1960, 844.) The heading 'Industry' covers all manufacturing and mining industries, and apparently also timber cutting and hauling. It apparently includes cooperative artisans, although they are not strictly 'employed', but excludes kolkhoz enterprises, and some small-scale auxiliary industrial enterprises which are attached to other branches of the economy. See *Trud* (1968), 22, 81, 84 (p. 84 shows a figure for workers in timber, woodworking and paper industry which is obviously too high to exclude timber cutting and hauling – compare the data for these industries in 1937 in *Industrializatsiya, 1933–1937* (1971), 382–9; 1,618,000 workers as compared with 1,594,000 in 1940).

ᵈ Covers building and erection work; capital repair of buildings and installations; organisations responsible for drilling; and project organisations.

Table 12. (cont.)

ᵉ Includes vehicle, urban electric and other transport (including civil aviation); and also loading and unloading organisations.

ᶠ Includes organisations responsible for wholesale and retail trade; public catering; supply and sales of materials and machinery; agricultural and other procurements.

ᵍ Includes science and scientific services; education; culture and art.

ʰ Includes physical culture and staff responsible for social security.

ⁱ Includes central banks and branches, state insurance and pawn shops. Does not include trade union staff administering social insurance (see *Chislennost'* (1936), 301, cited in Redding (1958), 226).

ʲ 'Staff of organs of state and economic administration, and organs of administration of cooperatives and voluntary organisations' (latter include party and Trade Union staff). This covers Ministries and local authorities and organs of economic administration; legal and juridical institutions; and cooperative and voluntary organisations. It does not include the administrative and managerial staff of enterprises of all kinds, or of schools, banks and other establishments, or, apparently, of science and scientific services; these appear under the appropriate branch of the economy. See *Nar. kh. 1988* (1989), 36–7. As compared with the series for administration in *Trud* (1936), 10–1, the present series excludes entertainment, publishing houses and geological survey (all now under Science and Education), and project organisations (now under Building); together these amounted to 164000 persons in 1928 and 268000 in 1932.

ᵏ Includes personnel in organisations responsible for housing (including factory housing), and for hotels and barracks; water and sewage, etc; also includes hairdressers and laundries; and undertakers. See *Trud* (1936), 26–31, 359–60, 364, 366; note that p. 359 states that coverage for municipal enterprises was widened in 1933 and again in 1935. There is, however, a great deal of ambiguity about these figures. Several different series have appeared:

	1928	1932	1933	1935 April 1	1935	1937	1940
(A) *Trud* (1936), 10–11, 26–31							
'Municipal enterprises'	117	237	373	222	509	..	..
Housing	..	..	..	132	..	..	..
Housing, cultural-welfare at enterprises	..	..	..	271	..	..	..
Total	..	..	..	625	..	..	..
(B) *Itogi* (1939), 104	..	394	..	..	..	754	..
(C) *Nar.kh. 1958* (1959), 658–9	147	661	..	..	..	1023	1221
(D) *Trud* (1968 and 1988)	158	711	..	..	..	1102	1516

The differences between (C) and (D) are due to the inclusion of members of cooperative artels (and kolkhozy?) in (D). But the other changes in coverage have nowhere been satisfactorily explained. In later years this item may include domestic servants (see G. Ofer, *The Service Sector in Soviet Economic Growth* (Camb., Mass., 1973), 27). In the 1939 population census the numbers employed in housing and municipal services was given as 913,000 (see table 11).

ˡ This category was included in the data published in *Trud* (1936), 10–11 and early hand-books; the figure for 1937 appears simply as 'other branches' in *Tretii pyatiletnii plan* (1939), 228.

Source:

Trud (1988), 30–1; 'agriculture' and 'forestry' have been deducted from this table, and 'domestic help and day labour' added.

Table 13. *Employment in industry, 1928–1940 (thousands)*

	1928	1932	1937	1938	1940
Large-scale socialised[a]	3096[1]	6481[1]	..	..	..
Small-scale socialised	408[1]	248[1]	..	..	..
	3504[1]	6729[1]	..	..	..
Timber cutting and hauling	331[1,b]	1140[1]	..	..	..
	(3835)	(7869)	..	..	..
All industry (excluding members of artels)	3773[2]	8000[2]	10112[2,4]	10357[4]	10967[2]
Members of artels	(566)	(1374)	(1529)	..	(2112)
All industry (including members of artels)[c]	4339[3]	9374[3]	11641[3]	..	13079[3]
Members of artels plus kolkhoz enterprises	..	..	..	(2494)	..
Auxiliary enterprises of non-industrial organisations	..	..	..	644[4]	..
Total	..	..	..	13495[4]	..
of which, large-scale	..	..	..	11710[4]	..
small-scale	..	..	..	(1785)	..

Notes:
[a] Excludes repair workers of Narkomput' and Narkomvod (railway and water transport); hired workers in industrial artels; fire prevention staff. Together these amounted to 491000 in 1935.
[b] Large-scale industry only.
[c] Excludes those working in industrial enterprises of kolkhozy, and in 'part of the small auxiliary industrial enterprises'. This whole series probably includes timber cutting and hauling.
Sources:
[1] *Trud* (1936), 10–1.
[2] *Nar. kh.* (1956), 190.
[3] *Trud* (1968), 81 and *Trud* (1988), 47.
[4] *Industrializatsiya, 1938–1941* (1973), 211–12.

Table 14. *Length of employment of workers in large-scale industry, 1929*

Industry and region	0–2 years %	3–5 years %	6–10 years %	11–15 years %	6–20 years %	21–25 years %	26–30 years %	30+ years %	Average no. of years
Metalworking and engineering									
Leningrad	13.5	23.4	23.4	14.3	7.6	5.8	4.8	7.2	11.3
Moscow province	13.1	22.7	23.4	16.2	8.3	5.8	4.6	5.9	11.1
Ukraine	9.5	23.2	25.6	15.8	8.6	5.7	4.7	6.9	11.7
Iron and steel									
Ukraine	15.9	30.4	22.9	12.5	5.9	4.5	3.4	4.5	9.2
Urals	12.3	22.2	21.7	17.2	8.3	6.2	5.7	6.4	11.7
Cotton									
Leningrad	11.7	28.9	18.9	13.7	9.3	6.9	4.5	6.1	11.3
Moscow region	10.5	17.8	18.5	16.9	10.8	8.9	7.3	9.3	13.9
Ivanovo region	11.6	16.4	17.8	16.8	11.4	9.1	7.3	9.6	13.9
Coal									
Donbass	24.4	24.7	21.4	11.5	6.4	4.5	3.4	3.7	8.7
Urals and Siberia	20.4	23.4	22.8	13.7	7.7	5.4	3.5	3.1	9.0

Source:
Rashin (1930), 64.

Table 15. *Young workers in large-scale industry, 1930–1933 (thousands)*

	Total number of workers	Under 18	18–22	Total under 23	Under 18	18–22	Under 23
					% of total		
1930	3116.2	127.8	641.9	769.7	4.1	20.6	24.7
1931	4252.4	327.4	1067.3	1394.7	7.7	25.1	32.8
1932	5271.3	521.8	1507.5	2029.3	9.9	28.6	38.5
1933	5139.7	483.1	1639.6	2122.7	9.4	31.9	41.3

Source:
Rashin (1930), 18; compiled from *Sots. str.* (1934), 344–5.

Table 16. *Women workers in large-scale industry, 1929–1939 (as % of total number of workers)*

	1 Jan. 1929	1 July 1932	1 Jan. 1933	1 Jan. 1934	1 July 1935	1 Nov. 1939
All large-scale industry	28.5	35.1	35.6	36.9	39.8	43.3
Power stations	..	11.0	13.4	16.8	16.8	20.9
Coal mining	7.7	16.5	17.1	19.4	24.1	24.8
Oil mining	0.4	4.4	4.6	7.8	9.3	15.4
Iron-ore mining	6.3	20.7	19.3	18.9	23.0	23.6
Iron and steel	7.1	18.7	20.3	20.3	23.4	24.9
Engineering and metalworking	8.9	21.4	22.6	24.1	26.2	31.7
Printing	22.6	40.9	44.0	48.7	51.1	57.8
Cotton	61.5	69.0	68.9	69.7	70.1	68.5
Clothing	63.9	80.1	81.2	82.5	82.6	83.4
Food	26.3	32.8	35.0	37.1	45.1	47.2

Sources:
Trud (1930), 10; Trud (1936), 95 ff.; *Industrializatsiya, 1938–1941* (1973), 214.

Table 17. *Social origins of workers in large-scale industry, 1929 (% of total)*

Industry and region	Manual workers	Peasants	White-collar workers	Merchants, artisans, etc.
Metalworking and engineering	58.7	33.3	5.5	2.5
Leningrad	51.8	38.6	7.1	2.5
Moscow region	54.7	37.9	5.5	1.9
Ukraine	62.5	26.8	7.0	3.7
Urals	71.3	19.9	4.8	4.0
Central industrial region	61.7	33.9	3.0	1.4
Other regions	57.6	33.8	5.4	3.2
Metallurgy	52.7	42.1	3.2	2.0
Ukraine	41.2	53.7	3.1	2.0
Urals	69.9	26.5	2.3	1.3
Other regions	55.4	38.4	3.9	2.3
Cotton	56.5	39.4	2.6	1.5
Leningrad	57.7	35.5	4.8	2.0
Moscow region	59.9	35.8	2.8	1.5
Ivanovo region	52.7	3.7	2.0	1.6
Coal-mining	34.4	62.3	1.9	1.4
Donbass	33.8	63.1	1.9	1.2
Urals	39.1	58.2	2.0	0.7
Siberia	36.6	58.7	1.3	3.4
Iron-ore mining	41.6	53.9	2.6	1.9
Ukraine	32.6	62.7	2.6	2.1
Urals	54.4	41.5	2.6	1.5
Oil	32.7	63.4	1.6	2.3
All industry	52.2	42.6	3.3	1.9

Source:
Trud (1930), 27.

Table 18. *Gross agricultural production by branch of production, 1909–13 –
1939 (million rubles at 1926/27 prices)*

	Grain	Potatoes and vegetables	Industrial crops	Total arable	Total livestock	Total arable and livestock
1909–13 average	3930	958[a]	443[b]	5331	4281	9612
1913	4566	1158	497	6221	4434	10655
1928	3641	1647	613	5901	5117	11018
1929	3584	1648	576	5807	4419	10226
1930	3757	1773	744	6274	3330	9604
1931	3237	1788	885	5910	2869	8779
1932	3237	1730	692	5659	2405	8064
1933	3757	1832	682	6271	2622	8893
1934	3930	1907	663	6500	3130	9630
1935	4335	2135	900	7371	3757	11128
1936	3237	1529	1068	5833	3864	9697
1937	5607?	2212	1215	9034	4249	13283
1938	4277?	1308	1144	6728	5089	11817
1939	4219?	1284	1205	6709	4383	11092

General note: This table is estimated on the basis of the revised data in physical terms. These have been converted to 1926/27 prices by using the prices set out in Wheatcroft (1984), 44, estimated from *Stat. spr. 1928* (1929), 274–81.

Arable production: for data in physical terms, see table 19. The estimates exclude straw and chaff, and wild and sown hay. Industrial crops include sunflower seeds, sugar beet, and flax and cotton fibre. We have used our estimates for grain and potatoes, and Soviet estimates for other crops. Note that we believe that grain production in 1937–9 may be exaggerated (see table 19, note f).

Livestock production: for data in physical terms, see Wheatcroft (1984), 43. This series includes: changes in draft stock and meat stock, meat and dairy production, eggs, hides, wool and manure.

Notes:

[a] For 1909–13 we have used Soviet revised figure for 1913; figure for 1909–13 not available.

[b] For sunflower seed in 1909–13, we have used Soviet revised figure for 1913; figure for 1909–13 not available.

Table 19. Agricultural production in physical terms, 1913–1940 (million tons)

(a) Grain, potatoes and vegetables

	Grain			Potatoes			Vegetables[1]	
	Soviet estimate in 1930s	Revised Soviet estimate	Our 'low' estimate[c]	Soviet estimate in 1930s	Revised Soviet estimate	Our estimate	Soviet estimate in 1930s	Revised Soviet estimate[4]
1909–13 (average)	67.6[1,a]	65.2[3]	68[d]	22.4[5,g]	22.4[10]	..	..	..
1913	80.1[1,a]	76.5[3]	79[d]	..	23.3[10]	29.9[j]	8.6[11]	8.6
1921	42.3[2]	36.2[4]	..	..	23.3[4]	..	..	..
1928	73.3[1]	73.3[4]	63[e]	46.4[6]	46.4[4]	45.2[k]	10.5[12]	10.5
1929	71.7[1]	71.7[4]	62[e]	45.6[6]	45.6[4]	45.1[k]	10.6[12]	10.6
1930	83.5[1]	83.5[4]	65±3%[e]	49.4[6]	49.4[4]	44.6[k]	13.9[12]	13.9
1931	69.5[1]	69.5[4]	56±9%[e]	44.8[6]	44.8[4]	40.6[k]	16.8[12]	16.8
1932	69.8[1]	69.8[4]	56±10%[e]	43.1[6]	43.1[4]	37.2[k]	17.5[12]	17.6
1933	89.8[1]	68.4[4]	65±4%[e]	49.3[5]	41.4[4]	41.3[b]	21.8[12]	17.4
1934	89.4[1]	67.6[4]	68[f]	51.0[6]	43.8[4]	43.8[b]	20.0[12]	17.6
1935	90.1[1]	75.0[4]	75[f]	69.7[9]	60.5[4]	60.5[f,r]	16.8[12]	12.4
1936	82.7[1]	55.8[4]	56[f]	(51.4)[h]	44.4[4]	44.4[f]	..	8.2
1937	120.3[1]	97.4[4]	97[f]	65.6[8]	58.7[4]	58.7[f]	..	15.4
1938	95.0[1]	73.6[4]	74[f]	42.0[7]	38.3[4]	38.3[f]	..	6.8
1939	106.5[19]	73.2[4]	73[f]	62.1[19]	40.7[4]	40.7[f]	..	9.7
1940	95.5[19]	(86.9)[b]	87[f]	84.2[19]	(64.7)[j]	64.7[m]	..	..

| | (b) Other food crops | | | | (c) Industrial crops | | | |
| | Sunflower seed | | Sugar beet | | Raw Cotton | | Flax fibre | |
	Soviet estimate in 1930s	Revised Soviet estimate	Soviet estimate in 1930s	Revised Soviet estimate	Soviet estimate in 1930s	Revised Soviet estimate	Soviet estimate in 1930s	Revised Soviet estimate
1909–13 (average)	..	..	9.7[5]	9.7[18]	0.68[5]	0.68[18]	0.26[5]	0.26[18]
1913	..	0.74[15]	10.9[16]	10.9[18]	0.74[16]	0.74[18]	0.45[16]	0.33[18]
1921		0.58[4]	..	0.5[4]	..	0.03[4]	..	0.16[4]
1928	2.127[13]	2.13[4]	10.14[17]	10.1[4]	0.82[17]	0.79[4]	0.32[17]	0.32[4]
1929	1.764[13]	1.76[4]	6.25[17]	6.2[4]	0.86[17]	0.86[4]	0.36[17]	0.36[4]
1930	1.629[13]	1.63[4]	14.02[17]	14.0[4]	1.11[17]	1.11[4]	0.44[17]	0.44[4]
1931	2.506[13]	2.51[4]	12.05[17]	12.1[4]	1.29[17]	1.29[4]	0.55[17]	0.55[4]
1932	2.268[13]	1.13[4]	6.56[17]	6.6[4]	1.27[17]	1.27[4]	0.50[17]	0.50[4]
1933	2.354[13]	1.14[4]	8.99[17]	9.0[4]	1.32[17]	1.32[4]	0.55[17]	0.36[4]
1934	2.077[13]	1.15[4]	11.36[17]	9.9[4]	1.18[17]	1.20[4]	0.53[17]	0.37[4]
1935	1.92[17]	1.22[4]	16.21[17]	16.0[4]	1.71[17]	1.77[4]	0.55[17]	0.40[4]
1936	..	1.12[4]	16.83[a]	16.4[4]	2.4[a]	2.47[4]	0.60[a]	0.33[4]
1937	2.08[14]	1.75[4]	21.86[14]	21.6[4]	2.58[14]	2.58[4]	0.57[14]	0.36[4]
1938	1.67[19]	1.61[4]	16.68[5]	16.2[4]	2.69[5]	2.63[4]	0.55[5]	0.31[4]
1939	2.92[19]	2.07[4]	21.0[19]	14.3[4]	2.79[19]	2.70[4]	0.63[19]	0.38[4]
1940	3.3[19]	(2.41)[m]	21.0[19]	(16.9)[o]	2.70[19]	(2.19)[p]	0.57[19]	(0.27)[q]

Notes:

[a] In the 1920s, Gosplan applied a 19 per cent correction coefficient to the pre-revolutionary data and obtained 81.6 million tons for the 1913 sown area with 1909–13 average yield, and 94.4 million tons for the year 1913 (see G. Krzhizhanovskii et al. (1930), 183, and Pyatiletnii plan, I (1930), 144; see also Wheatcroft (1974), 157–80). These figures were revised to those shown in the table above from 1934 onwards.

[b] Source note 3 gives 1938–40 (average), pre-1939 frontiers, as 77.9 million tons; combining this with harvests for 1938 and 1939 given in this column, we obtain 86.9.

Table 19. (*cont.*)

c   Assuming that uncorrected data for 1909–13 and 1913 are correct.

d   The reasons for rejecting the 1960 revision are set out in Wheatcroft (1974), 171–2.

e   We have reduced the official figures by a rising correction coefficient between 1928 and 1932, to allow for the increasing distortion in the official estimates even before the notorious switch from 'barn harvest' to 'biological yield' was introduced. For the crucial year 1932 these lower estimates are confirmed by archival data (see Tauger (1991), 70–89; using the archival data Tauger even puts the 1932 harvest at the very low figure of 50 million tons or less).

f   For 1934–9 we have used the current official data as compatible with the data for earlier years with corrections removed. *But grain harvests for 1937–40 are probably exaggerated.*

g   This estimate is for field-grown potatoes only, and excludes potatoes grown in peasant and urban household plots; later figures include all potatoes. The comparable figure for all potatoes was estimated in Gukhman (1925), 130, as 29.9 million tons. Vyltsan (1970), 112, estimates 1909–13 (average) harvest at 30.6 million tons.

h   *Sots. sel. kh.* (1939), 68, gives 1933–7 (average) as 57.4 million tons; from this and the annual figures for 1933–5 and 1937 the 1936 figure can be estimated.

i   1938–40 average was 47.9 million tons (*Sel. kh.* (1960), 201); 1940 figure has been estimated from this figure and figures for 1938 and 1939.

j   Gukhman's estimate in 1925 (see note g above).

k   We have applied a small and increasing reduction coefficient to the current official figures for 1928–32 to allow for the exaggeration already present in these figures. However, there is some evidence that the 1928 and 1929 figures were exaggerated to a greater extent than we have indicated; *Ekonomicheskoe obozrenie*, 1, 1930, 144, gives only 39.9 million tons for 1928, and 1929 may be at the same level.

l   Includes all vegetables for feed as well as food except (a) potatoes, and (b) melons, pumpkins and other cucurbits (*bakchevye*).

m   1938–40 average was 2.03 million tons (*Sel. kh.* (1960), 200); 1940 figures obtained as in note b.

n   Estimated by deducting annual data for 1933–5, 1937, from data in 1933–7 in source note 5.

o   1938–40 average was 15.79 million tons (*Sel. kh.* (1960), 198); 1940 obtained as in note b.

p   1938–40 average was 2.51 million tons (*Sel. kh.* (1960), 199); 1940 obtained in note b.

q   1938–40 average was 0.32 million tons (*Sel. kh.* (1960), 199); 1940 obtained as in note b.

r   The sudden jump in this year may be due to fuller statistical coverage.

Sources:

1 See Wheatcroft, Davies and Cooper (1986), 282–3.   2 *Nar. kh.* (1932), xxxviii–xxxix.   3 *Sel. kh.* (1960), 196.   4 *Nar. kh.* (1987), 208.
5 *Sots. sel. kh.* (1939), 68.   6 *Sel. kh. 1935* (1936), 467, 1428.   7 *Sots. sel. kh.* (1939), 68.   8 *Tret'ii pyatiletnii plan* (1939), 218.
9 *Sots. str.* (1936), 345.   10 *Sel. kh.* (1960), 201.   11 Gukhman (1925).   12 *Tekhnicheskie kul'tury* (1936), 85.   13 *Sel. kh. 1935* (1936), 390.
14 *Tret'ii pyatiletnii plan* (1939), 218.   15 *Sel. kh.* (1960), 200.   16 *KTs...na 1928/29* (1929), 409.   17 *Sots. str.* (1936), 345.
18 *Sel. kh.* (1960), 198–9.   19 See Zaleski (1980), 584–7, 597–8.

Table 20. *Number of animals, 1914–1940 (millions; 1 January of each year)*

	Horses	Cattle	Sheep and goats	Pigs
1914[a]	37.0	55.6	90.3	19.8
1916[1,b]	34.2	51.7	88.7	17.3
1922[c]	25.7	40.9	73.7	13.1
1923[c]	23.3	41.8	68.0	10.4
1928	32.1	60.1	107.0	22.0
1929	32.6	58.2	107.1	19.4
1930	31.0	50.6	93.3	14.2
1931	27.0	42.5	68.1	11.7
1932	21.7	38.3	47.6	10.9
1933	17.3	33.5	37.3	9.9
1934	15.4	33.5	36.5	11.5
1935	14.9	38.9	40.8	17.1
1936	15.5	46.0	49.9	25.9
1937	15.9	47.5	53.8	20.0
1938	16.2	50.9	66.6	25.7
1939	17.2	53.5	80.9	25.2
1940	17.7	47.8	76.7	22.8

Notes:
[a] Estimated by applying 1914:1916 ratios estimated by Vainshtein (*Ocherki po istorii statistiki* (1960), 112–15) to the data for the spring-summer period (see Davies (1980), 420).
[b] Data evidently based on 1916 livestock census.
[c] Lowest figures for livestock numbers in post-civil war period.
Sources:
Nar. kh. (1987), 253, except where otherwise stated.
[1] Sel. kh. (1960), 263.

Table 21. *Number of animals by social sector, 1 January 1938(millions)*

Owned by	Cattle	Pigs	Sheep and goats
Kolkhozy[1]	14.8	6.3	22.8
Sovkhozy[2]	2.6	1.8	5.6
Other state organisations[3]	0.6	0.7	0.9
Collective farmers[4]	25.8	13.1	31.6
Other individuals, etc.[3]	7.1	6.2	5.7
Total[5]	50.9	25.7	66.6

Sources:
[1] *Kolkhozy* (1939), 96.
[2] Estimated by deducting animals owned by kolkhozy from data for animals owned by kolkhozy and sovkhozy in *Sel. kh.* (1960), 265.
[3] Residual from data in *Sel. kh.* (1960), 265, 264.
[4] Number of animals per 100 households (*Kolkhozy* (1939), 106) multiplied by number of collectivised households (18.7 million, intermediate between data for 1 July 1937, and 1 July 1938 (*Kolkhozy* (1939), 1)).
[5] *Sel. kh.* (1960), 263.

Table 22. *Grain collections, 1927/28–1939/40 (million tons)*[a]

	Total collections	Remainder of harvest (low estimate)
1927/28	11.05[1]	51
1928/29	10.79[1]	52
1929/30	16.08[1]	46
1930/31	22.14[1]	42
1931/32	22.84[2]	33
1932/33[b]	18.78[3]	37 or less
1933/34[b]	23.29[3]	42
1934/35[b]	26.25[3]	42
1935/36[b]	28.39[3,c]	47
1936/37	(27.6)[d]	(28)
1937/38	31.94[4]	65
1938/39	29.09[4]	45
1939/40	30.71[4]	42

Notes:

[a] Includes centralised and decentralised collections and milling levy up to 1932/33; compulsory deliveries, sovkhoz transfers, payment in kind to MTS, return of seed loan, state purchases and milling levy from 1933/34 onwards.

[b] Listed as calendar year, but according to the notes 'includes the period of collections from the harvest of the corresponding year, and the completion of the collections does not always coincide with the end of the calendar year' (*Sel. kh.1935* (1936), 1430). If this is true for 1935 up to 20 December only, the figure seems remarkably high.

[c] Preliminary figure; grain collections and purchases up to December 20 or 31 1935.

[d] Obtained as residual from data in table and in *Sel. kh.* (1960), 196.

Sources:

[1] See Davies (1980), 427.

[2] *Ezhegodnik khlebooborota za 1931–32, 1932–33* (1934), 5.

[3] *Sel. kh. 1935* (1936), 215.

[4] Cited from the archives in M. A. Vyltsan, *Sovetskaya derevnya nakanune Velikoi Otechestvennoi voiny* (1970), 136.

Table 23. *Effect of weather on the deviation of grain yield from trend, 1904–1940 (tsentners per hectare)*

	Trend of grain yield[a]	Actual grain yield	Deviation of actual grain yield from trend[b]	Predicted agro-meteorological deviation of grain yield from trend[c]
1904–8 (average)[d]	6.93	6.71	−0.22	−0.13
1909–13 (average)[d]	7.30	7.68	+0.38	+0.31
1920–4 (average)[d]	8.12	6.42	−1.70	−0.68
1925–9 (average)[d]	8.49	7.88	−0.61	−0.10
1929	8.64	7.42	−1.22	+0.46
1930	8.71	7.80	−0.91	+0.84
1931	8.78	6.58	−2.20	−1.75
1932	8.86	7.04[e]	−1.82	−0.55
1933	8.93	6.86	−2.07	+0.29
1934	9.01	6.88	−2.13	−0.67
1930–4 (average)	8.86	7.03	−1.83	−0.37
1935	9.08	7.53	−1.55	+1.01
1936	9.15	5.78	−3.37	−1.28
1937	9.23	9.40	+0.17	+0.70
1938	9.30	7.36	−1.94	−0.62
1939	9.38	7.40	−1.98	−0.92
1935–9 (average)	9.23	7.49	−1.73	−0.22

Note:
[a] The actual yield in 1883–1915 was linearly extrapolated to 1940.
[b] First column minus second column.
[c] To obtain these predictions, grain yields were correlated with temperature and rainfall variables in critical months in 1883–1915 for six places (Moscow in NCR, Kiev and Odessa in SPR, Kazan and Saratov in CPR, and Orenburg in EPR). This index was used to predict agro–meteorological deviations (deviations due to good or bad weather) from the trend of the grain yield.
[d] Annual data by region for 1908–1928 will be found in Davies (1990), 283 (Wheatcroft).
[e] Yield in 1932 is almost certainly an overestimate.
Source:
Wheatcroft (1977), 44–5.

Table 24. *Soviet and Western indexes of industrial production, 1928–1940 (1928 = 100)*

	1928	1932	1937	1940	Annual rate of growth 1928–40 (%)
Soviet official:					
gross production[1]	100	202	446	642	16.8
net production[2]	100	237	585	..	21.7[h]
Seton[3,a]	100[e]	181	380	462	13.6
Hodgman[4,b]	100[e]	172	371	430	12.9
Nutter[c]					
civilian industry (1928 prices)[5]	100[e]	144	266	286	9.2
civilian industry (1955 prices)[6]	100[e]	141	233	227	7.1
all industry including armaments (1928 prices)[7]	100[e]	150	279	312[d]	10.0
Kaplan–Moorsteen:					
civilian industry[8]	100	154	249	263	8.4
Unofficial Soviet estimate (1987) (in 1980 $)[9]	100[f]	..	217[g]	..	9.0[i]

Notes:

a Estimated by combining growth rates of key sectors, using comparable data from other countries in order to obtain weights (see Davies (1978), 48–9).

b Large-scale industry only, excluding armaments, using wage-bill weights for 1934 (see Davies (1978), 43–8).

c All Nutter's estimates are for net production.

d Not strictly comparable with rest of series, as it was calculated using a geometrical average of 1928 and 1955 prices; in 1928 prices, it would be a few percentage points higher.

e Base-year is 1927/28.

f Base-year is 1929.

g 1938.

ʰ 1928–37 annual average.
ⁱ 1929–38 annual average.

Sources:

1 See table 25.
2 *Problemy ekonomiki*, 9, 1940, 62 (Krasnolobov).
3 Seton (1956–7), 30.
4 Hodgman (1954), 89.
5 Nutter (1962), 525–6.
6 Nutter (1962), 527–8.
7 Nutter (1962), 326.
8 Kaplan and Moorsteen (1960), 237.
9 *Mezhdunarodnaya ekonomika i mezhdunarodnye otnosheniya*, 11, 1987, 151 (estimates by B. Bolotin).

Table 25. Gross production of large-scale and small-scale industry, 1913–1940: Soviet official data (billion rubles, 1926/27 prices)[1]

	1913	1927	1928	1932	1933	1937	1940
Large-scale industry							
Group A	4733	6271	7777	21663	23861	53270	..
Group B	6312	7221	9056	17180	18169	36896	..
Total	11045	13492	16833	38843	42030	90166	..
Small-scale industry							
Group A	721	684	700	1480[a]	685	1984	..
Group B	4483	3816	3900	3020[a]	3009	3382	..
Total	5204	4500	4600	4500[a]	3694	5366	..
All industry							
Group A	5454	6955	8477	23143	24546	55254	83900[2]
Group B	10795	11037	12956	20200	21178	40278	53600[2]
Total	16249	17992	21433	43343	45724	95532	137500[2]

Notes:
[a] These figures may be too high; they are evidently estimates made before the 1933 census of small-scale industry.
Sources:
[1] Buzlaeva (1969), 111, 113, citing 1938 industrial census, except where otherwise stated.
[2] Voznesensky (1941), 7–19.

Table 26. Employment in large-scale industry by size of plant and branch of industry, 1927 and 1936 (percentages)

	Up to 100 employed	101–500 employed	501–1000 employed	1001–5000 employed	>5000 employed	Total number of persons employed
Iron and steel						
1 Jan. 1927[1]	2.8		5.5	37.8	53.9	200003
1 Jan. 1936[1]	0.3		1.3	19.4	79.0	384010
Machine building & metalworking						
1 Jan. 1927[2]	5.6	19.1	12.7	36.3	26.3	494299
1 Jan. 1936[2]	2.7	11.5	9.4	33.5	42.9	2373701
Coal						
1 Jan. 1929[3,a]	0.2	1.4	3.3	18.4	76.7	306058
1 Jan. 1936[4]	0.3	3.6	13.0	46.0	37.1	493986
Footwear						
1 Jan. 1927[5]	9.7	28.1	27.7	11.2	23.3	23606
1 Jan. 1936[5]	3.0	15.5	10.2	42.1	29.2	108449
Food						
1 Jan. 1929[3,a]	28.2	30.6	23.8	17.4	0	316961
1 Jan. 1936[6]	13.0	43.8	23.4	17.0	2.8	798902
All large-scale industry						
1 Jan. 1927	7.8[7]	18.4[7]	12.1[7]	37.5[7]	24.2[7]	2760500[8]
1 Jan. 1929[3]	6.4	17.7	13.6	34.1	28.2	3207570
1 Jan. 1936[9]	4.8	18.7	13.6	37.0	25.9	7493600

Note:

a Data for 1 Jan. 1927, not available.

Sources:

[1] *Trud* (1936), 144.   [2] *Trud* (1936), 152.   [3] *Trud* (1930), 11.   [4] *Trud* (1936), 109.   [5] *Trud* (1936), 226.   [6] *Trud* (1936), 231.   [7] *Trud* (1930), 12.
[8] Calculated from *Trud* (1930), 7–8.   [9] *Trud* (1936), 73.

Table 27. *Industrial production in physical terms, 1913–1940, 1987*

	1913[a]	1928[b]	1932	1933	1936	1937	1940[c]	1987[k]
Electric power (billion kWh)[1]	1.9	5.0	13.5	16.4	32.8	36.2	48.3	1665
Crude oil (million tons)[2]	9.2	11.6	21.4	21.5	27.4	28.5	31.1	624
Coal (million tons)[3,d]	29.1	35.5	64.4	76.3	126.8	128.0	165.9	760
Pig-iron[4]	4.2	3.3	6.2	7.1	14.4	14.5	14.9	114
Rolled steel (million tons)[4]	3.5	3.4	4.4	5.1	12.5	13.0	13.1	134
Quality steel (million tons)[5]	0.04	0.09	0.68	0.89	2.06	2.39	2.79	..
Copper (thousand tons)[6]	31.1	30.0	45.0	44.3	100.8	97.5	160.9	..
Cement (million tons)[7,e]	1.52	1.85	3.48	2.71	5.87	5.45	5.68	137
Mineral fertilisers (million tons)[8,f]	0.07	0.14	0.92	1.03	2.84	3.24	3.24	36.31
Sulphuric acid (million tons)[9,g]	0.12	0.21	0.55	0.63	1.20	1.37	1.59	28.5
Metal-cutting machine tools (thousands)[10]	1.5	2.0	19.7	21.0	44.4	48.5	58.4	156[m]
Locomotives (standard units)[11]	265	478	828	941	1566	1582	1220	..
Equipment for metal industries (thousand tons)[12]	0	0	6.9	..	..	18.4	23.7	317[r]
Generators (thousand kW)[13]	0	75	1085	587	..	561	468	12600
Electric motors (thousand kW)[13]	0	259	1658	1385	1653	1833	1848	49700
Tractors (thousand 15 hp units)[14]	0	1.8	50.8	79.9	173.2	66.5	66.2	3460[m]
Lorries (thousands)[15]	0	0.7	23.7	39.1	131.5	180.3	136.0	..
Raw sugar (million tons)[16,h]	1.35	1.28	0.83	1.00	2.00	2.42	2.17	13.7
Cigarettes (billions)[17,i]	22.1	49.5	57.9	62.7	85.9	89.2	100.4	378
Vodka (million decalitres)[18,j]	118.9	55.5	72.0	..	89.7	92.5	44.3	123[o]
Cotton fabrics (million linear metres)[19]	2582	2678	2694	2732	3270	3448	3954	7945[p]
Woollen fabrics (million linear metres)[20]	105	101	89	86	102	108	120	690[q]

Notes

a Pre-1939 inter-war frontiers.

b Sometimes economic year 1927/28, not calendar year 1928.

c Some figures in this column are relatively too high by a small percentage, because they include part or all of the territory annexed in 1939 and 1940.

d Includes anthracite and brown coal.

e All types of cement.

f All types of mineral fertiliser.

g In monohydrate.

h Raw sugar (*sakhar-pesok*).

i *Papirosy* and *sigarety*.

j 40° alcohol equivalent.

k 1987 frontiers. We have given data for 1987 rather than later years, as the output of a number of products declined in later years. These figures therefore represent the maximum achievement of Soviet industry.

l In 100%-nutritional equivalent; comparable figure for 1940 is 0.8 million tons.

m Maximum production in 1980: 216,000. According to official figures, the value of the production of metal-cutting machine tools has increased from 62 million rubles in 1940 to 2,838 million rubles in 1987(!) (*Nar. kh. 1987* (1988), 130).

n Given as 51.9 million hp as compared with 1.5 million in 1940, so equivalent 1940 figure in 15 hp units is 100 thousand.

o Production in 1980 was 295 million decalitres.

p Million square metres – equivalent figure in 1940 was 2715.

q Million square metres – equivalent figure in 1940 was 155.

r 1986.

Sources:

NB: All data for 1987 was obtained from *Nar. kh. 1987* (1988), 120–237.

[1] *Promyshlennost'* (1957), 171. [2] *Promyshlennost'* (1957), 153. [3] *Promyshlennost'* (1957), 140. [4] *Promyshlennost'* (1957), 106.
[5] Clark (1956), 20, except 1940: *Promyshlennost'* (1957), 110. [6] Nutter (1962), 420. [7] *Promyshlennost'* (1957), 277.
[8] *Promyshlennost'* (1957), 192. [9] *Promyshlennost'* (1957), 196. [10] *Promyshlennost'* (1957), 207. [11] *Promyshlennost'* (1957), 220.
[12] *Promyshlennost'* (1957), 212.
[13] *Promyshlennost'* (1957), 214–15, except (for generators) 1933 and (for electric motors) 1933 and 1936: Nutter (1962), 441.
[14] *Promyshlennost'* (1957), 226. [15] *Promyshlennost'* (1957), 223. [16] *Promyshlennost'* (1957), 373.
[17] *Promyshlennost'* (1957), 372, except 1933 and 1936: Nutter (1962), 454. [18] *Promyshlennost'* (1957), 372. [19] *Promyshlennost'* (1957), 328. [20] *Promyshlennost'* (1957), 328, except 1913: Nutter (1962), 457, 492; and 1928: Wheatcroft and Davies (eds.) (1985), 368; both these figures purport to include small-scale industry.

Table 28. *Production of armaments in physical terms, 1929/30–1940*

	1929/30[a]	1 October 1930–31 December 1931[a]	1932	1933	1934	1935	1936	1937	1938	1939	1940
Machine guns (thousands)	9.7	41.0	45.0	32.7	29.2	29.6	31.9	42.3	77.1	113.7	96.5[1]
Rifles and carbines (thousands)	126	174	224	241	303	222	403	578	1175	1503	1461
Artillery systems											
Small (units)	344	1040	972	2884	2521	3395	3395	3768	7126	8485	..
Medium and large (units)	608	926	1602	1754	1602	988	952	1705	5214	8863	..
Total (units)	952	1966	2574	4638	4123	4383	4347	5473	12340	17348	15000[2]
Warships (thousand tons)[3],[b]	1.5	5.3	3.0	11.4	9.3	15.2	32.5	7.0	49.3	40.9	61.4
Tanks and tankettes (units)	170	740	3038	3509	3565	3055	4803	1559	2271	2950	2794
Combat aircraft (units)	204[4]	220	146	627	962	835	2798[4]	3432[4]	4033[4]	6470[4]	8232[4]
All aircraft (units)	899	860	1734	2952	3109	2529	3770	4435	5467	10382	10565

Notes:

[a] Original source gives slightly different dates; for explanation of our re-dating, see Davies (1987), table 1 note b.
[b] Includes both surface ships and submarines.

Sources: Cooper (1976), 46–50, Harrison (1985), 250, 252, except where otherwise stated.

[1] Calculated from *Istoriya Vtoroi Mirovoi voiny*, XII (1982), 168 and Kravchenko (1970), 317.
[2] *Istoriya Vtoroi Mirovoi voiny*, III (1974), 385.
[3] Estimated by J. M. Cooper from data in Berezhnoi (1988), and Dmitriev (1990).
[4] Batekhin (1988), 102, 144.

Table 29a. *Production of defence industry in value terms, 1913–1940: Gross production (million rubles at 1926/27 prices)*

	1930	1931	1932	1933	1937	1938	1939	1940
Gross defence production	384[1,a]	683[1,a]	1176[1,a]	1289[1,a,b]	8472[2,c]	11556[2,c]	16935[2,c]	23000[2,c]
Gross production of large-scale industry[3]	27699	34159	38831	42041	90166	100602	..	100602

Notes:
This series almost certainly exaggerates the growth rate between 1933 and 1937, as it shows total production of defence industry, including civil production, in 1937–40, but only defence production in 1930–3; it also excludes shipbuilding in 1930–3, and includes it in 1937–40.
Total production of defence industry, excluding shipbuilding, was 817 million rubles in 1930 and 2091 million rubles in 1933 (preliminary); and an implied figure for total production including shipbuilding in 1933 is 3,000 million rubles (see Cooper (1976), 51). On the other hand, the proportion of defence production in total defence industry production was certainly higher in 1937 than in 1933; and in 1937 a higher proportion of total defence production was manufactured in civilian industry than in 1933.
[a] Defence production only; includes armaments as such and military products of chemical industry. See also General Note above.
[b] Preliminary figure.
[c] Total production of defence industry commissariats.
Sources:
[1] RGAE, 4372/91/1824, 33.
[2] See Cooper (1976), 51.
[3] See Davies, Cooper and Ilič (1991), 37, 42 and (for 1937 and 1938) Buzlaeva (1969), 113.

Table 29b. *Production of defence industry in value terms, 1913–1940: Gross defence production compared with net production of all industry (million rubles)*

	1913[b]	1930[c]	1932[c]	1937[d]	1940[d]
Gross defence production[a]	233[1]	384[3]	1176[3]	6800[5]	16600[5]
Net production of all industry	4334[2]	14800[4]	20600[4]	65400[5]	73800[5]
Defence production as % of all industry	5.4	2.6	5.7	10.4	22.5

Notes:
As the armaments' industry primarily produces end-products, the amount of double-counting in the figures for gross production is likely to be rather small. But in industry as a whole the double-counting in gross production is extremely large. A comparison of gross production of armaments with net production of all industry therefore gives a more accurate indicator of the weight of armaments in industrial production. However, gross production of armaments includes transport costs, etc. which do not appear in net production of industry. On the other hand, overestimation is likely to be higher in the official figures for net industrial production used for 1930 and 1932, than in the official figures for armaments.

As different prices have been used for different columns, these figures do not show the change over time of armaments production in real terms.

[a] Includes military products of chemical industry as well as armaments as such. Data for 1930 and 1932 exclude shipbuilding. These figures all exclude civilian production of armaments industry, and data for 1930 and 1932 exclude armaments produced by civilian industry.

[b] 1913 prices; Russian Empire.

[c] 1926/27 prices.

[d] 1937 prices.

Sources:

[1] Estimated by P. Gatrell (private communication).

[2] Falkus (1968), 55.

[3] RGAE, 4372/91/1824, 33.

[4] *Sots. str.* (1935), xlv.

[5] Tables 57, 58; in 1937, gross defence production is assumed equal to twice the net figure.

Table 30. *Gross production of large-scale industry by regions, 1913–1939 (million rubles)*

	1912[1]		1928[2]		1933[3,d]		1939[2]	
	Amount	Per cent	Amount	Per cent	Amount	Per cent	Amount	Per cent
RSFSR								
Centre	1793	39.4	6759	42.9	15843	37.5	45456	39.3
North and North West	552	12.2	2058	13.1	6742	16.0	15992	13.8
South-East	504	11.1	1534	9.7	3964	9.4	10839	9.4
Urals and West Siberia	267[a]	5.9	1065	6.8	3458	8.2	10202	8.8
East Siberia and Far East	59[a]	1.3	275	1.7	718	1.7	(3227)[c]	2.8
Total RSFSR	3175	69.9	11569[b]	73.5	(30725)	72.7	85716	74.1
Ukraine plus Crimea	940	20.7	2928	18.6	7607	18.0	20080[f]	17.4
Belorussia	34	0.7	205	1.3	821	1.9	2051	1.8
Transcaucasus	317	7.0	616	3.9	1877	4.4	4032	3.5
Central Asia	84[a]	1.8	332	2.1	920	2.2	2646	2.3
Kazakhstan	..	..	89	0.6	311	0.7	1133	1.0
Total USSR	4549[a]	100.0	15746[c]	100.0	42261	100.0	(115658)	100.0

Notes:

1912 data are in current prices, data for 1928, 1933 and 1939 in 1926/27 prices.

[a] Data for Siberia and Central Asia are for the year 1908, and are therefore underestimated.

[b] Total adds to 11691, presumably because part of data for the economic regions refers to areas outside the RSFSR.

[c] Total adds to 15,861, presumably because certain regions have been double-counted under economic areas of RSFSR and under the other republics.

[d] Administrative regions of RSFSR regrouped by the present author, so they may not correspond to the regions used in the source for 1928 and 1939.

[e] Residual, including Crimea, which was responsible for 0.6 per cent of production in 1933, and possibly some other regions.

[f] Ukraine only.

Sources:

[1] *Dinamika*, I, iii (1930), 14–15.

[2] *Industrializatsiya, 1938–1941* (1973), 191–5.

[3] *Sots. str.* (1935), 32.

Table 31. *Annual rate of growth of industry, 1926–1940 (Percentage increase or decrease (−) as compared with previous year)[a]*

	1926	1927	1928	1929[c]	1930[d]	1931[e]	1932	1933	1934	1935	1936	1937	1938	1939	1940[3]
Official															
All industry[1,b]	34.4	31.9	19.1	20.0	22.0	20.5	14.7	5.5	19.1	22.6	28.7	11.2	11.8	16.0[2]	11.0[3]
Group A[1,b]	41.1	31.6	21.9	28.5	38.1	28.8	19.4	6.1	25.2	26.6	30.9	8.5	12.4	18.7[2]	13.8[3]
Group B[1,b]	30.5	32.1	17.4	14.4	10.1	12.8	9.7	4.8	12.2	17.4	25.6	15.0	11.1	12.2[2]	6.8[3]
Nutter (1928 prices)[4,f]															
All civilian industry	..	..	..	13.6	14.8	7.5	0.1	6.0	19.7	18.3	16.9	6.1	4.6	2.9	0.3
Intermediate products[g]	..	..	..	23.5	30.1	6.9	6.8	7.7	22.4	19.5	18.4	2.0	3.6	5.4	4.9
Machinery and equipment[h]	..	..	..	33.7	42.5	22.5	28.0	53.7	37.1	42.0	8.5	17.4	3.8	−4.3	−26.9
Consumer goods[i]	..	..	..	5.8	0.6	6.9	−9.4	−2.0	12.6	11.0	17.1	9.4	6.3	1.3	0.8
Nutter (1955 prices)[5,f]															
All industry	..	..	..	17.0	12.8	−3.5	6.8	1.9	16.2	22.7	10.4	2.3	1.1	1.7	−5.5
Intermediate products[g]	..	..	..	26.7	30.8	−10.2	14.2	2.4	16.3	18.2	16.3	−2.5	1.0	5.0	−1.1
Machinery and equipment[h]	..	..	..	30.2	35.1	1.8	3.5	18.4	27.9	51.4	−8.4	−0.8	−3.5	−8.9	−22.8
Consumer goods[i]	..	..	..	9.0	−7.5	0.9	1.6	−6.0	9.3	7.7	22.2	9.3	4.0	5.1	−1.6

Notes:

a Increases are given without a sign, decreases indicated by − sign.

b Estimated from Soviet data for gross production in value terms, in 1926/27 prices.

c For Nutter indexes, increase of economic year 1928/29 over economic year 1927/28.

d For Nutter indexes, 1929/30: 1928/29.

e For Nutter indexes, (calendar year 1931): (economic year 1929/30).

f Net production.

g Metals; fuel and power; chemicals; construction materials.

h Excludes Nutter's category 'miscellaneous machinery'; covers 42 items (1928 prices), 71 items (1955 prices); excludes armaments (see Nutter (1962), 574–8, for details).

i Covers food products industry as well as manufactured goods and durables.

Sources:

1 Except where otherwise stated, Buzlaeva (1969), 111, 113, citing 1938 industrial census.

2 See Zaleski (1980), 578–9.

3 Voznesensky (1941), 7–19.

4 Calculated from data in Nutter (1962), 525–6.

5 Nutter (1962), 527–8.

Table 32. *Freight by mode of transport, 1913–1945 (percentage share, measured in ton–kms)*

	Railways	Sea	River	Pipeline	Automobile	Air
1913	57	17	25	0.3	0.1	0
1924	74	8	15	0.8	0.4	0
1928	78	8	13	0.5	0.2	0
1937	82	8	8	0.8	1.4	0.04
1940	85	5	7	0.7	1.9	0.04
1945[a]	84	9	5	0.7	1.3	0.16

Notes:

International traffic by Soviet shipping is included. Automobile traffic includes not only that carried by common-carrier trucking organisations (which carried three per cent of the automobile traffic in 1940) but also by other state organisations as well as collective farms. On the other hand, traffic by industrial railways is not included. All these features mean that the share of railway transport in domestic traffic is understated here by about five per cent. Note also that these percentages do not precisely correspond to those published for other countries.

[a] 1945 frontiers.

Source:
Transport i svyaz' SSSR (1972), 17.

Table 33. *Railway traffic, 1913–1945*

	Freight ton-kms (billions)	Total passenger/km (billions)	Of which commuter passenger/km (billions)	'Conventional' ton/km (billions)
1913 (Empire)	76.8[1]	29.7[2]	1.9[2]	107.5
1913	65.7[1]	25.24[1]	1.5[2]	91.8
1913 (1945 frontiers)	76.4	30.3	..	106.7
1914 (Empire)	74.7[1]	38.5[11]	..	113.2
1915 (Empire)	83.0[3]	53.2[11]	..	136.2
1916 (Empire)	..	..	..	..
1917 (Empire[a])	63.0[4]	22.0	..	85.0
1918 (Empire[a])	14.1[4]	..	..	..
1919 (Empire[a])	14.8[2]	..	..	..
1919[a]	17.5	..	..	..
1920[a]	11.4	..	..	..
1921[a]	14.0	..	..	..
1921/22	16.0[3]	..	..	..
1922	18.2	9.4	..	27.6
1922/23	23.5[2]	13.9[2]	..	37.4
1923	26.2	12.8	..	39.0
1923/24	33.7[2]	15.4[2]	2.1[2]	49.1
1924	36.5	16.7	..	53.2
1924/25	47.4[2]	19.0[2]	2.7[2]	66.4
1925	52.6	20.5	2.8[13]	73.1
1925/26	68.9[2]	23.4[2]	3.2[2]	92.3
1926	73.5	22.8	..	96.3
1926/27	81.7[2]	22.1[2]	3.2[2]	103.8
1927	82.6	22.4	..	105.0
1927/28	88.2[2]	23.6[2]	3.7[2]	111.8
1928	93.4	24.5	3.8	117.9
1929	113.0	32.0	4.6[5]	145.0
1930	133.9	51.8	7.4[5]	185.7
1931	152.1	61.8	11.6[5]	213.9
1932	169.3	83.7	16.7[5]	253.0
1933	169.5	75.2	16.0[5]	244.7
1934	205.7	71.4	16.9[6]	277.1
1935	258.1	67.9	..	326.0
1936	323.4	77.2	17.9[6]	400.6
1937	354.8	90.9	21.4	445.7
1938	370.5	91.7[7]	..	462.2
1939	391.7	93.7	24.3[8]	485.4
1940	409.0[9]	..	..	..
1940 (1945 frontiers)	415.0	98.0	24.7	513.0
1940 (1940 frontiers)	412.3[9]	..	..	..
1940	431.9[10]	..	..	..
1941 (Jan.–June)	230.7[12]	41.3[12]	..	272.0
1941(July–Dec.[a])	155.9[12]	25.5[12]	..	181.4
1942[a]	217.8[12]	37.8[12]	..	255.6
1943[a]	238.8[12]	39.3[12]	..	278.1
1944[a]	280.3[12]	57.6[12]	..	337.9
1945 (1945 frontiers)	314.0	65.9	15.0	379.9

Table 33. (*cont.*)

Notes:
Tariff rather than operating ton/kms are used. These assume that consignments travel by the shortest route. In fact not all do, so operating ton/kms would be a fairer index of work actually performed. The difference between tariff and operating ton/kms would be greatest in times of crisis; in 1945 it amounted to 10.6 per cent (*Zheleznodorozhnyi transport*, 8, 1948, 20) but in more typical years it was about 5 per cent. The railways' own freight shipments are included in these figures so long as they were conveyed in commercial freight trains. A small amount of freight, amounting annually to about 3–4 billion ton/kms in the 1930s, was carried in exclusively railway–service trains and was therefore not included in the ton/km figures.
[a] Fluid frontiers compromise these figures.
Sources: Except where indicated, figures in the first three columns are from *Transport i svyaz' SSSR* (1972), 91–2.
  [1] NKPS, *Materialy*, CIV (1929), table 1, and *Transport i svyaz'* (1972), 91–2.
  [2] NKPS, *Materialy*, CIV (1929), table 1.
  [3] NKPS, *Materialy*, III (1922), table A (this series gives 1913 as 75.9 billion).
  [4] NKPS, *Materialy*, III (1922), table A and *Transport i svyaz'* (1972), 91–2.
  [5] Yakobi (1935), 36. Yakobi's passenger figures match those of *Transport i svyaz'* (1972), and of NKPS, *Materialy*, CIV (1929), table 1.
  [6] Vol'fson *et al.* (1941), 365. Vol'fson's figures match those of the other source.
  [7] Vol'fson *et al.* (1941), 365, Kim (1970), 413. *Transport i svyaz'* (1972) gives 84.9 billion.
  [8] Kim (1970), 384.
  [9] Kim (1970), 381, 384.
  [10] Kim (1970), 381. These are operating, not tariff, ton/kms.
  [11] Vasiliev (1939),92.
  [12] Konarev (1987), 489.
  [13] *Zheleznodorozhnyi transport v 3ei Stalinskoi pyatiletke* (1939), 220.

Table 34. *Railway freight tonnage and average length of haul, 1913–1945*

	Tons (million)	Average haul (km)
1913[a]	157.6	485
1924	70.7	517
1928	156.2	598
1937	517.3	686
1940	592.6	700
1945	395.2	794

Note:
[a] 1945 frontiers.
Source: *Transport i svyaz'* (1972), 95.

Table 35. *Railway route mileage and traffic density, 1913–1945*

	Route in operation (thousand kms)	Traffic density (million 'conventional' ton/kms per km)
1913 (Empire frontiers)	70.5	1.5
1913	58.5	1.6
1922/23	69.6	0.5
1923/24	73.9	0.7
1924/25	74.4	0.9
1925/26	74.6	1.2
1926/27	75.8	1.4
1927/28	76.9	1.5
1928	76.9	1.5
1929	76.9	1.9
1930	77.9	2.4
1931	81.0	2.6
1932	81.8	3.1
1933	82.6	3.0
1934	83.5	3.3
1935	84.4	3.9
1936	85.1	4.7
1937	84.9	5.2
1938	85.0	5.4
1939	86.4	5.6
1940 (1940 frontiers)	106.1	4.8
1943	81.7	..
1944	110.5	..
1945	112.9	3.4

Note: Traffic density is the average for the whole system under NKPS management, including narrow-gauge lines. Mileage is given for the year-end, while the traffic which produces the density figure is for the preceding twelve months. It should be noted that the average conceals a wide difference between busy and lightly-trafficked lines. In 1913, for example, some of the lines out of the Donbass were carrying more than seven million ton/kms per kilometre.
Sources:
1913–27: NKPS, *Materialy*, CIV (1929), 1, for mileage, which we have then divided into the combined ton/kms of commercial trains.
1928–45: *Transport i svyaz'* (1957), 28, with a similar process of division. 1943 and 1944 are from Kovalev (1981), 333.

Table 36. *Railway electrification: plans and achievement, 1930s (total mileage in kms)*

	Plan	Actual
First five-year plan: by 1 October 1933	456	347
June 1931 party resolution: by end of 1933	3757	347
July 1931 resolution of Council of People's Commissars: by end of 1934	3607	378
Second five-year plan: by end of 1937	5062	1632
Third five-year plan: by end of 1942	3472	1950

Notes:
The plans are obtained by adding electrification plans to existing electrified mileage; for plans, see Naporko (1957), 246, 253, 289, 322.
Kim (1970), 412, is the source for actual (year-end) electrification totals (including electrified lines in temporary operation). The 1942 achievement figure is estimated, based on the end-1940 mileage of 1865km and the approximately 100km known to have been completed during the war. *Transport i svyaz'* (1972), 89, gives the end-1945 electrified mileage as 2000km.

Table 37. *Railway labour force and labour productivity, 1913–1945*

	Operating workers (thousands)	Thousand conventional ton/kms per operating worker
1913 (Empire)	823[1]	130.6[1]
1913 (1945 frontiers)	846[3]	126[3]
1913	691[2]	132.8[2]
1924/25	801[1]	82.8[1]
1928	863[3]	137[3]
1932	1054[3]	240[3]
1937	1250[3]	357[3]
1940 (1945 frontiers)	1394[3]	368[3]
1945 (1945 frontiers)	1502[4]	253[4]

Note: Sources other than those below give somewhat different figures, especially for the 1930s. See Westwood (1993).
Sources:
[1] NKPS, *Materialy*, CIV (1929), table 1.
[2] Yakobi, *Zheleznye dorogi* (1935), 58.
[3] *Transport i svyaz'* (1972), 109.
[4] Hunter (1959), 383.

Table 38. *Waterways traffic, 1913–1945*

	Million tons	Billion ton/kms
1913	33	29
1913 (1945 frontiers)	35	29
1917	..	15
1924	9	8
1928	18	16
1932	44	25
1937	66	33
1940 (1945 frontiers)	73	36
1945 (1945 frontiers)	37	19

Source: Transport i svyaz' (1972), 17, 21.

Table 39. *Highway traffic, 1913–1945*

	Million tons	Billion ton/kms
1913	10.0	0.1
1913 (1945 frontiers)	10.0	0.1
1924	15.0	0.2
1928	20.0	0.2
1932	100.0	1.1
1937	569.1	5.9
1940 (1945 frontiers)	858.6	8.9
1945	420.0	5.0

Note: Only mechanical transport is included. The figures are said to include all departmental freight as well as that of collective farms. The figures up to 1932 have a ready-made look about them, and difficulties of collecting figures probably ensure the imprecision of this table. In 1940 *common-carrier* (public service) highway operations registered 15.5 million tons or 266 million ton/kms (*ibid.* 222).
Source: Transport i svyaz' (1972), 17, 21.

Table 40. *Public highway mileage, 1913–1945 (thousand kms; 31 December of each year)*

	Total all roads	Of which hard surfaced	Of which improved
1913	1310.6	24.3	..
1913 (1945 frontiers)	1450.0	37.3	..
1920	1450.0	25.0	..
1924	1060.0	23.1	..
1928	1452.1	32.0	..
1932	1493.7	44.5	0.5
1937	1502.0	83.9	3.2
1940 (1945 frontiers)	1531.2	143.4	7.1
1945 (1945 frontiers)	1529.1	155.3	10.2

Source: Transport i svyaz' (1972), 262.

Table 41. *Total factor productivity growth in the period 1928–1940 (1937 prices, annual average growth rates, per cent)*

A. GNP/NNP

	Bergson		Moorsteen and Powell		Ofer[a]
	(i)[b]	(ii)[b]	(i)[b]	(ii)[b]	
	L = 0.805	L = 0.704	L = 0.727	L = 0.542	L = 0.683
GNP/NNP	4.2	4.2	6.1	6.1	5.8
Total inputs	3.8	4.2	5.5	6.0	4.4
Total factor productivity	0.5	0.1	0.5	0.1	1.4
TFP share in GNP growth	12%	2%	8%	2%	24%

B. Sectoral

	Moorsteen and Powell		Powell	
	(i)[b]	(ii)[b]	(i)[b]	(ii)[b]
Non-agricultural sector	L = 0.777	L = 0.548		
Output	8.8	8.8		
Total factor productivity	0.9	0.4		
TFP share in output growth	10%	5%		
Non-agricultural, non-residential sector				
Output	9.0	9.0		
Total factor productivity	0.5	−0.6		
TFP share in output growth	6%	−6%		
Industry			L = 0.624	L = 0.550
Output			9.8	9.8
Total factor productivity			2.1	1.5
TFP share in output growth			21%	15%

Notes:
[a] Ofer states that he uses a particular set of Bergson's weights for shares in NNP and adjusts them for depreciation. He appears to have made an error in his calculations and have given a higher weight to labour, lower weights to capital and land than those implied by Bergson's NNP breakdown. The figures used here are based on the author's recalculations of Bergson's weights; Ofer's figures for the growth of total inputs and total factor productivity are 4.0 per cent and 1.7 per cent respectively.
[b] In column (i) it is assumed that the rate of return on fixed capital was 8 per cent, in column (ii) that it was 20 per cent; L is the resulting share attributable to labour in output.
[c] Bergson's estimates are for NNP, Moorsteen and Powell, and Ofer for GNP.
Sources:
Bergson: Bergson and Kuznets (1963), 6.
Moorsteen and Powell: Moorsteen and Powell (1966), 361, 371–3, 378–9.
Ofer: Ofer (1987), 1778–9.
Powell: Bergson and Kuznets (1963), 155, 172.

Table 42. *Total factor productivity growth in the period 1928–1937 (1937 prices, annual average growth rates, per cent)*

	Moorsteen and Powell		Powell	
	(i)[a]	(ii)[a]	(i)[a]	(ii)[a]
	L = 0.727	L = 0.542		
GNP	6.2	6.2		
Total factor productivity	1.8	1.2		
TFP share in GNP growth	29%	19%		
Non-agricultural sector	L = 0.777	L = 0.548		
Output	9.6	9.6		
Total factor productivity	2.7	2.0		
TFP share in output growth	28%	21%		
Non-agricultural, non-residential sector	L = 0.821	L = 0.614		
Output	9.8	9.8		
Total factor productivity	2.2	0.7		
TFP share in output growth	22%	7%		
Industry			L = 0.624	L = 0.550
Output			10.1	10.1
Total factor productivity			1.9	1.2
TFP share in output growth			19%	12%

Note:
[a] In column (i) it is assumed that the rate of return on fixed capital was 8 per cent, in column (ii) that it was 20 per cent; L is the resulting share attributable to labour in output.
Sources:
Moorsteen and Powell: Moorsteen and Powell (1966), 361, 371–3, 378–9.
Powell: Bergson and Kuznets (1963), 169, 178, 202.

Table 43. *Balance of payments, 1909–1913 and 1913 (million rubles at current prices)*

		1900–13 average	1913
1	Commodity trade balance	+279	+128
2	Interest and dividend payments and profits repatriated by foreign companies	−287	−401
3	Net tourist expenditures	−160	−292
4	Other payments	−12	−13
5	Current account balance [1−(2+3+4)]	−180	−578

Source:
Estimated from Gregory (1982), 97–8.

Table 44. *Foreign trade, 1913–1940 (millions of 'gold' rubles)*

	Exports	Imports
1913	1506	1375
1918	8	105
1919	0.1	3
1920	1.4	29
1921	20	211
1922	82	270
1923	217	143
1924	329	260
1925	586	827
1926	698	689
1927	725	758
1928	796	953
1929	924	881
1930	1036	1059
1931	811	1105
1932	575	704
1933	470	348
1934	418	232
1935	367	241
1936	310	309
1937	376	292
1938	293	313
1939	133	214
1940	306	313

Note:
'Gold' rubles are rubles with a gold content equivalent to that prevailing between 1897 and 1936.
Source:
data from *Vneshnyaya torgovlya* (1960), 14, converted to gold rubles using coefficients from *Vneshnyaya torgovlya* (1960), 9; in some years the export figures include some precious metals, these have been subtracted from the values in the original table (for further discussion see Dohan (1969), 720, 733).

Table 45. *Foreign debt and export of precious metals, 1924–1936 (million 'gold' rubles)*

Foreign debt		Net precious metals exports	
1924 (1 October)	156		
1925 (1 October)	213	1924/25	24
1926 (1 October)	305	1925/26	72
1927 (1 October)	392	1926/27	34
1928 (1 October)	485	1927/28	155
1929 (1 October)	615	1928/29	67
1930 (1 October)	865	1929/30	8
1931 (1 October)	1295	1930/31	110
1931 (31 December)	1400	1931	120
1932 (1 July)	1335	1932	103
1933 (31 December)	450	1933	111
		1934	119
1935 (October)	139	1935	49
1936 (July)	85	1936	19
		1937	239
		1938	139

Sources:
Foreign debt: Dohan (1969), 643. There are alternative values of 804 million rubles on 1 January 1929, 2371 million rubles on 1 January 1932; it is suggested that these higher figures reflect the accumulation of unsold products in the warehouses of Soviet trade missions abroad (*Byulleten' Prokopovicha*, CXXXII (1936), 131).
Net precious metals exports: Dohan (1969), 851–852.

Table 46. *Exports and imports by type of product, 1913 (million gold rubles)*

(a) Exports	
Grain and grain products	529
Other food and agricultural products	620
Timber and wood products	164
Minerals and fuel	74
Industry (excluding food processing)	117
Total	1506

(b) Imports	
Agricultural, food and timber products[a]	692
Minerals and fuel	105
Machinery	228
Metal products	94
Chemicals	69
Textiles	105
Other consumer goods	70
Other industrial goods	14
Total	1375

Note:
[a] Includes raw materials for textile industry, 16.0 per cent of total imports.

Source:
Vneshnyaya torgovlya (1960), 45–66, 204–36.

Table 47. *Soviet exports and imports by type of product, 1938 (million gold rubles)*

(a) Exports	
Grain and grain products	64
Other food and agricultural products	79
Timber and wood products	59
Minerals and fuel	35
Industry (excluding food processing)	57
Total	293
(b) Imports	
Agricultural, food and timber products[a]	99
Minerals	9
Machinery	108
Metal products	85
Other industrial goods	9
Other products	3
Total	313

Note: for gold rubles, see note to table 44.
[a] Includes raw materials for the textile industry, 9.9 per cent of total imports.

Source:
Vneshnyaya torgovlya (1960), 155–88, 368–401.

Table 48. *Grain exports, 1922/23–1938 (thousand tons)*

1913	9182[a]
1921/22	0[b]
1922/23	729
1923/24	2576
1924/25	569
1925/26	2016
1926/27	2099
1927/28	289
1929	178
1930	4764
1931	5056
1932	1727
1933	1683
1934	769
1935	1517
1936	321
1937	1277
1938	2054

Notes:
[a] Russian Empire.
[b] Only 115 tons export recorded.

Source:
Vneshnyaya torgovlya (1960), 84, 110, 144, 179.

Table 49. *Balance of trade, 1913–1940 (million rubles at current prices)*

1913	+131
1914	−224
1915	−596
1916	−625
1917	−665
1918	−97
1919	−3
1920	−27
1921	−191
1922	−188
1923	+74
1924	+69
1925	−241
1926	+9
1927	−33
1928	−157
1929	+43
1930	−23
1931	−294
1932	−129
1933	+122
1934	+186
1935	+126
1936	+6
1937	+392
1938	−91
1939	−374
1940	−34

Notes:
Data for 1913–24 are in 1913 prices.
Data have been adjusted for precious metal exports when available (see Dohan (1969), 720, 733).

Sources:
1914–17: see Baykov (1946), 6.
Other years: *Vneshnyaya torgovlya* (1960), 14.

Table 50. *Soviet international terms of trade, 1913–1938 (1913 = 100)*

	1913 weights	1927/28 weights
1924/25	100.9	105.3
1925/26	98.0	103.7
1926/27	104.3	108.4
1927/28	108.7	105.1
1929	103.8	103.2
1930	80.7	94.3
1931	67.5	83.7
1932	71.3	75.1
1933	72.8	77.4
1934	79.6	69.3
1935	76.1	76.4
1936	76.6	76.8
1937	92.8	89.8
1938	81.2	88.4

Source: derived from Dohan and Hewett (1973), 35, using import price index based on German machinery prices.

Table 51. *Soviet exports and imports, 1913–1938 (1913 = 100)*

	Exports	Imports
1918[a]	0.0	0.1
1919[a]	0.0	0.0
1920[a]	0.0	0.0
1921 (Jan.–Sept.)	0.0	0.1
1921/22	0.1	0.2
1922/23	0.1	0.1
1923/24	27.7	23.3
1924/25	25.9	42.5
1925/26	34.0	51.4
1926/27	40.0	53.9
1927/28	41.2	70.6
1929	54.1	68.0
1930	80.1	88.6
1931	90.1	111.0
1932	74.0	77.8
1933	71.0	52.9
1934	67.3	51.8
1935	59.9	54.8
1936	47.3	54.8
1937	46.3	50.9
1938	39.1	56.5

Sources:
1918–1922/23: *Vneshnyaya torgovlya* (1939), 11; 1923/24–1938: Dohan and Hewitt (1973), 24, 27.

Table 52. *Sources of Soviet imports, 1913–1940 (in percentage of total for each year)*

	France	Germany	UK	USA	Other
1913	7.3	47.5	12.6	5.8	26.8
1921/22	0.1	30.9	19.6	16.2	33.2
1922/23	0.4	41.3	25.0	3.0	30.2
1923/24	6.5	19.4	21.0	21.8	31.3
1924/25	3.1	14.2	15.3	27.9	39.5
1925/26	5.3	23.3	17.1	16.2	38.2
1926/27	7.6	22.6	14.2	20.4	35.2
1927/28	4.3	26.3	5.0	19.9	44.5
1929	4.8	22.1	6.2	20.1	46.7
1930	4.2	23.7	7.6	25.0	39.6
1931	3.5	50.2	9.0	28.1	9.3
1932	4.1	46.5	13.1	4.5	31.8
1933	6.6	42.5	8.8	4.8	37.4
1934	9.4	12.4	13.5	7.7	57.0
1935	7.5	9.0	9.3	12.2	62.0
1936	7.6	22.8	7.1	15.4	47.0
1937	6.5	14.9	4.7	18.3	55.7
1938	3.7	4.7	12.1	28.3	51.2
1939	2.9	5.7	11.4	30.7	49.3
1940	0.1	29.0	0.9	31.0	38.9

Source:
Vneshnyaya torgovlya (1960), 13, 21, 23, 27, 37.

Table 53. *Labour productivity in large-scale industry, 1913–1921*[a]

	Production (million rubles 1913 prices)	Employment (millions)	Labour input (adjusted for hours worked)	Output/ labour (rubles)[b]	Per cent of 1913[b]
1913	6391	2.44	2.44	2619	100
1914	6429	2.48	2.40	2679	102
1915	7056	2.58	2.50	2822	108
1916	7420	2.87	2.84	2613	100
1917	4780	2.89	2.57	1860	71
1918	2160	2.25	1.91	1131	43
1919	955	1.54	1.28	746	28
1920	818	1.54	1.32	620	24
1921	1080	1.30	1.10	982	37

Note:
[a] Figures relate to USSR pre-1939 territory.
[b] Column 1 divided by column 3.
Sources: Gross value of output of census industry from *Planovoe khozyaistvo*, 5, 1929, 173 (Gukhman); labour input from Mints (1975), 39; hours worked from Strumilin (1964), 365.

Table 54. *Capital stock in large-scale industry, 1914–1923 (million pre-war rubles)*

	Value of capital (1 Jan.)	Investment during year	Depreciation	Net increase
1914	3538	327	125	202
1915	3740	291	132	159
1916	3899	275	138	137
1917	4036	153	143	11
1918	4047	43	177	−134
1919	3913	32	231	−199
1920	3715	20	203	−183
1921	3532	19	187	−168
1922	3364	30	183	−153
1923	3211	42	113	−71
1923	3140 (1 Oct.)	83	114	−31

Sources:
Trudy TsSU, XXIX (1926), 95–7; *Tablitsy*, 31.

Table 55. *Grain production and procurement, 1909–13 to 1921[a] (million tons)*

	Production	Procurements	Residual
1909–13	67.8	–	–
1913	79.7	–	–
1914	67.8	5.0	62.8
1915	74.3	8.2	66.1
1916	62.5–65.5[b]	8.9	53.6–56.6[b]
1917	59.5–62.5[b]	2.5	57.0–60.0[b]
1918	..	1.8	..
1919	..	3.5	..
1920	44.5[c]	5.9	38.6
1921	38.0[c]	3.8	34.2[c]

Notes:
[a] USSR pre-1939 territory.
[b] There are major problems of comparability between the 1916 (and subsequent) data and the pre-1916 data. Wheatcroft has advised that the data for 1916 and 1917 (including the Southern Consumer Region, which was omitted in official publications) be corrected by between five and ten per cent, to bring the production figures into closer conformity with the corresponding figures for earlier years. Wheatcroft (1980), 217–21.
[c] The official (TsSU) figures are comparable with the pre-war uncorrected data, but the SCR was again excluded. The data in Table 55 incorporate an allowance of 2.5 million tons for grain production in this region. Wheatcroft (1980), 478.
Sources: Wheatcroft (1980), 216, 478; Wheatcroft, 'Balance of grain production' (n.d.), 5; Malle (1985), 407; N. D. Kondratiev *Rynok khlebov i ego regulirovanie vo vremya voiny i revolyntsii* (1922), 128.

Table 56. *Gross industrial production, 1913–1921/22 (USSR pre-1939 territory) (million rubles, 1913 prices)*

	Large-scale	Group A	Group B	Small-scale	Total
1913	6391	2582	3809	2040	8431
1914	6429	2626	3703	2000	8429
1915	7056	3359	3697	1600	8656
1916	7420	4170	3250	1800	9220
1917	4780	2667	2113	1600	6380
1918	2160	980	1180	1500	3660
1919	955	551	404	1000	1955
1920	818	396	422	900	1718
1920/21	1080	416	664	1000	2080
1921/22	1435	629	806	1100	2535

Source:
Planovoe khozyaistvo, 5, 1929, 173, 191.

Table 57. *Real GDP by sector of origin, 1937–1944 (billion rubles and 1937 factor cost)*

	1937	1940	1941	1942	1943	1944
Agriculture	63.0	69.9	42.3	25.3	30.4	45.0
Industry:	65.4	73.8	70.3	51.1	59.2	66.5
defence industry	3.4	8.3	14.2	28.1	35.0	38.7
civilian industry	62.0	65.5	56.2	22.9	24.2	27.8
Construction	10.5	10.6	6.9	3.2	3.4	4.4
Transport, communications	16.8	19.3	17.8	10.2	11.8	13.7
Trade, catering	10.4	11.1	9.3	3.8	3.5	4.1
Civilian services	33.1	42.0	35.3	22.1	23.4	28.8
Military services:	3.7	7.3	10.4	16.6	17.3	17.9
army, navy	3.4	6.8	9.8	15.8	16.6	17.2
NKVD	0.3	0.5	0.6	0.8	0.7	0.7
NDP	202.9	234.0	192.3	132.4	149.1	180.5
Depreciation	9.4	13.6	14.0	11.7	11.8	11.7
GDP	212.3	247.6	206.3	144.1	160.9	192.2

Source:
Harrison (1993a), Table 1.

Table 58. *Real burden of defence outlays, 1940–1944 (billion rubles, at 1937 factor cost)*

	1940	1941	1942	1943	1944
GDP	247.6	206.3	144.1	160.9	192.2
Net imports	0.0	0.0	9.0	30.9	35.6
Defence outlays:	45.3	66.9	110.1	133.8	145.3
Munitions	16.6	28.3	61.6	82.3	90.2
Pay	6.8	9.8	15.8	16.6	17.2
Food	9.9	14.1	16.1	19.0	19.1
Clothing, etc.	4.4	5.1	6.4	5.3	6.3
Fuel	1.5	2.1	2.4	2.7	3.1
Transport	0.9	1.1	1.4	2.6	3.0
Construction	2.4	2.6	2.0	1.1	1.5
Other, including repairs	2.7	3.8	4.5	4.2	4.8
Defence outlays, less net imports	45.3	66.9	101.1	102.9	109.7
Defence outlays, % of GDP:					
Domestic supply	18	32	70	64	57
Foreign supply	0	0	6	19	19

Source:
Harrison (1993), Table 4 and D–1.

Table 59. *Employment, 1940–1945 (millions, annual average)*

	1940	1941	1942	1943	1944	1945
Agriculture	49.3	36.9	24.3	25.5	31.3	36.1
Industry:	13.9	12.8	8.8	9.1	10.3	11.7
Defence industry	1.6	1.8	2.4	2.6	2.8	2.2
Civilian industry	12.4	11.0	6.4	6.5	7.5	9.5
Construction	2.6	2.5	1.8	1.7	2.1	2.3
Transport, communications	4.0	3.5	2.4	2.4	3.0	3.6
Trade, catering	3.3	2.8	1.7	1.7	2.1	2.5
Civilian services	9.1	7.7	4.8	5.1	6.5	7.7
Military services:	5.0	7.1	11.3	11.9	12.2	12.1
Army, navy	4.7	6.7	10.8	11.4	11.7	11.6
NKVD	0.4	0.4	0.5	0.5	0.5	0.5
Total working population	87.2	73.4	55.1	57.5	67.4	76.0

Source:
Harrison (1993a), Table 2.

Table 60. *Recruitment into public sector employment, by sector of economy, 1942 (thousands)*

	Vocational training	Conscripts	NKVD *spetskontingent*	Urban population not at work
Defence industry	175	129	68	346
Mining, metallurgy	93	223	88	98
Transport	77	64	5	173
Construction, etc	49	65	41	38
Light industry	33	7	9	412
Other	69	43	29	148
Total	495	530	240	1215

	Rural population	Other		Total
Defence industry	82	52		853
Mining, metallurgy	101	14		617
Transport	123	4		445
Construction	82	1		275
Light industry	139	4		603
Other	32	15		336
Total	558	90		3129

Note: The source lists 31 commissariats and chief administrations, including the following:
Defence industry: Aircraft Industry, Ammunition, Armament, Mortar Armament, Shipbuilding, Tank Industry
Mining, metallurgy: Coal Industry, Oil Industry, Ferrous Metallurgy, Nonferrous Metallurgy
Transport: Transport, River Shipping, Maritime Shipping
Construction: Construction, Defence Industry Construction, Construction Materials, Timber Industry.
Light industry: Light Industry, Textile Industry, Food Industry, Meat and Dairy Industry, Fishing Industry
Source:
RGAE, 4372/42/986, 118.

Table 61. *Estimated net output per worker in material production, 1940–1944 (rubles, at 1937 factor cost)*

	1940	1941	1942	1943	1944
Industry	5300	5490	5780	6490	6470
Defence industry	5300	7840	11640	13310	13940
Civilian industry	5300	5110	3570	3730	3700
Agriculture	1420	1150	1040	1190	1440
Construction	4150	2730	1840	2030	2110
Transport, communications	4880	5050	4340	4830	4570
Trade, catering	3340	3290	2250	2060	1980

Source:
Harrison (1993a), Table 3.

Glossary of terms and abbreviations

ADK	Andreev, Darskii and Khar'kova (see Bibliography)
art.	article (*stat'ya*)
Bolsheviks	more revolutionary section, headed by Lenin, of Russian Social Democratic Labour Party (so-called from the Russian *bol'shinstvo*, because they obtained a majority of the votes at one stage in the 1903 Congress)
Cobb-Douglas production function	see Box on Production function, Chapter 9, p. 193
construction (*stroitel'stvo*)	capital construction, exclusive of installations and machinery (i.e. building work)
conventional ton/km (*uslovnyi tonno-kilometr*)	combined traffic measure, treating 1 passenger/km (q.v.) as equal to 1 ton/km (q.v.)
CBR (crude birth-rate)	annual number of live births per 1,000 population
CDR (crude death-rate)	annual number of deaths per 1,000 population
CPR (Central Producer Region)	Central grain-surplus region
Dneproges (Dneprovskaya gidroelektricheskaya stantsiya)	Dnepr Hydro-electric Power Station
Donbass (Donetskii ugol'nyi bassein)	Donets coal basin
EPR (Eastern Producer Region)	Eastern grain-surplus region
excess deaths	premature deaths due to violence, famine or epidemics

Gerschenkron effect	see Box, Chapter 2, p. 32
Goelro (Gosudarstvennaya komissiya po elektrifikatsii Rossii)	State Commission for the Electrification of Russia
Gosplan (Gosudarstvennaya Planovaya Komissiya)	State Planning Commission
gross production (*valovoe proizvodstvo*)	total output of goods by an economic unit or aggregated output of groups of units (so output used by another unit is double-counted)
Group 'A' industry	Capital goods (producer goods)
Group 'B' industry	Consumer goods (including industrially processed food products)
GULag or GULAG (Glavnoe upravlenie lagerei)	Chief Administration of Corrective-Labour Camps, responsible for forced labour
index numbers	see Box, Chapter 2, p. 31
industry (*promyshlennost'*)	mining and manufacturing industry (Russian term excludes building industry, transport, etc.)
infant mortality	annual death rate in first year of life per 1,000 live births
KGB (Komitet gosudarstvennoi bezopasnosti)	Committee of State Security (post-war successor to NKVD)
khozraschet (*khozyaistvennyi raschet*)	economic accounting (= profit-and-loss accounting)
kolkhoz (pl. *kolkhozy*) (*kollektivnoe khozyaistvo*)	collective farm
KTs	*Kontrol'nye tsifry* (see Bibliography)
kulak	more prosperous peasant (Russian word for 'closed fist' or 'tight fist')
kustar' (pl. *kustari*)	artisan
large-scale industry (*krupnaya promyshlennost'*)	normally included industrial units employing 16 workers or more when using mechanical power, or 30 workers or more otherwise; all other industry was classified as 'small-scale'. Also known as 'census' (*tsenzovaya*) industry

Laspeyres index	price index weighted by prices of initial year (see also Box on Index number problems, p. 32)
LCL	less-than-carload (goods wagon load) rail traffic
Mensheviks	less revolutionary section of Russian Social Democratic Labour Party (from *men'shinstvo* – minority) see Bolsheviks
MTS (Mashino-traktornaya stantsiya)	Machine-Tractor Station
nadel (pl. *nadely*)	arable land alloted to households in main fields of village
Nar. kh.	*Narodnoe khozyaistvo* (see Bibliography)
NCR (Northern Consumer Region)	Northern grain-deficit region, importing grain from producer regions
NEP (Novaya ekonomicheskaya politika)	New Economic Policy
net production (*chistoe proizvodstvo*)	total output of economic unit or group of units *less* inputs (i.e. = value-added)
NKPS (Narodnyi komissariat putei soobshcheniya)	People's Commissariat of Ways of Communication [i.e. of Transport]
NKVD (Narodnyi komissariat vnutrennikh del)	People's Commissariat of Internal Affairs; responsible for administration of forced labour
NRR (net reproduction rate)	Annual excess of births over deaths per 1,000 population
Paasche index	price index weighted by prices of current year (see also Box on Index number problems, p. 32)
passenger/km (passenger-kilometre)	movement of 1 passenger over 1 kilometre
People's Commissar (*narodnyi komissar*)	government Minister, member of Sovnarkom (q.v.)

Politburo	political committee of central committee of Communist Party, effectively supreme centre of power
population deficit	excess deaths (q.v.) plus loss in population due to temporary fall in birth rate
prodrazverstka (prodovol'stvennaya razverstka)	'food-quota allocation' (central food collection plan, usually for grain, broken down to village or household as compulsory quotas) (often translated 'grain requisitioning')
production function	see Box, Chapter 9, p. 193
promysly	'industry' (all economic activity of peasants outside own farm)
Rabkrin (Narodnyi komissariat raboche-krest'yanskoi inspektsii)	People's Commissariat of Workers' and Peasants' Inspection
R & D	research and development
RSFSR (Rossiiskaya Sovetskaya Federativnaya Sotsialisticheskaya Respublika)	Russian Soviet Federative Socialist Republic, largest constituent republic of USSR (q.v.)
ruble *(rubl')*	unit of currency, at par = £0.106 or $0.515 (inter-war period)
'scissors' *(nozhnitsy)*	ratio of retail prices of manufactured goods to prices received by peasants for their produce, graph of which resembled open blade of a pair of scissors during 1922–3 (for 'scissors' crisis' of 1923, see Chapter 1)
SCR (Southern Consumer Region)	Southern grain-deficit region, importing grain from producer regions.
Sel.kh.	*Sel'skoe khozyaistvo* (see Bibliography)
small-scale industry *(melkaya promyshlennost')*	see Large-scale industry
Socialist Revolutionaries (SRs)	Peasant-revolutionary party
Sots. sel. kh.	*Sotsialisticheskoe sel'skoe khozyaistvo* (see Bibliography)
Sots. str.	*Sotsialisticheskoe stroitel'stvo* (see Bibliography)

sovkhoz (pl. *sovkhozy*) (*sovetskoe khozyaistvo*)	soviet [i.e. state] farm
Sovnarkom (Sovet Narodnykh Komissarov)	Council of People's Commissars – government of the Soviet Union, composed of People's Commissars (q.v.) and agencies such as Gosplan (q.v.)
SPR (Southern Producer Region)	Southern grain-surplus region
Stakhanov movement	drive for higher labour productivity, launched after Aleksei Stakhanov achieved record coal output in the night-shift of August 30–31 1935
Stat. spr.	*Statisticheskii spravochnik* (see Bibliography)
stazh	length of employment
syndicates (*sindikaty*)	joint organisations of industrial firms controlling sales (= cartels)
ton/km (ton kilometre)	movement of 1 ton over 1 kilometre
tsentner	0.1 tons
TsIK (Tsentral'nyi Ispolnitel'nyi Komitet)	Central Executive Committee of Soviets of USSR
TsOS (Tsentral'nyi Otdel Statistiki)	Central Department of Statistics of VSNKh (responsible for industrial statistics, 1918–31)
TsSK (Tsentral'nyi Statisticheskii Komitet)	Central Statistical Committee attached to Ministry for Internal Affairs (pre-revolutionary)
TsSU (Tsentral'noe statisticheskoe upravlenie)	Central Statistical Administration (1918–1930; re-established March 1941) – *see* TsUNKhU
TsUNKhU (Tsentral'noe upravlenie narodno-khozyaistvennogo ucheta)	Central Administration of National-Economic Records (statistical agency, formed in December 1931 attached to Gosplan, continued to March 1941) – *see* TsSU
Turksib (Turkestano-Sibirskaya Zheleznaya Doroga)	Turkestan-Siberian Railway

uchet	records
usad'ba (pl. *usad'by*)	household plot around cottage
USSR (SSSR – Soyuz sovetskikh sotsialisticheskikh respublik)	Union of Soviet Socialist Republics, inaugurated in 1922, by 1941 had sixteen constituent republics; dissolved end of 1991
VSNKh (Vesenkha) (Vysshii sovet narodnogo khozyaistva)	Supreme Council of Nationa Economy, in charge of industry, 1918–1931, divided into three People's Commissariats January 1932 (these were later subdivided)
zemstvo (pl. *zemstva*)	rural local government elected institution (pre-revolutionary)

Notes

1 CHANGING ECONOMIC SYSTEMS: AN OVERVIEW

1 Gerschenkron (1965).
2 See *Economic History Review*, 2nd series, XXXV (1982), 104–5 (Gatrell); *Russian Review*, XI (1984), 231–59 (Pintner); Davies (1990), 146–7.
3 The orthodox view is presented in Bovykin (1988); for the 'new direction', see *Voprosy istorii kapitalisticheskoi Rossii* (1972) and more recently, *Voprosy istorii*, 3, 1989, 44–61 (V. V. Polikarpov).
4 *Slavic Review*, XLVII (1988), 514.
5 Shanin (1985), 200.
6 *Slavic Review*, XX (1961), 576 (Black).
7 Seton-Watson (1952), 377–9.
8 Gerschenkron (1965), 141.
9 Von Laue (1966), 36, 233; Geyer (1987), 11, 345–6; Lieven (1983), 153–4.
10 'The Next Tasks of Soviet Power' in Lenin (1936–8), VII, 313–35; and speech of 18 May 1918, in Lenin (1936–8), VII, 380–3.
11 For a detailed account of the economic system of War Communism, see Carr (1952), ch. 17; for currency circulation, see Davies (1958), 9, 31.
12 See Szamuely (1974), 18–19; Gimpel'son (1973), 158–62.
13 Dobb (1946), 122; for the alternative view, see Roberts (1971), 20–47.
14 P. K.Kaganovich, December 1919, cited in *Slavic Review*, XLV (1986), 678–9 (Lih).
15 Nove (1982), 48. The different assessments are carefully discussed in Malle (1985); see also Davies (1989a), 997–1002.
16 For the civil war economy of the South, see Kenez (1977), 94–102, 159, 162, 287–91.
17 Lenin, (1941–62), XXX (1950), 308–9 (2 February).
18 Davies (1958), 38–45; on the 'false start' of 1920 generally, see Davies (1989a), 1004–6.
19 For these developments see Carr (1952), 271, 280–3, and Davies (1989a), 1008–11.
20 Lenin, (1941–62), XXXIII (1950), 72 (Moscow party conference, October 1921).
21 See Gregory in Davies (1990), 337.
22 See Davies (1990), 154–7 (Gatrell and Davies), 189–211 (Cooper and Lewis).
23 Davies (1990), 110–11, 285 (Harrison); grain marketings are measured in terms of non-rural utilisation. For a debate about the level of grain marketings between

J. F. Karcz and R. W. Davies, see *Soviet Studies*, XVIII (1966/7), 399–434; XXI (1969/70), 314–29; XXII (1970/1), 262–94.

24 Davies (1990), 324–5, 331.

25 This view is criticised by Harrison, as far as the influence of intra-peasant differentiation is concerned, in Davies (1990), 112–3, 361 note 20.

26 Harrison in Davies (1990), 113, 287, 361, note 22.

27 For further discussion, see Harrison in Davies (1990), 113–14 and 361–2, notes 25–7.

28 For example, Conquest (1986), 87–93.

29 See Carr and Davies (1969), 291–2, 773–5, and table 18.

30 For example, Nove (1982), 138–42.

31 On this, see Davies (1989a), 1022, 1024; and (1980), 39–40.

32 Gerschenkron (1965), 144–60; for a similar view applied to the dilemmas of foreign trade, see Dohan in Davies (1990), 212–33.

33 *Rodina*, 7, 1989, 80–4; see also his article in *EKO*, 10, 1989, 66–83.

34 See Carr in Feinstein (1967), 278.

35 Gorinov (1990), and see his article in *Voprosy istorii KPSS*, 1, 1990, 18.

36 See Tucker (1973), ch. 12, and Cohen (1974), ch.9.

37 *Slavic Review*, XXXIII (1974), 766; see also *Journal of Political Economy*, March–April 1974, 346–7 (Gisser and Jonas).

38 Hunter and Szyrmer (1992); the quote is from p.90. For discussion of earlier versions of Hunter's model, see *Slavic Review*, XXXII (1973), 237–91 (Hunter and others), XXXIV (1975), 790–803 (Davies/Wheatcroft and Hunter); Davies (1984), 16–33, 52–63 (Hunter/Rutan, Harrison and Wheatcroft).

39 See Davies (1989b), chs. 3 and 4. For a good Russian study written from this point of view, see Goland (1991).

40 Davies (1990), 127–8 (Gatrell and Davies).

41 See Carr (1958), 290–7, 305–8; Davies (1980), 30.

42 See, as examples of a large literature, the discussion between Mark Tauger and Robert Conquest, in *Slavic Review*, L (1991), 70–89, and LI (1992), 192–4; see also the exchange between Conquest and Davies in *Détente*, 9–10 (1987), 44–5; 11 (1988), 36; 12 (1988).

43 Economic developments in this period are surveyed in Harrison (1985), ch. 1.

44 For the size of the army, see Tupper (1982), 103, 202; for armaments' production, see Harrison (1991), 52.

45 The residual is in turn sometimes known as 'technical progress' because this is assumed to be its main component).

46 F. Seton in *American Economic Review*, LXIX (1959), 1–14.

47 Barsov (1969), *passim*; Ellman (1975), 844–63.

48 Millar and Nove in *Problems of Communism*, XXXV (1976), 49–62; for further criticism of Barsov's findings, see D. Morrison (1982), 570–84.

49 See Ellman (1975), 859.

2 THE CROOKED MIRROR OF SOVIET ECONOMIC STATISTICS

1 *Istoriya sovetskoi gosudarstvennoi statistiki* (1960), 51–5; Gozulov (1972), especially pp. 52–4; Wheatcroft (1980), I, 1–37.

2 See the chapters on different sectors of the economy in *Istoriya sovetskoi gosudarstvennoi statistiki* (1960). For the collection of pre-revolutionary industrial statistics, see the introductory chapters to the three volumes of *Dinamika* (1929–30).

3 *Sobranie uzakonenii, 1918*, art. 611.

4 *Balans ... 1923–24g. (Trudy TsSU, XXIXX (1926)); Vsesoyuznaya perepis', I–LVI* (1928–33); *Melkaya promyshlennost' ... 1929,* I (1933) and II–III (1932).

5 Stalin (1946–51), VI (1947), 214–15 (report to XIII party congress, 23 May).

6 *Sobranie zakonov, 1926,* II, art. 19 (5 January), art. 32 (4 February).

7 For Groman's appointment, see *Sobranie zakonov, 1927,* II, art.5 (dated 28 December 1926).

8 *Sobranie zakonov, 1928,* II, art. 43 (dated 3 March).

9 See Carr and Davies (1969), 76–8; Wheatcroft (1980), 311.

10 See Davies (1980), 66–7.

11 See Davies (1989b), 119–22, 406–11.

12 *Sobranie zakonov, 1930,* art. 97.

13 *Sobranie zakonov, 1931,* art. 488 (dated 17 December).

14 Osinskii was confirmed as TsUNKhU director on 11 January 1932 (*Sobranie zakonov, 1932,* II, art. 15).

15 See Wheatcroft in Fitzpatrick and Viola (1987), 156.

16 RTsKhIDNI, 17/3/911, 22–3 (Politburo session of 16 December).

17 RTsKhIDNI, 17/3/911, 22–3, and 17/3/913, 3, 29 (Politburo session of 16 January 1933).

18 *Sobranie zakonov, 1933,* II, art. 29 (dated 21 January).

19 *Pravda,* 20 June 1933.

20 *Sobranie zakonov, 1935,* II, arts. 118–19 (dated 8 August).

21 He was dismissed from TsUNKhU on 23 May 1937 (*Sobranie zakonov, 1937,* art. 143).

22 TsUNKhU was renamed TsSU in January 1941, and in August 1948 it was restored to its pre-1930 status of an independent government department separate from Gosplan. But by 1948 it was under very firm political control.

23 Gerschenkron (1951), 46–7, 52.

24 See, for example, Chamberlin (1934), 76; some émigré economists, however, accepted the official harvest figures – e.g. Yugov (?1942), 49–50.

25 Clark (1939); his revised estimates are printed in Jasny (1962), 19.

26 *Journal of Political Economy* (April 1953) (Kaplan).

27 Bergson (1961), 198–201.

28 Khanin (1991a), 146.

29 Estimated from Moorsteen and Powell (1966), 622 (civilian plus military industry). Nutter's estimated rate of growth is lower.

30 Khanin (1991b); Khanin does not give his own estimate for construction.

31 Moorsteen and Powell (1966), 622.

32 Khanin criticises the rate of growth of Moorsteen's machinery production series, without offering an alternative figure (Khanin (1991b)); it is not clear how this criticism is compatible with Khanin's figure for the rate of growth of industrial production as a whole, which agrees with Moorsteen and Powell.

3 NATIONAL INCOME

1 Stalin (1940), 366.
2 On Russian and Soviet economic mobilisation in the two world wars, see chapter 12.
3 In this chapter I refer sometimes to GNP (gross national product), sometimes to GDP (gross domestic product). The difference between the two is net investment income from abroad (GNP = GDP + foreign investment income). This was an important distinction for the market economies, and for Russia before 1917, but the Soviet Union had no significant foreign assets or liabilities in the inter-war years, so Soviet GNP and GDP were interchangeable.
4 Others involved include Roman Bernaut, Janet G. Chapman, Hans Heymann, Oleg Hoeffding, Richard Moorsteen, Nancy Nimitz, Raymond P. Powell and Lynn Turgeon. See further chapter 2.
5 See Wiles (1962), 245.
6 *Nar. kh. 1961* (1962), 140, 597.
7 Davies (1990), 239–44 (Gregory).
8 Davies (1990), 247 (Gregory). Per capita income (below) is based on population figures from Davies (1990), 332.
9 The net harvest of food grains in 1913 was 17 per cent above the logarithmic trend for 1885–1913; the average for 1909–13 was just 4 per cent above this trend. The net output of food grains, in 1913 prices, is given by Gregory (1982), 235.
10 Gregory, in Davies (1990), 337, suggests 107 per cent of 1913 actual national income as a figure for 1928 national income, after upward revision to meet Davies and Wheatcroft's first objection. This is raised to 111 per cent of 1913 permanent income as follows. In 1913, agriculture contributed 50.7 per cent of national income at 1913 prices (Gregory (1982), 73); in 1909–13 gross agricultural production in 1926/27 prices averaged 93 per cent of the 1913 level (Wheatcroft, Davies and Cooper (1986), 281). Therefore, permanent national income in 1913 was roughly 3.5 per cent below actual 1913 national income.
11 On the basis of population figures within pre-1939 and contemporary frontiers from ADK (1990a), 41, I multiply Bergson's, and Moorsteen and Powell's index numbers for 1940 by 0.9.
12 The figures which follow are taken or calculated from Clark (1957), 247; Jasny (1961), 444; Bergson (1961), 128, 153; Moorsteen and Powell (1966), 622. On Clark and Jasny, see chapter 2, where it was shown that Jasny's 'real' 1926/27 prices (so-called to distinguish them from the steadily inflating '1926/27' prices of Soviet official statistics) were in practice equivalent to Bergson's 1937 factor costs; thus the coincidence between Bergson and Jasny apparent from these figures was no accident.
13 *Mirovaya ekonomika i mezhdunarodnye otnosheniya*, 11, 1987, 145–7 (IMEMO). The element of international comparison, however, seemed to generate a number of anomalies; see Harrison (1992a), 16.
14 *Kommunist*, 17, 1988, 85 (Khanin).
15 Harrison (1993b).
16 This picture is a more optimistic one that that of Harrison (1992a), table 6, for two reasons. First, in previous work I began from actual rather than permanent 1913 national income, and I used Gregory's estimate of a 10 per cent decline in

GNP per head for 1913–28. Secondly, my earlier estimate lowered Moorsteen and Powell's figures for GNP in 1938–40, substituting my own (from Harrison (1991), table 2), but my own revision of their work was partly in error; here I return to the original estimates of Moorsteen and Powell. As a result, present series show GNP per head as constant in 1928 compared with 1913, and in 1940 compared with 1937, rather than declining in each sub-period.

17 For Russian national income per capita at 1913 prices, see Gregory (1982), 56–7.
18 This is for several reasons, any one of which would be compelling. First, because productivity differences between countries tend to be wider in the traded goods sector than in largely untraded services, GNP comparisons based on exchange rates tend to exaggerate the income gap between rich and poor countries; see Marer (1985), 75–7. Secondly, exchange rates are rendered volatile by speculative movements of foreign currency. Thirdly, exchange rates are affected by the varying commercial policies pursued by governments, and also by instruments of exchange control.
19 Marer (1985), 86; United Nations and EUROSTAT (1986), I, 7.
20 Harrison (1992a), table 2.
21 The competing estimates are surveyed in Harrison (1992a), 16–17.
22 Harrison (1992c), 9.
23 For these and following figures, see Moorsteen and Powell (1966), 333–9.
24 Moorsteen and Powell (1966), 367, 369.
25 Wheatcroft, Davies and Cooper (1986), 268–70.
26 For more detailed discussion of unfinished construction as an indicator of the investment process, with a wider sample across countries and periods, but with more preliminary data, see *Economics of Planning*, XIX, no. 2 (1985) (Harrison).
27 For relevant figures of personal consumption and national income, 1913 and 1928, see Davies (1990), 337 (Gregory).
28 Davies (1990), 285–6 (Harrison).
29 Davies (1990), 244–5 (Gregory).
30 Morrison (1989), 184.
31 For farm consumption in kind, 1928–40, see Bergson (1961), 167.
32 Chapman (1963), 166.
33 Chapman (1963), 166–7.
34 Bergson (1961), 252.
35 Bergson (1961), 256–7.
36 For more detailed evaluation of the comparability of the price structures of 1913 and 1937, note that Gregory's estimate of the consumption share in NNP in 1928, in 1913 prices, ranges from 73.2 to 76.7 per cent (Gregory (1990), 337). By comparison, from Bergson and at 1937 prices, the share of consumption in NNP in 1928 can be put at 81.6 per cent (table 5). Therefore, in 1937 non-consumption goods were relatively not only much cheaper than in 1926/27 or 1928, but also slightly cheaper than in 1913.

4 POPULATION

1 See Volkov (1930), 14; we have added an estimate of 2.2 million to the census figures to include the population of Khiva and Bukhara in Central Asia, which was not included in the census (see Lorimer (1946), 36).

2 See Volkov (1930), 7–48. This modified the earlier corrections by V. Zaitsev in Groman (1927), II.
3 See data cited in Lorimer (1946), 116.
4 See data cited in Wheatcroft (1976a), 16.
5 According to Volkov (1930), 35, population on 1 January 1914 amounted to 139.9 million (excluding Khiva and Bukhara); this is the equivalent of 142.4 million including Khiva and Bukhara (Lorimer (1946), 30). On this estimate the population in mid-1913 would therefore be approximately 141.2 million. According to an alternative estimate by Gukhman in *Planovoe khozyaistvo*, 8, 1926, the correct figure for 1 January 1914 is 139.7 million, giving 138.5 for mid-1913 (see also Vainshtein (1960), 250–4, and Danilov (1970), 244). We have taken the average of 141.2 and 138.5 million for the mid-1913 figure used for the comparison of per head figures in this book. Our figure for the population of the whole Russian Empire excludes Finland and the Kingdom of Poland. (See Zaitsev's estimate in Groman (1927), II, 91; the equivalent figure excluding Khiva and Bukhara is 165.1 million.)
6 See Lorimer (1946), 31–2; and Volkov (1930), 268–71.
7 See Ptukha (1960), 279–347, especially p. 297.
8 See Lorimer (1946), 35–6, 27; Wheatcroft (1976a), 10. Migration from the Western areas separated from Soviet Russia after the revolution was even more intensive, amounting to 19.2 per cent of the natural increase in population; 76 per cent of this migration was emigration abroad.
9 Lorimer (1946), 42.
10 Volkov (1930), 49–94.
11 Volkov (1930), 102–7, 216. The figure for the military includes all those not yet settled: demobilised soldiers, deserters, and those evacuated as sick or wounded. Volkov classified the whole army as 'on non-active service' at the end of 1917.
12 Volkov (1930), 184.
13 See Wheatcroft (1982b), 6, 8, citing *Statisticheskii sbornik po Petrogradu i Petrogradskoi gubernii* (Petrograd, 1922), and *Statisticheskii ezhegodnik g. Moskvy i Moskovskoi gubernii* (1927), II, 88.
14 According to Volkov, the urban population increased from 20.4 million on 1 January 1914 (using the 1897 definition) to 25.6 million at the beginning of 1918 (also using the 1897 definition). It then declined to 21.4 million on 1 January 1921; but the latter figure is based on the wider definition of 'urban' in the census instructions for that year, so the decline was considerably greater than these figures indicate (Volkov (1930), 270–1). According to Gukhman (1925), population of towns as defined in 1897 declined from 20.4 million on 1 January 1914 to 15.1 million on 1 August 1920; population of towns and urban settlements together, using the 1921–3 definitions, declined from 25.4 million to 20.1 million (see also Volkov (1930), 203).
15 See Maksudov (1989), 187, and Lorimer (1946), 39.
16 For various estimates see Lorimer (1946), 40 (Kohn and Golovine); Kaminskii (1974), 114–22; Volkov (1930), 49–130. Urlanis (1960), 381, gives a total of 1.81 million, the same as Volkov, but assumes that as many as 1.4 million of these were killed in action (Volkov's figure is 0.7 million – see p. 61 above).
17 In Saratov CDR increased from 29 in 1914 to 34 in 1917; in Moscow it remained unchanged at about 24 (see data in Wheatcroft (1982b), 9, 12).

18 Urlanis' estimate for Red and White armies together, including 0.45 million deaths from illness, is 0.8 million (Urlanis (1960), 399), Polyakov's for the Red Army alone 1.2 million (Polyakov (1986), 101–3).

19 See data from Volkov cited in Lorimer (1946), 41.

20 See Wheatcroft (1981), for an analysis of conditions in Moscow, Petrograd and Saratov (Saratov was in the centre of the famine zone); and Wheatcroft (1982b), 6, for monthly CDR in Petrograd.

21 For details, see Danilov (1970), 246–7; Polyakov (1986), 96–8.

22 2.6 million in Lorimer (1946), 30 (Volkov's figures adjusted to include Khiva and Bukhara); 3.6–4.2 million in Danilov (1970), 244–5; 4.7 million in Polyakov (1986), 94, 98 (the 1917 figure is for autumn 1917).

23 Danilov (1970), 246.

24 See Wheatcroft (1976b), 130–1; both before the war and in the 1920s the age of marriage was higher in the town than in the countryside.

25 See Wheatcroft (1976b), 135; the number of registered abortions was 5 per 100 births in 1925, and increased to 21 per 100 births by 1929.

26 *Strana sovetov* (1967), 257. There is some doubt about this figure. The life-tables for the USSR for 1926/27 give the higher figure of 187 for the European USSR, and the figure for the USSR as a whole was presumably higher. See Wheatcroft (1976a), 15.

27 The legalisation of abortion also tended to reduce infant mortality.

28 ADK (1990a), 35, 37. The alternative suggestion was made by the statistician Kurman in the 1930s that the population was overestimated by 1.5 million, because the census took place over a period of one week in the towns and 15–20 days in the countryside. This is rejected by most authorities (Kurman was anxious to explain away the low level of the population in the 1937 census – see the discussion of the 'Kurman gap', below). For Kurman's memorandum, see *Sots. issl.*, 6, 1990, 22–4; his proposition is criticised in ADK (1990a), 35.

29 See Lorimer (1946), 31–3.

30 See Lorimer (1946), 41–3.

31 For details see Lorimer (1946), 123–5.

32 For details see Lorimer (1946), 113–19.

33 Maksudov (1989), 217–23.

34 Estimated from Lorimer (1946), 134.

35 *Vestnik statistiki*, 7, 1990, 41.

36 RGAE, 105/1/10, 20.

37 ADK estimate the population on 1 January 1930 at the higher figure of 157.4 millions because they believe that the population on 1 January 1927, a few days after the census, was not the 147.1 millions derived directly from the census by Lorimer but as high as 148.6 million (see figure 3). Danilov gives a figure of 156.4 for 1 January 1930, but believes that the true figure may be somewhat smaller (*Arkheograficheskii ezhegodnik* (1970), 251).

38 *Sots. issl.*, 10, 1991, 3–5 (Zemskov). These figures do not apparently include peasants who died on route to exile.

39 *Pravda*, 16 September 1988. A lower figure, 1.3 million, is obtained by deducting the number of peasants exiled outside their own region (2.1 million) from the total number exiled in 1930–2 (3.4 million – see *Soyuz*, 26, 1990); to this should be added an unknown number of peasants exiled within their own region in 1933.

40 Estimated from data in *Sots. issl.*, 10, 1991, 4–5.
41 *Voprosy istorii*, 7, 1989 (Abylkhozhin, Kozybaev and Tatimov). Their estimate of total abnormal loss of Kazakhs in 1931–3 is 1.75 million; allowing for migration, Maksudov accepts 1.3–1.5 million, and Ellman 1.3 million (see *Soviet Studies*, XLII (1990), 812–3 (Nove) and XLIV (1992), 914, note 2 (Ellman)).
42 *Sots. str.* (1936), 545.
43 Estimates by P. I. Popov cited in Pisarev (1962), 97.
44 The relevant decisions and decrees were published in *Trud*, 4 June 1992.
45 See *Sots. issl.*, 2, 1991, 75 (Zemskov). We have not entered here into various complications about the comparability of these figures.
46 See Bacon (1992b); on *ssyl'nye*, see *Sots. issl.*, 11, 1990, 3 (Zemskov).
47 See *Sots. issl.*, 2, 1991, 74–5 (Zemskov), correcting a higher estimate in *Sots. issl.* 8, 1990.
48 *Sots. issl.*, 8, 1990, 37, 42.
49 *Sots. str.* (1936), 542.
50 See ADK (1990a), 326; and Kurman's memorandum, reprinted in *Sots. issl.*, 6, 1990, 24.
51 See ADK (1990a), 36; Kurman reprinted in *Sots. issl.*, 6, 1990, 24.
52 ADK (1990a), 36.
53 Wheatcroft, Davies and Cooper (1986), 273, suggest it should be reduced by 'at most 2½ million', i.e to a figure somewhat in excess of 167.5 million. According to Conquest (1986), 302, it was 'probably about 167.2 million'.
54 See *Sots. issl.*, 8, 1990, 49–51.
55 Memorandum from Voznesenskii, head of Gosplan, and Sautin, head of TsUNKhU, to Stalin and Molotov, 21 March 1939 (RGAE, 1562/329/256, 38, cited ADK (1990a), p.38). No serious justification was proposed for these changes.
56 *Sots. issl.*, 8, 1990, 51 (Polyakov, Zhiromskaya and Kiselev).
57 *Slavic Review*, XLIV (1985), 517–36. Low fertility is defined as the age-specific fertility reported for 1938–9; high fertility as the age-specific fertility in the European USSR in 1926–7. Similarly low mortality is defined as the reported level of mortality for 1938–9; and high mortality as the mortality rates for 1926–7 in the USSR as a whole as estimated by Lorimer.
58 *Zven'ya*, I (1991), 85.
59 See Ellman (1991), 377–8. Ellman and Maksudov have suggested that the estimates by ADK do not allow sufficiently for increased deaths from famine in Kazakhstan, and from dekulakisation generally, in 1930–2; even if their total estimate of deaths in 1927–36 is correct, the number attributed to 1933 alone is therefore too high (Ellman (1992), 913–5). Maksudov's total estimate of deaths of children born in 1927–38 roughly coincides with that by ADK.
60 RGAE, 1562/20/193, 57a; somewhat different figures for 1937 are given in RGAE, 1562/20/108, 39.
61 For executions in 1937–8, see *Kommunist*, 8, 1990, 103. For Tsaplin's figures, see Tsaplin (1989), 181. He argues that according to the registration data the population should have amounted to 168.8 million in the 1939 census (162 + 6.8), whereas in fact it amounted to only 167.5; he attributes the missing 1.3 million to deaths of persons in the hands of the NKVD.
62 See Wheatcroft (1976a), 15. Infant mortality declined rapidly in the immediate post-war years, falling to 81 per thousand by 1950.

63 ADK (1990b), 25–7; 1939 figure was revised from 168.9.
64 *Nar. kh.* (1956), 17.
65 Cited in *Istoriya SSSR*, 2, 1989, 133.
66 *Vestnik statistiki*, 10, 1990 (referred to here as ADK ((1990b)). Their account does not, however, include the detailed calculations which lay behind their estimates.
67 *Istoriya SSSR*, 2, 1989, 132–9; he derives the population at the end of 1945 from L. E. Polyakova, *Tsena voiny* (1985).
68 *Voenno-istoricheskii zhurnal*, 3, 1990, 14. These figures are presented in greater detail by G. F. Krivosheev, *Voenno-istoricheskii zhurnal*, 2, 3 and 4, 1991.
69 According to the Soviet demographer Urlanis, direct war deaths in Germany amounted to over 4 million military deaths (including 0.5 million Germans from Austria, Czechia, Poland and Alsace-Lorraine), 0.5 million deaths from bombing, 0.3 million in camps; 0.5 million German allies also died, making 5.5 million in all (see *Istoriya SSSR*, 2, 1989, 133). Moiseev claims however that deaths amounted to 5.5 million in military units of German nationality, and satellites lost a further 1.2 million (*Voenno-istoricheskii zhurnal*, 3, 1990, 16).
70 *Istoriya SSSR*, 2, 1989, 138.
71 Volkogonov (1989), II, ii, 26–7; according to L. Rybakovskii in *Politicheskoe obrazovanie*, 10, 1989, 96–8, a post-war commission concluded that there had been 10 million military deaths, *plus* 2.8 million prisoners who had died up to 1941 December *plus* 11 million civilians who died on occupied territory, making a total of over 25 million. This figure apparently excludes civilian excess mortality in Soviet territory.
72 Deaths of military personnel are discussed in more detail in Bacon (1992a); Bacon also argues that Moiseev's figures are too low.
73 *Politicheskoe obrazovanie*, 10, 1989, 96–8.
74 Data estimated from *Istoriya SSSR*, 12, 1989, 136–42 (N. Bugai), *Novaya i noveishaya istoriya*, 2, 1989, 26–43 (V. S. Parsadonova). These figures do not include deportations from the Baltic states.

5 EMPLOYMENT AND INDUSTRIAL LABOUR

1 Except where otherwise stated, the sources for the material in sections I(A) and (B) may be found in the chapter by Perrie and Davies in Davies (1990), 29–45.
2 Becker (1985), 187–8.
3 See data in Davies (1990), 30.
4 See Davies (1990), 40, and 348, note 81.
5 Domestic labour: for 1913 see Davies (1990), 253 (referring to the Russian Empire); for 1926/27, see *Trud* (1930), 1.
6 See Davies (1990), 66–75 (Shapiro).
7 *Nar. kh.* (1932), 410–11 (total excluding agricultural workers).
8 See Carr and Davies (1969), 454.
9 Lorimer (1946), 101.
10 In 1926, 2,196,000 out of 8,490,000 workers and employees in non-agricultural occupations lived in the countryside (see Lorimer (1946), 74). In 1939, 14.2 out of 38.4 million workers and employees lived in the countryside (estimated from data in RGAE/1562/336/242, 5–9 and summary table 25); as 'manual and white-

collar workers' includes those working on state farms, these figures somewhat exaggerate the proportion of non-agricultural personnel living in the countryside.

11 According to Lorimer (1946), 149–50, about 23 million of the net increase by 29.6 million between 1926 and 1939 was due to migration.

12 Number of pupils in various forms is from *Nar. kh. 1958* (1959), 814–15; the number in each age-group of the population is estimated from data in Lorimer (1946), 231 (for 1926 census) and in RGAE, 1562/336/604, Form N 11 (from 1939 census).

13 Estimated from table 12 and data in *Nar. kh. 1958* (1959), 674.

14 For the increase in the number of pupils and teachers, see *Nar. kh. 1958* (1959), 812–5.

15 According to the KGB, 786,098 persons were executed for counter-revolutionary and state crimes in 1930–53 (*Pravda*, 14 February 1990); how many of these executions took place in 1930–41 was not stated. Many other executions associated with the mass repressions may have taken place under other heads of the criminal code.

16 See Wheatcroft (1976b), 81.

17 *Trud* (1968), 22. However, this figure includes technical and other specialist personnel, which rose very rapidly in this period.

18 Crisp (1978), 357.

19 Crisp (1978), 391; Davies (1990), 38 (Perrie and Davies); 79 per cent of male workers and only 44 per cent of female workers were literate.

20 Crisp (1978), 372–3; *Trud* (1930), 28–9.

21 Crisp (1978), 372–3, 367–8.

22 Smith (1983), 16.

23 Crisp (1978), 412, citing a study by the Russian economist Tugan-Baranovsky.

24 See Smith (1983), 13.

25 It was 300 per 1000 in Moscow and 250 in St Petersburg as compared with the national average of 273 (see Kaiser (1987), 52 (Bater)).

26 Smith (1983), 43; however, the number of working days per year were 20–30 less than in Britain, Germany or the US, owing to the prevalence of religious holidays.

27 *Slavic Review*, XLVII (1988), 514.

28 According to the 1929 survey, 52.2 per cent of workers came from working-class families, 20.6 per cent held land; in the case of the coal industry, where ties with the land were closer, the respective percentages were 34.4 and 24.6 per cent (*Trud* (1930), 28–9; Barber (1978), 8–14).

29 A 1929 survey of building workers showed the following (in percentages):

	Permanent workers	Migrant workers
In industry before 1928	37.1	35.9
Working-class parents	37.6	9.2
Own agriculture in countryside	19.9	90.0

Sources:
Trud (1932), 83, 85; *Izmeneniya* (1961), 152, 180, 194 (Gol'tsman).

30 On the role of the factory engineer, see Carr (1958), 378–9, and Carr and Davies

(1969), 578–80; on the foreman, see *Predpriyatie*, 12, 1926, 13–4 (S. Gastev), 22 (Kotel'nikov).

31 See Bergson (1944), 60; the quartile ratio, which is a measurement of equality, increased substantially in seven out of eight industries studied.

32 For 12 industries for which data are available for the whole period, covering 76 per cent of industrial workers, the percentages were as follows:

1913	30.7	1922/23	34.7
1915	36.0	1923/24	32.8
1917	39.7	1924/25	34.2
1918	41.2	1925/26	34.3
1921/22	38.0	1926/27	35.0

For all census industry, the percentage increased from 25.2 in 1913 to 29.5 per cent in 1926/27 (*Ocherki* (1957), 244–5, 206).

33 According to Soviet estimates:

	Women as percentage of numbers of workers[a]		Real wages: all workers $(1913 = 100)$[b]
	1913	1926/27	1926/27
Metalworking	4.8	10.2	85.0
Mining	8.0	14.5	75.0
Woodworking	8.2	16.4	108.2
Printing	9.1	22.1	106.8
Food	21.3	26.8	158.1
Paper	36.7	29.3	126.0
Chemicals	31.3	31.2	127.3
Textiles	56.1	60.2	120.0
All industry	25.2	29.5	99.6

Sources:
[a] *Ocherki* (1957), 206–67 (Mints).
[b] *Ekonomicheskoe obozrenie*, 10, 1927, 144–7 (Kheinman).

34 This did not, however, result in equal earnings for men and women, as female labour was concentrated in the less remunerative jobs. According to surveys of the central bureau of labour statistics, the average daily earnings of adult women increased from 63.4 per cent of adult male earnings in March 1926 to 67.2 per cent in March 1928; the equivalent percentage for June 1914 was only 51.1 (*Statistika truda*, 9–10, 1928, 2–48 (Rashin)).

35 A Soviet economist wryly commented: 'We are maintaining a definite policy of eliminating the pre-revolutionary gaps in the payment of male and female labour. But generally the shift in the former relationships of wage payments between the producer goods and consumer goods industries is the result of the disruption of the planned control of wages, a disruption due to market conditions.' (*Ekonomicheskoe obozrenie*, 9, 1929, 147 (Kheinman)).

36 See Carr (1952), 104.

37 *Trud* (1936), 98, 371; according to this source '"the normal length of the working day" refers to the number of hours of work which are fixed for the given worker

by existing legislation or the conditions of the labour contract'. These figures are for adult workers. According to *Trud* (1930), 37, the actual average length of the working day amounted to 7.45 hours in 1926/27 and 1927/28, including 0.1 hours overtime, and 7.37 including 0.13 hours overtime, in 1928/29; this figure presumably includes adolescents, who worked a shorter day.

38 See Carr and Davies (1969), 495–500.
39 Vdovin and Drobizhev (1976), 97; for total employment in industry, see table 13.
40 *Izmeneniya* (1961), 20.
41 *Proekt vtorogo piatiletnego plana* (1934), 502–3.
42 *Tretii pyatiletnii plan* (1939), 228.
43 Vdovin and Drobizhev (1976), 106–7.
44 Estimated from Rashin in *Izmeneniya* (1961), 17.
45 *Bol'shaya sovetskaya entsiklopediya*, XVII (1974).
46 Estimated from *Izmeneniya* (1961), 50, and Vdovin and Drobizhev (1976), 146.
47 Sul'kevich (1939), 32–3.
48 Stanley (1968), 13. For these regions and towns, see Maps 1 and 3.
49 Vdovin and Drobizhev (1976), 167.
50 To be more precise, the average worker who was a member of a trade union had. The 1932–3 trade-union census did not include workers (about a fifth of the total) who were not union members, and who may well have included in their number a higher proportion of new workers than the members of trade unions did.
51 Vdovin and Drobizhev (1976), 113, calculate from figures in *Trud* (1968), 22, that 66.8 per cent of manual and white-collar workers in large-scale industry in 1932 had a length of employment of under five years.
52 Vdovin and Drobizhev (1976), 113.
53 Estimated on the basis of the figures cited above, producing the following totals of 1928 workers still employed: in 1932 2,499,000 out of 6,007,000; in 1937 2,163,000 out of 7,924,000; and in 1940 1,964,000 out of a total of 8,290,000.
54 *Izmeneniya* (1961), 138.
55 *Trud* (1936), 107.
56 *Planovoe khozyaistvo*, 6–7, 1932, 152.
57 *Devyatyi vsesoyuznyi s"ezd professional'nykh soyuzov* (1933), 411.
58 Vdovin and Drobizhev (1976), 134.
59 *Molodezh' SSSR* (1936), 131–3.
60 *Industrializatsiya, 1938–1941* (1973), 214, citing a TsUNKhU report.
61 Vdovin and Drobizhev (1976), 130.
62 Vdovin and Drobizhev (1976), 136. The authors point that the frequent assertion that women comprised 82.8 per cent of the increase in the number of employed people between 1933 and 1937 (as stated in *Problemy ekonomiki*, 6, 1939, 157) is inaccurate. Allowing for the natural decrease in the number of employed people, the majority of whom would have been male, men and women must have entered the workforce during this period in roughly equal numbers.
63 Tverdokhleb (1970), 140.
64 Vdovin and Drobizhev (1976), 136.
65 *Profsoyuznaya perepis', 1932–33* (1933), 20; *Izmeneniya* (1961), 174.
66 *Zhenshchina* (1936), 79.
67 *Trud* (1936), 6; *Sostav novykh millionov* (1933), 48–9.
68 *Trud* (1930), 28–9.

69 *Puti industrializatsii*, 1, 1930, 38. As pointed out on p. 93 above, the impression of the social composition of workers given by the 1929 trade-union census may exaggerate the proportion of hereditary proletarians in the workforce. With the 'class struggle' developing in the countryside, some workers may have concealed their rural origins. On the other hand, the findings of this census concerning social origin are similar to those of the all-Union census of 1926.
70 *Istoricheskie zapiski*, LXXXVII (1971), 15.
71 *Sostav novykh millionov* (1933), 15.
72 *Itogi vypolneniya* (1933), 174.
73 *Sostav novykh millionov* (1933), 48–9.
74 *Sostav novykh millionov* (1933), 3–4.
75 *Trud* (1930), 27.
76 *Industrializatsiya, 1938–1941* (1973), 248.
77 Vdovin and Drobizhev (1976), 119.
78 Sonin (1959), 143.
79 *Pyatiletnii plan* (1929), 335.
80 Tverdokhleb (1970), 335.
81 43.6 per cent in 1932 and 56.1 per cent in 1937, according to Zaleski (1980), 392.
82 *Statistika truda*, 5–6, 1928, 16; *Trud* (1936), 342.
83 Vvedenskii (1932), 22, 24.
84 *Zhilishchno-bytovoe stroitel'stvo v Donbasse* (1930), 12.
85 *Kommunal'noe khozyaistvo*, 19–20, 1931, 38, 45.
86 Zaleski (1980), 536.
87 Tverdokhleb (1970), 229.
88 Tverdokhleb (1970), 347.
89 British ambassador, Moscow, to Foreign Office, 7 February 1936; PRO N870/63/38.

6 AGRICULTURE

1 *Osnovnye elementy* (1930), 23–41, gives a figure of 8.2 per cent; for somewhat lower figures, see Wheatcroft (1980), 233–5.
2 *Osnovnye elementy* (1930), 90–107.
3 For a detailed discussion of this question, see Wheatcroft in *Soviet Studies*, XXVI (1974), 157–80.
4 See Wheatcroft (1986), 12.
5 Davies (1990), 90–1 (Wheatcroft).
6 See Davies (1990), 278.
7 See data cited in Davies (1990), 359, note 78 (Wheatcroft).
8 *Sots. sel. kh.* (1939), 24.
9 *Pravda*, 7 November 1929.
10 Thus the average live weight was estimated as follows (kilograms):

	Pigs	Cattle
1926/27[a]	112	376
1932[b]	55/79	223
1939[c]	82	236
1940[d]	85	238

Sources:

[a] *Sdvigi* (1930), 190–1; refers to all animals.

[b] *Sel. kh. 1935* (1936), 524; refers to animals delivered to the state for meat. The higher figure for pigs refers to pigs reared for bacon; the lower figure to other pigs.

[c] *Sots. str.* (1939), 380; collective-farm animals.

[d] *Sel. kh.* (1960), 368; all animals.

11 *Nar. kh.* (1932), 144.

12 In 1928 an average two-thirds of all food calories and nearly two-thirds of protein by weight were obtained from grain and grain products (Wheatcroft (1976), 94–5); the proportion of calories and protein obtained from grain was somewhat higher in the towns, somewhat lower in the countryside.

13 See Wheatcroft, Davies and Cooper (1986), 282–3; and Tauger (1991), 70–89.

14 See Jasny (1949), 731–2; the instruction was eventually published in 1944 in *Slovar'-spravochnik po sotsial'no-ekonomicheskoi statistike* (1944), 90.

15 Calculated from *Sots. str.* (1935), 367.

16 *Sotsialisticheskaya rekonstruktsiya sel'skogo khozyaistva*, 1, 1936, 20 (Chernov); and see Vyltsan (1978), 142, who reports that at the beginning of 1937 satisfactory crop rotation could be found on only one-third of all collective farms.

17 *Sel'skoe khozyaistvo ot VI k VII s"ezdu sovetov* (1935), 99–101; Vyltsan (1978), 139; *Byulleten' Prokopovicha*, CXXXIII (January–February 1937), 17; Jasny (1949), 494–501, 511. In the fertile and treeless steppe areas manure was used not as fertiliser but as fuel.

18 See Davies (1980), 25–6; these data are taken from a 1927 sample census of peasant households supervised by V. S. Nemchinov.

19 Estimated from Moorsteen and Powell (1966), tables T1, T-12 and T-23 (total net fixed capital minus net fixed non-agricultural capital, plus value of livestock).

20 *Nar. kh.* (1932), 188–9; *Sots. str.* (1935), 367.

21 See Wheatcroft (1985), Appendix 3d.

22 Stalin (1946–51), XII, 154.

23 *Resheniya*, II (1967), 145–9.

24 *Bol'shevik*, 10, 31 May 1930, 81–3 (S. Uzhanskii).

25 *Sots. str.* (1935), 302; Jasny (1949), 458; *Sel. kh.* (1960), 409.

26 *Sots. sel. kh.* (1939), 24.

27 *Proizvoditel'nost'* (1939), 34–8, 44–7; and for mechanisation generally, see the account in Jasny (1949), ch. 19.

28 See Jasny (1949), 481–2, 493–4.

29 See Wheatcroft (1985), Appendix 3a. Soviet sources variously treat one tractor drawbar horsepower as equivalent to 1.33 or 2 animal hp.

30 Based on data in Jasny (1949), 458, excluding combine-harvesters and lorries. The horse-equivalent horse power of combine harvesters amounted to 4.3 million hp (see *Sots. str.* (1939), 24, 88).

31 See Jasny (1949), 457–8. The nominal horse power of the Soviet lorries amounted to 5.4 million hp, but Jasny estimates this as the equivalent of only 1.5 million tractor hp owing to the shorter period for which farm lorries were used.

32 In 1932–6, the People's Commissariat of Agriculture of the USSR trained 1,738,000 tractor drivers, 243000 combine operators and 106000 lorry drivers; in addition, in 1930–1, 177000 tractor drivers were trained from collective farms alone (excluding state farms, etc.) (see Vyltsan (1959), 57, 22).

33 Annual turnover of tractor drivers was 49 per cent in 1932, and fell to 23 per cent in 1935 (*Istoriya SSSR*, 5, 1964, 7 (Zelenin)). Turnover was 137 per cent in large-scale industry and 306 per cent in building in 1932, and 86 per cent and 235 per cent respectively in 1935 (*Trud* (1936), 95).

34 *Trud* (1968), 129 (on 1 July).

35 *Trud* (1968), 262–3, 280–1. These figures somewhat exaggerate the increase, as the figures for 1941 include the territory acquired in 1939–40.

36 *Trud* (1968), 268–9, 286–7.

37 For examples, see Nove (1982), 259–60.

38 Jasny (1949), 4.

39 For details, see Wheatcroft (1977) and Wheatcroft (1982).

40 The effect of the weather up to 1929 is further discussed in Davies (1990), 92, 102 (Wheatcroft).

41 A. V. Chayanov (1926), pp. 7, iii.

42 For sown area, see *Posevnye ploshchadi, 1938* (1939), 21–2; for number of households, see *Kolkhozy* (1939), 1. In addition, allotments with a sown area of 1.11 million hectares were cultivated by employees of state farms and other organisations; a mere 0.86 million hectares were cultivated by non-collectivised individual peasants.

43 *Posevnye ploshchadi, 1938* (1939), 21–2.

44 *Kolkhozy* (1939), xi; the figure for potatoes and vegetables was estimated by us as a residual, using data for total production (*Kolkhozy* (1939), 81). According to postwar Soviet data, in 1940 total production by the non-socialised sector (including individual peasants on the territories acquired by the Soviet Union in 1939–40) amounted to as much as 43 per cent of total gross production (Belyanov (1970), 53–4; the author derives this figure from data in *Sel. kh.* (1960), 21, 22, 23, 24, 84, 85, but does not explain how he made his ca.culations).

45 *Kolkhozy* (1939), 106.

46 Based on a survey of the budgets of 17,000 households in 28 regions and republics, which gave personal income per household, valued at free market prices, as 5,843 rubles (*Kolkhozy* (1939), 114).

47 *Pravda*, 13 March 1935 (Stalin (1967), I (XIV), 54.

48 Decrees of 27 May, 8 July 1939 (*Sobranie postanovlenii* (1939), arts. 235, 316). This legislation is described in Volin (1970), 268–72.

49 See table 20, and data for collective and state farms, etc. in *Sel. kh.* (1960), 264, 265, which enable number individually owned to be estimated. Peasant money incomes continued to rise, owing to the increase in prices on the free market resulting from the worsening shortage of food available in socialised trade.

50 See Nimitz (1965); the 1927/28 Gosplan labour balance is in *Pyatiletnii plan*, II, ii (1930), 9.

51 *Proizvoditel'nost* (1939), 68, 137. The survey assumed a working year of 288 days.

52 The private sector was responsible for 33.3 per cent of agricultural employment and 27.8 per cent of gross output (Nimitz (1965), 36).

53 Moorsteen and Powell (1966), 370; figures are for net output and full-time equivalent employment (34.9 million persons on the agricultural sector produced 59 billion rubles net output (in 1937 prices); 36.7 million persons in the non-agricultural sector produced 159 billion rubles).

7 INDUSTRY

1 For production, see table 4; for labour force, see Davies (1990), 251. For the division of production between large-scale and small-scale industry, see Falkus (1968), 55.
2 For comparative data, see Mitchell (1978), 179–81.
3 See Davies (1990), 128, 146–7 (Gatrell and Davies); Gatrell (1982), 104–5.
4 This is a recent Soviet estimate: *Mirovaya ekonomika i mezhdunarodnye otnosheniya*, 11, 1987, 152.
5 *Annales*, November–December 1965; see Nove (1982), 14–5.
6 Data for coal, pig iron and cotton textiles: Khromov (1960), 45, 49, 58, cited in Crisp (1978), 402–4.
7 See Crisp (1976), 34–6.
8 The higher estimate is in *Vestnik statistiki*, 14 (1923), 152–3 (Vorob'ev); the lower estimate is in *Planovoe khozyaistvo*, 5, 1924, 173 (Gukhman).
9 See data in Davies (1990), 129, 135 (Gatrell and Davies).
10 *Planovoe khozyaistvo*, 5, 1929, 191; this figure includes small-scale industry.
11 See Strumilin (1958), 282–5; this figure is for industry planned by Vesenkha.
12 *Byulleten' Gosplana*, 5, 1923, 55ff; production in 1926/27 in fact amounted to 3 million tons.
13 See Davies (1989b), 13–14.
14 *Planovoe khozyaistvo*, 6, 1926, 55.
15 The rate of growth again somewhat increased in 1927/28 and 1928/29, but in these years the USSR was already moving into the post-NEP era of central planning. Even so, it should be noted that the high rate of increase until 1929/30 partly resulted from the continued taking up of spare capacity (see Davies (1989b), 82 and *Ekonomika i matematicheskie metody*, 2, 1968, 298–9 (A. Vainshtein and G. I. Khanin)).
16 Stalin (1946–51), XI, 250–1 (speech of November 1928).
17 Stalin (1946–51), XII, 80–1 (speech of April 1929).
18 *Nar. kh.* (1932), xlvi–xlvii. These figures include 'concessions' owned by foreign firms; in industry these had all been closed down by 1933.
19 *Melkaya promyshlennost'*, I (1933), pp. 22–3; see Davies (1989b), 79 note 85.
20 *Ekonomicheskaya zhizn'*, 27 March 1933 (V. Rossov).
21 Note that these figures include all artisan activities (*promysly*) and are therefore wider in their coverage than industry (*promyshlennost'*) as such.
22 The first plan was dated 1 October 1928 to 30 September 1933, but was (falsely) declared to have been completed by 31 December 1932. The third plan was broken off by the German invasion of 22 June 1941.
23 *Promyshlennost'* (1957), 10.
24 'Lukavaya tsifra', *Novyi mir*, 2, 1987, especially 188–9.
25 See Moorsteen (1962), 115, 119–21. In chapter 12 of the present volume, Harrison shows that the official index also underestimated the wartime growth of armaments production.
26 See Davies (1978), 40–3.
27 For production figures, referring to 1928 and 1937, see table 25; for labour force, referring to December 1926 and January 1939, see table 11.
28 The data on large-scale and small-scale industry in the next two paragraphs are

obtained from Kaufman (1962), 73–5 (for 1927/28) and *Industrializatsiya, 1933–1937* (1971), 382–91 (for 1937).

29 *Trud* (1936), 144.

30 On the armaments industry in the mid-1920s, see Davies (1987), 1.

31 Armaments production in the machine-building sub-sector of industry amounted to 1056 million rubles (RGAE, 4372/91/1824, 33); total machine-building and metal-working production amounted to 9408 million rubles (Davies, Cooper and Ilič (1991), 34). Armaments production was classified as part of the (a) machine-building and metal-working, and (b) chemical sub-sectors of industry.

32 See figures for the gross production of the People's Commissariats concerned in *Gosudarstvennyi plan . . . na 1941* ((1941)), 9.

33 1928/29, 1932: all industrial investment: Davies, Cooper and Ilič (1991), 52–3.
    Armaments investment: 1928/29: *Otchet . . . na 1928–1929* (1930) (figure for national economy allocation to other state industry, so may be somewhat larger than figure for investment);
    1932: RGAE 4372/91/1824, 34.
    1941 (plan): *Gosudarstvennyi plan . . . na 1941* ((1941)), 483–5 (these figures exclude a small amount of investment outside the fixed limits).

34 See Harrison (1985), 14, citing Clark (1956), 315–16.

35 Cooper (1976), 3.

36 See Holloway in Amann, Cooper and Davies (1977), 417–20; Orgill (1970), especially pp. 21–31; Cooper (1976), 11, 17.

37 RGAE, 4372/91/1050, 133–2 (meeting dated 10 August 1932).

38 See Harrison (1985), ch. 1, especially pp. 7–10.

39 *Promyshlennost'* (1957), 226, 232. For tractors in comparable 15 hp units, see table 27.

40 *Promyshlennost'* (1957), 223; for other years, see table 27.

41 See data in *Promyshlennost'* (1957), 127–9.

42 See *Promyshlennost'* (1957), 118, 122.

43 *Trud* (1968), 84–5.

44 Gerschenkron and Nimitz (1953), 52; netting out the inputs into the iron and steel industry, and the transfers within the industry, the index number rises to 505 (p. 68).

45 See also *Promyshlennost'* (1957), 110 and Clark (1956), 14–20; we have drawn heavily on Gardner Clark's classic study in these paragraphs. Broadly, the Soviet term 'quality steel' includes alloy steels plus carbon tool steels, and high-carbon steels used in machine-building; in Western terminology the term is not in regular use, and when it is used refers to a somewhat narrower category of steels (see Bergson and Turgeon (1955a), 1 and (1955b), 1).

46 This refers to the heading 'miscellaneous machine-building' in Shul'kin (1940), 20–4.

47 Clark (1956), 26–7; on the diversion of production to armaments, see Scott (1942), 103.

48 For the output of the main types of power equipment, see *Promyshlennost'* (1957), 214–15.

49 *Promyshlennost'* (1957), 234–5.

50 See Cooper (1975), *passim*.

51 *Sots. str.* (1936), 48–9.
52 Chapman (1963), 166; her estimate of consumer goods per head is based on the Kaplan–Moorsteen index (1950 prices).
53 See *Sots. str.* (1935), 291, for the stock of tractors, and *Na agrarnom fronte*, 1, 1930, 62–3 for the plan for 1932/33.
54 For some figures, see Davies (1976), 2, note 5; for data for the economy as a whole, see table 3.
55 See Wheatcroft (1985).
56 See Davies (1976), 4, note 1.
57 See Davies (1985).
58 On the influence of attitudes to technology, see, in addition to Cooper (1975), Bailes (1978) and Granick (1967).
59 Dodge (1960).
60 Jasny (1961).
61 See Wheatcroft and Davies (1985), 18–19, 418–21; and chapter 3 above.
62 See Davies (1989b), 516–17.
63 See Wheatcroft and Davies (1985), 21.
64 For details, see Davies (1989b), chapter 9; and Davies (1976), *passim*.
65 See Davies (1989b), 371–7.
66 See Arakelyan (1938), 71–2, and *Sots. str.* (1936), 384, 388.
67 See chapter 3. The relative under-allocation of investment to certain industries in 1935–8, notably iron and steel, exacerbated the problems.

8 TRANSPORT

1 See Nag .csuna (1987).
2 Text in Naporko (1957), 244–52.
3 *Sotsialisticheskii transport*, 1, 1937, 62.
4 *Sotsialisticheskii transport*, 4, 1940, 106.
5 *Transport i svyaz'* (1972), 98.
6 Orlov (1963), 39.
7 Yakobi (1935), 7, 18.
8 Yakobi (1935), 35.
9 NKPS, *Materialy*, XXIV (1923), 13.
10 Orlov (1963), 39.
11 Orlov (1963), 97.
12 Orlov (1963), 134.
13 Kim (1970), 88.
14 Orlov (1963), 135–6.
15 *Sotsialisticheskii transport*, 10, 1932, 54.
16 A blow-by-blow account of the 1931–4 railway situation, especially from the political point of view, is given in Rees (1987).
17 Orlov (1963), 225.
18 Kumanev (1976), 49.
19 Kim (1970), 384.
20 Danilov (1956), 385–6.
21 *Transport i svyaz'* (1957), 27. The industrial railways' mileage was 31000km in 1940, compared to the 106000km of the NKPS public railways. Most NKPS

tonnage originated in the industrial lines, and for statistical purposes entered or existed NKPS books at the NKPS/enterprise interchange sidings.

22 Orlov (1963), 258.
23 Orlov (1963), 185.
24 Orlov(1963), 185.
25 *Sotsialistcheskii transport*, 11, 1938, 53.
26 Orlov (1963), 188.
27 Kim (1970), 257.
28 Orlov (1963), 188.
29 Vasiliev (1939), 15.
30 Westwood (1993).
31 Orlov (1963), 206. According to this source, 64000 goods wagons were destroyed or damaged in 1934, declining to 14000 in 1937.
32 *Zheleznodorozhnyi transport v 3ei Stalinskoi pyatiletke* (1939), 57.
33 Kim (1970), 415.
34 Sidorov in *Istoricheskie zapiski*, XXVI (1948), 8.
35 Kim (1970), 395.
36 Orlov (1963), 173–6.
37 Westwood (1982), 212.
38 See Westwood (1982), for a long treatment of this phenomenon.
39 Orlov (1963), 178.
40 Derived from Association of American Railroads figures. The method of calculation does not precisely match the Soviet method. The US figures are in US tons, not metric tons.
41 The ailway purges are described in Rees (1992).
42 *Sotsialistcheskii transport*, 11, 1940, 79.
43 *Sotsialistcheskii transport*, 2, 1938, 22.
44 Kim (1970), 362.
45 Kim (1970), 163.
46 *Rechnoi transport* (1957), 65, 67.
47 *Transport i svyaz'* (1972), 21. 17.
48 *Transport i svyaz'* (1972), 170.
49 Orlov (1963), 57.
50 Orlov (1963), 127.
51 *Transport i svyaz'* (1972), 163.
52 Orlov (1963), 196.
53 *Transport i syvaz'* (1972), 263.
54 *Sovetskii transport* (1927), 216–17, 223.
55 Orlov (1963), 98.
56 Orlov (1963), 200.
57 Orlov(1963), 219.
58 Orlov (1963), 219.
59 Orlov(1963), 248.

9 TECHNOLOGY

1 Gatrell (1986), 154–67.
2 McKay (1970), 123.

3 Westwood (1982), 5–8.
4 See Cowie (1949), 36–42.
5 Davies (1990), 192 (Cooper and Lewis).
6 Bailes (1978), 38–9.
7 Gatrell (1986), 160.
8 Gregory (1982), 189–90.
9 Bailes (1978), 44–58; Lewis (1979), 6–7.
10 Bastrakova (1973); Mokshin (1972).
11 Mokshin (1972), 175–224.
12 Westwood (1982), 17–20, 34–51.
13 Gatrell and Davies (1987), 5.
14 Davies (1990), 209 (Cooper and Lewis).
15 Davies (1990), 202–3.
16 Carr and Davies (1969), 198.
17 Davies (1980), 10.
18 *Kontrol'nye tsifry* (1927), 444–5.
19 Carr and Davies (1969), 413.
20 Carr (1958), 272, 320–1.
21 See, for example, the resolution of the Fourteenth Party Congress of December 1925 on the report of the central committee: *Resheniya*, I (1967), 508.
22 Resolution of TsIK and Sovnarkom USSR of 16 March 1927 'On collective farms': *Resheniya*, I (1967), 591.
   However, it should be noted that the extent and nature of the difference between American and British technology has been a matter of vigorous debate amongst economic historians; for a brief introduction, see Willis and Primack (1989), 125–33.
24 McKay (1970), *passim*.
25 *Torgovo-promyshlennaya gazeta*, 27 May 1928.
26 Svennilson (1954), 99.
27 See Dodge (1960), 441.
28 Feinstein (1967), 295–6, 298; Cooper (1975), 110, 236; on the American model on the railways, see Westwood (1982), 92.
29 See remarks made by an engineer from Khar'kov about the engineering industry in *Torgovo-promyshlennaya gazeta*, 27 June 1928.
30 For a discussion of the issues, see Stewart (1978).
31 Dobb (1955) and (1956/7); this is also applicable when the savings rate is sub-optimal, see Sen (1968), xiii–xviii.
32 Clark (1956), 61.
33 Field (1983); (1985).
34 These two points on stocks are picked up by Dodge in his discussion of the Soviet tractor industry (Dodge (1960), 449).
35 This point was made by M. L. Sorokin, head of Avtotrest, who was a vigorous advocate of American technology (Cooper (1975), 262).
36 Field (1983), 409.
37 The classic text is Salter (1966).
38 Clark (1956), 49, 55.
39 Clark (1956), 254.
40 Astakhov, Grübler and Mookhin (1989), 6.

41 Sutton (1971).
42 Granick (1967), 171–206.
43 This was also encouraged by the institutional factors which created uncertainty about component supply.
44 Granick (1967), 177–81.
45 Astakhov et al. (1989), 7.
46 Granick (1967), 174.
47 Clark (1956), 119–89.
48 *Historical Statistics of the United States*, I (1975), 469; *Nar. kh.* (1956), 144; Svennilson (1954), 99.
49 Clark (1956), 81; Svennilson (1954), 132–3.
50 *The Soviet Aircraft Industry* (1955).
51 Amann, Cooper and Davies (1977), 417–20 and Amann and Cooper (1982), 370–5. Even Sutton, the most avid proponent of the influence of foreign technology on the Soviet economy, considers that the Soviet Union had an indigenous military technology by 1941 (Sutton (1971), 248).
52 Sutton (1968), 185–208 and (1971), 154–76.
53 Amann, Cooper and Davies (1987), 208 (Allinson).
54 Amann, Cooper and Davies (1977), 272–4, 276–82 and Amann and Cooper (1982), 131–44; Lel'chuk (1964).
55 Cooper (1975), 332.
56 Westwood (1982), 164, 171–2, 183, 200–1; the quotation is from p. 183.
57 *Soviet Studies*, XXXI (1979), 234–6 (Crouch).
58 Cooper (1975), 97.
59 Holliday (1979), 122, 130–2.
60 *Za industrializatsiyu*, 10 July 1935 (A. Khan'kovskii).
61 Lewis (1979), 6–26.
62 Bailes (1978), 337–80; Lewis (1979), 114–32.
63 See, for example, Westwood (1982), 183.
64 An exception was Seton (1959), 1–14.
65 Bergson uses 60 per cent in one set of weights (Bergson and Kuznets (1963), 19).
66 Bergson and Kuznets (1963), 19–20.
67 Harrison (1987).
68 Khanin (1988); Harrison (1993b).
69 Gregory (1982), 189–90.
70 Abramovitz and David (1973), 431; Floud and McCloskey (1981), 9, 22; Maddison (1987), 665; Maddison (1991), 38.
71 Moorsteen and Powell (1966), 294; this is not a problem solely in the Soviet case.
72 Seton (1959), 9.
73 Harrison (1985), 1–37.
74 Katz (1975), 584–5.
75 Bergson (1968), 22.
76 Feinstein (1967), 305.
77 Westwood (1982), 137.
78 Clark (1956), 283.
79 Granick (1967), 160.
80 Holliday (1979), 127.
81 Granick (1967), 143–70.

82 See, for example, Granick (1967), 104–7; this has been linked to on the job training.
83 Cooper (1975), 332.
84 Cooper (1975), 332.
85 See Granick (1967), 263–364.
86 See, for example, Clark (1956), 94–5.
87 Katz (1975), 585–7.

10 FOREIGN ECONOMIC RELATIONS

1 *Vneshnyaya torgovlya* (1960), 21, 23.
2 See McKay (1970).
3 Gregory (1982), 314.
4 Baykov (1946), 5–6.
5 *Vneshnyaya torgovlya* (1939), 11.
6 Carr (1952), 132.
7 *Resheniya*, I (1967), 50–2.
8 Carr (1952), 128.
9 Carr (1953), 463–6; Smith (1971), 49–63.
10 Dohan (1976), 219–20.
11 See the remarks of Lenin to the X Party Congress in March 1921: *Desyatyi s″ezd RKP(b)* (1963), 32.
12 *Resheniya*, I (1967), 181–3.
13 Carr (1958), 190–3, 443.
14 Carr and Davies (1969), 707.
15 Dohan (1976), 273, 382.
16 Reiman (1987), 39; it should be noted that the author himself has doubts on the reliability of the underlying archival source.
17 Dohan (1969), 475–80, 644–5, 867–9.
18 Various sources gives figures of between 70 and 100 for the number of concessions in operation in 1927; see, for example, Eventov (1931), 101; Fisher (1928), 354; Kas'yanenko (1972), 197.
19 Fisher (1928), 354.
20 *Industrializatsiya, 1928–1932* (1969), 270–1.
21 Sutton (1971), 95–7.
22 Fisher (1928), 354.
23 *Pyatnadtsatyi s″ezd*, II (1962), 1099.
24 Shanin (1964), 209–10; Erlich (1960), 27–30.
25 Preobrazhensky (1965), 104.
26 *Pyatnadtsatyi s″ezd*, ii (1962), 1443.
27 *Torgovo-promyshlennaya gazeta*, 15 September 1928.
28 *Pyatiletnii plan*, I (1929), 99.
29 Svennilson (1954), 292.
30 Tracy (1982), 127.
31 Baykov (1946), 18–19; Smith (1971), 65–73.
32 Dohan and Hewitt (1973), 49.
33 *Vneshnyaya torgovlya* (1939), 35.
34 *Resheniya*, II (1969), 221.

35 See, for example, *Resheniya*, II (1969), 221–2.
36 *Vneshnyaya torgovlya* (1960), 322, 355; Zaleski (1972), 254.
37 Davies (forthcoming), ch.9.
38 *Balance of payments* (1932), 12.
39 Baykov (1946), 47–48; Dohan (1976), 624–31; Williams (1992),151–64.
40 *Vneshnyaya torgovlya* (1939), 29.
41 Sutton (1968), 86–91; (1971), 23–7.
42 See Carr and Davies (1969), 962.
43 Aralov and Shatkhan (1930), 163.
44 Kas'yanenko (1972), 189.
45 Holliday (1979), 116–36; Sutton (1971), 74–9, 185–8.
46 Davies (1989), 397; Kas'yanenko (1972), 184; Sutton (1971), 363–72, in the most comprehensive study of Western technical assistance, identifies some 200 agreements between 1929 and 1945.
47 *Balance of Payments* (1932), 13.
48 *Pravda*, 30 April 1933; *Za industrializatsiyu*, 1, 3 and 11 March 1933.
49 Dohan (1969), 867.
50 *Byulleten' Prokopovicha*, CXXVIII (1936), 51.
51 I. P. Aizenberg, *Valyutnaya sistema SSSR* (1962), 65, cited by Dohan (1969), 609–10.
52 Dohan (1969), 610.
53 *Byulleten' Prokopovicha*, CXXVIII (1936), 50.
54 League of Nations (1937), 108.
55 Dohan (1969), 614.
56 See, for example, Holliday (1979), 181–5; Holzman (1974), 53–60.
57 Dohan (1976), 633–4.
58 Dohan (1976), 622, 626.
59 Dohan (1969), 617.
60 Dohan and Hewitt (1973), 24, 27. Comparisons of Russian and Soviet trade values and volumes are made difficult by the boundary changes which took place after the Revolution; the comparison here is with an adjusted figure for 1913; a straight comparison with the 1913 figure for the Russian Empire would show an even larger fall.
61 *Vneshnyaya torgovlya* (1960), 21, 23, 37.
62 Moorsteen (1962), 419–20, 449.
63 *Vneshnyaya torgovlya* (1960), 300, 306–8, 334, 339–41.
64 See, for example, Davies (forthcoming), ch.17.
65 See, for example, Wheatcroft, Davies and Cooper (1986), 279.

11 THE FIRST WORLD WAR AND WAR COMMUNISM, 1914–1920

1 See Struve (1930); Zagorsky (1928); Lih (1990); and Malle (1985).
2 Tereshkovich (1924); *Statisticheskie materialy po sostoyaniyu narodnogo zdraviya* (1926); McAuley (1991), 275–9.
3 *Izvestiya Vserossiiskogo Soyuza Gorodov*, no. 34, 1916, 179–222; Koenker *et al.* (1989), 73 (Brower); McAuley (1991), 264; see also Chapter 4, note 14.
4 Kohn (1932), 32–4; these figures exclude the Transcaucasus.

5 Polner *et al.* (1930); Polyakov (1986), 100.
6 *Izvestiya Vserossiiskogo Soyuza Gorodov*, nos. 31–2, 1916, 250–73; Kohn (1932), 32, 41; Polyakov (1986), 113–14; Wheatcroft (1986b), 20–1.
7 Kohn (1932), 18.
8 Volobuev (1964), 19.
9 *Ekonomicheskoe polozhenie* (1967), 59–60; Kohn (1932), 19–24. Some provinces, such as Ekaterinoslav, Perm and Petrograd escaped relatively lightly, but others – Kursk, Vologda, Vitebsk, Olonets and Kiev – were hard hit.
10 Bukshpan (1929), 241; Golovin (1939), II, 49; Feldman (1966); Hardach (1977), 178–9.
11 Kir'yanov (1971), 39.
12 Mints (1975), 47, 53.
13 According to the TsSU, output per person in large-scale industry increased by around five per cent between 1913 and 1916. *Sbornik statisticheskikh svedenii* (1924), 170–1.
14 *Trudy 1 s"ezda predstavitelei metalloobrabatyvayushchei promyshlennosti* (1916), 66.
15 Tarnovskii (1981).
16 Rosenberg (1985); Brovkin (1983).
17 Malle (1985).
18 Strumilin (1964), 367.
19 Malle (1985), 478–88.
20 Gregory (1982), 56–7.
21 According to a report submitted by leading industrialists, the value of capital equipment in private defence factories increased five-fold between 1913 and mid-1916. Allowing for price changes, the value of equipment may have trebled: Bovykin and Tarnovskii (1957), 21.
22 See also Strumilin (1958), 554–5, 558–9. However, some of Strumilin's methods are dubious. He applied a constant rate of depreciation of the capital stock, making no allowance for the fact that equipment and buildings depreciated at a much faster rate during wartime, and he assumed that investment in small-scale industry increased at the same rate as large-scale industry.
23 Volobuev (1962), 273n.
24 Petrov (1917), III, 44–7; *Vestnik finansov*, 31, 1917, 124–6, and 33, 1917, 190–1 (Sharii).
25 Izmailovskaya (1920); *Trudy TsSU*, XXVI (1926), i, 42; Anfimov (1962), 133–4; Gukhman (1929), 174–5.
26 Anfimov (1962), 114–15, 200.
27 Wheatcroft (1987), 18, 20–1; livestock numbers valued in pre-war prices. In *Istoriya sotsialisticheskoi ekonomiki* (1976), I, 312, the horse population is given as 34.2 million in 1916, falling to 28.7 million in 1920.
28 Derived from Polyakov (1967), 84–5; Vainshtein (1960), 228.
29 Strumilin (1958), 646–9.
30 *Zheleznodorozhnyi transport v 1913g.* (1925), xxxv–xxxvi; Strumilin (1958), 646, 657; Sidorov (1973), 608.
31 Strumilin (1958), 514, citing *Planovoe khozyaistvo*, 10, 1927.
32 Gukhman (1929), 174–5; Strumilin (1958), 506–8; McAuley (1991), 267–75.
33 Struve (1930); Wheatcroft (n.d.), 4.

34 Wheatcroft (n.d.), 10–13.
35 Wheatcroft (n.d.), 13–17.
36 See Volobuev (1962), 384–7 for an estimate of aggregate grain surplus, and for an indication of available surpluses in the North Caucasus, Don, Tauride, Kherson, Bessarabia and western Siberia.
37 The Rittikh levy envisaged the procurement of 12.6 million tons, but local objections reduced this to 5.3 million tons. For fuller discussion, see Struve (1930), 82–111, 329–467, and Lih (1990). The best study of the Provisional Government's grain monopoly remains Volobuev (1962), 383–468.
38 Shanin (1972), 157–9, 176; Malle (1985), 327–8.
39 Kabanov (1988), 111; Figes (1989), 277.
40 Malle (1985), 434–7. But note the qualifications she makes about Tambov and Ryazan' in 1920.
41 Kabanov (1988), 118–22; Figes (1989), 275, 270–84.
42 Polyakov (1967), 63–5; Wheatcroft (1987), 17.
43 Malle (1985), 340, 348, 373–5.
44 Figes (1989), 249–50, 253–60; Malle (1985), 376–7.
45 Malle (1985), 403–6; Figes (1989), 260–3, 269–70.
46 Polyakov (1967), 64; Wheatcroft (n.d.), 23.
47 Kabanov (1988), 157; Malle (1985), 456.
48 Figes (1989), 248.
49 *Trudy TsSU*, XXXVI (1926), i, 40–1; Gukhman (1929), 191; Malle (1985), 84–6.
50 TsGVIA 369/3/78, 170–2; 369/3/93, 1–11.
51 TsGVIA, 369/1/31, 105–9; 369/1/124, 10–16; Sidorov (1973), 252–332, 424–49; Neilson (1984).
52 Stone (1975).
53 Manikovskii (1930), II, 332–5; Kovalenko (1970), 117, 121, 253, 388.
54 Kovalenko (1970), 177, 232, 235–9, 250–1, 266–9, 281, 378–9, 392.
55 Derived from *Trudy TsSU*, XXVI (1926), i, 41.
56 Zagorsky (1928), 134.
57 *Trudy TsSU*, XXVI (1926), i, 38. Figures are for the gross value of output divided by the labour force, at a constant number of enterprises.
58 Malle (1985), 304–8.

12 THE SECOND WORLD WAR

1 Such official data have been repeated in many authoritative publications over the years; see, for a representative example, *Nar. kh.* (1987), 43–4.
2 A preliminary stage of this work is represented by Harrison (1991); the most important results were reported and analysed in Barber and Harrison (1991), 180–93.
3 In particular, an abridged version of *Nar. kh. 1941–5* (1959), originally circulated only within closed official circles, has at last been published as *Nar. kh. 1941–5* (1990). It contains data previously withheld from the public, including detailed industrial, agricultural, employment, and demographic statistics, and a somewhat truncated set of national accounts at 1940 prices, but little on the defence industry, and sections on defence-related branches such as nonferrous metallurgy have been cut out. The new estimates given below rely on the original

Nar. kh. 1941–5 (1959), together with other new archival sources, surveyed in Harrison (1993a).

4 Calculated from Bacon (1992a), 3, 8.
5 Bacon (1992a), 28.
6 Harrison (1990b), 572–3. This was the exact opposite of the more usual peacetime problem of hidden inflation, which led official index numbers to overstate real product growth.
7 Calculated from RGAE,71/25/7882, 4–20; Harrison (1985), 250–1; Byushgens (1992), tables 3 and 4 (Kostyrchenko).
8 Harrison (1990b), table 8.
9 Bacon and Harrison (1993).
10 RTsKhIDNI, 71/25/9250, 28.
11 E.g. *Istoriya Vtoroi Mirovoi voiny*, VI (1976), 350; *Istoriya sotsialisticheskoi ekonomiki*, V (1978), 275.
12 Harrison (1985), 175–82.
13 By November 1943 the numbers had recovered to 143 million, and to 170.5 million by the end of 1945. For 1941 and 1945, see ADK (1990b), 96, and for 1942–3 Mitrofanova (1984), 347–8.
14 *Nar. kh. 1941–5* (1959), 35–6.
15 At least, by the agrometeorological standards of 1886–1950, 1940–2 and 1944–5 were all good years, whereas 1943 was merely average. See chapter 6.
16 See further Moskoff (1990).
17 See Harrison (1985), 256–66.
18 Harrison (1985), 264.
19 Voznesensky (1948), 61.
20 The munitions and industrial goods supplied in Lend-Lease, if valued at the official exchange rate, probably amounted to 40–45 billion rubles. The gross value of output of Soviet industry, at current prices including turnover tax revenues, 1941–5, was probably of the order of 1000–1100 billion rubles. This yields a ratio of approximately 4 per cent.
21 This choice was further discussed by Harrison (1990a).
22 This composite list is assembled from Voznesensky (1948), 36–7, *Nar. kh. 1941–5* (1959), 78, *Istoriya Velikoi Otechestvennoi voiny*, II (1961), 498, Kravchenko (1970), 123–4, and Cooper (1976), 10–11, 15, 18, 20. For the aircraft, armament, and tank industries, the denominator is the number of enterprises, not the value of output.
23 Voznesensky (1948), 42–6.
24 Cooper (1991), 21–2.
25 Belikov (1966), 47; Kumanev (1974), 215.
26 For the official claim, see *Planovoe khozyaistvo*, 1, 1944, 7 (Kosyachenko).
27 *Istoricheskie zapiski*, LI (1978), 47 (D'yakov).
28 See Likhomanov, Pozina and Finogenov (1984), 111.
29 Kravchenko (1970), 115.
30 See Lerskii (1945), 20.
31 See further Harrison (1985), 53–63.
32 These figures are indicative, but not precise; not only are they heavily rounded, but there was much scope for inflating them by arbitrarily separating out smaller productive units within large complexes. The 'quinquennial' totals (actually,

only one of the periods listed lasted a full five years) are from *Nar. kh. 1941–5*
(1959), 32. A total of 7500 factories rehabilitated in the formerly occupied
territories is also given for the war years.

33 *Istoricheskie zapiski*, LI (1978), 43, 50 (D'yakov).
34 *Nar. kh. 1941–5* (1959), 52.
35 *Journal of Economic History*, XXXVIII (1978), 959 (Millar, Linz); Harrison
(1985), 160n.
36 See *Slavic Review*, XLVII (1988), 206 (Hunter); also chapter 6.
37 *Nar. kh. 1941–5* (1959), 36.
38 See further Harrison (1993a).
39 Bacon (1992a), 2.
40 Bacon (1992b), 1078. See further Harrison (1993a).
41 *Istoriya Vtoroi Mirovoi voiny*, IV (1975), 53.
42 Sokolov (1968), 215.
43 This is a retreat from the author's estimate of these numbers in Harrison (1991),
table G–4. As more detailed employment data become available, it is clear that
these earlier estimates of 'defence sector' employment were too sensitive to
assumptions about the input-output structure of the Soviet economy which are
either unrealistic or unsupported. See further Harrison (1993a).
44 Mitrofanova (1971), 186, 190.
45 Kravchenko (1970), 110–11.
46 See further Bacon (1992b).
47 These numbers are formed by estimates of the population in NKVD GULAG
camps, colonies, and labour settlements, less those subcontracted to work under
other commissariats, less an allowance for those unfit for heavy labour; see
further Harrison (1993a), table B-7.
48 *Istoriya sotsialisticheskoi ekonomiki*, V (1978), 203.
49 The total is derived from Mitrofanova (1971), 193, 428, 433; for shares of the
urban and rural populations in recruitment in each year, see *Istoriya sotsialisticheskoi ekonomiki*, V (1978), 203.
50 *Nar. kh. 1941–5* (1959), 421.
51 Rogachevskaya (1977), 183.
52 Voznesensky (1948), 90; *Istoriya Vtoroi Mirovoi voiny*, V (1975), 50, VII (1976),
43.
53 *Nar. kh. 1941–5* (1959), 40.
54 Hours worked are those for industry as a whole, less those in machine building
and metalworking (which in wartime was almost entirely defence industry),
calculated from *Nar. kh. 1941–5* (1959), 86–7.
55 Voznesensky (1948), 91.
56 *Nar. kh. 1941–5* (1959), 86.
57 Denison (1967), 59.
58 *Nar. kh. 1941–5* (1959), 89.
59 For evidence, see Harrison (1990b), 576.
60 Mitrofanova (1971), 498.
61 Zaleski (1980), 452.
62 Zaleski (1980), 688, 694.
63 Chernyavskii (1964), 70–1.
64 The population subject to bread rationing, given as 61.8 million in December

1942 and 67.7 million in 1943, in *Nar. kh. 1941–5* (1959), 441, is compared with population totals of 130 million in November 1942 and 143 million in 1943 (above).

65 Barber and Harrison (1991), 80–1.
66 Chernyavskii (1964), 77.
67 Salisbury (1971), 460.
68 Moskoff (1990), 171–6.
69 See further Moskoff (1990).
70 Chernyavskii (1964), 179, 186.
71 Harrison (1990a), 84.
72 Arutyunyan (1970), 361. I assume 2.15 cals/gm for bread and 0.75 cals/gm for potatoes.
73 For urban *kolkhoz* market food prices, see *Nar. kh. 1941–5* (1959), 435. In 1942 (when the *kolkhoz* market food price index stood at only 749 percent of 1940), farming households saved 13.7 billion rubles, nearly two-fifths of their cash income; non-farm households suffered a small reduction of cash savings (GARF, 687/48/5726, 183). After the war, in December 1947, the cash hoards acquired from wartime food sales would be devalued and rendered nearly worthless by means of a currency reform.
74 This concluding section relies on Gatrell and Harrison (1993), which represents the authors' collaboration in a comparative exercise. For the First World War, see chapter 11 in the present volume.

Bibliography

Place of publication is Moscow or Moscow–Leningrad unless otherwise stated. Major articles in periodicals and books are listed in the bibliography and in the text of the book under the name of the author; less important articles appear under the name of the periodical, or of the editor in the case of a book. Abbreviated titles used in the endnotes are given in brackets after the full title when the abbreviation may not be obvious, and also appear in the Glossary.

UNPUBLISHED MATERIALS

ARCHIVES

(Russian archives are referred to by initials of name of archive, followed by fond/opis'/delo, list)
Public Record Office, London (PRO)
Gosudarstvennyi arkhiv Rossiiskoi Federatsii (GARF, formerly TsGAOR)
Rossiiskii gosudarstvennyi arkhiv ekonomiki (RGAE, formerly TsGANKh)
Rossiiskii tsentr khraneniya i izucheniya dokumentov noveishei istorii (RTsKhIDNI, formerly TsPA)
Tsentral'nyi gosudarstvennyi voenno-istoricheskii arkhiv (TsGVIA)

UNPUBLISHED THESES AND PAPERS

Astakhov, A., Grübler, A. and Mookhin, A. (1989). 'Technology Diffusion in the Coal Mining Industry of the USSR: An Interim Assessment', unpublished *Working Paper* (IIASA, Laxenburg, Austria, July.

Bacon, E. and Harrison, M. (1993). 'The Real Output of Soviet Civilian Industry in World War II', unpublished *Working Papers*, 9303 (Department of Economics, University of Warwick).

Bacon, E. (1992a). 'Soviet Military Losses in the Great Patriotic War', unpublished *Working Papers*, 9230 (Department of Economics, University of Warwick).

Barber, J. (1978). 'The Composition of the Soviet Working Class, 1928–1941', unpublished *Discussion Papers*, SIPS no. 16 (CREES, University of Birmingham).

Bergson, A. and Turgeon, L. (1955a). 'Prices of Quality Rolled Steel in the Soviet Union, 1928–1950', unpublished RAND Research Memorandum RM–778–1 (Santa Monica).

358

Bergson, A. and Turgeon, L. (1955b). 'Prices of Ordinary Rolled Steel in the Soviet Union, 1928–1950', unpublished RAND Research Memorandum RM–767–1 (Santa Monica).

Cooper, J. M. (1976). 'Defence Production and the Soviet Economy, 1929–1941', unpublished *Discussion Papers*, SIPS no. 3 (CREES, University of Birmingham).

Cooper, J. M. (1975). 'The Development of the Soviet Machine Tool Industry, 1917–1941', PhD thesis (CREES, University of Birmingham).

Davies, R. W. (forthcoming). 'Crisis and Progress in the Soviet Economy, 1931–1933'.

Davies, R. W. (1987). 'Soviet Defence Industries during the First Five-Year Plan', unpublished *Discussion Papers*, SIPS no. 27 (CREES, University of Birmingham).

Davies, R. W. (1985). 'The Soviet Economic Crisis of 1932: the Crisis in the Towns', unpublished paper presented to the Annual Conference of the National Association of Soviet and East European Studies, 23–5 March 1985.

Davies, R. W. (1982). 'Capital Investment and Capital Stock in the USSR, 1928–1940: Soviet and Western Estimates', unpublished *Discussion Papers*, SIPS no. 22 (CREES, University of Birmingham).

Davies, R. W. (1978). 'Soviet Industrial Production, 1928–1937: The Rival Estimates', unpublished *Discussion Papers*, SIPS no. 18 (CREES, University of Birmingham).

Davies, R. W. (1976). 'The Soviet Economic Crisis of 1931–1933', unpublished *Discussion Papers*, SIPS no. 4 (CREES, University of Birmingham).

Dodge, N. T. (1960). 'Trends in Labor Productivity in the Soviet Tractor Industry: A Case Study in Industrial Development', unpublished PhD thesis (Harvard University).

Dohan, M. R. (1969). 'Soviet Foreign Trade in the NEP Economy and the Soviet Industrialization Strategy', unpublished PhD thesis. (MIT).

Gatrell, P. and Davies, R. W. (1987). 'The Industrial Economy', unpublished paper, 4th conference of the International Work Group on Soviet Economic History, Birmingham, 6–9 January 1987.

Gerschenkron, A. (1951). 'A Dollar Index of Soviet Machinery Output, 1927–28 to 1937', unpublished RAND Research Memorandum R–197 (Santa Monica).

Gerschenkron, A. and Nimitz, N. (1953). 'A Dollar Index of Soviet Iron and Steel Output, 1927/28–1937', unpublished RAND Research Memorandum RM–1055 (Santa Monica).

Goldsmith, R. W. (1955). 'The Economic Growth of Russia, 1860–1913', unpublished conference paper (International Association for Research in Income and Wealth).

Harrison, M. (1993a). 'Soviet Production and Employment in World War II: a 1993 Update', unpublished *Discussion Papers*, SIPS no.35 (CREES, University of Birmingham).

Harrison, M. (1992a). 'Russian and Soviet GDP on the Eve of Two World Wars: 1913 and 1940', unpublished *Discussion Papers*, SIPS no. 33 (CREES, University of Birmingham).

Harrison, M. (1992b). 'Soviet National Accounting for World War II: An Inside View', unpublished *Working Papers*, 9235 (Department of Economics, University of Warwick).

Harrison, M. (1992c). 'GDPs of the USSR and Eastern Europe: Towards an Interwar Comparison', unpublished *Working Papers*, 9244 (Department of Economics, University of Warwick).

Harrison, M. (1992d). 'Soviet Economic Growth Since 1928: the Alternative Statistics of G. I. Khanin', unpublished *Working Papers*, 9245 (Department of Economics, University of Warwick, 1992). Published in *Europe–Asia Studies* (formerly *Soviet Studies*) (Harrison (1993b)).

Harrison, M. (1991). 'New Estimates of Soviet Production and Employment in World War II', unpublished *Discussion Papers*, SIPS no. 32 (CREES, University of Birmingham).

Kaplan, N. and Moorsteen, R. (1960). 'Indices of Soviet Industrial Output', unpublished RAND Memorandum RM–2495 (Santa Monica).

Khanin, G. I. (1991b). 'Shkola Bergsona', unpublished ms.

Nagatsuna, K. (1987). 'A Utopian Ideologue in Soviet Industrialisation', unpublished working paper (CREES, University of Birmingham).

Nimitz, N. (1965). 'Farm Employment in the Soviet Union, 1928–1963', unpublished RAND Memorandum RM–4623-PR (Santa Monica).

Redding, A. D. (1958). 'Nonagricultural Employment in the USSR, 1928–55', PhD dissertation (Columbia University).

Rees, E. A. (1992). 'The Purge on Soviet Railways, 1937', unpublished *Discussion Papers*, SIPS no. 34 (CREES, University of Birmingham).

Rees, E. A. (1987). 'The Transport Crisis of 1931–1935', unpublished *Discussion Papers*, SIPS no. 29 (CREES, University of Birmingham).

Tupper, S. M. (1984). 'The Red Army and Soviet Defence Industry, 1934–1941', unpublished PhD thesis (CREES, University of Birmingham).

Tverdokhleb, A. A. (1970). 'Material'noe blagosostoyanie rabochego klassa Moskvy v 1917–1937 gg.', kandidatskaya dissertatsiya (Moscow).

Westwood, J. N. (1993). 'Russian Transport, 1913–1945', SIPS no.36 (CREES, University of Birmingham).

Wheatcroft, S. G. (1987). 'Agricultural Production, Capital Investment and Other Factors affecting Agricultural Production, 1908–1928', unpublished working paper (CREES, University of Birmingham).

Wheatcroft, S. G. (1986a). 'The Agrarian Crisis and Peasant Living Standards in Late Imperial Russia: a Reconsideration of Trends and Regional Differentiation', unpublished working paper (History Department, University of Melbourne).

Wheatcroft, S. G. (1986b). 'Public Health in Russia during the War, Revolution and Famines, 1914–1923: Moscow, Petrograd and Saratov', unpublished working paper (History Department, University of Melbourne).

Wheatcroft, S. G. (1985). 'The Soviet Economic Crisis of 1932: the Crisis in Agriculture', unpublished paper presented to the National Association of Soviet and East European Studies, 23–5 March 1985.

Wheatcroft, S. G. (1982a). 'The Use of Meteorological Data to Supplement and Analyse Data on Grain Yields in Russia and the USSR, 1883–1950', unpublished paper presented to the SSRC Work Group on Quantitative Methods in Economic History (Cambridge).

Wheatcroft, S. G. (1982b). 'Famine and Factors affecting Mortality in the USSR: the Demographic Crisis of 1914–1922 and 1930–1933', unpublished *Discussion Papers*, SIPS no. 20 (CREES, University of Birmingham), SIPS no. 21, *Appendices* (CREES, University of Birmingham).

Wheatcroft, S. G. (1980). 'Grain Production and Utilisation in Russia and the USSR Before Collectivisation', PhD thesis (CREES, University of Birmingham).

Wheatcroft, S. G. (1977). 'The Significance of Climatic and Weather Change on Soviet Agriculture (with Particular Reference to the 1920s and 1930s)', unpublished *Discussion Papers*, SIPS no. 11 (CREES, University of Birmingham)

Wheatcroft, S. G. (1976a). 'The Population Dynamic and Factors Affecting It in the Soviet Union in the 1920s and 1930s', part 1, unpublished *Discussion Papers*, SIPS no. 1 (CREES, University of Birmingham).

Wheatcroft, S. G. (1976b). 'The Population Dynamic and Factors Affecting It in the Soviet Union in the 1920s and 1930s', part 2, unpublished *Discussion Papers*, SIPS no. 2 (CREES, University of Birmingham).

Wheatcroft, S. G. (n.d.). 'The Balance of Grain Production and Utilisation in Russia before and during the Revolution', unpublished working paper (CREES, University of Birmingham).

PERIODICALS, NEWSPAPERS

Annales.
Bol'shevik (later *Kommunist*)
Byulleten' ekonomicheskogo kabineta prof. S. N. Prokopovicha (Prague)
Byulleten' Gosplana
Détente
The Economic History Review
EKO
Ekonomicheskaya zhizn'
Ekonomicheskoe obozrenie
Ekonomika i matematicheskie metody
Europe–Asia Studies (formerly *Soviet Studies*)
Istoricheskie zapiski
Istoriya SSSR
Izvestiya Vserossiiskogo Soyuza Gorodov
Journal of Political Economy
Kommunal'noe khozyaistvo
Kommunist (formerly *Bolshevik*, now *Svobodnaya mysl'*)
Mirovaya ekonomika i mezhdunarodnye otnosheniya
Na agrarnom fronte
Narodnoe khozyaistvo
Novaya i noveishaya istoriya
Novyi mir
Planovoe khozyaistvo
Politicheskoe obrazovanie
Pravda
Problemy ekonomiki

Predpriyatie: proizvodstvenno-ekonomicheskii i tekhnicheskii zhurnal
Puti industrializatsii
Rodina
Slavic Review (Urbana-Champaign)
Sotsialisticheskaya rekonstruktsiya sel'skogo khozyaistva
Sotsialisticheskii transport
Sotsial'nye issledovaniya (Sots. issl.)
Soviet Studies
Soyuz
Statistika truda
Torgovo-promyshlennaya gazeta
Trud
Vestnik finansov
Voenno-istoricheskii zhurnal
Voprosy istorii
Voprosy istorii KPSS
Za industrializatsiyu

BOOKS AND ARTICLES IN RUSSIAN

ADK (1990a) – Andreev, E., Darskii, L. and Khar'kova, T. 'Opyt otsenki chislennosti naseleniya SSSR 1926–1941 gg.', Vestnik statistiki, 7.
ADK (1990b) – Andreev, E., Darskii, L. and Khar'kova, T. 'Otsenka lyudskikh poter' v period Velikoi otechestvennoi voiny', Vestnik statistiki, 10.
Anfimov, A. M. (1962). Rossiiskaya derevnya v gody pervoi mirovoi voiny, 1914–1917 gg..
Arakelyan, A. (1938). Osnovnye fondy promyshlennosti SSSR.
Aralov, S. I. and Shatkhan, A. S. (eds.). (1980). Promyshlennyi import.
Arkheograficheskii ezhegodnik: 1968 (1970).
Arutyunyan, Yu. V. (1970). Sovetskoi krest'yanstvo v gody Velikoi Otechestvennoi voiny (2nd edn).
Balans narodnogo khozyaistva Soyuza SSR 1923/24 goda (1926). (Trudy TsSU, XXIX, i–ii).
Barsov, A. A. (1969). Balans stoimostnykh obmenov mezhdu gorodom i derevnei.
Bastrakova, M. S. (1973). Stanovlenie sovetskoi sistemy organizatsii nauki (1917–1922).
Batekhin, L. L. (ed.). (1988). Vozdushnaya moshch' rodiny.
Belyanov, V. A. (1970). Lichnoe podsobnoe khozaistvo pri sotsializme.
Berezhnoi, S. S. (1988). Korabli i suda VMF SSSR, 1928–1945: spravochnik.
Bol'shaya Sovetskaya Entsiklopediya (1974). XVII (3rd edn).
Bovykin, V. I. and Tarnovskii, K. N. (1957). 'Kontsentratsiya proizvodstva i razvitie monopolii v metalloobrabatyvayushchei promyshlennosti Rossii', Voprosy istorii, 2.
Bukshpan, Ya. M. (1929). Voenno-khozyaistvennaya politika.
Byushgens, G. S. (ed.). (1992). Samoletostroenie v SSSR, I.
Chayanov, A. V. (ed.). (1926). Problemy urozhai.
Chernyavskii, U. G. (1964). Voina i prodovol'stvie.
Chislennost' i zarabotnaya plata rabochikh i sluzhashchikh v SSSR (itogi edinovremennogo ucheta za mart 1936 g.). (1936).

Danilov, S. K. (ed.). (1956). *Ekonomika transporta.*
Danilov, V. P. (1970). 'Dinamika naseleniya SSSR za 1917–1929 gg.', *Arkheograficheskii ezhegodniki: 1968.*
Devyati vsesoyuznyi s″ezd professional'nykh soyuzov SSSR (1933).
Dinamika rossiiskoi i sovetskoi promyshlennosti v svyazi s razvitiem narodnogo khozyaistva za sorok let (1887–1926 gg.). (1930). I, iii.
Dmitriev, V. I. (1990). *Sovetskoe podvodnoe korablestroenie.*
D'yakov, Yu. L. (1978). 'Promyshlennoe i transportnoe stroitel'stvo v tylu v gody Velikoi Otechestvennoi voiny', *Istoricheskie zapiski*, CI.
Ekonomicheskoe polozhenie Rossii nakanune Velikoi Oktyabr'skoi sotsialisticheskoi revolyutsii, chast' tret″ya: sel'skoe khozyaistvo i krest'yanstvo. (1967).
Eshelony idut na vostok. (1966).
Ezhegodnik khlebooborota za 1931–32, 1932–33 i predvaritel'nye itogi zagotovok 1933 g. (tablitsy). (1934).
Gimpel'son, E. G. (1973). *'Voennyi kommunizm': politika, praktika, ideologiya.*
Goland, Yu. (1991). *Krizisy, razrushivshie NEP.*
Golovin, N. (1939). *Voennye usiliya Rossii v mirovoi voine*, II (Paris).
Gorinov, M. M. (1990). *NEP: poiski putei razvitiya* (Seriya 'Znanie', Istoriya, 2).
Gosudarstvennyi plan razvitiya narodnogo khozyaistva SSSR na 1941 god. (n.d. (1941)).
Gozulov, A. I. (1972). *Ocherki istorii otechestvennoi statistiki.*
Groman, V. (ed.) (1927). *Vliyanie neurozhaev na narodnoe khozyaistvo Rossii*, II.
Gukhman, B. A. (1928). 'Na rubezhe', *Planovoe khozyaistvo*, 7 and 8.
Gukhman, B. A. (1929). 'Na rubezhe', *Planovoe khozyaistvo*, 5.
Gukhman, B. A. (1925). *Produktsiya i potreblenie SSSR: k narodno-khozyaistvennomu balansu (1922/23 khozyaistvennyi god).*
Industrializatsiya SSSR, 1938–1941 gg.: dokumenty i materialy. (1973).
Industrializatsiya SSSR, 1933–1937 gg.: dokumenty i materialy. (1971).
Industrializatsiya SSSR, 1926–1928 gg.: dokumenty i materialy. (1969).
Istoriya sotsialisticheskoi ekonomiki SSSR. I (1976); V (1978).
Istoriya sovetskoi gosudarstvennoi statistiki. (1960).
Istoriya Velikoi Otechestvennoi voiny Sovetskogo Soyuza 1941–1945 (1965). VI.
Istoriya Vtoroi Mirovoi voiny, 1939–1945. (1975–82). IV (1975); V (1975); VI (1976); VII (1976); XII (1982).
Itogi vypolneniya pervogo pyatiletnego plana razvitiya narodnogo khozyaistva Soyuza SSR. (1933).
Itogi vypolneniya vtorogo pyatiletnego plana razvitiya narodnogo khozyaistva Soyuza SSR. (1939).
Izmailovskaya, E. I. (1920). *Russkoe sel'skokhozyaistvennoe mashinostroenie.*
Izmeneniya v chislennosti i sostave sovetskogo rabochego klassa. (1961).
Kabanov, V. V. (1988). *Krest'yanskoe khozyaistvo v usloviyakh 'Voennogo kommunizma'.*
Kaminskii, L. S. (1974). *Meditsinskaya i demograficheskaya statistika.*
Kas'yanenko, V. N. (1972). *Zavoevanie ekonomicheskoi nezavisimosti SSSR (1917–1940 gg.).*
Khanin, G. I. (1991a). *Dinamika ekonomicheskogo razvitiya SSSR* (Novosibirsk).
Khanin, G. I. (1988). 'Ekonomicheskii rost: al'ternativnaya otsenka', *Kommunist*, 17.

Khromov, P. A. (1960). *Ocherki ekonomiki perioda monopolisticheskogo kapitalizma.*

Kim, M. P. (ed.). (1970). *Zheleznodorozhnyi transport v gody industrializatsii SSSR (1926–41).*

Kir'yanov, Yu. I. (1971). *Rabochie Yuga Rossii, 1914-fevral' 1917 g..*

Kolkhozy vo vtoroi stalinskoi pyatiletke. (1939).

Konarev, N. S. (ed.). (1987). *Zheleznodorozhniki v velikoi otechestvennoi voine.*

Kontrol'nye tsifry narodnogo khozyaistva SSSR na 1928/1929 god. (1929).(*KTs ... na 1928/29*).

Kovalenko, D. A. (1970). *Oboronnaya promyshlennost' Sovetskoi Rossii v 1918–1920 gg..*

Kovalev, I. V. (1981). *Transport v Velikoi Otechestvennoi voine (1941–1945 gg.).*

Kravchenko, G. S. (1970). *Ekonomika SSSR v gody Velikoi Otechestvennoi voiny* (2nd edn).

Krzhizhanovskii, G. M., Strumilin, S. G., Kviring, E. I., Kovalevskii, N. A. and Bogolepov, M. I. (1930). *Osnovnye problemy kontrol'nykh tsifr narodnogo khozyaistva SSSR na 1929/30 god.*

Kumanev, G. A. (1976). *Na sluzhbe fronta i tyla.*

Lel'chuk, V. S. (1964). *Sozdanie khimicheskoi promyshlennosti SSSR. Iz istorii sotsialisticheskoi industrializatsii.*

Lenin, V. I. (1941–62). *Sochineniya*, 40 vols. (4th edn.).

Lerskii, I. A. (1945). *Vosproizvodstvo osnovnykh fondov promyshlennosti SSSR v usloviyakh otechestvennoi voiny.*

Likhomanov, M. I., Pozina, L. T. and Finogenov, E. I. (1985). *Partiinoe rukovodstvo evakuatsiei v pervyi period Velikoi Otechestvennoi voiny 1941–1942 gg.* (Leningrad).

Maksudov, S. (1989). *Poteri naseleniya SSSR* (Benson, Vermont).

Manikovskii, A. A. (1930). *Boevoe snabzhenie russkoi armii v mirovuyu voinu 1914–1918 gg.*, II (2nd edn).

Melkaya promyshlennost' SSSR po dannym Vsesoyuznoi perepisi 1929 g.. (1932–3). I (1933); II–III (1932).

Mints, L. E. (1975). *Trudovye resursy SSSR.*

Mitrofanova, A. V. (ed.). (1984). *Istoriya Sovetskogo rabochego klassa*, III, *Rabochii klass SSSR nakanune i v gody Velikoi Otechestvennoi voiny, 1938–1945 gg.*

Mitrofanova, A. V. (1971). *Rabochii klass SSSR v gody Velikoi Otechestvennoi voiny.*

Mokshin, S. I. (1972). *Sem' shagov po zemle. Ocherki o stanovlenii i razvitii sovetskoi nauki.*

Molodezh' SSSR. (1936).

Naporko, A. (ed.). (1957). *Zheleznodorozhnyi transport SSSR v dokumentakh Kommunisticheskoi partii i Sovetskogo pravitel'stva.*

Narodnoe khozyaistvo SSSR v Velikoi Otechestvennoi voine, 1941–1945 gg. (1990).

Narodnoe khozyaistvo SSSR v 1988 godu: statisticheskii ezhegodnik. (1989).(*Nar. kh. 1988* (1989).

Narodnoe khozyaistvo SSSR v 1987 godu : statisticheskii ezhegodnik (1988). (*Nar. kh. 1987* (1988)).

Narodnoe khozyaistvo SSSR za 70 let: yubileinyi statisticheskii ezhegodnik. (1987). (*Nar. kh.* (1987)).

Narodnoe khozyaistvo SSSR v 1961 godu: statisticheskii ezhegodnik. (1962).(*Nar. kh. 1961* (1962)).

Narodnoe khozyaistvo SSSR v 1959 godu: statisticheskii ezhegodnik. (1960). (*Nar. kh. 1959* (1960)).

Narodnoe khozyaistvo SSSR v 1958 godu: statisticheskii ezhegodnik. (1959). (*Nar. kh. 1958* (1959)).

Narodnoe khozyaistvo SSSR v Velikoi Otechestvennoi voine, 1941–1945 gg.. (1959).(*Nar. kh. 1941–5* (1959)).

Narodnoe khozyaistvo SSSR: statisticheskii sbornik. (1956) (*Nar. kh.* (1956)).

Narodnoe khozyaistvo SSSR: statisticheskii spravochnik 1932. (1932). (*Nar. kh.* (1932)).

NKPS. (1923–9). *Materialy po statistike putei soobshcheniya*, vyp. III, vyp. XXIV (1923), vyp. CIV (1929).

Ocherki po istorii statistiki SSSR. (1957).

Orlov, B. P. (1963). *Razvitie transporta SSSR* (1963).

Otchet Narodnogo Komissariata Finansov Soyuza SSR ob ispolnenii edinogo gosudarstvennogo byudzheta Soyuza Sovetskikh Sotsialisticheskikh Respublik za 1928–1929g.. (1930).

Petrov, G. P. (1917). *Promyslovoe oblozhenie*, III.

Pisarev, I. Yu. (1962). *Narodonaselenie SSSR.*

Polyakov, Yu. A. (1986). *Sovetskaya strana posle okonchaniya grazhdanskoi voiny: territoriya i naselenie.*

Polyakov, Yu. A. (1967). *Perekhod k NEPu i sovetskoe krest'yanstvo.*

Posevnye ploshchadi SSSR, 1938 g.: statisticheskii spravochnik. (1939).

Proekt vtorogo pyatiletnego plana razvitiya narodnogo khozyaistva SSSR (1934). I.

Profsoyuznaya perepis', 1932–1933 g. (1934). I.

Proizvoditel'nost' i ispol'zovanie truda v kolkhozakh vo vtoroi pyatiletke. (1939).

Promyshlennost' SSSR: statisticheskii sbornik. (1957).

Ptukha, M. V. (1960). *Ocherki po statistike naseleniya.*

Pyatiletnii plan narodno-khozyaistvennogo stroitel'stvo SSSR. I (1st edn, 1929); I, II (i); II (ii); III (3rd edn, 1930).

Pyatnadtsatyi s"ezd VKP(b), dekabr' 1927 goda: stenograficheskii otchet. (1962). II.

Rashin, A. (1930). *Sostav fabrichno-zavodskogo proletariata.*

Rechnoi transport SSSR (1917–1957). (1957).

Resheniya partii i pravitel'stva po khozyaistvennym voprosam. (1967–69). tom I, 1917–1928 gody (1967), tom II, 1929–1940 gody (1969).

Rogachevskaya, L. S. (1977). *Sotsialisticheskoe sorevnovanie v SSSR. Istoricheskie ocherki, 1917–1970 gg..*

Sbornik statisticheskikh svedenii po Soyuza SSR, 1918–1923 gg. (Trudy TsSU, 18, 1924).

Sdvigi v sel'skom khozyaistve SSSR mezhdu XV i XVI partiinymi s"ezdami: statisticheskie svedeniya po sel'skomu khozyaistvu za 1927–1930 gg.. (1931). (1st edn, 1930) (2nd edn).

Sel'skoe khozyaistvo ot VI k VII s"ezdu sovetov. (1935).

Sel'skoe khozyaistvo SSSR: ezhegodnik 1935. (1936). (*Sel. kh. 1935*).

Sel'skoe khozyaistvo SSSR : statisticheskii sbornik. (1960). (*Sel. kh.* (1960)).

Sharii, V. I. (1917). 'Dokhodnost' aktsionernykh predpriyatii za vremya voiny', *Vestnik finansov*, 31 and 33.

Shul'kin, L. P. (1940). *Potreblenie chernykh metallov v SSSR.*
Sidorov, A. L. (19??). 'Zheleznodorozhnyi transport Rossii v Pervoi mirovoi voine', *Istoricheskie zapiski*, XXVI.
Slovar'-spravochnik po sotsial'no-ekonomicheskoi statistike. (1944).
Sobranie uzakonenii i razporyazhenii RSFSR.
Sobranie zakonov i razporyazhenii SSSR (series 1 has been used except where series 2 is indicated as ii) (*Sobranie postanovlenii* from 1939).
Sokolov, P. V. (1968). *Voenno-ekonomicheskie voprosy v kurse politekonomii.*
Sokolov, V. (1946). *Promyshlennoe stroitel'stvo v gody Velikoi Otechestvennoi voiny.*
Sonin, M. Ya. (1959). *Vosproizvodstvo rabochei sily v SSSR i balans truda.*
Sostav novykh millionov chlenov profsoyuzov. (1933).
Sotsialisticheskoe sel'skoe khozyaistvo SSSR: statisticheskii spravochnik. (1939). (*Sots. sel. kh.*).
Sotsialisticheskoe stroitel'stvo Soyuza SSR (1933–1938 gg.): statisticheskii sbornik. (1939). (*Sots. str.* (1939)).
Sotsialisticheskoe stroitel'stvo SSSR: statisticheskii ezhegodnik. (1936). (*Sots. str.* (1936)).
Sotsialisticheskoe stroitel'stvo SSSR: statisticheskii ezhegodnik. (1935).(*Sots. str.* (1935)).
Sotsialisticheskoe stroitel'stvo SSSR: statisticheskii ezhegodnik. (1934). (*Sots. str.* (1934)).
Sovetskii transport 1917–1927. (1927).
Sovetskii tyl v Velikoi Otechestvennoi voine. (1970). II.
Stalin, I. V. (1967). *Sochineniya*, vols. I (XIV) – III (XVI), ed. R. H. McNeal (Stanford, California).
Stalin, I. V. (1946–51). *Sochineniya*, 13 vols.
Statisticheskie materialy po sostoyaniyu narodnogo zdraviya i organizatsii meditsinskoi pomoshchi v SSSR za 1913–1923 gg. (1926).
Statisticheskii spravochnik SSSR za 1928. (1929). (*Stat. spr. 1928*).
Strana sovetov za 50 let: sbornik statisticheskikh materialov. (1967).
Strumilin, S. G. (1964). *Problemy ekonomiki truda.*
Strumilin, S. G. (1958a). *Na planovom fronte, 1920–1930 gg..*
Strumilin, S. G. (1958b). *Statistiko-ekonomicheskie ocherki.*
Sulkevich, S. (1939). *Naselenie SSSR.*
Tarnovskii, K. N. (1981). 'Melkaya promyshlennost' v gody pervoi mirovoi voiny', *Voprosy istorii*, 8.
Tekhnicheskie kul'tury i kartofel', ovoshchi. (1936).
Tereshkovich, A. M. (1924). 'Vliyanie voiny i revolyutsii na psikhicheskuyu zabolevaemost'', *Moskovskii meditsinskii zhurnal*, 4.
Torgovlya SSSR za 20 let, 1918–1937 gg.. (1939).
Transport i svyaz' SSSR. (1972).
Transport i svyaz' SSSR. (1957).
Tretii pyatiletnii plan razvitiya narodnogo khozyaistva Soyuza SSR (1938–1942 gg.) (proekt). (1939).
Trud v SSSR: ekonomiko-statisticheskii spravochnik. (1932).
Trud v SSSR: spravochnik 1926–1930. (1930).
Trud v SSSR: statisticheskii sbornik. (1988).

Trud v SSSR: statisticheskii sbornik. (1968).
Trud v SSSR: statisticheskii spravochnik. (1936).
Trudy Pervogo S"ezda predstavitelei metalloobrabatyvayushchei promyshlennosti. (1916).
Trudy TsSU, see under *Balans narodnogo khozyaistva*; *Sbornik statisticheskikh svedenii*; *Vserossiiskaya promyshlennaya i professional'naya perepis'*
Tsaplin, V. V. (1989). 'Statistika zhertv stalinizma v 30-e gody', *Voprosy istorii*, 4.
Urlanis, B. Ts. (1977). 'Dinamika urovnya rozhdaemosti v SSSR za gody Sovetskoi vlasti', *Brachnost', rozhdaemost', smertnost' v Rossii i v SSSR.*
Urlanis, B. (1960). *Voiny i narodonaselenie Evropy.*
Vainshtein, A. L. (1960). *Narodnoe bogatstvo i narodnokhozyaistvennoe nakoplenie predrevolyutsionnoi Rossii.*
Vasiliev, M. (1939). *Transport Rossii v voine 1914–1918 gg..*
Vdovin, A. I. and Drobizhev, V. Z. (1976). *Rost rabochego klassa SSSR, 1917–1940 gg..*
Vneshnyaya torgovlya SSSR. Statisticheskii sbornik, 1918–1966. (1967).
Vneshnyaya torgovlya SSSR za 1918–1940 gg.: statisticheskii obzor. (1960).
Vol'fson, Ya., et al. (1941). *Ekonomika transporta.*
Volkogonov, D. (1989). *Triumf i tragediya: politicheskii portret I. V. Stalina,* vol. 1, pts i, ii, vol. 2, pts i, ii.
Volkov, E. Z. (1930). *Dinamika narodonaseleniya za vosem' desyat' let.*
Volobuev, P. V. (1964). *Proletariat i burzhuaziya v 1917 godu.*
Volobuev, P. V. (1962). *Ekonomicheskaya politika Vremennogo pravitel'stva.*
Voprosy istorii kapitalistichekoi Rossii. (1972). (Sverdlovsk).
Vserossiiskaya promyshlennaya i professional'naya perepis' 1918g.: Fabrichnozavodskaya promyshlennost' v period 1913–1918 gg.. (1926). 3 parts (*Trudy TsSU*, XXVI).
Vsesoyuznaya perepis' naseleniya 1926 goda. (1928–33). I–LVI.
Vvedenskii, A. S. (1932). *Zhilishchnoe polozhenie fabrichno-zavodskogo proletariata SSSR.*
Vyltsan, M. A. (1978). *Zavershayushchii etap sozdaniya kolkhoznogo stroya (1935–1937 gg.).*
Vyltsan, M. A. (1959). *Ukreplenie material'no-tekhnicheskoi bazy kolkhoznogo stroya vo vtoroi pyatiletke (1933–1937 gg.).*
Yakobi, A. (1935). *Zheleznye dorogi v tsifrakh.*
Zheleznodorozhnyi transport v 3ei Stalinskoi pyatiletke. (1939).
Zheleznodorozhnyi transport v Rossii v 1913 g. (ed. V. V. Rachinskii). (1925).
Zhenshchina v SSSR. (1936).
Zhilishchno-bytovoe stroitel'stvo v Donbasse. (1930).
Zven'ya. (1991). I.

BOOKS AND ARTICLES IN NON-RUSSIAN LANGUAGES

Abramovitz, M. and David, P. (1973). 'Reinterpreting Economic Growth: Parables and Realities', *American Economic Review*, LXVIII.
Amann, R. and Cooper, J. M. (eds.). (1982). *Industrial Innovation in the Soviet Union* (New Haven and London).

Amann, R., Cooper, J. M. and Davies, R. W. (eds.). (1977). *The Technological Level of Soviet Industry* (New Haven and London).

Atkinson, D. (1983). *The End of the Russian Land Commune, 1905–1930* (Stanford, California).

Bacon, E. (1992b). 'Glasnost' and the Gulag: New Information on Soviet Forced Labour Around World War Two', *Soviet Studies*, XLIV.

Bailes, K. E. (1978). *Technology and Society Under Lenin and Stalin. Origins of the Soviet Technical Intelligentsia, 1917–1941* (Princeton).

The Balance of Payments and the Foreign Debt of the USSR. (1932). Birmingham Bureau of Research on Russian Economic Conditions, Memorandum no. 4 (Birmingham).

Barber, J. D. and Harrison, M. (1991). *The Soviet Home Front, 1941–1945: a Social and Economic History of the USSR in World War II* (London).

Baykov, A. (1946). *Soviet Foreign Trade* (Princeton).

Becker, S. (1985). *Nobility and Privilege in Late Imperial Russia* (Dekalb, Illinois).

Bergson, A. (1968). *Planning and Productivity Under Soviet Socialism* (New York).

Bergson, A. (1961). *The Real National Income of Soviet Russia since 1928* (Cambridge, Mass.).

Bergson, A. (1953). *Soviet National Income and Product in 1937* (New York).

Bergson, A. (1944). *The Structure of Soviet Wages: a Study in Socialist Economics* (Cambridge, Mass.).

Bergson A. and Kuznets, S. (eds). (1963). *Economic Trends in the Soviet Union* (Cambridge, Mass.).

Brovkin, V. N. (1983). 'The Mensheviks' Political Comeback: Elections to the Provincial City Soviets in Spring 1918', *Russian Review*, XLII.

Carr, E. H. (1958). *Socialism in One Country, 1924–1926*, vol. 1 (London, 1953).

Carr, E. H. (1952–3). *The Bolshevik Revolution, 1917–1923*, vol. 2 (London, 1952), vol. 3 (London, 1953).

Carr, E. H. and Davies, R. W. (1969). *Foundations of a Planned Economy, 1926–1929*, vol. 1 (London).

Chamberlin, W. H. (1934). *Russia's Iron Age* (Boston).

Chapman, J. (1963). *Real Wages in Soviet Russia since 1928* (Cambridge, Mass.).

Clark, C. (1957). *Conditions of Economic Progress* (London, 2nd edn 1951, 3rd edn).

Clark, C. (1939). *A Critique of Soviet Statistics* (London).

Clark, M. G. (1956). *The Economics of Soviet Steel* (Cambridge, Mass.).

Cohen, S. F. (1974). *Bukharin and the Bolshevik Revolution: a Political Biography, 1888–1938* (London).

Conquest, R. (1986). *The Harvest of Sorrow: Soviet Collectivisation and the Terror Famine* (London).

Cooper, J. (1991). *The Soviet Defence Industry: Conversion and Reform* (London).

Cowie, J. S. (1949). *Mines, Minelayers and Minelaying* (London).

Crisp, O. (1978). 'Labour and Industrialisation in Russia', *Cambridge Economic History of Europe*, VII, ii (Cambridge).

Crisp, O. (1976). *Studies in the Russian Economy Before 1914* (London).

Davies, R. W. (1989a). 'Economic and Social Policy in the USSR, 1917–41', *Cambridge Economic History of Europe*, VIII.

Davies, R. W. (1989b). *The Soviet Economy in Turmoil, 1929–1930* (London and Cambridge, Mass.).

Davies, R. W. (1980). *The Socialist Offensive: the Collectivisation of Soviet Agriculture, 1929–1930* (London and Cambridge, Mass.).

Davies, R. W. (1958). *The Development of the Soviet Budgetary System* (Cambridge).

Davies, R. W. (ed.). (1990). *From Tsarism to the New Economic Policy: Continuity and Change in the Economy of the USSR* (London).

Davies, R. W. (ed.). (1984). *Soviet Investment for Planned Industrialisation, 1929–1937: Policy and Practice: Selected Papers from the Second World Congress for Soviet and East European Studies* (Berkeley).

Davies, R. W., Cooper. J. M., and Ilič, M. (1991). *Soviet Official Statistics on Industrial Production, Capital Stock and Capital Investment, 1928–41* (SIPS Occasional Paper No. 1, CREES, University of Birmingham).

Deane, P. and Cole, W. A. (1969). *British Economic Growth, 1688–1959: Trends and Structure* (Cambridge, 2nd edn).

Denison, E. F. (1967). *Why Growth Rates Differ: Postwar Experience in Nine Western Countries* (Washington, DC).

Dobb, M. (1955). *On Economic Theory and Socialism* (London).

Dobb, M. H. (1946). *Soviet Economic Development since 1917* (London).

Dohan, M. R. (1976). 'The Economic Origins of Soviet Autarky, 1927/28–1934', *Slavic Review*, XXXV.

Dohan, M. R. and Hewett, E.(1973). *Two Studies in the Soviet Terms of Trade, 1918–1970* (Bloomington).

Ellman, M. (1992). 'On Sources: a Note', *Soviet Studies*, XLIV.

Ellman, M. (1991). 'A Note on the Number of 1933 Famine Victims', *Soviet Studies*, XLIII.

Ellman, M. (1975). 'Did the Agricultural Surplus Provide the Resources for the Increase in Investment in the USSR during the First Five Year Plan?', *Economic Journal*, LXXXV.

Erlich, A. (1960). *The Soviet Industrialization Debate* (Cambridge, Mass.).

Falkus, M. E. (1968). 'Russia's National Income, 1913: A Revaluation', *Economica*, XXXV.

Feinstein, C. H. (1972). *National Income, Expenditure and Output in the United Kingdom, 1855–1965* (Cambridge).

Feinstein, C. H. (ed.). (1967). *Socialism, Capitalism and Economic Growth* (Cambridge).

Feldman, G. D. (1966). *Army, Industry and Labor in Germany, 1914–1918* (Princeton).

Field, A. J. (1985). 'On the Unimportance of Machinery', *Explorations in Economic History*, XX.

Field, A. J. (1983). 'Land Abundance, Interest/Profit Rates and Nineteenth Century American and British Technology', *Journal of Economic History*, XLIII.

Figes, O. (1989). *Peasant Russia, Civil War: The Volga Countryside in Revolution, 1917–1921* (Oxford).

Fisher, A. (1928). 'Foreign Concessions in Russia', in Chase, S., Dunn, R. and Tugwell, R. G. (eds.), *Soviet Russia in the Second Decade* (New York).

Fitzpatrick, S. and Viola, L. (1987). *A Researcher's Guide to Sources on Social History in the 1930s* (Armonk, New York).

Floud, R. C. and McCloskey, D. N. (eds.). (1981). *The Economic History of Britain Since 1700*, vol. 2 (Cambridge).

Gatrell, P. (1986). *The Tsarist Economy, 1850–1917* (London).

Gatrell, P. and Harrison, M. (1993). 'The Russian and Soviet Economies in Two World Wars: a Comparative View', *Economic History Review*, 2nd series, XLVI, no. 3.

Gerschenkron. A. (1965). *Economic Backwardness in Historical Perspective: A Book of Essays* (New York).

Geyer, D. (1987). *Russian Imperialism: the Interaction of Domestic and Foreign Policy, 1860–1914* (London).

Granick, D. (1967). *Soviet Metal-Fabricating and Economic Development: Practice versus Policy* (Madison, Milwaukee and London).

Gregory, P. R. (1982). *Russian National Income, 1885–1913* (Cambridge).

Hardach, G. (1977). *The First World War, 1914–1918* (London).

Harrison, M. (1993b). 'Soviet Economic Growth Since 1928: the Alternative Statistics of G. I. Khanin', *Europe–Asia Studies*, XLV.

Harrison, M. (1990a). 'Stalinist Industrialisation and the Test of War', *History Workshop Journal*, no. 29.

Harrison, M. (1990b). 'The Volume of Soviet Munitions Output, 1937–1945: a Reevaluation', *Journal of Economic History*, L, no. 3.

Harrison, M. (1987).'Macroeconomic Efficiency and Capital Formation in Soviet Industry Under Late Stalinism, 1945–1955', *Soviet Studies*, XXXIX.

Harrison, M. (1985a). 'Investment Mobilisation and Capacity Completion in the Chinese and Soviet Economies', *Economics of Planning*, XIX, no. 2.

Harrison, M. (1985b). *Soviet Planning in Peace and War, 1938–1945* (Cambridge).

Historical Statistics of the United States. Colonial Times to 1970 (1975). Vol. 1 (Washington).

Hodgman, D. R. (1954). *Soviet Industrial Production, 1928–1951* (Cambridge, Mass.).

Holliday, G. D. (1989). *Technology Transfer to the USSR, 1928–1937 and 1966–1975: the Role of Western Technology in Soviet Economic Development* (Boulder, Col.).

Holzman, F. D. (1974). *Foreign Trade Under Central Planning* (Cambridge, Mass.).

Hunter, H. (1988). 'Soviet Agriculture With and Without Collectivization, 1928–1940', *Slavic Review*, XLVII, no. 2.

Hunter, H. (1959). *Soviet Transportation Policy* (Cambridge, Mass.).

Hunter, H. and Szyrmer, J. M. (1992). *Faulty Foundations: Soviet Economic Policies, 1928–1940* (Princeton, New Jersey).

Jasny, N. (1962). *Essays on the Soviet Economy* (New York).

Jasny, N. (1961). *Soviet Industrialization, 1928–1952* (Chicago).

Jasny, N. (1949). *The Socialized Agriculture of the USSR: Plans and Performance* (Stanford).

Kaiser, D. H. (ed.). (1987). *The Worker's Revolution in Russia, 1917: the View from Below* (Cambridge).

Katz, B. G. (1975). 'Purges and Production: Soviet Economic Growth, 1928–1940', *Journal of Economic History*, XXXL.

Kenez, P. (1977). *Civil War in South Russia, 1919–1920* (Berkeley and London).

Koenker, D. (1989). *et al.* (eds.). *Party, State and Society in the Russian Civil War: Explorations in Social History* (Bloomington, Indiana).

Kohn, S. (1932). *The Cost of the War to Russia* (New Haven).

League of Nations (1937). *Balances of Payments, 1936* (Geneva).

Lenin, V. I. *Selected Works*, 12 vols. (London, 1936–8).

Lewis, R. A. (1979). *Science and Industrialisation in the USSR* (London and Basingstoke).

Lieven, D. C. B. (1983). *Russia and the Origins of the First World War* (London).

Lih, L. (1990). *Bread and Authority in Russia, 1914–1921* (Berkeley and Los Angeles).

Lorimer, F. (1946). *The Population of the Soviet Union: History and Prospects* (Geneva).

Maddison, A. (1991). *Dynamic Forces in Capitalist Development: a Long-Run Comparative View* (Oxford).

Maddison, A. (1989). *The World Economy in the 20th Century* (OECD, Paris).

Maddison, A. (1987). 'Growth and Slowdown in Advanced Capitalist Economies', *Journal of Economic Literature*, XXV.

Malle, S. (1985). *The Economic Organization of War Communism, 1918–1921* (Cambridge).

Marer, P. (1985). *Dollar GNPs of the USSR and Eastern Europe* (London).

McAuley, M. (1991). *Bread and Justice: State and Society in Petrograd, 1917–1922* (Oxford).

McKay, J. P. (1970). *Pioneers for Profit. Foreign Entrepreneurship and Russian Industrialization, 1885–1913* (Chicago and London).

Millar, J. R. and Linz, S. J. (1978). 'The Cost of World War II to the Soviet People: a Research Note', *Journal of Economic History*, XXXVIII, no. 4.

Mitchell, B. R. (1978). *European Historical Statistics, 1750–1970* (London and Basingstoke).

Moorsteen, R. (1962). *Prices and Production of Machinery in the Soviet Union, 1928–1958* (Cambridge, Mass.).

Moorsteen R. and Powell, R. P. (1966). *The Soviet Capital Stock, 1928–1962* (Homewood, Illinois).

Morrison, D. J. 'The Soviet Peasantry's Real Expenditure in Socialised Trade, 1928–1934', *Soviet Studies*, XLI, no. 2.

Moskoff, W. (1990). *The Bread of Affliction: the Food Supply in the USSR During World War II* (Cambridge).

Neilson, K. (1984). *Strategy and Supply: The Anglo-Russian Alliance, 1914–1917* (Cambridge).

Nove, A. (1990). 'How Many Victims in the 1930s?', *Soviet Studies*, XLII.

Nove, A. (1982). *An Economic History of the USSR* (London, 1969, revised Harmondsworth).

Nutter, G.W. (1962). *Growth of Industrial Production in the Soviet Union* (Princeton, NJ).

Ofer, G. (1987). 'Soviet Economic Growth, 1928–1985', *Journal of Economic Literature*, XXV.

Orgill, D. (1970). *T–34: Russian Armour* (London).

Polner, T. J. (1930). *Russian Local Government During the War and the Union of Zemstvos* (New Haven).

Powell, R. P. (1968). 'The Soviet Capital Stock and Related Series for the War Years', in *Two Supplements to Richard Moorsteen and Raymond P. Powell, The Soviet Capital Stock, 1928–1962* (The Economic Growth Center, Yale University).

Preobrazhensky, E. A. (1965). *The New Economics* (Oxford).

Reiman, M. (1987). *The Birth of Stalinism* (Bloomington).

Roberts, P. C. (1971). *Alienation and the Soviet Economy* (Albuquerque).

Rosenberg, W. (1985). 'Russian Labor and Bolshevik Power after October', *Slavic Review*, XLIV.

Salisbury, H. E. (1971). *The 900 Days: the Siege of Leningrad* (London).

Salter, W. E. G. (1966). *Productivity and Technical Change* (Cambridge).

Scott, J. (1971). *Behind the Urals: An American in Russia's City of Steel* (London and Cambridge, Mass., 1942, reprinted New York).

Sen, A. K. (1968). *Choice of Techniques*, 3rd edn (Oxford).

Seton, F. (1959). 'Production Functions in Soviet Industry', *American Economic Review*, XLIX.

Seton, F. (1956–7). 'The Tempo of Soviet Industrial Expansion', *Transactions of the Manchester Statistical Society*.

Seton-Watson, H. (1952). *The Decline of Imperial Russia* (London).

Shanin, T. (1985). *Russia as a 'Developing Society'* (London).

Shanin, T. (1972). *The Awkward Class: Political Sociology of Peasantry in a Developing Society: Russia, 1910–1925* (Oxford).

Smith, G. A. (1971). *Soviet Foreign Trade: Organisation, Operations and Policy, 1918–1971* (London and New York).

Smith, S. A. (1983). *Red Petrograd: Revolution in the Factories, 1917–1918* (Cambridge).

The Soviet Aircraft Industry (Chapel Hill). (1955).

Spulber, N. (1964). *Foundations of a Soviet Strategy for Economic Growth* (Bloomington).

Stalin, J. (1940). *Leninism*.

Stanley, E. J. (1968). *Regional Distribution of Soviet Industrial Manpower, 1940–1960* (New York).

Stewart, F. (1978). *Technology and Underdevelopment* (London and Basingstoke).

Stone, N. (1975). *The Eastern Front, 1914–1917* (London).

Struve, P. B. *et al.* (1930). *Food Supply in Russia during the World War* (New Haven).

Sutton, A. C. (1971). *Western Technology and Soviet Economic Development, 1930–1945* (Stanford).

Sutton, A. C. (1968). *Western Technology and Soviet Economic Development, 1917–1930* (Stanford).

Svennilson, I. (1954). *Growth and Stagnation in the European Economy* (Geneva).

Szamuely, L. (1974). *First Models of the Socialist Economic Systems: Principles and Theories* (Budapest).

Tauger, M. (1991). 'The 1932 Harvest and the Famine of 1933', *Slavic Review*, L.

Tracy, M. (1982). *Agriculture in Western Europe: Challenge and Response, 1880–1980* (St. Albans).

Tucker, R. C. (1973). *Stalin as Revolutionary, 1879–1929: A Study in History and Personality* (New York).

United Nations and EUROSTAT. (1986). *World Comparisons of Purchasing Power and Real Product for 1980*, 2 vols. (New York).

Volin, L. (1970). *A Century of Russian Agriculture: From Alexander II to Khrushchev* (Cambridge, Mass.).

Von Laue, T. H. (1966). *Why Lenin? Why Stalin? A Reappraisal of the Russian Revolution, 1900–30* (London).

Voznesensky, N. A. (1948). *War Economy of the USSR in the Period of the Patriotic War*.

Voznesensky, N. A. (1941). *Economic Results of the USSR in 1940 and the Plan of National Economic Development for 1941*.

Werth, A. (1964). *Russia at War, 1941–1945* (London).

Westwood, J. N. (1982). *Soviet Locomotive Technology During Industrialisation, 1928–1952* (London and Basingstoke).

Wheatcroft, S. G. (1974). 'The Reliability of Russian Prewar Grain Output Statistics', *Soviet Studies*, XXVI.

Wheatcroft, S. G. and Davies, R. W. (eds.). (1985). *Materials for a Balance of the Soviet National Economy, 1928–1930* (Cambridge).

Wheatcroft, S. G., Davies, R. W. and Cooper, J. M. (1986). 'Soviet Industrialization Reconsidered: Some Preliminary Conclusions About Soviet Economic Development Between 1926 and 1941', *Economic History Review*, 2nd series, XXXIX.

Wiles, P. J. D. (1962). *The Political Economy of Communism* (Oxford).

Williams, A. J. (1992). *Trading with the Bolsheviks: the Politics of East–West Trade* (Manchester and New York).

Willis, J. F. and Primack, M. L. (1989). *An Economic History of the United States*, 2nd edn (Englewood Cliffs).

Yugov, A. (n.d.). *Russia's Economic Front for War and Peace* (London [? 1942]).

Zagorsky, S. O. (1928). *State Control of Industry in Russia during the War* (New Haven).

Zaleski, E. (1980). *Stalinist Planning for Economic Growth, 1933–1952* (London and Basingstoke).

Zaleski, E. (1971). *Planning for Economic Growth in the Soviet Union, 1918–1932* (Chapel Hill).

Index

374

For EU product safety concerns, contact us at Calle de José Abascal, 56–1°,
28003 Madrid, Spain or eugpsr@cambridge.org.

www.ingramcontent.com/pod-product-compliance
Ingram Content Group UK Ltd.
Pitfield, Milton Keynes, MK11 3LW, UK
UKHW042316180425
457623UK00005B/19